CENTRE FOR INTERNATIONAL ECONOM

The Looming Corporate Calamity

Restoring Corporate Legitimacy

The Case for Fundamental Reform

Richard Tudway
2014
www.richardtudway.com

Published by
Heterodox Publications Limited

Restoring Corporate Legitimacy

Heterodox Publishing Limited
London UK
www.hdxeconomics.com

Heterodox Publishing Limited is dedicated to developing markets for publications which explore alternative insights into the governance of major economic and global institutions.

About the Cover Photograph
The photograph on the cover is what remains of the once glorious ocean going liner the SS United States. Her main route was conveying passengers in luxury from New York to Southampton, but competition from the airline industry put her out of business. Notable passengers included the Duke and Duchess of Windsor and former President Bill Clinton. Many attempts have been made to restore her to her former glory. Sadly at the time of the publication of this work she still is in danger of being scrapped. Below is a photograph of Peter Clarke, publisher of this work, arriving with his family in Southampton from New York.

Text & Cover Design by James Honess
While working with Richard Tudway on this book, I am also studying for a degree in Computer Science at Sussex University. It's been a great pleasure having the opportunity to aid in the creation of this fantastic book.

Contents

Preface

The Modern Corporation – an Unanchored Monolith

What is this book about? It explores the role played by the larger publicly traded corporations that operate in our social and economic space. This arises in part because of the way the corporation has been transformed over the past hundred years or so. Changes in the law, especially in Anglo American jurisdictions, have played a major part. But what we expect corporations to do and how we expect them to behave has also shaped our thinking. Needless to say corporate governance lies at the heart of all these concerns. We need to understand why this is so important.

Limited liability is the point of departure. Prior to limited liability corporate endeavour was commonly, though not exclusively, an activity undertaken by unincorporated individuals - or partners. This activity was essentially unlimited in terms of liability. If things went wrong then the person or persons who were *the business* were responsible. This is the essence of unlimited liability. The responsibilities that fell upon those persons reflected the underlying morality of the day. Each person was ultimately responsible for his or her actions.

The Advent of Limited Liability

One simple example will suffice. If the meat prepared and sold by the butcher turns out to be unfit for human consumption then the butcher would be accountable for his actions in selling the meat to them. That was very much the world at the time Adam Smith was writing his *Wealth of Nations*. This state of affairs locked every commercial action into to a known and mostly predictable code of behaviour. There were few loopholes or exceptions. The market was unforgiving. The errant butcher would soon be out of business as customers bought elsewhere. An example, perhaps, of Adam Smith's *invisible hand* at work promoting the social responsibility of business.

Limited liability fundamentally transforms this. It introduces by stealth and over a lengthy period of time another *person*. This other *person* as we shall see is a mysterious creation. His arrival radically shifts the goal posts. The question on the minds of all at this point must be – what is this other *person* and how did he get there? The mindboggling answer is that the *person* turns out to be a fictional *personification* of a real person. Something lawyers ended up confecting in law to solve a specific problem associated with limited liability. This *fictional* person arises because when the enabling legislation was passed something odd happened. The activity which had previously been clearly

i

performed by a *real* person or persons under unlimited liability ceases to apply in quite the same way under limited liability.

The Origins of the Corporate Person

How this comes about is a juridical paradox. Under limited liability something which did not previously exist, now exists. In our example the butcher is the *real* person who prepares the meat and sells it to his customer. He is replaced by another person who is not a *real* person but nevertheless exists as a fact of law. If the butcher sells poor quality meat to his customer and this results in a legal action - the legal liability changes. It is no longer the person who actually sold the meat that is legally responsible. It is another party, the *corporate person*, to whom complainants will seek redress.

Stripping out everything else this is the most significant and little understood development that occurs as a direct result of limited liability. A new party, the *corporate person* has been created. Aside from the matter of criminal negligence on the part of the *real* person who sold the meat, the party that is now responsible for the matter of the meat is no longer the party who sold the meat. As if by sleight of hand the *corporate person* is now the central player. But this is only the beginning of a remarkable journey as we are going to discover. It subtly transforms the company's sense of corporate responsibility as it does so.

The Role of the Shareholder

Once a distinction is established between the *real person* and the fictional or *corporate person* other things happen. We need to consider the role and the position of the *shareholders* in this transition. When a limited liability company is first created a specific type of corporate *vehicle* is created in law. This *vehicle* is separate in law from the parties that create it. The parties that create the company are commonly, though mistakenly, referred as the *owners* - though they are of course the *shareholders*. Imagine that Smith the butcher decides to create a limited liability company. In doing so he creates a *vehicle* through which his future commercial activities will then be conducted.

In creating the company he is obliged by law to hold a claim on the company in the form of shares in exchange for cash. The shares represents the value of whatever Smith has paid for the creation of XYZ Ltd. XYZ Ltd has, at birth, a *proprietor* or more correctly a *shareholder,* and a sum of money that has been paid in exchange for the shares. This sum of money is the capital of the XYZ Ltd and is *owned* by the company, not as we will discover, by the *shareholder*. At this point XYZ Ltd begins to trade lawfully. From a legal standpoint XYZ Ltd will be responsible for what it purchases (meat carcases for example), what it sells, the revenue it receives and its disbursements and any actions that might arise against it in law.

The Corporate Holy Trinity

In a start-up situation Smith is likely to perform all executive functions on behalf of XYZ Ltd. Someone has to do this. The company is an *inanimate fictional* entity in law. It can perform no actions except through the mediation of a *real person*. Smith is therefore the proprietor of the company, the shareholder and the director – a holy trinity of sorts. He operates the company and does everything for the company. This became the position in law in Britain (and elsewhere) at the moment that the law of limited liability was enacted in the mid 19th century. To sum up: there is an entity called a company; a shareholder called Smith; paid up capital in the company resulting from Smith buying shares in the company and money in the firm's bank account at the outset equal to the value of Smith's shares. Furthermore the commercial activities of the company are controlled and managed by Smith but the company is responsible for all liabilities resulting from its activities. A remarkable development! As things progress the situation will again change, again in a very significant way.

We can now see clearly who the different *players* are in the limited liability company. This evolves as we move forward in time. We need to understand the nature of the changes that take place and why they are important. Remember before limited liability *the partners,* (or individuals), were in essence inseparable from the company through which the business was conducted. They were the *aggregate identity* of the company. For all practical purposes they would have shared common values. Mostly unprompted they would acknowledge *their* collective corporate responsibility for *their* actions. The *aggregate* sense of obligation in terms of their behaviour as individuals is of great importance as we move forward in time.

Preserving the Aggregate Identity

Once limited liability occurs some odd things also happen to the *aggregate* nature of the company and its activities. Imagine Smith is a partner in an unlimited liability company which then elects to become a limited liability entity. This would have been a common event. It happened frequently at the time limited liability was first enacted. Under unlimited liability Smith and his partners would have been the *aggregate* expression of their collective actions. All the partners would have felt a similar sense of obligation about these matters. This is the essence of unlimited liability – *joint and several responsibility*. But once the event of limited liability occurs the *aggregate identity* begins to fade. It does so because of the nature of the limited liability company. Once the unlimited liability partnership of which Smith was part becomes a limited liability company some might ask - what now is the purpose of the company's *aggregate* nature. This thought had crossed the mind of Adam Smith well before the introduction of limited liability. He warned, with great intuitive insight, that any dilution of individual or collective liability, would fundamentally and adversely transform behaviour. How right he was.

The act of limited liability is silent on these matters. The *aggregate* nature of corporate endeavour is accorded no explicit role. In Britain the matter was never seriously debated. Elsewhere, however, the matter was considered carefully. In certain European jurisdictions and further afield laws were passed which effectively protected and nurtured the *aggregate* sense of corporate endeavour. In these jurisdictions there was an awareness that without legal requirements being explicitly set out the *aggregate* sense of corporate endeavour under limited liability would wilt. This development was seen to be potentially harmful.

Two-Tier Board Structures

For larger limited liability entities laws were thus enacted which required such companies to institute two-tier board structures. The upper board, the supervisory board, would be responsible for ensuring that shareholders, employees and other stakeholder interests were properly taken into account. In this way the *aggregate* sense of corporate responsibility would be preserved. In Anglo American jurisdictions this did not happen. As a result the limited liability company gradually detaches itself from its shareholders, other stakeholders and its customary social obligations. The corporation develops in a distinctly different fashion. It certainly responds to changing social and economic circumstances differently. This may explain the emergence of CSR (corporate social responsibility) reporting in the 1980s in Anglo American jurisdictions. Corporations felt compelled to justify their actions to an increasingly sceptical public. It explains why today many view this type of reporting as little more than an elaborate design to justify irresponsible and unsustainable behaviour.

In various European and Nordic jurisdictions and elsewhere the history is different. The role of the shareholders, employees and other stakeholders in the governance of the corporation is better preserved. The *aggregate* sense of corporate responsibility remains an integral part of the corporation's governance culture. In Anglo American jurisdictions this culture has withered and died. Institutional investors, dominant in these jurisdictions, are not a progressive or proactive force in governance. These differences as we are going to discover have had a fundamental role to play in shaping governance systems in all jurisdictions and ultimately the way in which the corporation responds to changing economic and social challenges.

How the Corporate Person Transforms Corporate Behaviour

In jurisdictions that have chosen to protect the *aggregate* nature of the commercial endeavour the corporation appears able to internalise and respond to social, economic and technological concerns in a more credible fashion. In Anglo American jurisdictions, in contrast, responsiveness has been enfeebled. The *aggregate* nature has given way to the now all-powerful *corporate person*. Corporations in Anglo American jurisdictions have become progressively disconnected from the communities around them. They no longer have a natural or organic means for internalising these concerns. The *corporate person* has also grown massively in importance and presence. It is portrayed by those who speak for it, the directors, as a *corporate citizen* - alas an inanimate fictional entity in law unable to align itself naturally to citizen values. The credibility gap in terms of public perceptions of the importance of these issues grows wider by the day. Meantime the directors cling to the questionable doctrine of *shareholder value* as the principal if not exclusive metric of measuring company performance.

The failure in Anglo American jurisdictions to identify and preserve the *aggregate* values that are part and parcel of the corporation and its DNA has grave consequences. This may explain the divergence between what corporations do and what society expects of them. This divergence inevitably undermines corporate legitimacy. The gap cannot be bridged by exercises in CSR. These fundamental matters are explored in this book as we try to settle how best to articulate sustainable reforms to the way in which tomorrow's corporation is governed.

Acknowledgements

I owe thanks to friends, colleagues, students and other associates who have helped in shaping my views on corporate governance. They have in their different ways sharpened my insight into the hidden role of prejudice and political orthodoxy in concealing from sight the many problems and difficulties associated with it. I am also conscious of the fact that, as with everything else, ideas are explored through the eyes of a particular observer. The individual observer inevitably has his own particular slant on things. This results in some things being overstated, others being understated, sometimes even ignored. Likewise I too am an observer of events. I have nevertheless tried hard and conscientiously to resist so*ft-soap* and the easy take on events in addressing this task. This is a pervasive problem.

My task is complicated, immeasurably, by language. The challenges of translating Asian concepts of the corporation into the different European and English languages are always present. Within and between the speakers of the English and other European languages and traditions, there are also hidden differences of understanding and meaning where corporate matters are being explored. Superficial similarities of understanding run alongside more fundamental misunderstandings.[1] Some of these elusive events and their impact are explored.

I became interested in the phenomenon of corporate governance during work I was doing in Russia and Ukraine, following the collapse of the USSR. This first triggered my interest in the nature of the corporation, the act of shareholding and corporate governance.[2] In both Russia and Ukraine mass privatisations, were being undertaken with many privately owned entities, some very large businesses indeed, emerging from former state control. As a bystander I was able to watch the American *rules of the game* being applied by the new owners. Within the blinking of an eye in terms of time new corporate entities had sprouted across the full spectrum of commercial and industrial activities from banking and insurance through coal, gas and oil to processing, manufacturing and retailing.

The new style shareholders and board directors began to look closely at what they could and couldn't do within the law (and sometimes outside it!) as they began to address the problems of raising new capital from the market place to develop their businesses. Needless to say there was no local capital market developed enough to enable these new business leaders to raise equity. Local banks were chary about entering into lending agreements with corporations which might, in the event, be difficult if not impossible to enforce. These gaps were filled mostly by western investors keen enough, (or rash enough!), to place reliance on undertakings in public offer documents, declarations made in audited accounts, the reliability of shareholder registers and perhaps most importantly the processes of governance and the integrity of individual board directors.

The tales of anger and disenchantment are almost legendary. A combination of weak if not nonexistent enforcement of corporate law, indifference to the niceties of investor protection and outright criminality caused me to look more closely at how such things occurred in these transitional economies when they generally didn't in Anglo American jurisdictions which I felt I knew and understood. Well I didn't! As I looked I began to realise that my preconceptions were far from accurate. Looking at the development of railroad and oil industries in the US in the 19th century I soon realised that patterns of behaviour were little different to those I found myself watching in the **FSU** (former Soviet Union) much later. And then we had Enron and its racketeering alongside a slew of other examples of massive and systemic abuses of corporate governance particularly in the US but also in other jurisdictions. I began to understand why institutions had, in *path dependent*[3]fashion developed so distinctively in Anglo American jurisdiction when compared with European and other OECD jurisdictions. In short the *rules of the game* have evolved everywhere to protect wealth from corporate abuse of investors and other stakeholders.

I also soon discovered that they had all developed from the same font, more or less, in terms of corporate creation but had evolved in markedly different ways thereafter. It was at the point that I realised that these differences needed to be explored rather than rely on one single model of development – the Anglo American model – as the model towards which all other would inevitably develop. I hope that this book takes those that are interested in these matters further down the road of real critical understanding.

Singling out particular individuals to thank is difficult and sometimes invidious. I am bound, however, to record my thanks to TUAC, (the Trade Union Advisory Committee to the OECD and their many trade union affiliates worldwide), the Global Labour University and the ActTrav (Workers Action) Group of the ILO. They have provided help and encouragement in the exploration of these issues. Concerned as they are with worker and more broadly citizen wellbeing they rightly have a compelling interest and concern for improving corporate governance everywhere and protecting citizen interests. The effects of poor corporate governance as evidenced by the global financial crisis triggered by events on Wall Street continue to paralyse economic growth. My own efforts, unambiguously, support theirs. We all deserve better and must strive to together in achieving that end. I must also acknowledge the many lengthy exchanges I have had with Andrew Linden of the RMIT University in Melbourne, Australia. Andrew's deep insight into the socio-political issues of corporate governance in Rhineland and Anglo American jurisdictions has helped to sharpen my own thinking.

I must also acknowledge the dedication of my publisher and the graphics, layout media expert James Honess. Heterodox Publications has been a source of inspiration and support throughout. Without constant penetrating questioning from Peter Clarke, its editor in chief, this publication might never have come about. I have also a debt to pay to a wide number of friends and colleagues who, with patience and affection, have encouraged me to continue in the face of many challenges. David and Janice Henwood, as lay commentators, have contributed to the shaping of a number of thoughts as we have walked together on the South Downs. So too has my friend and colleague Dennis Jones in our various discussions. Though I alone am responsible for the ideas that have emerged I am grateful to have had this support and encouragement throughout. Finally I thank my wife for her stoic patience throughout this long trek.

Notes

[1] An example, of which there are many, would include the concept of the "board" as in board of directors. In English speaking domains the term board is a reference to the single unitary executive organ that runs the company. In other European and Nordic languages the term "board" is often a reference to an independent supervisory board which plays no direct role in the running of the company. Its role is supervisory. This difference can and does lead to confusion and misunderstanding.

[2] Though I had read carefully the British Bullock Report *The Report of the Committee on Industrial Democracy* (1997) which investigated British corporate governance. Its recommendations were never implemented.

[3] *Path dependency* may be defined as the tendency of a past or traditional practice or preference to continue even if better alternatives might be available: 'we've always done it this way and this is the only way to do it'!

Foreword

The Challenge of Unaccountable Power

Disclosures about the scale of corporate complicity in surveillance and eavesdropping have rocked the world. It is a chilling reminder of Lord Acton's[1] memorable words when he warned:

> *Power tends to corrupt, and absolute power corrupts absolutely. Great men are almost always bad men.*

Evidence disclosed by Edward Snowden's leaked material[2] put on public view not only the scale of state engagement in illegal surveillance of citizens activities - with elected politicians and the public at large unaware of the existence of these operations - but also the complicity of some of the largest publicly traded corporations in America (and by implication Britain)[3] in these illegal acts. Some of the best known names in the world handling data have illicitly shared secrets with the state about how they legally gather and use information as part of their legitimate business activities.

The famous Google[4] mission statement jingle *Do No Evil* is a reference to its commitment never to share details of its own secret information sourcing and encryption technology. It reveals the scale of deception. When the Chinese authorities put pressure on Google to share this information with them, as a condition of operating in the Chinese market, Google protested loudly to the rest of the world. It claimed that it could not and would not betray the confidence and trust of its customers. The Chinese government were, in the event, mostly refused access.[5] But in secret it now appears that Google and other major IT providers have shared this information with the NSA[6] (National Security Agency) of the US, the British GCHQ (Government Communications Headquarters) and others. The sense of public outrage is understandable. But there is a lesson that this saga has so far failed to explore. How could these events have occurred with commercial organisations that were properly and effectively governed? There is yet no answer to that question. We are again left to conclude that the role of NEDs (non executive directors) has again failed to operate as an effective countervailing influence. It is yet further damning proof that the effectiveness of unitary board structures in Anglo American jurisdictions has past its *sell by date.*

The Transatlantic Trade and Investment Partnership (TTIP) is yet a further example of pervasive, unseen, unaccountable corporate power. The aim of the TTIP is to remove the regulatory differences between the US and European nations. The US is less regulated than the EU in areas like food safety and other areas of consumer protection. Will regulatory harmony mean that EU citizens will be expected to make concessions? Nobody yet knows. Once ratified the treaty would enable the largest corporations to sue governments who take legal action to defend their citizens against perceived wrong doing. This will happen through a secretive panel of corporate lawyers not the courts. They will be empowered to overrule even the will of parliaments. Citizen protection will inevitably be undermined. The mechanism through which this is achieved is known as *investor-state dispute settlement*. It is already being used in various parts of the world to the detriment of citizens. Yet there has been no thorough, open, public debate in the US or Europe about these matters. One asks why? Might the answer be another example of Orwellian apathy? Who can tell?

Notes

[1] John Emerich Edward Dalberg-Acton, 1st Baron Acton, KCVO, DL (10 January 1834 – 19 June 1902). He was an English Catholic historian, politician, and writer. Source: Wikipedia.

[2] Edward Joseph "Ed" Snowden (born June 21, 1983) is an exiled American computer specialist and former CIA employee and NSA contractor. He disclosed classified details of several top-secret United States and British government mass surveillance programmes to the press. He is living in Russia under temporary political asylum and is considered a fugitive from justice by American authorities. Source: Wikipedia.

[3] Though precise details have not yet been disclosed British incorporated internet access providers are also implicated.

[4] While many companies have ethical codes that govern their conduct in contrast, Google claims to have made "Don't Be Evil" a central pillar of their identity as part of their self-proclaimed core values. The words: "Don't be evil" form part of the sixth point in these Core Values, and in full it states: "Do the right thing: don't be evil. Have respect for honesty and integrity. Our business practices are beyond reproach. We make money by doing good things." This commitment is often referred to by the more imperative *Do no evil.*

[5] Eventually because of pressure from the Chinese authorities Google shut down its mainland Chinese operation and operated from Hong Kong which can still be accessed from the mainland, if you know how!

[6] A reference to the Prism and Tempora programmes in the case of the NSA and GCHQ respectively.

Int.1   Introduction

Orthodoxy means not thinking – not needing to think. Orthodoxy is unconsciousness

(George Orwell *1984* written in 1949)

The issues surrounding the debate on corporate governance rank as some of the most important we all face whether as citizens of particular sovereign states, investors in international traded stocks, policy makers trying to make sense of these developments, students of the global economy trying to understand them or simply the man in the street puzzled by what happens. The reasons for this are both simple and complex, and frequently misunderstood. At one level corporate endeavour is seen to be a straightforward matter of finding profitable and efficient ways of satisfying market need. The law lays down a framework of rules within which corporate entities are governed in competitive markets. Corporations do the rest. It all sounds very simple. How wrong we are in that assumption.

At yet another level the way in which corporate power is exercised, by whom and for whose benefit, reveals a web of different and often conflicting views about the corporation and the purposes and processes of its governance. Needless to say there is a great deal of public misunderstanding and possibly misrepresentation about these matters. As Masahiko Aoki with great insight makes clear "the end of corporate history for corporate law"[1] is far from being a reality, (Aoki 2010).[2] We approach a point in history when many of these matters will be challenged. Reflecting on the prophetic sentiments expressed by a former President of the World Bank, James Wolfenshon, 'the proper governance of companies will be as crucial to the world economy as the proper governing of countries. The two go together.'[3] How right Wolfenshon was. How much there is to be done.

Int.2   The spirit of laissez faire

Trying to explain how we arrived at where we are calls for an examination of the history and evolution of political ideologies. The current guiding orthodoxy of market capitalism is that the economic system should be as free from government intervention or moderation as possible. It should be driven by the market forces. This has by stealth become not just a set of guiding principles but an all-embracing ideology encompassing wealth, celebrity

1

and progress for the common good. For many this is a matter that can no longer be accepted as the norm for development. The global economic and financial crisis is a symptom of this phase in the evolution of financial market capitalism. Whilst it has brought about a sharp decline in the pace of growth of the global economy the underlying orthodoxy remains mostly unchallenged and unchanged.

We can better understand how we have arrived from where we were by examining developments historically. Classical Smithsonian orthodoxy centred on the belief the human beings are naturally motivated by self-interest.[4] When they are not interfered with in their economic activities, a balanced system of production and exchange based on mutual benefit emerges. Laissez-faire (*leave it alone* in translation from the French) in contrast originated in 18th century France. Economists such as Francois Quesnay (1694-1774) and Victor Riqueti-Marquis de Mirabeau (1715-89) were influential in its development. They opposed, for example, subsidies and discriminatory economic measures features of the notorious mercantilist system which then prevailed. Taking a somewhat different tack to Adam Smith they emphasised the bounty of nature and the innate goodness of humankind. They asserted that governments should leave the individual alone except when social liberties are infringed.

In the 19th century, this philosophy became the dominant economic thinking in the Western world. In contrast, and with far less fanfare, the influence of Frederich List in German development shaped a key strategic and interventionist role for the state and may explain what is sometimes referred to as the German social market economy.[5] The concepts undergirding the social market economy are profoundly significant as we shall discover. They also have a critical bearing on what we should expect from corporate governance.

Int.3   Responding to negative externalities

But there were counter forces in the making. These were shaped by the growing disparities in the distribution of wealth, the treatment of working people under the factory system, disregard for public safety and wellbeing, and monopolistic competition which began to emerge. As the 19th century rolled out, opposition to *laissez faire* economics sharpened its focus. Governments in all industrialised countries intervened on behalf of working people and the population at large.[6] Factory acts and environmental laws were enacted. Anti monopoly legislation was passed. Early in the 20th century monopolies in the US were broken up. In the post World War ll period the nationalisation of large scale industries and services in Europe took place *in the public interest*.

Keynesian economics, which offered a range of fundamental alternatives, advocated government intervention in the national economy, in appropriate circumstances. It was a powerful counter to the *laissez-faire* school of economic thought and was spurred by the great depression of 1930s. From the 1970's onwards, however, the pendulum has swung back. Keynesianism was forced to retreat in favour of a new variant of *laissez-faire* economics (rebranded the 'market economy' or 'free enterprise'). This heralded widespread deregulation of business practice, financial and labour markets, and trade. It is well evidenced by the globalisation of the world economy. A somewhat mixed blessing.[7]

Market forces, as we are reminded by Hall, (2013)[8] have penetrated deep into institutional life. 'It has shaped a popular culture which extols celebrity and promotes the value of private gain and possessive individualism'. It has also shaped how corporations behave and the manner in which they respond to the challenges of inclusive corporate governance and accountability. As we will discover there is happily a greater variety in terms of general practice than we might expect. That fact will be explored in the following chapters. These differences are to be welcomed and better understood. Only in that way can we move forward.

Int.4   Taming the corporation

The corporation, as Teubner[9] (1994) reminds us, was a fiery fighter for political and economic freedom in the 19th century. Today corporations seem very different. They are often seen as obstacles to progress across a wide front. Finding ways of 'taming the corporation' without impairing its capacity to create wealth poses dilemmas is now at the forefront. Sad to say the response to the challenge of governing the corporation more effectively is not matched by a critical enough assessment of what good and effective corporate governance might entail. Worse there is evidence that policy makers and opinion influencers alike, especially in English speaking countries, suppress or otherwise discourage these thoughts.[10] This book aims to address these most important shortcomings. It takes its cue from Allen and Gale's (2002) important contribution to the debate about the relative effectiveness of different corporate governance systems in different jurisdictions.[11]

It also does this by examining a series of selected case studies. These cases explore different aspects of failure (and success) in respect of corporate governance and evidence from different cultural and governance perspectives. These are embedded in the text in Chapter 10. They should be used by readers and students alike to sharpen their insight into the issues exposed and explored. The aim is to generate a wider understanding of why institutions have evolved differently and what changes need to be encouraged as we strive to generate better and more effective governance.

Perceptions and public reactions about these matters have evolved in different global jurisdictions in different ways. In Anglo American jurisdictions concerns have focused historically and currently mostly (if not exclusively) on strengthening *external* mechanisms designed to protect shareholders (or investors) and thereby enhance the prospects for economic growth and development. The uppermost aim has been to boost the liquidity of capital markets as a mechanism for raising equity and debt finance and the buying and selling of securities. Whether these provisions offer a necessary and a sufficient condition for success is increasingly in doubt. There are also doubts about the validity of casting shareholders and/or institutional investors in a *role of primacy* in the governance process.

Shareholders as institutional investors are, in the end, expected to play a crucial monitoring role in governance. On too many occasions for comfort they have been caught 'sleeping on the job'. We are bound to ask how the global financial crisis which first broke in 2008 could have inflicted the damage that it has if the external disciplining mechanism in capital markets had been functioning properly. The immediate answer is that institutional investors have failed to protect themselves from abuse, and the millions of savers and investors they ultimately represent. This is evidenced by the trillions of dollars worth of shareholder value that has been directly and indirectly destroyed.[12] As we shall discover these represent failures in corporate governance in general and a wholesale breakdown of directors' fiduciary duties for which there are, as yet, no viable remedies in place.[13]

Int.5　　　　　　Co-determination in the work place

In contrast models elsewhere, most notably the social market models in *Rhineland*[14]jurisdictions and elsewhere in Europe and the Nordic countries, have been more concerned about the *internal* institutional framework within which governance of the largest corporations takes place. This also embraces the promotion of *co-determination*[15] in the work place. Through the mechanism of the supervisory board there is mostly clear evidence that effective supervision has managed to prevent the worst excesses that have become increasingly evident in Anglo American jurisdictions. As Allen & Gale (2002) remind us *Rhineland* corporations have been better at protecting long term wealth and ensuring a better and more effective form of governance benefitting shareholders, institutional investors, stakeholders and employees alike. Whilst the

German economy was adversely impacted by the global financial crisis it has proved surprisingly resilient.[16] The reasons that explain this need to be understood.

Variants of both the Anglo American and the *Rhineland* models are to be found elsewhere. For example Japanese and South Korean models reflect aspects of the *Rhineland* model. The Japanese model can be seen as explicitly favouring stakeholders rather than shareholders. In the case of South Korea this also runs alongside French-style *dirigiste* tendencies where the state plays a leading role in protecting and promoting *commanding-height* industries[17] and protecting the interests of labour. Various adaptations of the *Rhineland* and Anglo American and French models are to be found in other jurisdictions. Chinese and Russian models are yet to be finally settled but like Brazil, Indonesia and other emerging market economies they will be looking at wider aspects of performance (rather than ideological considerations) in determining how best to encourage progressive corporate governance and sustainable development.

As we shall see Anglo American jurisdictions may generally be typified as *laissez faire* in the sense that the prime concern has been to protect shareholders and investors through statutory laws otherwise leaving the directors of the corporation to manage governance through a raft of hard, soft[18] or *comply or explain* codes of practice. This stands in contrast to *Rhineland* and Nordic jurisdictions where there has been far greater emphasis on formal, independent *ex ante* supervision of the actions of the executive board of management. Models elsewhere, notably in French speaking jurisdictions have favoured a more interventionist approach in terms of both law and regulation – a hybrid lying between Anglo American *laissez faire* and *Rhineland* independent supervision and workplace co-determination. There are important lessons to be learnt from understanding the differences and similarities.

Int.6   The portrayal of the corporation

There is another dimension to this question. Certainly the largest corporations, (including state-run corporations) exercise huge power over the lives of all – power which in too many cases fails the tests of accountability transparency and inclusivity. Corporations are commonly portrayed in law as if they had an existence analogous to that of human beings.[19] This is a dangerous, if compelling, illusion. Bob Diamond[20] in his inaugural *Business Today* address speaks about this. He places great emphasis on Barclays Bank and Corporate Citizenship. See the full text of his speech at Appendix 5. It merits close reading. It is full of high sounding intent but little substance.

My reply to his address was published in The Guardian newspaper in November 2011. See Figure 1 *infra*. Corporations cannot act as if they were human beings.[21] This is because they are, in essence, inanimate fictional legal entities, not citizens or real persons. They rely instead on directors, managers (and in some instances shareholders), to represent them within a framework of soft and hard law and regulation. This leads us to the most controversial issues in the corporate governance debate. If corporations are not natural persons then governance structures must take account of the plurality of stakeholder interests of which the corporation is their focus. It cannot be left to directors or managers, alone, as members of unsupervised unitary boards, to interpret how best corporations should be governed.[22]

As we shall see issues of corporate governance have a long pedigree. There can be little doubt, however, that events over the past decade and a half tell us that the scale of the problem is worsening. This has occurred against the backdrop of new regulatory and accountability reform initiatives, especially in Anglo American jurisdictions. These have in turn been triggered by a rising tide of crises. These stretch back to Enron and include several other large scale failures in the governance arrangements notably in the US and the UK. This includes, most notably, the recurrent governance and risk management problems of BP. It includes also the widespread problems of abuse and multiple governance failures associated with particular banks and financial institutions. The consequences of these failures triggered the wider global financial crisis which first broke in November 2007. It continues to blight most OECD countries and global output. It is a long way from being resolved as the 2014 world economic assessment of the IMF bears witness.

There are important and perplexing issues which flow the status of the corporation. This applies regardless as to whether the corporation is portrayed as a *fictional person,* an *aggregate entity* with real persons behind the corporation, or simply as a *nexus of contracts.*[23] The manner in which the corporation is governed is therefore crucially important. The range of challenges that effective governance pose are explored in the following chapters. The conclusions drawn invite a full, frank and comprehensive debate if the governance arrangements of the corporation are to be fundamentally improved. Reform needs to meet, unambiguously, the priority of ensuring that the governance arrangements address the fundamental challenge of corporate legitimacy and CSR (corporate social responsibility). This can only be credibly achieved if shareholders along with other legitimate stakeholders are empowered and required by law to play a proactive *ex ante* role in the decision taking of the corporation. Nothing less will do. Failure to act will leave the corporation effectively unaccountable in terms of its operations a state of affairs which will undermine still further its social and economic legitimacy.[24]

6

As a subset of the general concerns about shareholder responsibilities there is the separate challenge of how to ensure that institutional investors play an 'engaged' role in the companies in which they are invested. This is complicated by the appearance of hedge funds and private equity funds along with the wider use of derivatives and other aspects of complex financial engineering – all of which weaken the primary objective of effective corporate governance.

Int.7   A personal muse

Finally on a personal note I have been examining corporate structures, how they have evolved, how they operate and how they are regulated for a lengthy period of time. I have been helped in this task by friends and colleagues alike. During this experience it has become clear that entities which may be the size of micro limited liability businesses - whose ownership is clearly reflected in both the shareholding arrangements and the management of the business - change in very fundamental ways as the limited liability entity evolves to become a publicly traded corporation or when companies are subsequently nationalised or otherwise become state-owned entities. In countries which have developed institutions which protect private property they all start their lives either as partnerships or limited liability companies but as they evolve they change in many subtle and material ways.

In many jurisdictions there has been a failure to understand the significance of these changes for society as a whole. What I have written aims to expose that ignorance, restore our perspectives and ultimately secure a better quality of decision-making and accountability in our increasingly globalised world. What I am also very conscious is the extent to which corporate governance if in some respects one of those *off limits* matters. We should never forget what George Orwell says about orthodoxy and unconsciousness.

7

Figure 1

Letter published in The Guardian newspaper dated 10 November 2011

Business as usual for Barclays boss Bob Diamond

Bob Diamond's lecture (Banks can be good citizens, 4 November) is an example of the sort of sophistry and deception we are all subjected to. Corporations are inanimate fictional entities in law. Corporations are not citizens, and it's absurd, but intentional, that they are portrayed as if they were. Directors like Diamond and his other managers are effectively the corporation we all know as Barclays plc. It is to them we should be asking the question about their own actions as citizens. Putting this irrelevant corporate entity in between is intended to suggest there is another entity which the directors and managers are there, in some sense, to tame. This is a smoke screen: a grand deception.

What we need is proper, thorough-going supervision with independent supervisory boards made up of representatives of the shareholders and stakeholders about which Diamond speaks so fondly. These supervisory boards would make their voice clear on what the corporation should or should not be doing to make money. They would also settle the vexed issue of executive pay. But Diamond wants none of that sort of democratic control and accountability. He wants to continue to control the business, at the same time daring to suggest they are all working to make Barclays Bank plc a better citizen. Pull the other leg, Mr. Diamond. You just want the clamour to go away and to get back to making money at everyone else's expense.

Richard Tudway

10 November 2011
Centre for International Economics
London

Notes

[1] A reference to the thesis of Hansmann H and Kraakman R *The End of History for Corporate Law* Yale Law School Working Paper No. 235; NYU Working Paper No. 013; Harvard Law School Discussion Paper No. 280; Yale SOM Working Paper No. ICF - 00-09.

[2] See: Aoki M *Corporations in Evolving Diveristy*, OUP 2010

[3] Attributed to James D Wolfenshon President of the World Bank, 1999.

[4] See: The Wealth of Nations, London, 1776.

[5] Frederich List's principal work is entitled *Das Nationale System der Politischen Ökonomie* (1841) and was translated into English as *The National System of Political Economy*.

[6] It is even suggested that Queen Victoria, in the age of the railway, was so appalled by the environmental damage in the Black Country of "Midlands" England (as it became known) that she protested to ministers and insisted on blinds being drawn in the carriages of her train when she passed through this scarred landscape of England's *green and pleasant land*.

[7] See: Micklethwait J and Wooldridge *A Future Perfect: The Challenge of Hidden Promise of Globalisation*, which offers a glowing if fanciful account of possibilities. London 2000

[8] See Stuart Hall *The Neoliberal victory must be challenged. We start today*". The Guardian, Comment & Debate, 24 April 2013.

[9] See: Teubner G *Enterprise Corporatism: New Industrial Policy and the 'Essence' of the Legal Person* in Wheeler S ed. A Reader on Law of the Business Enterprise, OUP 1994.

[10] Amid a wealth of "status quo" protective documentation where corporate governance is concerned there is one well documented historical example of this. It involved the decision of the Board of GM to ban managers and employees from reading Peter Drucker's *Concept of the Corporation* (1948 and 1972). They did so because he urged GM to treat workers as a *resource* rather than a *cost*. In contrast Japanese management embraced the concept. The Japanese auto industry prospered: GM, as we know, went into long term decline. See Aoki (2011) *op cit* pages 7 and 8.

[11] See: Allen F and Gale D *A Comparative Theory of Corporate Governance* December 2002.

[12] See: Richard Tudway *Corporate governance in a radically changed world – a fresh look at the Rhineland model,* Global Labour Column, No 36 October 2010.

[13] Senior bankers, in the wake of the global financial crisis, have escaped prosecution despite evidence of gross negligence.

[14] This is a reference to jurisdictions in countries which border the River Rhine in Europe and include notably Germany amongst other countries.

[15] A reference to the arrangements whereby working people are represented by their trade unions at different levels in the conduct of the affairs of the corporation through Works Councils and direct board representation.

[16] See: Beck Stefan and Scherrer Christoph, *The German Economic Model Emerges Reinforced from the Crisis* Global Labour Column, Number 29, August 2010.

[17] A reference to the sponsorship role of government in the affairs of a wide range of so called strategic industries.

[18] *Hard law* is statutory; *soft* law refers to the fact that *soft* laws are discretionary rather that statutory.

[19] The portrayal of the corporation as an entity which can be sued, in cases of corporate manslaughter, has arisen because of the difficulties of attributing culpability to individual directors. Though this has certainly helped families of victims to secure compensation for loss of life it has had the unintended effect of dampening further the prospects of establishing in law the guilt of real persons such as directors who act *for an on behalf of the corporation*, a device which is seen to protect them, unfairly, from personal liability.

[20] The CEO of Barclays Bank who resigned in July 2012 following the LIBOR scandal and its impact on Barclays Bank.

[21] The efforts made by corporate management to portray the corporation of a responsible corporate citizen bears witness to this phenomenon.

[22] The principal reason for this is the asymmetry of information which the Anglo American system creates, maintains and exploits and the fact that NEDs (non-executive directors) provide little more than the appearance of good governance and are mostly incapable of supervising the actions of executive directors.

[23] The nexus of contracts argument retains a hold on the imagination of many who argue that the company is a non regulatable entity – a site within which consenting parties contract between one another.

[24] See: Tudway R & Pascal A-M *Beyond the Ivory Tower: From Business Aims to Policy Making.* Public Administration and Development Vol 26, No 2, May 2006.

Chapter 1

An overview of the scope of the book

1.1   Summary

This book has two principal aims.

- First, to provide for readers and students alike with a comprehensive framework for examining and understanding the provenance and evolution of corporate governance traditions in different jurisdictions and the legal arrangements which support these traditions.

- Second to make an assessment of comparative corporate behaviour in different jurisdictions and draw conclusions about the imperatives in respect of reform.

In this respect the book distinguishes itself from the many books, originated in the English language, which are limited mostly to examining the history and evolution of corporate governance in English speaking (or more accurately Anglo American) common law jurisdictions.[1]

The book will seek to examine not only the evolution of corporate governance in Anglo American jurisdictions[2] but corporate governance in other non English-speaking non common law jurisdictions and, where appropriate, the governance of SOEs (state-owned industries), SWFs (sovereign wealth funds) other forms of corporate organisation and endeavour and their respective achievements. In this way it aims to provide a richer and more complete insight into corporate governance traditions, co-determination and performance outturns in alternative cultural settings covering Europe, Asia and the Americas. These matters are investigated in Chapters 1 to 5.

It will also seek to assess the impact of societal expectations on corporations and corporate behaviour in different jurisdictions. It will assess these behaviours that are exposed and set out the conclusions that can be fairly drawn. Chapters 6 to 10 focus on these matters. Specifically Chapter 10 includes a selection of case studies which explore different aspects of corporate behaviour. Finally this wide ranging analysis of experience drawn from the public record will be synthesised and conclusions drawn in respect of the fundamental reforms to corporate governance that need to be addressed. These matters are addressed in Chapters 11 to 14. Each chapter contains questions for review and other tasks that readers are encouraged to undertake. These aim at deepening our understanding of the underlying issues.

1.2   Corporate governance – the dominance of the Anglo American model

As Allen and Gale (2002)[3] remind us the paradigm of the Anglo American corporate governance model has been exhaustively reported upon. The literature is wide and for the most part uncritical in the sense that it accepts the orthodoxy of the Anglo American model. This book seeks, in contrast, to explore wider paradigms. It is comparative in treatment. In doing so it will examine four key interconnected matters on which the performance of the corporation ultimately depends. It will also help us to develop more critical insights into different governance systems and how they impact upon the delivery of performance.

The interconnected matters are as follows.

- The common and civil law identity of the corporation and the role of the director in the stewardship of the company in different jurisdictions.[4]

- How capital markets in general and the banking system in particular[5] have evolved in different jurisdictions to provide safeguards to investors from the errant behaviour of directors or controlling shareholders and promote the efficient use of capital.

- How the framework of checks and balances, supported by *hard* law and *soft*, (comply or explain) law, has developed to promote corporate accountability, transparency and compliance with the law.

- How benchmarks against which the performance of different governance systems have developed and their assessment.

The Anglo American model has, without doubt, been dominant in terms of defining the high ground of the debate on corporate governance.   Anglo American analysts traditionally stress the importance of strengthening the *external* role of capital markets in

12

disciplining management and the legal arrangements which undergird markets. The EMH[6] (Efficient Markets Hypothesis) is seen as the ultimate justification of reliance on capital markets. This ensures that the price of a security reflects accurately all information about that security and thereby protects the investor. Though widely discredited for its failure to detect much less discipline errant management, it remains fundamental to the perception of good governance.

This fact explains the focus of attention in the literature on common law precedents that have evolved in Anglo American jurisdictions in regard to the *external* mechanisms of control by capital markets. It also goes some way to explaining the relative paucity of detailed knowledge about governance in other jurisdictions. The book will seek to shed light on why analysts have paid less attention to the wider role of direct or *internal* mechanisms of shareholder and stakeholder intervention in corporate governance that is commonplace in other jurisdictions.

In Anglo American jurisdictions institutional investors (or more specifically portfolio managers), and more recently hedge funds and equity funds have become progressively dominant in the ownership of publicly traded corporations[7] as individual investors (and often founder) shareholders have gradually sold out. But there have been other processes at work. First institutional investors who replaced earlier shareholders, including founder shareholders, have progressively become *detached* from the everyday affairs of the corporation in which they are invested. Second they have become dispersed in terms of the proportion of shares held by any one institution.[8] This development reflects in *path-dependent* fashion the control mechanisms that have evolved in Anglo American jurisdictions. It has also lead to some of the most widely reported criticisms of the shortcomings of the Anglo American system of corporate governance and explains the curiosity to know and understand more about the behaviour and performance of corporations in other jurisdictions.

These features of corporate governance are not necessarily reflected in the institutional settings or social, political or regulatory priorities in the other jurisdictions examined. This is most strikingly the case in *Rhineland*, Nordic and Japanese and South Korean jurisdictions amongst others. Yet as we will see the Anglo American model has emerged in the second half of the 20th century as the dominant benchmark against which performance elsewhere is judged though this is now more fundamentally questioned.[9]

The activities of the OECD Roundtable on Corporate Governance and the Principles of Corporate Governance published by the OECD[10] well exemplify the perhaps unconscious presumption of convergence towards Anglo American best practice. The OECD

Principles of Corporate Governance can be downloaded at www.OECD.Org. The author's contribution to the OECD's on-line consultation on Corporate Governance and the Financial crisis and the Review of Corporate Governance by Trade Union Experts are set out in Appendices 1 & 2. The TUAC formal debate on Corporate Governance is contained in Chapter 7. The presumption of convergence is unhelpful because it has the effect of stifling debate on alternatives. This book will seek to redress this imbalance.

1.3   The governance of the corporation

Chapters 2, 3 & 4 examine the corporation and evolution as a legal construct mostly through the lens of English law. Chapter 5 looks closely at the role of directors in the governance process and how this has been shaped. The corporation is an entity that has existed in different forms throughout the centuries in different jurisdictions.[11] Its history is well documented and whilst issues of governance do not feature widely in this history[12] this is for one fairly straightforward reason. As unlimited liability entities, or partnerships such corporate structures were run and managed by the partners in the interests of the partnership. This state of affairs is fundamentally different to the arrangements which mostly exist in modern times.

The most important single difference is that most corporations and certainly publicly quoted corporations are limited liability entities in one form or another.[13] In Anglo American jurisdictions they are managed by a unitary board of directors who report, mostly, *ex post*, to shareholders or institutional investors, through the institution of the AGM (Annual General Meeting) according to conditions laid down in the Memorandum and Articles of Association (Mem & Arts).

Looking back historically it would be fair to conclude that disputes about the affairs of the corporation would have been mostly settled by the partners. Even when limited liability was introduced in Europe in the 19th century[14] life would have been little changed for those parties, previously partnered in unlimited liability entities who then found themselves shareholders in limited liability companies. Ways of resolving disputes and other differences existed. There are, of course, a number of well documented cases of systematic financial abuse and fraud[15] which, without doubt, helped to shape the distinctive preoccupations in Anglo American jurisdictions with investor protection.[16] Such protection arrangements were strengthened and deepened as corporations evolved.

1.4   Ambiguity and confusion in corporate law

During this evolution in English law the twists and turns of the interpretation of the corporation and its identity are plagued with ambiguity and confusion. Arguments in law saw the corporation partly as an *aggregate* entity in which the proprietorial rights of the shareholder appeared unchanged through to the portrayal of the corporation as an independent fictional entity in law owning its own assets. The role of the directors has followed a similarly tortured journey from a position where they were clearly the handmaidens of the shareholders to a position where it is evident that they have no clear duty of care to shareholders. It is little wonder that the corporation and its governance remains mired in confusion. This is fully explored.

As shareholders themselves became less closely connected with the everyday running of the business it fell to the directors they appointed to the board of the company to take over its stewardship. Chapter 5 explores this. In some instances the key director would be the chief executive. This might possibly have been an entrepreneur, incentivised by some share in the equity of the corporation whose task it was to make a success of the business. Some external directors might also be appointed to ensure that the interests of shareholders were properly represented and their interests protected. But the dynamic of change powered first by the industrial revolution and later through international trade and investment was to transform this picture almost beyond recognition.

Yet what remains is a picture confused by ambiguity with directors trapped in a time warp in terms of the nature of their fiduciary duties and to whom they owe their duty of care. Had these potential problems been identified clearly at an earlier stage steps could have been taken to resolve these matters an event that occurred in other jurisdictions. But the obsession with *one size fits all* then as now continues to misinform and distort public policy. Chapter 6 attempts to explore and assesses the different types of corporate structure and how they have evolved. This provides the important international perspective – a helpful and practical step in the direction of settling many of the underlying governance issues.

Chapters 7 to 10 will inspect closely how companies actually operate and how they respond to the reputational challenges they face and the drivers of societal expectations. These matters have shaped public concern issues centred on corporate governance. The different approaches in addressing how best to address societal expectations in different jurisdictions are explored in Chapters 8 and 9. The unitary board structures, a classic feature of Anglo American governance, will be contrasted with variants which include the two-tier independent supervisory board structures in *Rhineland*countries in Europe and the Nordic countries and the hybrid structures in Japan and other Asian jurisdictions. A key aspect of this debate centres on co-determination in the work place.

Chapter 10 provides insight into how firms behave and how they seek to portray themselves. Specifically the chapter will examine how they view themselves in terms of the CSR (corporate social responsibility) initiatives they adopt. This chapter will also explore the particular challenges facing corporations where ethical behaviour is concerned. This work is supported by a selection of Case Studies. These cases examine various aspects of corporate behaviour the drivers of those behaviours and the corporate response to the challenges they find themselves facing.

Chapters 11 to 14 seek to assemble the bits of the jigsaw. Chapter 11 makes a synthesis of different jurisdictional paradigms. In doing so it underscores how institutional structures are *path dependent* enabling us to see and better understand the strengths and weaknesses of different preferences. As a natural follow through Chapter 12 attempts to capture and explain how the corporation of tomorrow might look. Chapters 13 & 14 draw the key conclusions that flow from the earlier analysis and set out priorities in respect of corporate governance reform.

Notes

[1] Anglo-American common law traces its roots to the medieval concept that the law as handed down from the King's courts represented the common custom of the people. It evolved chiefly from three English Crown courts of the twelfth and thirteenth centuries: the Exchequer, the King's Bench, and the Common Pleas. These courts eventually assumed jurisdiction over disputes previously decided by local or manorial courts, such as baronial, admiral's (maritime), guild, and forest courts, whose jurisdiction was limited to specific geographic or subject matter areas. Equity courts, which were instituted to provide relief to litigants in cases where common-law relief was unavailable, also merged with common-law courts. This consolidation of jurisdiction over most legal disputes into several courts forms the framework for the modern Anglo-American judicial system.

[2] The term Anglo American jurisdictions refers to the common law evolution of the laws governing corporations and directors and the protection of shareholders which has evolved in English speaking jurisdictions, most notably the US and Canada, Britain and Ireland, South Africa (and other former African colonial countries). India, Australia, New Zealand and Hong Kong.

[3] See: Allen F and Gale D *op cit.*

[4] The common-law system is distinct from the civil-law systems which predominate in Europe, the Nordic countries and in areas colonised by France, Spain and Portugal.

[5] A reference to the role of banks most notably in *Rhineland* jurisdictions.

[6] The EMH (Efficient Market Hypothesis) affirms that financial markets are *informationally efficient*. This is now widely challenged by evidence of market rigging and other abuses in financial markets.

[7] A reference to corporations whose shares are quoted on stock markets when compared with non-quoted (public and privately held) corporations whose shares do not trade.

[8] Shareholdings held by institutions in publicly traded companies in Anglo American jurisdictions is unlikely, in practice, to exceed 5%.

[9] See: Hall P & Soskice D (2002) and Amable B (2003) *Varieties of Capitalism.*

[10] See: The OECD *Principles of Corporate Governance,* OECD 2004

[11] The term corporation derives from Roman Law. Examples include the Roman Catholic Church in Europe which was established under canon law through the Gregorian Reformation (1075-1120). Oxford and Paris universities were established in the 13th Century with Harvard chartered in 1636. Significantly corporations were not permitted under Islamic law though the *Waaf* was a form of corporate body which emerged in the 8th and 9th centuries. See: Kuran T *The absence of the corporation in Islamic law. Origins and persistence.* American Journal of Comparative Law 2005, 53: 758-834. Quasi-corporate forms in Japan were dynastically controlled by a professional administration. This addressed some of the problems of continuity and transferability embodied in the concept of the European corporation. See: Ikegami E *The Taming of the Samurai. Honorific Individualism and the Meaning of Modern Japan,* 1995, Harvard University Press.

[12] Though there are some notable and important examples which are explored in later chapters.

[13] Different jurisdictions have different types of limited liability company though mostly the distinction made is between private and public and publicly listed corporations.

[14] Limited Liability was introduced in Britain in 1856 following the Joint Stock Companies Act of 1844 Act. The 1844 Act created a Registrar of Joint Stock Companies. However, there was still no limited liability to shareholders and members could still be held responsible for unlimited losses by the company even though widespread use of Deed of Settlement Companies effectively shielded investors from unlimited liability risk.

[15] See: Mackay C, *Extraordinary Popular Delusions and the Madness of Crowds* (1841). This provides an account of some of these remarkable events.

[16] See: Tudway R *The Juridical Paradox of the Corporation* Annual of Corporate Law 2002.

Chapter 2

Corporations their ownership and governance

2.1 Summary

Chapter 2 is challenging. It is theoretical and historical in its treatment. It draws heavily on the legal debate as it has developed in Britain and America. It is nevertheless crucial to our understanding of the corporate form and how this has evolved in those jurisdictions. It is divided into three separate but closely connected sections.

It examines the concept of the corporation and the history of the development of the corporation under English and American law and its relationship with shareholders and directors. In explaining the birth of the limited liability corporation it explores the framework of laws which govern corporations and the different approaches to governance and its institutionalisation within the corporation that have arisen in Anglo American jurisdictions and jurisdictions elsewhere.

2.2 The origins of the corporation

Whilst corporate activity has its origins in antiquity it appears mostly to have been a European phenomenon. As we have seen earlier it has no straightforward historical parallels in Islam or elsewhere in Asia. Over the centuries the corporate form can be identified in numerous different guises. Its advent reflects amongst other objectives the need for collaborative endeavour over generations, joint pooling of capital, and joint sharing of commercial risks. Sometimes corporate ventures were supported by Royal Prerogative or by Charter and Acts of Parliament – even earlier by the Roman Church. The bulk, by far, reflected everyday practical needs of commerce as market-driven economic activity itself expanded and broadened out. This is first described and analysed by Adam Smith in his celebrated Wealth of Nations.[1]

The enactment of limited liability in 1856 was a major turning point in English law. It was then followed by almost half a century of confusion about the status of the corporation and its relationship with the shareholders. This was resolved in a ground breaking ruling of the British House of Lords in Salomon versus Salomon in 1897.[2] One major consequence of the Salomon judgement was the definition of the company as an entity separate from its shareholders. This was a judgment of fundamental significance in terms of the evolution of the corporation and the role of directors in its stewardship. Needless to say developments elsewhere took different paths. In exploring these matters we need to look closely at what a corporation is.

2.3   What is a corporation?

The corporation is concisely defined by Eisenberg (1989), a distinguished American academic jurist, in the following terms.

> *A corporation is a profit seeking enterprise of persons and assets organised by rules. Most of these rules are determined by the unilateral actions of corporate organs or officials. Some of these rules are determined by market forces. Some are determined by contract or other forms of agreement. Some are determined by law*[3]

This can, alternatively, be explained in the following terms. The first point to stress is that it is clear that the corporation is in a real sense a creature of *concession*. It is determined by law. This is consistent with the view that its existence depends on *enabling* legislation even though corporate forms existed long before legislation, as we understand it today, provided for their existence.[4] But even in the very earliest times corporations were *granted* as a form of *concession* either by the Church or by the Realm before the state passed comprehensive enabling legislation during the 19th century. This is a point of significance as we are going to discover. An extension of this argument is that the corporation is a *real* or *aggregate* entity – an existence which is defined by the *corporators*[5]without whom corporations would not exist. This conceptualisation of the corporation has shaped in a fundamentally different way approaches to corporate governance in Anglo American and European jurisdictions and elsewhere - a matter to which we will return as the argument develops.[6]

The second point turns on the source of the rules that govern the corporation. These consist of a panoply of *hard* and *soft* (sometime referred to as *comply or explain* rules), some of which are again enacted as self regulatory by laws[7] or by the state. Others are a direct consequence of market forces and are often initiated by governments. These cover competition, the environment, employment, equal opportunity and anti-discrimination laws amongst others. The third point is a reference to the corporation as a profit seeking enterprise of assets and people. This too is highly significant. The profit-seeking element serves only to identify the very broadest purposes of the endeavour. Whilst generally correct it does not rule out corporate endeavour which is **not** associated with profit seeking as an end in itself.

The fourth point concerning persons and assets is also of crucial importance. This acknowledges shareholders whose role it is to provide seed capital and possibly later development capital to the corporation. This is a role that changes fundamentally as the corporation matures. It may also refer to the role of capital and labour which enables the corporation to productively generate its output. This point will grow in importance as we explore further the nature of corporate endeavour.

Fifth and finally there is within the definition a reference to corporate organs and officials. The organs of the corporation are a reflection of the different control structures within the corporation. The most important in Anglo American jurisdictions is the Board of Directors. In *Rhineland* and Nordic jurisdictions the upper board is the Supervisory Board whose members represent the interests of shareholders and other key stakeholders. This board is distinct from the Executive Board that runs the business. This is of paramount importance.

In Anglo American jurisdictions board officials are drawn from the executives who run the company supplemented by other, sometimes, external or independent directors. Together they oversee the running the corporation. They are also the focus of power and decision taking within the corporation.[8] These officials not only determine the commercial direction of the corporation but are also responsible[9] for ensuring that the corporation complies with the *hard* and *soft* rules which form part of its operating environment and determine its *license to operate*[10], or in alternative terms its socio-economic legitimacy.

There remains a further aspect which will now be explored – the notion that the corporation is a *fictional entity* created in law and by implication an entity which is literally mindless and has to have officials to interpret, decide and pursue its purposes. This as we are to discover is the source of enduring controversy and confusion.

2.4   The corporate person

The portrayal of the corporation as a creature of *concession* and a legal *fiction* is not by any means the end of the story. It contrasts with another view of the corporate personality. This is embedded in the history of the corporation and the private individuals behind it. It presents a challenge to the *fictional* theory of the corporation. As stated earlier this is sometimes referred to as *aggregate* or *realist* concept of the corporation. The important point is that it represents a long standing European view of corporate entities.[11] It sees the corporation as existing independently of its shareholders and is therefore not an entity which is exclusively beholden to its shareholders.[12]

Rather it is an entity which is run by managers whose role it is to interpret its interests and purposes, its duties and obligations. The *realist* theory is unclear on whether the corporation is *concessionary* entity and thus liable to state regulation but it most certainly acknowledges that the corporation has interests which may be wider than that of narrowly promoting or protecting shareholder value. Japanese and South Korean reflect a similar view. This as we shall see opens up fundamental difference between European Asian and Anglo American concepts of the corporation and the way they are governed.

Returning to the Eisenberg definition we can see that it mostly fits the description of the corporation in the modern world. What of course the definition fails to explain is the difference between the corporation as a *fictional* entity when compared with the *realist* or *aggregate* portrayal nor the impact that economic development has played in shaping the environment in which the corporation operates and hence our interpretation of the underlying definition. These matters will be dealt with as we progress. We now turn briefly to events which brought about the separation of *ownership* from *control* and the particular response in Anglo American jurisdictions to this development.

2.5 The separation of ownership from control

We need to understand why the observation about the *separation of ownership from control* articulated by Berle and Means (1932) in their seminal work first came about.[13] As limited liability corporations grew in scale and importance the role of the shareholder began to change also. This gave rise to the concept of the *management–run* corporation. We should remember, in passing, that in the European tradition this would have posed fewer surprises because of the role of management in the running the limited liability corporate entity and the particular governance arrangements that had been instituted to address these challenges.[14] This is important.

Founder shareholders in Anglo American jurisdictions gradually reduced or sold out entirely their stakes to dispersed institutional investors leaving power increasingly in the hands of directors and managers. As this happened the appearance of separation of *ownership* from *control* became more clearly an operating reality. We can also begin to understand the influences that shaped thinking in Anglo American jurisdictions about how best to respond to this development. It also explains the factors that have shaped the focus of academic research in Anglo American jurisdictions in the period thereafter.

2.6   The corporation as a contracting site

There were also other significant theoretical developments. The unique economic insight of Coase (1937) into the firm (another colloquial term for a company or corporation) contested the failure of neo classical economics to address its organisational nature and purpose.[15] He questioned the assumption in classical economic theory that markets alone determined prices. He further observed that there were uncertainties in contracting in the market place. In the absence of perfect knowledge he pointed out that the managers of firms could exploit these transaction costs more effectively than individual contractors. This marks a huge step forward in thinking about the purpose and operating reality of the corporation and the role of management in that process.

Alchian and Demsetz[16] (1972) developed Coase's insight. They questioned the primary role of the entrepreneur as an organiser of individual contracts within the firm replacing it instead with a concept of the firm simply as *nexus of contracts* in which individual factors of production competed. This appeared to rehabilitate the proprietorial role of the shareholder. The actions of the firm are monitored, according to their model, by the shareholders who assess the performance of the firm and by definition the contribution of different factors of production in that process, including management.

Importantly this perception also recognised that the firm's management may not necessarily focus on enhancing shareholder outturns. From this backdrop Jensen and Meckling (1976) developed the concept of the *agent and principal*.[17] They argued that in order for the shareholders to ensure that management performed effectively, they incurred agency costs. These costs are incurred by shareholders in acquiring sufficient information to maintain an effective check on the behaviour of management. This line of argument was extended further by Williamson[18] (1975) strengthening the case for shareholder (or investor) *primacy* on the grounds that they buy their shares with no contractual assurances that management will, for example, seek to maximise profits or otherwise enhance shareholder value.

2.7   The corporation as a non regulatable entity

A significant inference from this line of reasoning is that it has the effect of diminishing the role of the state in regulating the affairs of corporations. The role of the state is effectively reduced to facilitating private contracting arrangements by providing default rules (exemplified by Table A in the Memorandum and Articles under English law) which apply in the absence of any agreement to the contrary. These influences have critically determined the pattern of corporate governance priorities in Anglo American jurisdictions and specifically the stance of institutional investors who have become the largest single investors in US and UK listed companies. Institutional investors prefer market related resolutions. In this w\ay they minimise the monitoring costs they might otherwise incur if they had to oversee management directly.

But things began to change in the light of experience. Disquiet at aspects of corporate governance provided ammunition to those who challenged the shareholder supremacy model. These sentiments have encouraged the development of alternative stakeholder efficiency arguments on the grounds that inefficiencies in the contractual renegotiating process allow management to take advantage of stakeholders, such as employees, who end up bearing a larger proportion of the risk than they had previously thought. Institutional investors, in contrast, rely on being able to protect their interests by formal mechanisms such as the obligation, in the case of listed companies, to submit public accounts audited by independent accountants and to comply with other listing obligations such as the issue of profits warnings.

The aim of these provisions is to protect investors from unexpected shocks and other management misdemeanours. As we move further in time the malfunctioning of these mechanisms has become increasingly more apparent. The impetus for change has been ratcheted up as a result of the massive destruction of shareholder wealth in the wake of the global banking crisis. The perception that the crisis was in large measure driven by failures in corporate governance has gradually crystallised. The plight of stakeholders, such as employees, has been totally ignored.

2.8 Developments in non Anglo American jurisdictions

The Anglo American path of development in terms of corporate governance is not reflected in the same way elsewhere. In the capitalist world notable differences can be identified between the United States and Britain, Germany and other *Rhineland* and Nordic[19] countries. The centre-piece of the *Rhineland* model is the supervisory board which separates clearly supervision from execution. France and Japan both represent variants of the *Rhineland* model. *Rhineland* habits and practices derive directly from 19th century legislation in Germany.[20] This recognised the importance of ensuring that as limited liability corporations became larger and shareholders increasingly at a distance from the day to day operations of the corporation that all corporations above a specified size would be obliged to create a separate supervisory board. The aim of this was to ensure that the interest of shareholders and other stakeholders were properly represented.[21]

Mostly importantly it is recognition that there is *no one size fits all* solution where corporate endeavour is concerned.[22]

Developments in France reflect in some measure similar influences that were at work in Germany. The absence of a strong investment oriented private banking system led France to favour the creation of *commanding heights* nationalised industries whose funding would depend directly upon the state rather than private capital markets. This was a feature of French post war reconstruction.[23] The institutional failures of Third Republic (1870 – 1940) in general, and the economic crisis of the 1930s were catalysts which reshaped French institutions from 1945 onwards.[24]

Capital markets also worked in a subtly different way in these jurisdictions. Banks themselves became increasingly shareholders in limited liability corporations. This in turn was instrumental in breaking the classic Anglo American distinction between *debt* and *equity*. It also explains in large measure the very fundamental differences in the financing of industrial expansion in Germany and elsewhere.[25] In post war Germany banks established investment funds and began to perform functions superficially similar to that of investment banks and institutional investors in Anglo American jurisdictions but with important differences.

Banks were themselves represented on the boards of those corporations in which they were invested. As a generalisation it would be fair to say that they were mostly long-term patient investors. Their role as board directors was to ensure that the executive directors and managers of the corporation behaved at least broadly in accordance with their own long term commitments as investors. This is a very significant difference. It portrays *Rhineland* investors as being both more strategic and more proactive. It also explains why *Rhineland* capital markets have evolved differently when compared with those in Anglo American jurisdiction and why institutional investor behaviour is fundamentally different as between the different jurisdictions. This is an outstanding example of *path dependency* in determining culture, institutional designs and commercial priorities.[26]

Variants of the *Rhineland* model have been replicated as we will discover in many other parts of the world. Indian traditions together with those in many parts of English-speaking Africa and the Middle East reflect a mix of British and French influence. In Central and South America, Spanish and broader Napoleonic influences have also been important. Both the Japanese *keiretsu* and the South Korean *chaebol* models of developments, though unique in themselves, may also have drawn inspiration from the *Rhineland,* Nordic and French models. How different types of corporate structure have evolved in Anglo American jurisdictions and elsewhere will be explored more fully in a later chapter.

2.9   Conclusions

This chapter has traced the historic origins of the corporation as a concessionary collective unlimited liability endeavour. This transformation is triggered by the introduction of limited liability in the mid 19th century. In Anglo American jurisdictions this development has resulted in unending legal confusion about the relationship between the company and shareholders and the issue of ownership. We have also traced the development of the role of the director. During this period we have also seen how the within the framework of the limited liability corporation shareholders have become progressively detached from the corporation. Finally we have examined how different jurisdictions have responded to these developments.

The detachment of shareholders from the corporation is supported in Anglo American jurisdictions by common law precedents establishing in the first instance that the limited liability company, if properly incorporated, owns its own assets. Common law also supports the conclusion that shareholders are not in any real sense owners of the corporation. The shares they own as shareholders are not titles to ownership of the underlying assets but non specific claims to participate in the profits of the company. This leaves the company in the strange position of owning itself. A matter for further investigation.

Questions for review

1. Why in the text does it speak about corporations as creatures of *concession*?

2. What is the difference between the company as a *fictional* representation and its representation as a *real* or *aggregate* entity?

3. What in your view is the most important element in Eisenberg's definition of the corporation?

4. What in your view is the most important dynamic change which has occurred to corporations in the past 150 years or so?

5. How did limited liability impact upon the act of shareholding?

6. What in your view has been the foremost concern in Anglo American capital markets and why has this arisen?

7. What is the significance of Coase's theory about the reasons why firms exist?

8. What insight does the *nexus of contracts* representation provide?

9. What does it mean to say that the governance of the corporation developed along different *path dependent* lines in different jurisdictions?

10. What is the essential difference between governance of corporations in Anglo American jurisdictions and those in *Rhineland* jurisdictions?

11. What in your view is the significance of the comment that corporations may not be profit-seeking entities?

12. What is a stakeholder and how are stakeholders different from shareholders?

Learning Tasks

I   Explain why governance priorities in Anglo American jurisdictions have tended to focus primarily on investor and shareholder interests?

II   What features would you expect to discover in a stakeholder capitalist system?

III   How would you assess whether an independent director was *independent*?

IV   How do boards control the corporation they represent?

V   Is there a case for independent supervisory boards and worker representation?

VI   Do large scale limited liability enterprises behave in the same way as small limited liability enterprises?

Figure 2   **Comparative Corporate Structures**

Jurisdictions

	Anglo American	**Rhineland/European**
Legal Traditions	Common Law	Roman/Civil Law
Legal Status	Fictional Entity	Real Entity
Ownership	Shareholders (ambiguously)	The *aggregate* Corporation
Control	Management (de facto)	Supervisory Boards
Supervision Directors	Unitary Board (with Independent Executive Board)	Supervisory Board overseeing
Shareholders	Ex post reliance on AGM	Shareholders and Stakeholders represented on Supervisory
Boards Supervision	Institutions not engaged	Banks, and Workers significantly
Shareholding by Banks and Insurers	Highly dispersed	Large holdings still held
Capital Access	Stock Markets	Bank Finance debt and equity
Investment Climate	Short-termist	Long-termist and patient

Figure 3

Letter to the Financial Times   10 October 2008

OECD must now tackle corporate governance issue

From Mr Richard Tudway

The global financial crisis heightens the importance of addressing what needs to be done to remedy defects in the arrangements of corporate governance and accountability. Moves in the US and the UK to effectively nationalise banking entities previously in private ownership provide abundant evidence of the failure of Anglo-American corporate governance model to protect shareholder value, and the economic welfare of citizens at large.

A short while ago Gordon Brown, in an address to the Labour party conference, spoke, non-specifically, about the need for "a new settlement". Any new settlement must surely include a fundamental review of the Organisation for Economic Co-operation and Development corporate governance arrangements.

The justification for independent supervisory board structures in promoting effective accountability of managers and company directors is overwhelming. In launching such an initiative the OECD and its advisers need to show courage in opposing the ideological resistance of the US to moves to improve and strengthen wider stakeholder interests through independent supervision. European Union nations, which generally support independent supervision, need to stand their ground if the opportunity to debate these issues afresh is not lost until the next crisis!

Richard Tudway

Centre for International Economics, London WC1, UK

Figure 4

Letter to the Financial Times   15 October 2008

OECD to unveil a road map on good governance

From Mr Marcello Bianchi

Richard Tudway (Letters, October 10) is correct in linking the current financial crisis to failures in corporate governance. And weak oversight by boards is certainly part of it. Against this background, the secretary-general of the Organisation for Economic Co-operation and Development, Angel Gurría, recently launched a global drive to improve corporate governance.

The initiative will build on the OECD principles of corporate governance and also engage international organisations, business associations and other key stakeholders. The task is to address immediate reactions to present malpractices and to establish a longer-term road map for effective implementation and monitoring.

The OECD will make a statement on its findings and recommendations about the corporate governance lessons from the financial crisis following the next meeting of the OECD steering group on corporate governance, on November 19-20.

Through this effort, the OECD will play an important role in fostering a sound business culture and rebuilding confidence discredited by bad corporate governance practices in individual companies.

Marcello Bianchi

Chairman, OECD Steering Group on Corporate Governance

Notes

[1] Smith A *The Wealth of Nations*, op.cit (1776). Smith supported the idea of private companies (or *copartneries*). In the private unlimited liability partnerships each partner was "bound for the debts contracted by the company to the whole extent of his fortune". Such a potential liability, he took the view, would concentrate the mind.

[2] See: Salomon v Salomon & Co Ltd [1897] AC 22 , HL

[3] See: Eisenberg M A *The Structure of Corporation :Law* (1989) 89 Colum L Rev 1461 at 1471.

[4] A major aspect of enabling legislation in Britain took the form of the Companies Act of 1844 which standardised acts of incorporation.

[5] *Corporator* is a term which broadly describes shareholders and other stakeholders such as employees and creditors all of whom are viewed as being part and parcel of the corporation in terms of rights.

[6] The *real* or *aggregate* view of the corporation has its roots in Roman and Civil law and explains important differences in the portrayal of the corporation in Europe and in Anglo American jurisdiction.

[7] An example would include the self regulatory Cadbury Code in Britain agreed by a committee of industrialists and recommended to other corporate directors as *best practice*.

[8] Though delegation of powers to lower levels of middle management mean that chains of command may be long – a matter of continuing controversy. It is also frequently used to excuse the failure of top management to respond to failure and abuse at lower levels within the organisation. This was often cited in the News Corp phone hacking hearings to explain and justify the lack of detailed knowledge on the part of the Murdochs.

[9] Responsibility as we are going to discover is often problematical in corporations when things go wrong and specific responsibility cannot be lawfully attributed to a particular individual. This is a particularly distressing aspect of corporate manslaughter cases, and in cases of risk management of major environmental events.

[10] *License to operate* is an almost rhetorical term which is intended to imply legitimacy in terms of corporate behaviour and economic and social acceptability.

[11] The concept of the *Societas* or association emphasises the real persons behind the corporation. The Corporation in this analysis has no independent existence. This line of reasoning predates by centuries the enactment of limited liability. Limited liability had the effect of complicating the picture of ownership.

[12] Whilst this is portrayed as a significant difference between Anglo American and European law the fact is that corporate law in Anglo American jurisdictions is notably indeterminate on the question of who owns the limited liability corporation. It appears clear on examination of the law that shareholders do **not** own the assets of the corporation and directors have a fiduciary duty to the corporation and **not** its shareholders. But myths prevail.

[13] See: Berle A A and Means G C *The Modern Corporation and Private Property*, New York, 1932.

[14] This is a reference to the practice in *Rhineland* jurisdictions to require certain types of corporate entity, by law, to appoint independent supervisory boards and to foster co-determination in the work place.

[15] See: Coase R H *The nature of the firm* Economica(1937)

[16] See: Alchian A and Demsetz H *Production, Information Costs and Economic Organisation* (1972) 62 American Economic Review.

[17] See: Jensen M C and Meckling M*Theory of the Firm: Management Behaviour Agency Costs and Ownership Structures* (1976) 3 Journal of Financial Economics.

[18] See: Williamson, Oliver E. (1975). *Markets and Hierarchies: Analysis and Antitrust Implications*. New York: The Free Press.

[19] Nordic is a reference to the Scandinavian countries of Denmark, Sweden, Norway and Finland.

[20] This occurred as a result of the First Joint Stock Modification Law [Erste Aktiennovelle] of 1871 which made two-tier board structures mandatory.

[21] In 1917 this took on a new significance in a pronouncement from Walter Rathenau who elaborated the concept of the company *in itself* (das Unterhemen an sich). He saw the company as having broad social obligations to create and preserve jobs and serve the needs of the state. See *Vom Aktienwesen,* Rathennau W, Berlin 1917.

[22] Significantly however two-tier board structures have been increasingly adopted by small and medium sized companies as a preferred form of governance.

[23] See: Murphy A, *Corporate ownership in France – the importance of history.*

[24] See: Meisel N, *Lessons from France's Corporate-Governance Experience for Developing Countries and Emerging Economies* OECD Development Centre, March 2002. The *Trente Glorieuse* (thirty glorious years) of post war reconstruction in France (1945 – 1975) were triggered by the recognition that France still retained most of the features of small-scale capitalism. Its pre-war financial system and corporate governance institutions were judged to be incapable of rising to the challenge of modernisation. Similar developments were triggered in Italy and other southern European countries.

[25] This matter is discussed by Calomiris C: *The Costs of Rejecting Universal Banking: American Finance in the German Mirror 1870 – 1914.* This explains also why German banks in the 1920s and 30s proposed debt for equity swaps with many large corporations which otherwise faced bankruptcy.

[26] See: Franks J, Mayer C and Wagner, H 2006. *The Origins of the German Corporation - Finance, Ownership and Control* Review of Finance, Oxford University Press.

Chapter 3

The evolution of the corporation

3.1 Summary

Chapter three looks at issues of evolution through a specifically British lens. This is because of importance of British law, historically, in determining the unique legal and operational environment of the corporation and everything else around it in English-speaking jurisdictions. In doing so it examines the principal influences that have shaped in *path dependent* fashion the relationship between the corporation, the shareholders and the directors and twists and turns in its evolution.

It also examines the framework of laws governing directors in the discharge of their fiduciary duties and how these have evolved historically in the context of disinterested trusteeship and the problems that this leaves unresolved. The chapter also examines how these matters have evolved in other jurisdictions and the factors that have influenced these developments and the differences that have emerged.

3.2 Company Creation

Before exploring more deeply the history of the evolution of the corporate form it may be instructive to recall what happens in English law when a limited liability company is born. Firms can be bought electronically, off-the-shelf, usually from a legal firm who specialises in these activities. [1] The firm's documentation consists of a standard form Memorandum, Articles of Association and a document referred to as Table A. [2] The Memorandum contains details of the shareholders at the time of purchase by the new shareholder(s) (the person(s) buying the company). The name of the company, randomly generated at the time of purchase, can be changed by resolution of the shareholders from XYZ Ltd to ABC Ltd. The shareholders are charged with the responsibility of appointing directors. They may be from their own ranks or elsewhere. The Companies Act requires directors to discharge certain tasks by law such as providing an Annual Return and submitting Accounts in respect of Profit & Loss and a Balance Sheet.

The authorised capital is also stipulated in terms of the number and the nominal value of shares that can be issued. This again can be altered (increased or decreased) by simple resolution. On the basis of this documentation the company can obtain a bank account and then begin to trade, such is the ease of incorporation under English law. Every subsequent development of the company can, in theory, be handled through this basic constitutional document unless and until the company changes its status and, for example, seeks stock exchange listing as a public corporation. The appearance of a *Holy Trinity*[3] embodying the company, shareholder and director is appealingly simple. But things are never as straightforward as we shall see.

3.3   Early corporate forms

Historically the most common British corporate form was the partnership. Each partner was an agent of his fellow partner bearing joint and several collective responsibility for the actions of the partnership, and the debts of the undertaking. This was the dominant form through which wealth was created in Europe as the Enlightenment gathered momentum.[4]

As we move forward in time examining events in England more closely there was evidence, however, of mounting difficulty in maintaining the integrity and coherence of *joint and several* responsibility. Deed of Settlement companies had already emerged as an alternative to partnership formations. These legal constructions were designed to circumvent the basic intention of partnership. They were a socio-economic reflection of the growing distance of some equity partners from the everyday running of the business, a factor which ultimately led to the introduction of limited liability in the mid19[th] century. The intricacies of this lengthy debate preceded the passage of the Joint Stock Companies Act of 1844, which preceded the Act of Limited liability in 1855.[5]

3.4   The Concept of Trusteeship and Fiduciary Duties

During this evolution the role of the director was shaped. In its shaping the director is portrayed historically as a trustee acting on behalf of other parties. This bedrock in trusteeship has endured the many other changes that have occurred as concepts of capitalism and democracy have evolved. The contemporary duties of the director reflect still, in some important measure, the notion that he or she is a trustee of others' interests. This is a role where *disinterested loyalty* and *good faith* remain significant considerations in law and practice.

Yet corporations have expanded and developed beyond all recognition, along with stock markets for the issue and trading of shares and the purchase and sale of listed companies. So too has the act of shareholding with the wholesale institutional investment industry now a dominant force in Anglo American jurisdictions and individual shareholding now a small proportion of total shares in issuance. Directorship, nevertheless, remains caught in a curious time warp straddling at least two mutually incompatible criteria from the point of view of any objective, credible and progressive evaluation of directors' performance: on the one hand the director as a clean pair of disinterested hands; on the other a risk seeking commercial decision taker.

3.5   Sorting out the status of the corporation

These problems have run alongside other inconsistencies, most notably the portrayal of the company in English law in the late 19th century and the issue in particular of to whom the director owes his duty. Following the Foss v Harbottle judgement[6] in England in the late first half of the 19th century the company was portrayed as an independent entity with its own assets subject to the control of the directors. To this day this remains a source of confusion.

A half century was to pass before the English House of Lords ruling in the Salomon[7] case in 1897 categorically established that a lawfully incorporated limited liability company was an entity separate in law from the shareholders. Shareholder ownership rights were, as a consequence, viewed as a right to participate in the profit generated by the enterprise, but not a claim on the assets of the company nor any rights in the management of the company. Uncertainties, however, still surround the matter.

From this the doctrine of the separation of *ownership* from *control* was articulated in the 1930's. The doctrine was in some respects a necessary consequence of limited liability, heightened by the development of capital markets in Anglo American jurisdiction. Its advent remains the source of many problems in the area of corporate governance. The separation of ownership and control confirmed by the Salomon judgement has resulted in misunderstandings about the real identity of the corporation, the proprietary rights of shareholders, and the function of the director in 'promoting the success of the company'.

3.6   Corporate identity in non Anglo American jurisdictions

Whilst there are differences between different English language jurisdictions in the treatment of these matters, the fundamental problem of the identity of the corporation, as it has evolved, remains an obstacle to progress. Jurisdictions, notably *Rhineland* and *Nordic* amongst others, have adapted in different ways to the governance challenges posed by the separation of *ownership* and *control*. The same is true in Asian and South American jurisdiction. The failure to satisfactorily address this ambiguity in law in Anglo American jurisdictions is an obstacle to progress though it has certainly satisfied other ideological ambitions.[8]

Shareholders of publicly traded corporations continue to be portrayed as proprietors when this is simply not the case. One is bound to ask why the myth of shareholder ownership of the corporation continues to exercise such sway over public perceptions. Shareholders continue to be portrayed, misleadingly, as enjoying *primacy* in terms of their illusory ownership rights. This continues to hamper the debate in Anglo American jurisdictions about governance of publicly traded corporations and the role of directors, shareholders and other stakeholders in that process. The relevant legal judgments, interpretations in common law and statutory changes to the law will now be explored in a bid to understand better the impact of these developments and the conclusions drawn.

3.7   The company and role of the director

We start with an oddity where the company is concerned. Under English law the word *company* is without formal legal definition[9] even though Eisenberg, in the American context, defines it very clearly, as we saw earlier. In common parlance the word company otherwise reflects the Eisenberg definition in all jurisdictions. It refers to those associated for economic purposes to carry on a business for gain. The director, who is responsible for the stewardship of the company, is again not defined in English law.[10] The contemporary powers of the director arise because of the separation of the personality of the corporation, the company being construed in law as a legal person in *personification[11]* and separate from the shareholders.

These powers were crystallised[12] by various landmark judgements in the 19th century in Britain. As mentioned earlier, these include *Foss v Harbottle (1843)* which translated the doctrine of the separate legal personality into a rule of procedure governing shareholder rights to sue; *Salomon* (1897) which established, categorically, the separateness of the company as a legal entity and its assets from the shareholders and, in between, the passing of the law of limited liability in 1855.[13]

This is important to our understanding. As artificial legal entities companies can only operate through the medium of human beings who take decisions for them. In larger companies these decisions are taken by those officers who provide the collective leadership of the company, namely the board of directors. Directors can thus be viewed as creatures of legal and practical necessity if a semblance of corporate democracy,[14] administrative efficiency and commercial coherence was to be established in companies which had not only grown in size and economic importance but where shareholders were increasingly remote from their day-to-day operations. This is a development which has gathered pace. As it has done so it has created a wave of new concerns which centre on the governance of the company, and the role of directors and shareholders in that process.

3.8   The separation of ownership from control

As already reported the growing distance of shareholders from the company in which they were invested was first explored systematically by Berle and Means (1932). This centred on the 200 largest US corporations of the day.[15] They argued that the separation of ownership and control, combined with the growing dispersion of share ownership, resulted in shareholders no longer being able to control the development and conduct of company commercial policy.

John Parkinson (1994) in his seminal work on corporate power and responsibility observes that this separation might encourage management 'to pursue economically sub optimal goals' and would definitely weaken the mechanisms that regulate the corporation, 'the design of which is premised on shareholder involvement'.[16] Though something of a digression the earlier claim made by Dodd (1932) in response to the Berle and Means study went much further.[17] Dodd argued, most controversially, that in any case the proper purpose of the corporation was not confined to making profit for shareholders. In the lengthy ensuing debate the argument was made that shareholders might have surrendered the right that corporations should be operated in their sole interest opening the door to another concept of the corporation and its purposes.

3.9   The drift of power to the directorate

The Berle and Means thesis could not, however, have foreseen the scale of change in the period since in Anglo American jurisdictions. As the British ONS (Office of National Statistics) confirmed in 1999 this has been characterised by the growth of global institutional investors as shareholders; the market for control played by stock exchanges in the trading of public shares; market-driven mergers and acquisitions of corporations, and the dwindling power of individual shareholdings as a proportion of the total.[18] As PIRC (2007) the British pensions and investment consultancy points out the effectiveness of the institutional investment industry in monitoring their investment interests remain a matter of enduring concern.[19]

In marked contrast the Securities Update (2006) reports a new development in terms of shareholder activism: the rise of hedge funds and equity funds as aggressive, activist small-scale strategic shareholders in selected public companies. Securities Update also observes that such activity can be 'a very disruptive and unpredictable force' which is not motivated by the desire to improve corporate governance.[20] The rise of private equity investment and their fund managers is seen as weakening not only corporate governance but also fostering rationalisation strategies designed to maximise short-term cash flow at the expense of longer term development.[21]

3.10   Identifying the interests of the corporation

Returning to the role of the director, Sealy (1967) argues that directors were appointed to manage the company's affairs.[22] This offered a practical solution to the obvious problem in which individual self-serving shareholders might otherwise, by their actions, tyrannise smaller shareholders, extract rents as in the Hollinger case, 2006[23] even though the vast bulk of smaller corporations and even some larger corporations are managed by directors who are also shareholders.[24] Just as importantly, it provided a basis whereby the directors could reach collective decisions regarding the commercial affairs of the company in an efficient, business-like fashion, having regard to the best interests of the company.[25]

This formulation, as it will be seen, invited disputes and misunderstandings as to what precisely the notion of 'the best interests of the company' might mean. It also threatened, as Parkinson (1994) observes, to drive a wedge between the company as a separate entity, the focus of directors duties and the interests of shareholders, especially where those interests become misaligned.[26] In understanding how this might arise, the historical underpinnings and the evolution of the role of the director will now be explored.

3.11   The historic overhang of partnership

In understanding the role of the director, Davies (1997) states that it is a function deeply rooted in partnership law in which each partner is the agent of his fellow partner.[27] This portrayal of the director has a long history. During the 19th century as Stokes (1994) explains the director was portrayed both as a trustee[28] as well as an agent of the shareholder. This portrayal is well illustrated in English law in *Isle of Wight Rly Co v Tahoudin* in the fourth quarter of the 19th century.[29] The judgement confirmed that the company, in general meeting, was constitutionally speaking supreme. The directors, acting as agents of the shareholders, were obliged as fiduciaries to act strictly in accordance with shareholders' decisions and the control of the general meeting.[30]

This appeared to confirm the fundamental principle that shareholders should either have the right to manage or to appoint others to manage on their behalf, for their exclusive benefit. They were also empowered to challenge transactions that were unconstitutional or were judged not to be in their interests. Legal arrangements reflected these *shareholder-friendly* arrangements. Companies could be sued in their own right, raise debt in their own right and even sue their own members. With the possession of a common seal this also facilitated a distinction between the company and its members thus conferring on members a form of limited liability from the acts of the company.[31]

3.12   Shifting perceptions of shareholder rights

Shareholding rights like other property rights were, in the 19th century, ascendant. Honore (1961) in his discussion of *incidents* cites the historic rights of property owners to 'possess, use, manage, and receive income' amongst other rights and to enjoy 'freedom from expropriation'.[32] But this portrayal in law of the relationship between director agent and shareholder principal was to change as a direct consequence of redefining the company in law. Companies which historically had been portrayed both as *aggregate* entities, owned by their members, typically as partnerships; *real* or *natural* entities reflecting the view that they existed separately from the members, typically in Charter Companies and unincorporated "deed of settlement" companies; and both *fictional* and, (following limited liability), *real* entities also were to face a fundamental change in design.

The enactment of Limited Liability in 1855[33] effectively, if unintentionally, *reified[34]* the company by reconstituting it as a separate legal entity from the shareholders even though, as Davies (1997) argues[35] this was not clearly grasped or understood at the time, by jurists, or the population at large.[36] In tandem with the earlier *Foss v Harbottle* judgment, limited liability thus *cleansed* in the words of Ireland (1996) shareholders from the company.[37] This cleansing had, inevitably, a far reaching impact on the role of the director in terms of those interests it was his first duty to protect. Whilst historically the director had owed his duty to the shareholder, by the mid 19th century, common law and the change in statute law granting limited liability had the combined effect of refocusing directors' duties on the company, an inanimate, fictional legal entity.[38] This is evidenced by the ongoing debate about the meaning and relevance of section 14 of the British Companies Act 1985, a matter explored more fully as we proceed.

3.13　　　Corporations as inanimate mindless fictional entities

The impact of this development was to have significant practical repercussions. As a contemporary comment Parkinson (1993) observes that 'it is doubtful whether an inanimate object can meaningfully be said to have interests, or if it could what they would be.[39] A relevant supplementary question might be asked: if the company gives expression to interests, by doing some things and not others - who causes those choices to be made? The answer to that question highlights the difficulties that arise from the disconnection of shareholders from any direct *ex ante* involvement in the commercial affairs of the company - and the dominant role of directors in determining outturns.

Awareness of this practical reality has, of course, shaped the *path dependent*[40] development of capital markets in Anglo American jurisdictions. As earlier stated, this development was first systematically explored by Berle and Means though some of the implications can be challenged.[41] How these different developments have impinged upon the evolution and focus of directors' duties will be considered in Chapter four.

3.14　　　　　　　Conclusions

This chapter has compared and contrasted the apparent simplicity of the limited liability company under English law at the point of creation and the manner in which this entity evolves into something far more complex. The path of common law interpretation has one way or another determined the outturn in English corporate law and elsewhere in English speaking jurisdictions. The simplicity of the *holy trinity* arrangement of ownership at the outset has given rise to a range of conflicting common law judgements about the nature of the company and the relationship between the company, the directors, the shareholders and other stakeholders. The gradual re-interpretation of the corporation in law has also created uncertainties as to true nature of the directors' accountability and ultimately the fiduciary duty of the director.

The confusions that have arisen in Anglo American jurisdictions appear to have arisen from the aim of trying to establish a *one-size-fits-all* solution to the issues of ownership of limited liability companies. One important consequence of common law evolution is that the limited liability company emerges as an entity separate in law from the shareholders, the shareholders detached from the everyday operations of the company and the directors having a duty to the company not the shareholders.

In other jurisdictions, notably *Rhineland* and Nordic amongst others, the corporate governance challenge posed by the separation of ownership from control has evolved differently with the institutionalisation of the supervisory board.

Questions for review

1. Why is directorship grounded in trusteeship and how does this impact upon directors' duties?

2. What did the Foss v Harbottle and the Salomon judgment settle in terms of the ownership of the company?

3. What caused the separation of ownership from control?

4. What has caused changes in shareholder rights over time?

5. Why does Ireland speak about the *cleansing* of the shareholders from the corporation?

6. Why are corporations referred to as mindless fictional entities?

7. How have Anglo American capital markets fostered the separation of ownership from control?

8. At the time a company is formed the control and ownership relationships appear clear. What causes this to change as they grow in size and importance?

9. Why has the issue of ownership and control not arisen in *Rhineland* and Nordic jurisdictions?

10. Why in Anglo American jurisdictions does the myth of shareholder ownership persist?

Learning Tasks

I   How would you design a system which would provide effective control over corporate actions?

II   How would you define the ownership arrangements in a large publicly held corporation?

III   Do independent supervisory boards provide better governance and accountability?

Figure 5
Letter to The Economist   9 July 2010

I refer to Schumpeter's measured piece *Two Cheers for Sarbanes Oxley* (The Economist 3 July 2010). In what is otherwise a sensible and realistic assessment of the overall benefits of *Sarbox* I am nevertheless struck by the myth of shareholder ownership which, it is argued, *Sarbox* has strengthened. This is surely a mistaken inference. *Sarbox* is a response to the failure of shareholders to act as responsible owners - not a mechanism designed to strengthen their ownership rights. There is more in this than meets the eye!

The fact, in law, is that the shareholders do not own the corporation. One direct consequence of limited liability is that the assets of the corporation are owned by the corporation – a fictional legal entity – and **not** the shareholders. The granting of limited liability in the 19th Century and the landmark Salomon versus Salomon judgement [British House of Lords] 1897 establishes this legal principle. The subsequent evolution of common law mostly supports this conclusion in Anglo American jurisdictions.

Misunderstandings about these matters continue to hold back the debate about the governance, especially of publicly traded corporation. Shareholders own shares but the shares only represent claims on the profits of the corporation. They confer no rights of ownership, except in narrowly defined circumstances. In Anglo American jurisdictions they confer no significant *ex ante* super*visory* rights - a sine qua non of meaningful ownership.

What proprietary rights shareholders may have are further weakened by the fact that shares in many publicly traded corporations are held today by a wide number of dispersed short-term profit seeking institutional investors who are not, in reality, committed shareholders. This compromises still further any meaningful concept of ownership.

Our collective failure to address this reality continues to hold back the debate on effective reform of both the ownership arrangements of publicly traded corporations and their governance. *Sarbox* does not alter this reality.

Richard Tudway

Centre for International Economics

Notes

[1] This refers to a standard off the shelf limited liability private company.

[2] For companies registered after 1 October 2009 Table A has been replaced by the Companies Act 2006 Model Articles, in line with companies (Model Articles) Regulations 2008.

[3] The *holy trinity* describes the relationship between God the Father, the Son and the Holy Spirit. It is extended as a metaphor to describe the relationship of unity between the Shareholders, the Directors and the Company at the outset of its life.

[4] The Enlightenment developed simultaneously in France, Britain and Germany, the Netherlands, Italy, Spain and Portugal and the American colonies throughout the 17th and 18th centuries and thereafter. The movement was buoyed by the success of the American Revolution when breaking free from the British Empire. Most of Europe was fundamentally affected. The authors of the American Declaration of Independence the United States Bill of Rights, the French Declaration of the Rights of Man and the Citizen were all motivated by Enlightenment principles.

[5] See: Davies P *Principles of Modern Company Law* Chapter 1, 6th edition 1997.

[6] Foss v Harbottle (1843) 2 Hare 461

[7] Salomon v Salomon *op. cit.*

[8] Very specifically the debate in Anglo American jurisdictions favoured the notion of the corporation existing only in terms of *a nexus of contracts* and not as a real socio-economic entity. This has given way to the portrayal of the corporation as a fictional person and ultimately to a corporate citizen – a triumph of *methodological individualism.*

[9] The word "company" is not formally defined in English law though the term implies an association of persons for committed to some common object. See: Davies P *op cit* Chapter 1 p 3. See also the comments of Judge Buckley in Re Stanley [1906] 1 Ch. 131 at 134 who famously stated '*the word company has no strictly legal meaning'.*

[10] There is no definition of the term 'director' in the British Companies Act beyond stating that it '*includes any person occupying the position of director by whatever named called'.*

[11] Personification is a figure of speech in which inanimate objects or abstractions are endowed with human qualities or are represented as possessing human form.

[12] It is appropriate to observe that the crystallisation of this doctrine occurred over a lengthy period of time during which there was a definite lack of clarity in law and practice about these matters. See: Sealy L *The Director as Trustee* Cam LJ 83 [1967] which examines the role of the trustee in 'deed of settlement' companies.

[13] The Limited Liability Act 1855 consolidated the following year in the Joint Stock Companies Act 1856.

[14] A broad analogy can be found in constitutional law. In a parliamentary democracy, legislative sovereignty rests with the parliament, while administration is left to the executive arm of government subject to parliamentary oversight. It is a limited parallel but provides some useful insight. The directors of the company and the board to which they are elected are not sovereign but have limited powers which are subject to the authority of the general meeting of members. See: Davies P *op cit* page 15 for a discussion of this point.

[15] Berle and Means *op cit* revealed in their study that 44% of the companies examined had no individual ownership interest. This they defined as being about 20% - a level viewed as providing a minimum necessary for shareholder control. These corporations they classified as being effectively "management controlled" because of the scale of shareholder dispersion.

[16] See: Parkinson J *Corporate Power and Responsibility* (1994) page 53 in particular, for a discussion of these matters. See also Chapter 1 page 47 where Parkinson, notwithstanding, observes that Berle and Means may have exaggerated the extent to which management could escape shareholder control and underestimated the importance of both product markets and the market for control in disciplining management. These matters are explored in a subsequent chapter which addresses the disciplining effectiveness of market control mechanisms.

[17] See: Dodd E M, *For Whom Are Corporate Managers Trustees?* 45 Harv. L. Rev 1145,1148 (1932)

[18] See: "Share Holding" *A Report on the Ownership of Shares*, ONS (Office of National Statistics) 1999. Institutional investment in UK quoted public companies had risen by 1999 to 81% of the total of all equity in issue.

[19] See: "Institutional Investment in the UK 6 years on" PIRC 2007. Note replies to question 21 in particular.

[20] See: Securities Update published by May Brown Rowe and Maw, 21 April *2006 Hedge Funds and Institutional Shareholder Activism.*

[21] See: Global Labour Column Number 44 December 2010, Goncalves, J R B and Caporale M A M. *Private Equity Investments and Labour: Current trends and challenges of trade unions.*

[22] The concept of 'management' carries with it a certain ambiguity. Directors, as managers, in their earliest existence were trustees rather than profit seeking managers. In the period since the passing of limited liability the notion of trusteeship has inevitably lost prominence though the importance of 'trust and loyalty' has remained an important fiduciary aspect of directors' duties, sitting sometimes awkwardly alongside the idea of directors as "risk takers and profit seekers". This is dealt with by Sealy *op cit.* especially page 86.

[23] Rents being a term which describes fees and other rewards, over and above agreed dividends, which are effectively "extorted" from the company by a particular shareholder who has the power to do so. An example would include (Lord) Conrad Black's fraudulent diversion of funds from the media company Hollinger Inc he controlled as a shareholder and director. See http://news.bbc.co.uk/1/hi/business/4447538.stm.

[24] An example of a very large publicly quoted company managed in this way is News Corp the media group led by Rupert Murdoch. Through his family trust, Rupert Murdoch, remains a large minority shareholder in News Corp. See: http:// www.newscorp.com/operations/newspapers.html

[25] In Gramophone and Typewriter Ltd v Stanley (1908) Judge Buckley had cause to express the view that 'Directors are not, I think, bound to comply with the directions even of all the corporators acting as individuals', a reflection which underscores the requirement that directors should always have regard to the best interests of the company and not necessarily those of the shareholders.

[26] This is explored by Parkinson J *op cit* pages 76 and 77. He expresses the view than an inanimate entity like a company cannot have interests, as such, and that therefore the enterprise's purposes can only be explained in terms of 'serving human interests or objectives'. See also Dignam A and Lowry J *Company Law* (2005) page 133 which examines the impact of section 151 of the Companies Act 1985 and the "larger purposes" criteria. This protects directors who can always claim that they are acting in the best interests of the company where their actions are challenged. See: Brady v Brady [1988] BCLC 20, CA, at 40 which examines a specific case where the "removal of deadlock" between owners and directors was achieved in a bid to protect the company's interests.

[27] See: Davies P *op cit* pages 19 and 81.

[28] The importance of the "trustee" origins of directorship explains, historically, the fiduciary nature of the director as agent to the shareholder principal. See: Stokes M *Company Law and Legal Theory* The Law of Business Enterprise ed. Wheeler S OUP 1994, page 88.

[29] See: Isle of Wight Rly Co v Tahourdin (1883) 25 ChD 320 CA.

[30] See: Dignam J and Lowry J *op cit*, para 13.4. They point out that the Companies Clauses Consolidation Act 1845 provided that directorial authority to manage the affairs of the company was subject to the 'control and regulation' of the general meeting.

[31]. See Davies P *op cit*, page 21 - 22 for a discussion of how legal forms were creatively used in this period.

[32] See: Honore A M *Ownership* in A G Guest, ed. Oxford Essays in Jurisprudence (First Series) (Oxford Clarendon Press, 1961) Chapter V.

[33] In the following year consolidated in the Joint Stock Companies Act 1856.

[34] *Reification* arises in the treatment of an analytic or abstract relationship as though it were a concrete entity. Taking an association of individuals who make up the "company" (typically a partnership) and then separating the "company" from those individuals as occurred following the passing of the law granting limited liability to shareholders had the effect of creating a fictional *reified* legal entity called a "company".

[35] See: Davies P *op cit* Chapter 2 for a discussion of these points. See also: Pollock Frederick (Sir) (1911) *Has the Common Law Received the Fictions Theory of Corporations?* 27 Law Quarterly Review. Sir Frederick explores the impact of fictions and real entities on the development of English common law. He concludes that the fiction theory was never applied in English law but rather that the concession theory of the firm was adopted in common law to explain the nature of the corporate personality.

[36] The implication of limited liability as Davies P *op cit* points out was not decisively clarified until *Salomon op cit* .See Chapter 5 of Davies for a discussion of this point.

[37] See: Ireland P *Corporate Governance, Stakeholding and the Company: Towards a Less Degenerate Capitalism.* Journal of Law and Society Vol 23, 1996. Ireland argues that by the 1850's companies were viewed as 'entities in their own right with a completely autonomous existence'. See page 289.

[38] Though one that was portrayed in common law, as maintained by Pollock (1911), as a concession-based aggregate entity – a matter of abiding, contemporary, confusion.

[39] See: Parkinson J *op cit* page 76 – 77.

[40] Path dependence is a metaphor from the physical sciences. In its narrow conception it explains why specific institutions and behaviour are influenced by specific historical events. The behaviour of capital markets and their organisation would be an example. This fully explored in Nelson R and Winter S (1982) *An evolutionary theory of economic change.* Harvard Economic Press. 1982

44

[41] See: Corey L *The House of Morgan* (New York) G Howard Watt, 1930. Corey, responding to the limitations of the Berle & Means thesis explores the manner in which major financial institutions, using a complex network of relationships and powers, formal and informal – and unrelated specifically to shareholding - were able to secure effective corporate control.

Chapter 4

The Great British Fudge

4.1   Summary

Chapter four takes us to the heart of the confusion over the status of the corporation. It examines the odd manner in which legal problems with the corporation have been addressed in the context of British and American law and the problems that remain unresolved. It explores the implications of defining the corporation simply as a legal fictional person. It also looks at the manner in which corporate liability can be deliberately avoided through the creation of "subsidiary" companies by the parent company. The discourse is partly chronological in terms of key historical legal judgments and partly interpretive in terms of contemporary debate and understanding of these matters. It is, unavoidably, technical and legalistic.

It aims to lay bare the mysteries of the limited liability corporate form, how the role of shareholding is transformed by limited liability and the consequences, and why *path dependency* has evolved in different ways in different jurisdictions. It also identifies why there is a powerful case for reform.

4.2   Company Creation

This is a tale of juridical confusion and contradiction which continues to blight our understanding of the corporation in Anglo American jurisdictions and how best it should be governed. As we have seen earlier the evolution of the director from agent of the shareholder to agent of the company was a slow and uncertain process. Grantham (1998)[1] observes that when Queen Victoria ascended the throne in 1837 there were two principal vehicles for undertaking substantial commercial operations – 'the corporation and the unincorporated[2] joint stock[3] company'. Halsbury in the early 20th century states that corporations, which in some instances dated back at least two centuries, owed their existence to Royal Charter or Acts of Parliament.[4]

These corporations enjoyed a separate legal existence from their members or shareholders, a status conferred upon them by Charter or Act of Parliament. They were in every respect very different from other entities. In contrast as Davies (1997) and Ireland (1985) point out the unincorporated joint stock company was little different in law from a partnership.[5] The key feature of its legal construction was that of an *aggregated* association with unlimited life, whilst at the same time inseparable from its members.[6] These undertakings were thus effectively governed by partnership law.

4.3   Trying to get round unlimited liability

But this too, as a portrayal, is far from straightforward. The members of traditional partnerships owned the assets and were *jointly and severally* responsible for the debts incurred by the company. The members were clearly owners with legal ownership entitling them to control and benefit from the company. But as already stated social and economic developments had by then taken a different turn. As Davies (1997) explains unincorporated *deed of settlement* associations or companies flourished during this period often as a device for circumventing the drawbacks of partnership and the legal complications associated with incorporation. The chaotic growth of these undertakings compromised the underlying principle of joint and several responsibility enshrined in partnership.[7]

The response of the Crown law officers of the day was to hold back on legitimate applications for incorporation. Their actions, as Dubois (1938) explains, fostered further growth of unincorporated associations which the Bubble Act of 1720 had been specifically designed to halt.[8] The Joint Stock Companies Act of 1844 aimed, though failed, to redress these adverse developments whilst sidestepping the growing public demand for limited liability. The eventual enactment of limited liability some 11 years later shifted the focus of public policy concern away from partnership as a legal form with the enactment of a standardised incorporation with limited liability. Though unanticipated by law makers at the time it was also to decisively influence the development of the doctrine of *separation of ownership and control,* a matter which will be examined afresh.

4.4   Foss v Harbottle and half a century of confusion

As already stated, the matter of ownership and control was first impacted by the *Foss v Harbottle* judgement in 1843. This had the effect of establishing a clear distinction between the shareholders as proprietors, on the one hand, and the company and its assets on the other. It also had the effect of underscoring the key role of the directors in managing the affairs of the company – effectively at the expense of shareholders. It was not, however, until the beginning of the 20th century, following the 1897 *Salomon* judgment, that this was crystallised.

Directors, as Stokes (1994) argues, were by this time accorded the exclusive rights to manage the day to day business of the company, to the exclusion of the shareholders.[9] Shareholders were, as a consequence, unable to issue instructions to directors on how to run the business.[10] It should be remembered that throughout much of the 19th century the common law view was that the directors were straightforwardly the agents of the company's shareholders, who were themselves portrayed as associated owners of the company. This signalled a major ground shift.

In rationalising the wider ramifications of these developments in terms of common law, the English courts presented a subtle interpretive change. It reasoned that managerial autonomy flowed from the construction of the company's articles of association. This was in turn portrayed as a contract between the shareholders and the company binding the two parties together. These provisions are currently reflected in English law by section 14 of the Companies Act 1985.[11] It offers the appearance, at least, of resolving the legal disconnection between the company and the shareholders.[12] But there is a well known difficulty with this portrayal. As Lowry and Dignam (2005) observe, 'the provision fails to take account of the company's status as a separate legal entity'.[13] The wording of the provision provides for the constitution to be 'signed and sealed by each member' (or shareholder). There is no mention, however, of the company acting likewise. It is not, in reality, a legal contract between the shareholders and the company as a separate legal entity. It is a truly odd state of affairs which has never been remedied. Some would say it constitutes significant legal fudge.

The contract's implication was that although the company was a separate legal entity, in reality the company and the shareholders were bound together through the memorandum and articles of association. This accommodated the concern that shareholders might suffer disadvantage from the shift of focus of directors' duties to the company. Binding them together constitutionally was construed as meaning that the directors were effectively acting for both parties in the name of the company.

The observation can be expressed in alternative terms. *Foss and Harbottle* in 1843, the enactment of limited liability in 1856, and the *Salomon* judgement in 1897 turned upon its head the notion that the directors had any direct obligations to the shareholders per *se*. The uncomfortable consequences of these legal developments were mitigated in common law by the interpretation that the company and the shareholders were in any case connected by contract as if they were a single party. The reality of things, as we have seen, is very different. In understanding how different – the significance of *separation of ownership and control* will now be examined.

4.5   The consequences of separation of ownership and control

In understanding how the doctrine of *separation of ownership and control* evolved two principal features of its development will be examined. First, the 19th century view, as already stated, viewed the directors, for the most part, as the agents of the shareholders. The company in general meeting was constitutionally supreme. This is well illustrated by the *Isle of Wight Rly*[14] judgment in 1883. The judgement continued, if mistakenly, to uphold the traditional view that the directors should act strictly in accordance with the decisions of the general meeting of members. The judgment reflected well the confused understandings of the day. As Davies (1997) explains, the court refused in the case in question to grant the directors an injunction to restrain the holding of a general meeting. To get a lie of the land - one purpose of the meeting was for the shareholders to appoint a committee to reorganise the management of the company. The judge, in his summing up, stated that it would be:

> *'a very strong thing [for the directors] to prevent shareholders from holding a meeting of the company, if the majority of them think that the course of action taken by the directors, in a matter ultra vires[15] of the directors, is not in the best interest of the company'.*

The interpretation of the law in this case is clear. First the directors are definitely portrayed as hand maidens of the shareholders. But the strength of this position, as it has been shown, was soon to be decisively challenged. Second, the supremacy of the shareholder was effectively reversed four years later in the landmark *Salomon* judgement.[16] This established in common law the principle that the company was an entity entirely separate from the shareholders. The company owned its assets, not the shareholders. Progressively, the duty of the director was portrayed as one owed to the company in terms of the management of its assets, and *not* the shareholders. This duty would be executed, according to Stokes (1994), without the interference of the shareholders[17] on a day to day basis, though subject to the constitutional provisions of the AGM (annual general meeting). The AGM whilst it empowered the shareholders to vote to re-appoint existing directors, or appoint new ones, effectively allowed for little else and certainly nothing in terms of *ex ante* debate.

The development clearly identifies the rise not only of the doctrine of the *separation of ownership and control*. It is a development that raises fundamental questions about the nature of ownership. Specifically it raises the question whether shareholders have any meaningful claims to ownership of the company. This is a controversial matter to which the discussion will return. In understanding the nature of this controversy and how it arose, the intentions behind the Joint Stock Companies Act of 1844 will now be examined. In doing so it will explore how the bid to re-establish members' collective responsibility led to further confusion, and ultimately to the realignment of the company and its ownership.

4.6   The impact of the Joint Stock Companies Act 1844

Davies (1997) explains that the Joint Stock Companies Act of 1844 was built upon three main principles. First it made a distinction between private partnerships and joint stock companies. Second, it provided for incorporation by means of simple registration.[18] Third it provided for 'full publicity' a matter judged to be the best safeguard against the growing problem of financial fraud.[19] The passing of the act arose, as already explained, from difficulties with the enforcement of partnership agreements in *deed of settlement* companies.

These companies, as Sealy (1996) points out, were in reality unincorporated ventures and had grown significantly in size and importance throughout the early 19th century.[20] At the height of the *railway mania* in the 1840's the ordinary man in the street, as The Times (1840) points out, 'was aware as never before of companies and their role in the generation of wealth'.[21] This had led to an expansion of the stock market in London and other provincial exchanges, an awakening of investor interest on the part of unsophisticated share buyers, growth in the trade of share often issued illegally,[22] and a sharp rise in business liquidations - developments which heavily influenced policy makers in the drafting of the 1844 Act.[23]

Because of the sheer volume of these unincorporated ventures the practicality of holding individual partners responsible for the debts of the company had become impossible. Collective responsibility was unenforceable. This difficulty was exacerbated by the transferability of shares in the growing market for shares. The passing of the Act regularised the position of the registered company. It did this by granting separate legal status to any venture which met the requirements of the law. The aim was to rationalise the unwieldy "conglomerates", consisting of multiple ventures - often with hundreds or thousands of different members[24] that had gradually developed - into separate incorporated, unlimited liability, joint stock companies. This had the neat surface appearance of restoring the personal liability of members until which time the hotly contested law on limited liability was eventually passed, a decade later, an event which was to fundamentally change everything.[25]

4.7   The consequences of limited liability and the Salomon judgement

The 1844 Act aimed at re-affirming the underlying premise of collective responsibility in partnership. It did so by limiting the size of such companies, remembering that the growth of companies had been a major factor undermining the collective responsibility of the members.[26] The objective as Stokes (1994) argues was to restore the notion of the company as an unlimited liability entity, with the members as partners in its collective ownership.[27] The act was, in the event, widely criticised for being cumbersome and unnecessarily complicated. It failed, in the event, to achieve its main objectives. Davies (1997) reports that estimates indicated that fewer than half the provisional registrations lodged ever succeeded in attaining complete registration.[28]

But other and more far reaching changes were afoot. They were embodied in the Joint Stock Companies Act 1856.[29] As Dignam and Lowry (2005) argue this had the effect of formalising the company as a *reified* legal entity separate from the limited liability conferred on shareholders.[30] In the period thereafter, as Davies (1997) reports, there was a rise in statutory incorporations,[31] a positive development. Against that, however, the enactment of limited liability was followed by forty years of legal confusion and ambiguity about its implications for shareholder ownership of the company. The confusion, as already stated, was brought to a head in the landmark *Salomon* ruling in 1897.[32] In the original hearing, Broderip v Salomon (1895), the Judge in his summing up found in favour of Mr Broderip's claim ruling that Mr Salomon had created the company with the sole intention of transferring the business to it. He therefore concluded that the company was, in reality, his agent and he, as principal, was liable for the unsecured creditors.

The Court of Appeal followed a different tack. Lord Lindley took the view that Mr Salomon had abused the privileges of incorporation and limited liability which Parliament had intended only to confer on 'independent bona fide shareholders, who had a mind and a will of their own and were not mere puppets'. He further stated that the legislative process had 'never contemplated an extension of limited liability to sole traders or a fewer number than seven (shareholders)'. Though there were seven members in the case of Salomon & Co, six were there, it was argued, to enable the seventh to carry on the business with limited liability. Lord Lindley effectively treated Salomon & Co as a trustee for Arun Salomon.

4.8   The House of Lords judgment

In the subsequent House of Lords appeal the reasoning was fundamentally different. It rejected the argument from agency and the implications of fraud on the part of Arun Salomon. Lord Halsbury in summing up his doubts about the two earlier verdicts stated:

> *'The learned judges appear to me not to have been absolutely certain in their own minds whether to treat the company as a real thing or not. If it was a real thing; if it had a legal existence, and if consequently the law attributed to it certain rights and liabilities in its own constitution as a company, it appears to me to follow as a consequence that it is impossible to deny the validity of the transaction into which he [Arun Salomon] has entered.'*

The case was thus settled in favour of Arun Salomon. The judgement was also to decisively redefine the meaning of proprietorship, establishing clearly in law the separateness of the corporation and the ownership of its assets, from the shareholders. It was also to hasten the arrival of *separation of ownership and control*, despite continuing uncertainty over the status of the company. It has also been subject to wide criticism in the period since.[33] Perhaps the most important of those criticisms is that it has left unresolved the critically important issue of the relationship between the company and the shareholder which, as we have explored, is only speciously resolved by the provisions of section 14 of the Companies Act 1985.

There is also the problem that arises when one corporation spawns another corporation for the purposes of liability avoidance. As Farrar (2005 and 1998) argues, the concept of the corporation is 'inadequately justified in terms of principle and policy'.[34] This is particularly evident in the case of corporate groups[35] which may be used to foster specious circumvention of tort liability[36] through the creation of subsidiaries for that purpose. This has also fostered confusion and inconsistency where judicial moves to lift and 'pierce the veil' arise.[37] Farrar argues that to accommodate the corporation into the rest of corporate law is futile: it is simply 'an elaborate exercise in rule interpretation and application law'. This jurisprudential flaw is explored in an alternative argument advanced by Rixon (1986).[38] He poses the question in the following terms: if it is the duty of the directors and shareholders, in general meeting, to act for the good of the company – then what is the company for this purpose? As a fictional entity in law the response to that crucial question is impossible to answer. It is literally anybody's guess. Not a promising backdrop for effective corporate governance.

4.9   Continuing confusion over the legal concept of the company

Until the *Salomon* judgment in 1887 the courts, following the passage of limited liability in 1856, continued to favour the view that the limited liability company was in essence a form of incorporated partnership, indistinguishable from its members or shareholders. This was a commonly held view. As Geldart (1911) reminds us the idea that the company had a separate legal personality was not accepted in contemporary law.[39] Following limited liability the widely shared understanding was that it was the shareholders who were incorporated, rather than the company, because it was the shareholders who benefited from limited liability.[40] Whilst under the Joint Stock Companies Act of 1844 Act genuine partnership was a precondition of unlimited incorporation, limited liability triggered a fundamental change which had the effect of detaching the shareholders from the company.

As we have seen it was not until the *Salomon* judgement that the position in law was definitively clarified. *Salomon* reformulated the underlying corporate concept. It established clearly the company as a legal entity separate from the shareholders. The company thus moved from being an association of individual incorporated shareholders to something that more closely resembled the earlier charter corporation, with the company being viewed as an independent entity (whether fictional or real) separate from the shareholders. This passage, as it has been shown, was preceded by forty years of confusion following the *Foss v Harbottle* judgment in 1843. The clarification offered by *Salomon* established the basic common law interpretation which has governed limited liability companies for a century and almost two decades since.

Whilst the status of the limited liability company was finally settled by *Salomon*, the proprietorial status of shareholders remained mired in ambiguity and controversy. If, as Rixon (1986) argues, the shareholders enjoy limited liability and the company is an independent legal entity owning its own assets, what does it mean to speak of shareholders as owners of the company?[41] This is a persistent conundrum.[42] In common parlance, at least, shareholders are often portrayed as if they were owners. Because of this, as Ireland (1996) reminds us shareholders are constantly exhorted to play a more proactive role in the governance of the company.[43] A similar ambiguity arises over the issue to whom the directors owe their duty. Directors are, again, commonly portrayed as owing their duty to and being accountable to the shareholders when in law this is not the case. Despite, or because of these ambiguities, the realignment of company ownership and the emergence of the doctrine of separation of *ownership* from *control* was an inevitable consequence. These matters are now addressed.

4.10   The shareholders in the backseat

Doubts and confusions about the status of the company and the role of shareholders within the power sharing arrangements under the company's constitution are now mostly settled. But they are settled only in the sense that in practice the directors and the management are responsible on a day to day basis for the running of the company. Shareholders are left to play a largely peripheral role in its affairs as passive recipients of dividends, determined at the discretion of the directors. Major, residual concerns about issues of corporate power, corporate governance and the accountability of directors and management flourish and undermine the legitimacy of the corporation.[44]

The separation of *ownership* from *control* as we have seen has a common sense ring about it when viewed both from a legal perspective, and from the practical standpoint of running the company. It continues, nonetheless, to pose concerns in Anglo American jurisdictions about the viability of corporate governance arrangements and the accountability of companies. This problem is compounded by the scale, complexity and geographical reach of modern global corporate entities. Corporations begin to enjoy a form of non jurisdictional existence – a truly alarming development.

4.11   The imperatives of corporate control and organisation

Given the scale of many corporate operations, day to day commercial control is delegated to smaller groups of directors and senior managers who inevitably work at distance even from board directors, and have no contact with shareholders. This, as it has been shown, appears as a natural consequence of limited liability. The company is defined as a separate legal entity, with the directors performing the management role of the company and its assets. Without the company's separate legal personality it would certainly be argued that shareholders should not benefit from limited liability.[45] Following this line of reasoning it is difficult to avoid the conclusion that the price of formalising shareholder protection through limited liability is that the shareholders are *cleansed* from the company, as Ireland[46] (1996) puts it. They are effectively purged from any direct position of control. The company is thus left in the hands of the directors who are there to run it and to account, only *ex post*, for their actions.

This act of *cleansing* brings with it however the difficulty that has been referred to earlier. In the contemporary context it definitely threatens the exclusivity of the shareholders in terms of both the debate on corporate governance and seemingly unresolved issue of ownership. With institutional shareholders in publicly quoted companies acting as portfolio managers rather than shareholders in the traditional sense of the term – how can such shareholders insist upon *primacy* ahead of other stakeholders in the governance of the company? An arresting response to this question is that the company is not an entity owned by anyone. It is in essence as Bratton (1994)[47] explains, a comprehensive nexus of contracts[48] between many different parties, including shareholders.

This legal device appears to circumvent ownership ambiguities associated with the *reified* concept of the company.[49] It also resolves the difficulties surrounding the somewhat fanciful portrayal of the company as a contracting party with its shareholders through the articles of association. Finally it appears to resolve the problem associated with corporate governance by reducing governance to one that is settled by the disciplining forces of capital markets, with the price of securities effectively valuing governance, putting better run companies at a premium when compared with less well run companies which will trade at a discount. But this too raises further difficulties on the corporate governance front.

4.12   Fictional versus real entity interpretation of the corporation

The *nexus of contracts* model, dominant in the two decades to the turn of the millennium has increasingly lost its appeal as an explanation of how corporate power is justified, monitored and controlled.[50] There has been, as a result, a resurgence of interest into the nature of the company, as a *real* or natural entity. The legitimation of directors' power that derives from this, and the challenge of promoting effective corporate governance are again at centre-stage. As Stokes (1994) explains the debate over the company and the legitimation of managerial power is far from resolved. The *nexus of contracts* model of the company conflicts with the theory prevailing in case law.[51] This, as it has been demonstrated, treats the company as an artificial entity, separate and distinct from its shareholders. Only in this way can the incident of limited liability be seen to derive from the separate corporate personality. If this view of the company is reduced to a mere contractual association it is difficult to explain why the shareholders should not be responsible for the full extent of any debts as they would be in an unlimited liability partnership.

In trying to move the argument forward towards more promising territory Stokes examines the merits of the natural entity or *realist* model of the corporation. The *realist* model of the corporation recognises the independent existence of the company. It is also capable of portraying the directors as the *brains*[52] of the organisation whose task it is to formulate and execute policy, with shareholders no longer representing, in most instances, the original investors of capital but increasingly only those who buy and sell securities in a multitude of third party transaction across global stock markets, as institutional shareholders. This brings us closer to understanding that the real challenge of governance is to ensure that the *brains* of the organisation are properly and effectively supervised and that the interest of shareholders and stakeholders alike are reflected in those deliberations. In drawing these inferences it is important for us to understand the act of shareholding, how this has been transformed over time, and the role of capital markets in that process.

4.13   Shareholdership and the company's assets

Historically the act of owning a share in a company was portrayed as the owners' share in the common property of the company.[53] Because of this shareholders were viewed, straightforwardly, as the beneficial owners of the company. As Davies (1997) states, rather oddly, it is evident that the members' share(s) in a *deed of settlement* company entitled them to an equitable interest in the assets even though *the exact nature of this interest is not crystal clear* [italics added].[54] Though the Companies Act of 1844 did nothing formally to change this when companies incorporated under the law, earlier judgements had already compromised this straightforward view of shareholding and the shareholder. As Grantham (1998) points out there was evidence of a shift in perception in Bligh v Brent[55] in the 1830's, a judgment which predates Foss versus Harbottle by more than a decade, and the much later Salomon judgement.[56] The shareholders were still viewed as the owners, and rather like ordinary partners they had no *severable*[57] interest in the company's assets.

By the beginning of the 20th century the notion that the shareholders had no direct interest in the assets of the corporation was better established. In Borland's Trustees v Steel Brothers & Co Ltd [1901] it was argued that because of a provision in the articles of association the company had a right, in the express circumstances of shareholder bankruptcy, to purchase back the shares at 'a reasonable price and not exceeding the par value of the share'. This application was resisted by the bankrupt's trustee. The court reasoned differently arguing that if the agreement was valid then the transaction could take place with the company buying back the share, and thereby cancelling the liability. By so doing this was seen as re-affirming that shareholders do not have a direct claim on the company's assets. The judge stated that:

"A share is the interest of a shareholder in the company measured by a sum of money, for the purpose of liability in the first place and of interest in the second but also consisting of a series of mutual covenants entered into by all the shareholders inter se in accordance with [section 14]. The contract contained in the articles of association is one of the original incidents of the share. A share is not a sum of money .... but is an interest

measured by a sum of money and made up of various rights contained in the contract, including the right to a sum of money of a more or less amount."[58]

The underlying theory being expressed is that the contract, as constituted by the articles of association, defines the nature of the rights. As Davies (1997) states, again somewhat quizzically, 'these are not purely personal rights but, instead confer *some sort* [italics added] of proprietary interest in the company though not in its property'.[59] As the judge stated categorically over forty years later in Short v Treasury Commissioners (1948) 'shareholders are not, in the eyes of the law, part owners of the undertaking'.[60] This case and its profound implications are now examined.

4.14   Severing shareholder interest from the assets of the company

In the 1837 Bligh v Brent[61] case the view expressed suggests that whilst the shareholders may have no interest in the assets of the company, they nevertheless own a share of the company. The 1901 Borland's Trustees v Steel Brothers & Co Ltd case appears to leave little room for doubt about the matter. The shareholder owns a proprietary interest in the company which issued the shares, though not in its property. In this portrayal shareholders have rights *in* the company, as well as against it. In terms of legal theory this distinguishes shareholders from debenture holders, for example, whose rights are also defined by contract[62] but are rights *against* the company.[63]

In subsequent legal interpretation, thinking shifted away from the issue of whether or not shareholders had an interest in the company, as such, to their rights as shareholders to a dividend; to a return of residual capital on the winding up of the company, and to voting at general meetings.[64] This marks a significant conceptual change. As Ireland (1995) argues this establishes a formal disconnection between the company and its assets as a separate entity in itself, and the shares in issue which represent those net assets in terms of value.[65]

This is well illustrated in the third, early post-war example, a case already mentioned. In Short v Treasury Commissioners[66] (1948) it was contended that the shareholders had a right to the entire value of the company, which in the particular instance was greater than the value of the individual shares.[67] The court ruled, however, that the shareholders had no right to compensation in respect of the difference between the value of the company and the value of their shares. They were thus deemed not to be part owners of the assets of the undertaking. They were entitled to compensation for the value of the expropriated shares, but not the value of the company.

Much of the past and continuing confusion that has arisen over the link between the act of shareholding and claims on the assets of the company derive from a fundamental misunderstanding of the act of shareholding. Shareholders are not, in many specific instances, the providers of capital to the company. Institutional investors, as shareholders, are more often than not solely involved in the trading of titles to a share in profit.[68] They are often not direct investors in the company. They are, in perhaps clearer terms, owners of *second hand* shares[69] issued by a company which trade in the stock market. This is a matter of fundamental significance since it has the effect of transforming the meaning of shareholding and the behaviour of those shareholders.

4.15   Shareholders as the owners of residual profit sharing rights

The law establishes clearly, therefore, the separation of the shareholders interests from the assets of the corporation. It also empowers the directors to manage the business of the company.[70] The status of the shareholder is thus reduced to that of a residual claimant to some part of the profits generated by the company in the form of a dividend, an amount determined at the discretion of the directors. Shareholders do have powers they may exercise to discourage shirking on the part of directors, or other actions which might foster a misalignment of their interests from those being pursued by the directors on behalf of the company. The most obvious is the termination of existing directors' contracts, and the appointment of new directors. This can be achieved by ordinary resolution, a power which may not be taken away by the articles of association.

As we have seen there are strong practical reservations, however, about how far shareholders, have any real influence on the conduct of directors, or the delegation[71] of powers by directors to managers of the company.[72] Art 70 of Table A of the English Articles of Association is sometimes cited as empowering shareholders to give the board directions by special resolution.[73] This, however, may be little more than a rhetorical claim, and in any case one unlikely to be used because of dispersed institutional shareholding. Even assuming the potential of Art 70 to bring about, for example, a change in commercial policy this is a matter institutional shareholders would be cautious about launching.[74] It has also to be acknowledged that there are, as Eisenberg (1976) argues, practical commercial reasons for limiting shareholder involvement in the running of the company.[75] These provisions are surely sensible.

As already mentioned the underlying commercial imperative is that the directors have to reach collective, commercially sensitive, decisions about the direction of commercial policy in a timely and efficient manner. This is something that would be impractical to involve institutional shareholders in trying to settle, even if there was a willingness to do so.[76] One consequence of these considerations is that the involvement of institutional shareholders is, in most instances, effectively restricted to that of a passive *ex post* recipient of a residual benefit, determined by management discretion. Institutional shareholders have little or no involvement in the businesses in which they are invested. Perhaps worse they often see little point in trying to force the hand of management where they are unhappy about performance. Hostile resolutions are not commonly supported by institutional investors. An easier and cheaper solution is to sell the stock and invest elsewhere - a matter to which we will return.

This popular perception explains why institutional shareholders are sometimes judged to be little more than *absentee landlords*. This accusation in turn explains why they are exhorted to act as responsible investors and find better and more effective means of monitoring directors' actions. Only in this way, so the argument runs, can they expect to improve the awareness of directors of wider issues that may influence shareholder value. An argument of equal if not greater importance is that this is the only way shareholders can justify the *primacy* of their treatment in the context of the governance of the modern corporation, a status that has the effect of excluding other stakeholders.[77] The realisation of the goal of closer engagement with directors remains, however, elusive so far as most institutional shareholders and the companies in which they hold shares are concerned.[78] In order to understand why this is the case there is a need to examine the role of capital markets and how the habits and practices of institutional shareholders have been shaped by those markets. To this we now turn.

4.16   Capital markets and the growth of institutional shareholders

As already stated financial institutions (pension funds, insurance companies, unit trusts, investment trusts and more recently equity funds, venture capitalists and hedge funds) are the principal institutional shareholders who own the bulk of the shares in publicly quoted companies. This is increasingly a global phenomenon, but the scope and scale of developments as already reported is far more pronounced in Anglo American jurisdictions. Institutional shareholders have acquired an increasing proportion of the quoted equity of public companies in Anglo American jurisdictions. As a result the UK equity market has become very largely *institutionalised*. In 1999[79] over 81% of quoted equities were held by British and overseas institutional investors. This is a figure which has risen steadily from the 1960's when it stood at around the 60% level. The same general trend, though less pronounced is apparent in other non Anglo American jurisdictions. The development has also generated concerns about short-termism in capital markets a matter first explored by Marsh (1990).[80] These concerns have intensified in the period since.

The significance of institutional shareholding is two-fold. First, it reflects the particular way in which savings, in aggregate, are invested in the UK and other economies, which are similarly structured, notably the US and other English speaking jurisdictions. Second, as reported by Philips and Drew (2001) it reflects the prevalence of funded occupational pension schemes in the UK (and the US) which in the UK have a cumulative value greater than 100% of GDP, a proportion far higher than in France or Germany and a number of other smaller OECD countries.[81] It is the first of these two observations that merits close attention. Shareholding has been transformed in the UK and other similar jurisdictions. A number of factors explain the structural nature of these changes.

One very important factor is that because of the doctrine of separation of *ownership* from *control* first and subsequent generation shareholders have progressively surrendered their shareholdings in major publicly quoted companies to institutional shareholders. This development may be seen as an example of *path dependence* in terms of the consequence of the separation of ownership from control. Significantly the scale of institutional shareholding in German industry was less than 25% in 1999, not just because of relative small proportion of national savings that are channelled into occupational pensions.[82] It is also smaller because individual and corporate shareholdings in German industry have retained their vitality and commitment[83] when compared with the UK and other Anglo American jurisdictions. This offers another example of *path dependence* in terms of shareholder behaviour. These matters have, as might be expected, a significant bearing on laws governing directors' directors duties' and their evolution a matter to which we now turn.

4.17   Conclusions

This chapter has explored the derivation of the corporation as a separate entity in law and the problems this creates which cannot be satisfactorily resolved. It explores the web of complexity and confusion that has arisen in English law and the particular issues that arise with corporate groups. These issues have held back effective reform. The company, an inanimate fictional entity, has to rely on the directors to settle what it wishes to do and to give expression to those wishes by its actions.

The shareholders or institutional investors have been effectively *cleansed* from the corporation, their ownership claims wholly compromised. Institutional investors are commonly referred to as *absentee landlords* and short-termist in behavioural terms reflecting the reality that their shareholdings are only claims on prospective profits generated by the company.

This contrasts sharply with the *Rhineland* and Nordic concepts of the corporation as a *real* or *aggregate* creation whose commercial functions are driven by an executive board which is overseen by an independent supervisory board. The supervisory board is there to represent shareholder and stakeholder interests. Similar concerns are also reflected in governance arrangements in Asian jurisdictions. Until the shortcomings in Anglo American jurisdictions are effectively addressed the legitimacy of the corporation will remain overshadowed.

Questions for review

1. How and why did the corporate form emerge first in Europe?

2. How did existence of the corporate form facilitate economic development?

3. What is the defining feature of partnership?

4. Who owned the corporate entity prior to the introduction of limited liability?

5. What do the concepts of unlimited and limited liability entail?

6. Why was there confusion in English law about the status of the corporation?

7. Did the Foss v Harbottle judgement help to clarify the status of the corporation?

8. What was the defining significance of the Salomon judgement?

9. How did passing of limited liability facilitate economic development?

10. Explain the concept of separation of *ownership* from *control*?

11. Explain the problem of corporate groups and the phenomenon of *piercing the veil*?

12. What was the significance of the Joint Stock Companies Act of 1844?

13. How can some shareholders tyrannise others?

14. Do shareholders own the corporation?

15. What is the difference between a founding shareholder and an institutional investor?

16. What is a share and what rights does it confer on the holder?

Learning Tasks

I   How would you characterise differences in the portrayal of the corporation in Anglo American jurisdictions and elsewhere?

II   How have shareholders become detached from corporations in Anglo American jurisdictions? How would you seek to reverse this situation?

III   How would you seek to enhance the legitimacy of the corporation?

IV   Should limited liability be withdrawn from shareholders of certain types of corporation?

V   If corporations are concessions in law how does this affect their purposes?

Figure 6
Letter to the Financial Times   8 June 2010

I refer to your editorial entitled Board Democracy in the Financial Times dated 1 June 2010.

One cannot easily dispute the proposals for sharpening the tools available to shareholders have you make and the reasons for making them. What is striking however is how far short they fall from acknowledging the cause of the wider democratic deficit in corporate governance and what needs to be done to redress this.

Empowering shareholders (and other stakeholders) has to go far beyond enabling them to select and reject board directors on an annual basis. If effective shareholder stewardship is to become a reality we have to address the fact that in many publicly held corporations they have no means of exercising *ex ante* influence over directors. They get to know about things that have gone wrong, for example, about the same time as everyone else. This is unacceptable. Any reforms need as a matter of urgency to address this institutional flaw.

The Combined Code and its reliance on non executive directors offers no effective remedy to group-think. What is needed is a separate supervisory institution which represents the interests of shareholders and other stakeholders alike. Relying on unitary boards to properly exercise this function is illusory.

What is long overdue is a thorough review of how publicly held corporations are governed in non-Anglo American jurisdictions. The Swedish model, as with so much else Swedish, might provide some fundamental insight into matters we continue to brush under the carpet.

Richard Tudway

Centre for International Economics

Figure 7   The legal evolution of the corporation

	Anglo American	**European**
Legal System	Common Law	Civil Law
Early Corporate Historical Concept	Aggregate	Aggregate
Later	Real	Aggregate
Post Limited Liability	Fictional Construct	Aggregate
Shareholders	Progressively Detached	Represented by Supervisory Board
Ownership of Assets	Corporate Entity	Aggregate
Supervision	Unitary Board	Supervisory Board (of larger corporations)

Notes

[1] See: Grantham R *The doctrinal basis of the rights of company shareholders* Cam L J 57(3) 1998 p 557.

[2] Such unincorporated businesses were effectively organised as deed of settlement companies and shared a resemblance to the joint stock company model as eventually proposed in the 1844 Joint Stock Companies Act. See Davies P *op cit* Chapter 2 for a discussion of these points.

[3] Remembering that "stock" was used in the sense of "stock in trade" and not the later sense of "stocks and shares." See Davies P *op cit* page 20 for a discussion of this point.

[4] See: Halsbury's Laws of England (4th edition) Vol 9 para 1209 [published between 1973 and 1987].

[5] See: Davies P *op cit* page 31. See also: Ireland P *The Triumph of the Company Legal Form* 1856-1914 in Adams (ed) Essays for Clive Schmitthof (Professional Books), Abingdon, England 1985.

[6] Though as already stated such unincorporated entities could by the ingenious use of a *deed of settlement* enjoy many of the advantages of incorporation including effective limited liability. See Davies P *op cit* page 29 for a discussion of this point.

[7] The reality was that unincorporated *deed of settlement* companies could effectively issue their own debt with the members enjoying protection from liability. See: Davies P *op cit* page 31 onwards for a discussion of this point.

[8] The growth in the scale of unincorporated associations was itself a consequence of the obstacles created by the authorities to incorporation. The passing of the Bubble Act 1720 had the effect of suppressing the establishment of incorporated companies. See: Dubois A B *The English Business Company after the Bubble Act 1720 – 1800* , New York, 1938. See also: Davies P *op cit* p 28.

[9] See: Stokes M *op cit*, page 87 for a discussion of this point.

[10] See: Automatic Self Cleaning Filter Co v Cuninghame [1906] 2 Ch 24 CA. The case concerned whether the directors were bound to give effect to a shareholder resolution. The Court of Appeal affirmed that the directors were not the agents of the shareholders, though they were agents of the company. This shift in the agency relationship fostered fears that directors might be encouraged to act in their own interest rather than those of the shareholders. This was an uppermost concern explored in the Berle and Means thesis *op cit*.

[11] Preceded by s 20(1) of 1948 Companies Act, s 16 of the 1862 Companies Act and the original wording in the 1844 Joint Stock Companies Act and most recently updated by the 2006 Companies Act.

[12] Remembering that the Joint Stock Companies Act of 1844 adapted the deed of settlement contract into a common contract, with the later Joint Stock Companies Act of 1856 introducing a provision along lines which have remained more or less unchanged since. They now form section 14 of the Companies Act 1985 updated in the Companies Act 2006.

[13] See Lowry J and Dignam A *op cit* para 8.16

[14] See: Isle of Wight Rly Co v Tahourdin (1883) 25 Ch. D *op. cit*. See also: Stokes M *op cit.* who explains that the traditional legal model illustrated in the Isle of Wight case portrays the directors as agents of the company with the shareholders as principals and owners of the company. This has the implication that the company is simply a manifestation of the shareholders.

[15] *Ultra vires* means literally "beyond the power (of)." It refers in the case of corporate law to actions taken by directors which are beyond their powers and are therefore deemed to be illegal.

[16] Salomon v Salomon [1897] A C 22 ; 66 L. J.193 H.L. *op cit* remembering that Lord Halsbury stated that the important question [decided by the HL judgment] was whether, in truth, an artificial creation of the legislature had been validly constituted in the case of Salomon & Co Ltd. If that condition was satisfied then the company becomes a person at law, independent and distinct from its members.

[17] See: Stokes M *op cit* in her assessment of the traditional model of the company. This shows that the directors of the company were treated as agents of the company, whose powers could be revoked by shareholders. See: page 87 for a discussion of this point.

[18] Thus avoiding the cumbersome process of securing a special Act of Parliament or Charter.

[19] See: Davies P *op cit* page 38.

[20] See: Sealy L S *Perception and Policy in Company Law Reform* in Feldman and Meisel (ed) Corporate and Commercial Law: Modern Developments (Lloyds of London Press, London 1996) pages 11-13 which comment on the explosive growth of unincorporated businesses.

[21] In 1845 some 1,520 companies were provisionally registered, mostly railway companies, more than half of which did not go beyond the first stage of paying a parliamentary deposit. See: The Times 14 April 1840 as discussed in Parliamentary Papers 1846 XLlll_l. See also: Bryer R A *Accounting for the Railway Mania of 1845 – A Great Railway Swindle* (1991) 16 Accounting, Organisation and Society, 437.

[22] Davies P *op cit* reports on the widespread share abuse of the period on page 32. See also Lobban M *Nineteenth Century Frauds in Company Formations – Derry v Peek in Context* (1991) 112 LQR, 287.

[23] See: Davies P *op cit.* An analysis of the background circumstances which led to the legislation is provided in Chapter 3.

[24] See: Grantham R *op cit* page 558 for an account. See also: Gower L C B *Some contrasts between British and American corporation law* 69 Harv L R 1369, 1372.

[25] The unlimited liability of particular members ceased three years after they had transferred their shares by registered transfer to another party. See: Davies P *op cit.* chapter 2 page 38.

[26] See: Grantham R *op cit.* Page 558 summarises the aims of the Act.

[27] Another underlying presumption was that these arrangements best satisfied the notion of a competitive market regulated by the Rule of Law which in turn legitimised private economic power. See: Stokes M *op cit* pages 82 and 83 for a discussion of these matters.

[28] See: Davies P *op cit.* chapter 2 page 40, footnote 30.

[29] The Act incorporated the provisions of the Limited Liability Act of 1855.

[30] Separate legal personality and limited liability are not, of course, the same thing but limited liability is the logical consequence of the existence of a separate legal personality – a crucial matter. See: Dignam A and Lowry J *op cit* para 2.18 page 21 for a discussion of this fundamental point.

[31] Davies P *op cit* reports that over 100 statutory incorporations occurred during the last 40 years of the 19th century

[32] Salomon v Salomon *op cit* AC 22 , HL

[33] See: Freund-Kahn Sir O (1944) *'Some Reflections on Company Law Reform'* (1943-1944) MLR 54. He condemned the Salomon judgment as 'calamitous' for failing to 'mitigate the rigidities of the folklore of the corporate entity in favour of the legitimate interests of the company's creditors'.

[34] See: Farrar J *Corporate Governance Theory, Principle and Practice* 2nd ed 2005, and Bond Law Review Vol 10 issue 2 1998 where he explores the manner in which the law of limited liability has been subverted.

[35] A corporate group is a collection of parent and subsidiary corporations that function as a single economic entity through a common source of control

[36] The tort liability avoidance is achieved by corporation A creating another corporation, corporation B for which corporation A has no responsibility because Corporation B is a separate legal entity.

[37] See: Ottolenghi S *From peeping behind the veil to ignoring it completely*, 1990 MLR 338

[38] See: Rixon F *Competing interests and conflicting principles: an examination of the power of alteration of articles of association* (1986) MLR 446.

[39] This is a legal oddity since legal entities being other than human had been established in early Roman law. The State, ecclesiastical bodies and educational institutions had long been recognised as legal entities distinct from their members. See: W Geldart (1911) *Legal Personality* LQR, 27, 94 for a discussion of this matter. See also: Dewey J *The Historic Background of Corporate Legal Personality* Yale Law Review (6) 1926, 655 – 67.

[40] The Act of 1855 provided for the limited liability of the members or shareholders on complete registration. These provisions were incorporated in the Joint Stock Companies Act of 1856. As Salomon v

Salomon was to establish 40 years later, the company was a separately incorporated entity in law from the shareholders - from which the limited liability of shareholders derives. See: Davies P *op cit* pages 44 and 45 for a discussion of this point.

[41] See: Rixon F (1986) *op cit* who explores the equivocation between treating the corporation as a separate legal person and equating the corporation with the shareholders.

[42] Significantly in the Second Reading of the Company Law Reform Bill, 6 June 2006 the British Secretary of State, in his comments along with other parliamentarians during the debate, continues to refer to the shareholders and the company as if they were one and the same, when in law they are clearly not.

[43] See: Ireland P *Company Law and the Myth of Shareholder Ownership* MLR Vol 32 (1999) page 62 footnote 6 in particular which addresses this confusion.

[44] Fears about corporate power and accountability would not in the economic and market conditions of the time have given rise to the pervasive concerns that are currently felt about these issues and raise fundamental questions about the legitmation of corporate power. See: Stokes M *op cit* page 86 for a discussion of this point.

[45] As it has already been noted, however, shareholders in unincorporated entities, prior to the enactment of limited liability, enjoyed a form of limited liability through asset partitioning. See: Getzler J and Macnair M *The Firm as an Entity before the Companies Acts: Asset Partitioning by Private Law.* Corporate forms existed long before the arrival of the joint stock limited liability company. This allowed private law to construct a "nexus of contracts" company with a veil drawn between investors and traders.

[46] See: Ireland P *op cit* JLS Vol 23 1996

[47] See: Bratton W W. *The New Economic Theory of the Firm* The Law of the Business Enterprise ed Sally Wheeler 1994 page 138.

[48] The nexus of contracts is often portrayed as an innovation of the 1970's. This is mistaken. See: Getzler J and Macnair M *op cit* who argue that the English courts have, by long tradition, acknowledged the "artificial legal personality" and the role played by asset partitioning.

[49] Regardless as to whether the *reification* is expressed in terms of a fictional entity or a real (or natural) entity. See: Stokes M *op cit* pages 88 – 90 for a discussion of this matter. See also: Dicey A V *Law and Public Opinion* (1st ed, 1905), p 165.

[50] The collapse of Enron is a lasting example of the limitations of reliance on financial market controls where abuse extended from management to market *gatekeepers* and other market making financial intermediaries. See: http//specials.ft.com/enron/

[51] See: Ashby Rly Carriage & Iron Co v Riche [1875] LR 7 HL 653. In this case the House of Lords eventually decided that the doctrine of *ultra vires* would apply to unincorporated deed of settlement companies, which subsequently registered as joint stock companies with limited liability and with memorandum and articles of association, even though such unincorporated entities had no recognised corporate personality before incorporation. See: Davies P *op cit* page 203 and Stokes M *op cit* page 91 for discussions of this matter.

[52] See: Stokes M *op cit* page 90 who points out that the theory was first popularised by the German realists who made a connection between the natural entity theory of the corporation and the theory of the state. The organic theory of the corporate personality has also affected company law in other areas most notably in seeking to establish evidence of the "directing mind and will of the company" in cases of corporate manslaughter. See: Lennard's Carrying Co v Asiatic Petroleum Co Ltd [1915] AC 705. See also: Pollock F (Sir) (1911) *op cit* pages 219 – 235 who discusses the conflicting interpretations of the corporation either as fictional entity or a real or natural entity in the context of English law.

[53] The exception being the company created by Charter which had an identity separate from its shareholders. See: Grantham R *op cit* p 562 where this matter is addressed.

[54] See: Davies P *op cit.* page 299.

[55] Bligh versus Brent (1836) Y & C 268. See also: Watson v Spratley (10 Ex 222) decided in 1854. The courts declared 'a share to be an interest only in profits' with the implication that shareholders had no direct interest in the assets of the company.

[56] See: Grantham R *op cit* page 562 footnote 48 which notes the case of Bligh versus Brent. It was argued in that case that shareholders had no *severable* interest in the company's assets which was understood at the time as meaning, only, that shares were not regarded as realty, (or real estate).

[57]*Severable* is defined in law as something that is capable of being separated from other things to which it is joined and maintaining nonetheless a complete and independent existence. This suggests that shares were not, for example, viewed as realty (or real estate).

[58] Borland's Trustees v Steel Brothers & Co Ltd [1901] Ch 279,288. Approved by C.A. in Re Paulin [1935] 1 K B 26 and by H. L.

[59] See: Davies P *op cit*. p 299 onwards.

[60] See: Evershed L J in Short v Treasury Commissions [1948] 1 K. B. 122 C. A.

[61] Bligh v Brent (1837) 2 Y & C Ex 268

[62] Though not by use of the articles of association but within the terms of the debenture.

[63] Remembering that the charge is secured against the company's property and never the company itself. See: Davies P *op cit* p 301 for a treatment of this issue.

[64] See: Davies P *op cit* chapter 9 p 178 onwards which explores this evolutionary background.

[65] As Ireland points out the confusion arises over the dichotomy between 'companies as owners of assets and shareholders as owners of shares'. See: Ireland P *op citCompany Law and the Myth of Shareholder Ownership* (1999) MLR 62 at page 32.

[66] See: Short versus Treasury Commissioners *op cit.* See also: Grantham R *op cit* p 563 for a discussion of this point.

[67] With the implication that the NAV (net asset value) of the company was higher than the company's capitalisation, with the shares not reflecting the underlying value of the company.

[68] This is a common error. Parkinson J *op cit* for example makes this error in arguing that shareholders are owners 'by virtue of being contributors to the company's capital' [page 34]. This is incorrect as a generalisation though footnote 109 goes some way to qualifying and explaining the position.

[69] The term second hand aims to make a distinction between shares that are issued by the company to shareholders in exchange for cash and shares that are simply traded between different parties in the stock market.

[70] As foreseen in Art 70 of Table A of the Articles of Association, British Companies Acts 1985 – 1989.

[71] The widespread delegation of managerial power in the modern corporation complicates still further the theoretical powers of shareholders to influence management behaviour. See: Parkinson J *op cit* Chapter 1 for a discussion of these matters.

[72] Persistently the courts maintain that it is for the shareholders, who appoint the directors, to use their legal powers to discipline erring directors as foreseen under the provisions of section 303 Companies Act 1985.

[73] Whilst Art 70 mentions 'any directions given by special resolution' [of the general meeting], there are no other indications as to what such a special resolution might cover. Its potential significance is also diminished by the rest of the relevant section which states clearly that 'the business of the company shall be managed by the directors who may exercise all the power of the company'. This may justify the description of the provision as being "rhetorical" rather than real.

[74] Institutional shareholders would have an eye to section 741 (2) Companies Act 1985 which addresses the issue of Insider Trading in any moves to encourage closer commercial involvement in the affairs of the company.

[75] Reducing management discretion has to be weighed against management costs, delay and error. See: Eisenberg M A *The Structure of the Corporation: A Legal Analysis* (1976) at 15 for an assessment of the

different skills of the investor on the one hand when compared with those of the business manager. Whilst a case might be made for extending shareholder involvement in areas where investment expertise might be uppermost, this does not apply across the range of business skills and expertise needed to run most businesses.

[76] Though this is discussed in a later section, the rules regarding Insider Trading could be a factor discouraging closer involvement in by institutional investors in the commercial affairs of the company in which they hold shares. See: Parkinson J *op cit* page 173 for a discussion of these matters. See also: Company Securities (Insider Dealing) Act 1985 section 1.

[77] See: www.valuebasedmanagement.net/articles_oecd_corporate_governance_principles2004.html for an inspection of the OECD's Framework for Corporate Governance which enshrines the *primacy* of shareholders rights to the exclusion of other stakeholders.

[78] It is further complicated by Shadow Director and Insider Trading concerns. See: Dignam A and Lowry J *op cit* pages 289 – 290 for a discussion of Shadow Directors and section 5.34 on Insider Trading. See also: Davies P *op cit* Chapter 17.

[79] Source: ONS (Office of National Statistics) *op cit* "Share Ownership". A Report on the ownership of shares at 31/12/99, page 8.

[80] See: Marsh P *Short-termism on trial* (International Fund Managers Association) 1990.

[81] See: Phillips and Drew '*Pension fund indicators, a long term perspective on pension fund investment 2000*' August 2001, page 13. The German pension assets to GDP ratio stands at around 18% with the French ratio at around 5%.

[82] Quoted in Phillips and Drew *op cit.*

[83] This is well exemplified in recent years by the activities of Volkswagen, the large German car manufacturer and its single and most active shareholder Porsche, the small luxury German car manufacturer. The chairman of the supervisory board of Volkswagen Ferdinand Piech at the time was also a board member of Porsche. Piech wanted to increase Porsche's shareholding in Volkswagen from 27.4% where it was to greater than 50%. This move was designed to prevent a hostile rival takeover by private equity funds. What this tale illustrates is the importance of "primary" shareholder culture in German industry when compared with institutional investors in the British and American contexts. See also the comments by Sir John Rose, chief executive of Rolls Royce Plc and the danger he highlights of transforming Britain into an "aircraft carrier" for foreign companies, a reference in the last analysis to the behaviour of institutional investors. This was reported in the Financial Times 10 February 2007 page 1.

Chapter 5

The Role of the Director

5.1   Summary

Building upon the analysis in chapters two, three and four, Chapter five will examine the role of the director as agent of the company. This creates challenges in distinguishing appearance from reality. It is sometimes referred to as the *agency problem* and starts its life in Anglo American jurisdictions. In all jurisdictions the evolution of fiduciary duties has been fundamentally influenced by considerations of fairness and impartiality. These are a historic overhang of the concept of trusteeship. But there are other significant differences between jurisdictions which will be explored

As we have seen Anglo American jurisdictions see the behaviour of board directors and senior managers as being monitored and disciplined principally, though not exclusively, by financial markets. This explains the very great importance placed upon accurate and transparent disclosure of financial information by the corporation and ever more demanding responsibilities on the chief executives and chief financial officer to guarantee proper disclosure.[1] The behavioural aspects of directorship have been tempered by the development of other soft and hard laws and the *comply or explain* corporate codes that have evolved. On balance the philosophy of *laissez faire* where commercial decision taking is concerned continues to favour *non intervention* by the courts as exemplified by something referred to as the *business judgement rule.*

In contrast in European *Rhineland* and Nordic jurisdictions the primary disciplinary focus is the supervisory board which has a legal duty to represent shareholders and other stakeholders. The *agency problem* does not arise. Elsewhere as we have seen there are variants of these different approaches. But in all of these different jurisdictions there is increased scrutiny of the behaviour of directors.[2] In Anglo American jurisdictions there is a high level of concern about the quality and effectiveness of boards but this has not always been matched with credible and enforceable remedies. In European *Rhineland* and Nordic jurisdictions both supervisors and executive board members are also subject to closer scrutiny.[3] Directors' duties in Japan resemble arrangements in the Rhineland and Nordic models. In all these non Anglo American jurisdictions there is an explicit recognition of the importance of ensuring that directors are seen to be acting in the interests of shareholders and other stakeholders alike.

5.2   The concept of fiduciary duties

Fiduciary duties, as we have seen earlier are grounded in trust. The presumption is that directors will not seek to benefit from their position of trust. This is rooted in history before the introduction of limited liability when directors were portrayed as trustees. This has brought with it some curious paradoxes in modern times. The current interpretation of these obligations in the British context can be portrayed in the following terms. Directors are expected to act in the best interests of the company; to do so under the constitution of the company; to avoid conflicts of interest and not to profit from their position as director.

As we have already explored the first paradox is that the directors have a duty to the company and not the shareholders.[4] This is a matter of on-going confusion. A second problem arises in interpreting what exactly the interests of the company might be in any particular situation. This paradox has been unsatisfactorily resolved under English law by treating the company not as an entity in itself but by *identifying* the interests of the company with those of the shareholders. This significant legal fudge has already been explored.[5] Thirdly the issue of conflicts of director interest is highly problematical and difficult to monitor effectively since breaches of that duty rely on directors to reveal. This is an area where further reform is urgently required. The British CLRSG (Company Law Reform Steering Group) which was set up in the aftermath of the Enron scandal had ample opportunity to address the conflicting and confused background[6]. In the event it largely failed to do so.

5.3   The duty of care

The duty of care is perhaps the most notorious examples of a fiduciary obligation which is bereft of any objective standards of assessment. Whilst progress has been made in certain specific technical areas such as insolvency the wider question of *competence* remains unresolved. The Barings Bank case in 1995, following spectacular losses resulting from the unauthorised dealings of Nick Leeson, a company employee, led to an application for one of the directors of Barings to be disqualified. The case in defence was that because of the size of the firm's operation his role was *reactive;* he relied on delegation to excuse personal liability.[7]

This view was challenged on the grounds that collectively and individually the directors had a duty to acquire a sufficient knowledge of the company's business in order to discharge their responsibilities. Whilst this has had the effect of focussing more closely on the issue of skill and competence there remains the need to lay down clear tests which could then be applied in settling such contested matters. On that front there has been little progress. The spirit of the *business judgement rule*[8] in Anglo American jurisdictions remain strongly entrenched. Judges refuse to second-guess the decisions of directors even though this objection becomes increasingly less acceptable.[9] The Banking Crisis in 2008 which provided ample evidence to challenge the competence of individual directors has not, to the dismay of the public at large, materialised. Individuals have been pilloried for their failures but not prosecuted for incompetence.

5.4   The principal/agent problem

Three sets of principal/agent problems arise in the structure of large corporations. These are described by Davies[10] (2000) in the following terms. Those arising between management and shareholders as a class; those between majority and minority shareholders; and those between the controllers of the company (whether management or shareholders) and non shareholder stakeholders. The types of conflict that may arise are very different in each set of circumstances. It will also determine the emphasis of legislative and policy attention.[11]

How the *principal agent* problem arises and how it can be remedied takes us to the heart of a number of fundamental difficulties. The reason why boards of directors have become the principal mechanism through which the company is managed is because it is impractical to leave these decisions to large number of shareholders to settle. This is broadly the legal position in most Anglo American jurisdictions. Shareholders may, for example, challenge directors' recommendations. But because of the dispersed nature of shareholding these powers are in any event mostly theoretical or rhetorical. They cannot be enforced. In other jurisdictions the situation is very different.

This, as we shall see, ignores number of alternative solutions like appointing separate and independent supervisory boards whose task it would be to assess *ex ante* management board decisions and settle thereby whether the best interest of shareholders and other stakeholders is served by the proposed action in question. This matter is dealt more fully later.

5.5   Conclusions

Directors in whatever jurisdiction wield great power. These powers have increased disproportionately where the *separation of ownership and control* is at its greatest as in Anglo American jurisdictions. It is the failure to have addressed this asymmetry in terms of power that undermines confidence in the Anglo American model. The business judgment rule is an unhelpful distraction.

In contrast the *Rhineland* and Nordic models have fashioned more effective control mechanisms. These mechanisms allow the supervisory board to challenge and to examine *ex ante* the decisions proposed by the executive board. This very specifically covers top executive remuneration but also broader questions of commercial development and the attendant risks.

None of these features exist within the Anglo American framework of governance. *Supervision* is continuously confused with *execution*. This continues to result in examples of governance failures which are not satisfactorily addressed.

Questions for Review

1. What is the nature of the *principal/agent* problem and why does it arise?

2. Explain the nature of fiduciary duties and comment upon its relevance in determining directors duties in modern times?

3. The role of the director is portrayed as one which aims to protect the interest of all shareholders, whether large or small block holders, in their commercial management of the company. How far can this be realistically achieved?

4. Explain the key differences between Anglo American board arrangements and those found in European, Nordic and Japanese corporations?

5. How effectively can shareholders bring management to account under Anglo American arrangements?

6. How can shareholder and stakeholder interests most effectively be represented?

7. What is the *Business Judgement Rule*? Can it be challenged and if so how?

8. 'The role of the judiciary is not to decide upon matters of commercial acumen where directors are concerned but whether or not directors have used proper and effective procedures in reaching in their decisions.' Comment upon this statement.

Learning Tasks

I   What in your view would be the most effective way of directing a corporation?

II   How would you go about deciding what qualities an NED should have to effectively contribute as a director?

III   How would you see an independent supervisory board operating alongside a board of management?

IV   How should the powers of directors be defined?

V   How would you go about making directors accountable for their decisions?

Figure 8

The Companies Act 2006 Directors Duties

172   Duty to promote the success of the company

(1) A director of a company must act in the way he considers, in good faith, would be most likely to promote the success of the company for the benefit of its members as a whole, and in doing so have regard (amongst other matters) to

(a) the likely consequences of any decision in the long term,
(b) the interests of the company's employees,
(c) the need to foster the company's business relationships with suppliers, customers and others,
(d) the impact of the company's operations on the community and the environment,
(e) the desirability of the company maintaining a reputation for high

standards of business conduct, and

(f) the need to act fairly as between members of the company.

(2) Where or to the extent that the purposes of the company consist of or include purposes other than the benefit of its members, subsection (1) has effect as if the reference to promoting the success of the company for the benefit of its members were to achieving those purposes.

(3) The duty imposed by this section has effect subject to any enactment or rule of law requiring directors, in certain circumstances, to consider or act in the interests of creditors of the company.

Figure 9
Letter to The Economist   10 March 2013

Schumpeter's piece entitled Companies' Moral Compass, [The Economist 9 March 2013] seems to point the way to progress! The points made by Colin Meyer of Said Business School, Oxford, are obviously correct for those who understand how the jurisprudence governing corporations has evolved historically. Corporations are indeed fictional entities in law. More than that however: shareholders do not (and cannot), under limited liability, be the owners of the corporation's assets. Because the shareholders do not own the assets of the corporation they are not *owners* in any recognisable sense of that term of the corporation. But these misunderstandings persist and distort everything we have to say about the corporation and its direction. The Economist, at least until now, has done little to dispel this myth.

Since shareholders, at least in Anglo American jurisdictions, have no clear proprietorial rights, especially where publicly traded companies are concerned, this raises fundamental issues not just about the ownership of the corporation but its purposes. It undermines the popular belief that the role of the director is to *maximise shareholder value*. If this is not true then it also raises questions about the purpose of governance arrangements for the corporation. Once the fallacy of *shareholder primacy* is exposed we are bound to ask the question – what should the governance arrangements of corporations aim to achieve?

It seems clear that boards in Anglo American jurisdictions, as they are currently instituted, are failing to address a number of concerns. There are at least two points that need to be emphasised. First the role of independent supervision of the company's activities is confused with the day to day running of the business. Mixing executive and non executive directors on single boards simply doesn't work as the evidence proves beyond reasonable doubt. Second the confusing of these two separate functions results in there being no effective mechanism in place for the internalisation of wider stakeholder and shareholder concerns, parties who have a direct and enduring interest in the affairs of the corporation.

Colin Mayer recommends the creation of separate trusts. This might well be a way forward. More generally what is needed – and exists under our very noses in *Rhineland* and Nordic jurisdictions – are separate and independent supervisory boards. Their role as directors is to ensure that the wealth of the corporation is properly husbanded in the interests of parties other than either semi-detached institutional investors, or worse still self serving directors.

Richard Tudway

Centre for International Economics, London

Notes

[1] This has been reinforced by the Sarbanes Oxley Act in the US a response to fraud in Enron involving senior directors.

[2] It is reported that the directors of the US company Yahoo sacked the chief executive Carol Bartz to prove that they are not the *doofuses* (an American term for idiots) that she claimed they were. A similar event is reported in respect of Hewlett Packard (the computer manufacturer) which fired two CEOs in quick succession to avoid a similar charge. In the case of the phone-hacking scandal the board of News Corporation are accused of inaction by shareholders because of their failure to address the crisis within the board. See: The Economist 17 September 2011 page 67 for an account of this event.

[3] The scrutiny is however mostly a private matter involving the directors and may be criticised for not being sufficiently transparent.

[4] This as we have seen was established under Foss v Harbottle (1843). As a general rule individual shareholders are not empowered to initiate proceedings for a wrong to the company. This may result in large scale shareholders tyrannising smaller shareholders or shareholders relying on directors to initiate action in respect of actions that they have themselves taken on behalf of the company.

[5] As already reported this arises under section 14 of the British Companies Act 1985. The wording of the section allows for the constitution of the company to be 'signed and sealed by each member'. There is no mention of the company, a separate entity in law. Despite this contradiction the judiciary holds that the company is a party to the contract.

[6] See Annex C Volume 1 of the Report of the Company Law Reform Steering Group – Statement of Directors Duties (2001).

[7] The bank collapsed in 1995 after one of its employees, Nick Leeson, lost £827 million ($1.3 billion) as a result of speculative and unlawful investing in futures contracts at the bank's Singapore office.

[8] The *business judgement rule* assumes that the directors of a corporation are presumed to be motivated in their conduct by a *bona fide* regard for the interests of the corporation whose affairs the shareholders have committed to their charge. To challenge the actions of a corporation's board of directors, a plaintiff assumes the burden of providing evidence that directors, in reaching their challenged decision, breached any one of the three main conditions governing their fiduciary duty - good faith, loyalty, or due care.

[9] The issue at stake is whether the director(s) was thorough in assessing the matter he acted upon and not whether his decision of a good one or a bad one. It is a matter of professional process.

[10] See Davies P, *The Board of Directors, Composition, Structure, Duties and Powers* OECD 2000

[11] For example given that dispersed shareholder is a common feature of listed corporations in Britain and America the remedies that have been developed reflect the concerns that tend to arise, notably the inability of shareholders to exercise effective influence over management. Where concerns centre on large block shareholdings the focus of legislation and policy focus will be different. Where the problem centres on the relationship between controllers and non-shareholder stakeholders again the focus of legislation and policy will be different.

Chapter 6

Corporate structures – an international overview

6.1   Summary

Chapter 6 is mainly descriptive and covers a range of different jurisdictions. There are a variety of different corporate structures other than limited liability companies. How the business enterprise sector is populated raises some unexpected diversity. By far the most popular by type of structure, however, is the limited liability companies. The reasons that explain this are explored. Historically other types of enterprise endeavour can also be identified. These include *mutuals*[1] and other forms of not for profit entities, co-operatives and SOEs (state-owned industries). More recently they also include SWF (Sovereign Wealth Funds).

These different structures will be examined with a view to establishing how far different types of structure determine different power-sharing, governance arrangements and development strategies.

6.2   Generalisations

The following generalisation about corporate structures can be made as follows.

- First the world is mostly and increasingly populated by limited liability companies with and without direct state shareholder participation and state-owned enterprises which themselves are either wholly owned state companies, or companies in which there is some proportion of non-state participation in corporations which are otherwise state controlled.
- Second Anglo American and other English speaking jurisdiction are almost exclusively populated by private limited liability corporations and publicly traded corporations. State ownership is of relatively minor importance. There exist in these jurisdictions examples of mutually owned ventures (such as credit unions) co-operatives and newer forms of social enterprise (often companies limited by guarantee) and other not for profit enterprises.

- Third in Europe and the Nordic countries state-owned enterprises still play a significant if diminishing role alongside the private enterprise sector which consist again of private and publicly traded corporations. Again there are examples of cooperatives and other forms of not for profit enterprises including SWFs.
- Fourth there are transitional economies the most significant of which are China India, Indonesia, Brazil and Russia – with a clustering of smaller countries such as Cambodia and Vietnam and others in South America where the emerging private sector is still distinctly overshadowed by state ownership. Again forms of ownership other than limited liability are beginning to emerge.

6.3   Anglo American and English-speaking Jurisdictions

The limited liability company has played a key role in economic development. It has also provided a mechanism for attracting development capital. The depth and liquidity of Anglo American capital markets is often cited as a reflection of the sophistication of financial capitalism in Anglo American jurisdictions compared with European and other jurisdictions. There has been a move away from unlimited liability corporate forms which were common in the professional services industry in favour of limited liability. This has been in response to the rising exposures faced by partners in these firms. The co-operative form has also retreated in Anglo American jurisdictions though this may now be changing.

Mutuals, or member owned organisations, also fell sharply in the 1980's as a result of deregulation of the banking industry. This encouraged many British building societies to re-establish themselves as publicly traded banking corporations. The Co-operative Group in Britain, following a period of decline in all its main sectors of activity has recovered ground in retailing and elsewhere. There have also been signs of growth in social enterprise companies, (often companies limited by guarantee) in healthcare and public sector delivery. These developments are often linked to CSR (corporate social responsibility) initiatives sponsored or otherwise funded by larger publicly trading companies and in some cases the state.

As already reported there are widespread concerns about corporate governance within traditional publicly listed corporations. These concerns are driving the debate on alternatives. Corporate forms like the John Lewis Partnership (a British company whose assets are held in a trust in which all members are owners) operates in the high-end department store sector and food retailing. It is widely regarded as a highly successful business with unique governance and co-determination arrangements in the workplace.

The Partnership is widely viewed as a model in terms of its governance when compared with orthodox limited liability entities.[2]

Finally because of concerns about corporate governance in Anglo American jurisdictions there are also concerns about the orientation of CSR and the support of other arms-length initiatives. These initiatives are often portrayed as being in response to exogenous threats and opportunities to the funding company rather than any systematic strategic board-driven assessment of the sustainability challenges facing the company.

6.4   State owned enterprises

State ownership is a common organisational form in many countries. It may also be referred to as public ownership, government ownership or state property. They represent property interests that are vested in the state, rather than individual companies or communities. State ownership may refer to state ownership or control of any asset, industry, or enterprise at any level, national, regional or local (municipal); or to common (full-community) non-state ownership. The process of bringing an asset into public ownership is called nationalisation or municipalisation. The reversal process is sometimes referred to as privatisation or denationalisation.

In primarily market-based economies, government-owned assets are often managed and run like joint-stock corporations with the government owning a controlling stake of the shares. This model is often referred to as an SOE (state-owned enterprise). An SOE may resemble a not-for-profit corporation as it may not be required to generate a profit. Governments may also use profitable entities they own to support the general budget. SOE's may or may not be expected to operate in a broadly commercial manner and may or may not have monopolies in their areas of activity. The creation of a government-owned corporation from other forms of government ownership may be a precursor to privatisation. The attention of readers is drawn to the OECD Guidelines on Governance of State Owned Enterprises. This can be downloaded from the OECD website.

Figure 10

Table 1. Equity holdings by public authorities (according to size of holding in 2008), US$ billion

	1998	2003	2008
Japan	434.5	553.0	777.8
France	171.6	184.4	387.4
United States	131.0	124.7	335.7
Norway	46.9	124.6	312.6
United Kingdom	159.6	187.3	280.8
Germany	184.2	141.2	269.4
Italy	133.0	123.8	182.1
Netherlands	47.3	46.9	136.5
Poland	42.6	35.5	124.4
Spain	64.3	64.1	122.4
Rest of OECD	338.2	530.9	778.8
Total OECD	*1753.2*	*2116.5*	*3708.0*

Source: OECD Financial Accounts Statistics.

6.5   Sovereign Wealth Funds

A sovereign wealth fund (SWF) is a state-owned investment fund comprising financial assets such as stocks, bonds, property, precious metals, or other financial instruments. SWFs invest globally. Most SWFs are funded by foreign exchange assets. Some sovereign wealth funds may be held by a central bank, which accumulates the funds in the course of its management of a nation's banking system. This type of fund is usually of major economic and fiscal importance. Other SWFs represent state savings that are invested in various entities for the purposes of investment return.

The accumulated funds may have their origin in, or may represent, foreign currency deposits, gold, special drawing rights (SDRs) and International Monetary Fund (IMF) reserve positions held by central banks and monetary authorities, along with other national assets such as pension investments, oil funds, or other industrial and financial share holdings. These are assets of the sovereign nation that are typically held in domestic and different reserve currencies (such as the dollar, euro, pound, and yen). Such investment management entities may be set up as official investment companies, state pension funds, or sovereign oil funds, among others.

There have been attempts to distinguish funds held by sovereign entities from foreign-exchange reserves held by central banks. SWFs can be characterized as *maximizing long-*

term return, with foreign exchange reserves serving short-term *currency stabilisation*, and liquidity management. Many central banks in recent years possess reserves greatly in excess of needs for liquidity or foreign exchange management. Moreover it is widely believed most have diversified into assets other than short-term, highly liquid monetary ones, though almost no data is publicly available to back up this assertion. Some central banks have even begun buying equities, or derivatives of differing ilk (like overnight interest rate swaps).

6.6   Concerns about SWFs

There are several reasons why the growth of sovereign wealth funds is attracting close attention. Some countries worry that foreign investment by SWFs raises national security concerns because the purpose of the investment might be to secure control of strategically important industries for political rather than financial gain. These concerns have led the EU to reconsider whether to allow its members to use *golden shares* to block certain foreign acquisitions. This strategy has largely been excluded as a viable option by the EU, for fear it would give rise to a rise in trade protectionism. In the United States, these concerns are addressed by the Exon–Florio Amendment to the Omnibus Trade and Competitiveness Act of 1988.

The inadequate transparency of SWFs is a concern for investors and regulators. This might include the size and source of funds, investment goals, internal checks and balances, disclosure of relationships, and holdings in private equity funds. Many of these concerns have been addressed by the IMF using the *Santiago Principles*[3] which set out common standards regarding transparency, independence, and the governance of these entities.

6.7   The Norwegian SWF

The Norwegian SWF is in many respects an exception. The Government Pension Fund – Global (*Statens pensjonsfond – Utland*, SPU) is a fund into which the surplus wealth produced by Norwegian petroleum income is deposited. The fund changed name in January 2006. It was previously known as *The Petroleum Fund of Norway*. The fund is commonly referred to as *The Oil Fund* (*Oljefondet*). In June 2011, it was valued as the largest pension fund in the world remembering that it is not a pension fund as such. It derives its financial backing from oil profits and not pension contributions. As of March 2013 its total value is NOK4.182tr ($712.7bn). It holds one percent of global equity markets. With 1.78 percent of European stocks invested, it is probably the largest single owner of public equity in Europe.

The purpose of the petroleum fund is to invest parts of the large surplus generated by the Norwegian petroleum sector. This derives in part from taxes of oil and gas companies, but also license exploration payments as well as the State's *Direct Financial Interest* and dividends from the partly state-owned Statoil. Current revenue from the petroleum sector is expected to decline in coming decades. The Petroleum Fund was established in 1990 after a decision by the country's legislature to counter the effects of the forthcoming decline in income and to smooth out the disruptive effects of highly fluctuating oil prices.

The fund is managed by Norges Bank Investment Management (NBIM), a part of the Norwegian Central Bank on behalf of the Ministry of Finance. It is currently the largest pension fund in Europe. It is also larger than the California public-employees pension fund (CalPERS), the largest public pension fund in the United States. The Norwegian Ministry of Finance forecasts that the fund will reach NOK4.3tr ($717bn) by the end of 2014. In a parliamentary White Paper in April 2011 the Norwegian Ministry of Finance forecast that the 2030 value of the fund might well reach NOK7.4tr ($1.3tr). Since 1998 the fund has been allowed to invest up to 40 percent of its portfolio in the international stock market. In June 2009, the ministry decided to raise the stock portion to 60 percent. The Norwegian Government has decided that up to 5 percent of the fund should be invested in real estate, beginning in 2010.

Due to the large size of the fund relative to the relatively small number of people living in Norway (4.9 million people in 2010), the *Petroleum Fund* has become a major political issue, dominated by three main concerns:

- Whether the country should use more of the petroleum revenues for the state budget instead of saving the funds for the future. The main matter of debate is to what degree increased government spending would increase inflation.
- Whether the high level of exposure (around 60 percent in 2008) to the highly volatile, and therefore risky, stock market is financially safe. Others claim that the high differentiation and extreme long term of the investments will dilute the risk and that the state is losing money due to the low investment percentage in the stock market.
- Whether the investment policy of the Petroleum Fund is ethical.

Part of the investment policy debate is related to the discovery of several cases of investment by *The Petroleum Fund* in highly controversial companies, involved in businesses such as arms production and tobacco. The Petroleum Fund's Advisory Council on Ethics was established 19 November 2004 by Royal Decree. Accordingly, the

Ministry of Finance issued a new regulation on the management of the Government Petroleum Fund which also includes ethical guidelines.

According to its ethical guidelines, the Norwegian pension fund cannot invest money in companies that directly or indirectly contribute to killing, torture, deprivation of freedom, or other violations of human rights in conflict situations or wars. Contrary to popular belief, the fund is allowed to invest in a number of arms-producing companies. This is because only certain kinds of weapons (such as nuclear arms) are banned by the ethical guidelines as investment objects.

An investigation by the Norwegian business newspaper *Dagens Næringsliv* in February 2012 showed that Norway has invested more than $2bn in 15 technology companies producing technology that can and has been used for either filtering, wiretapping, or surveillance of communication in various countries, among them Iran, Syria, and Burma. Although surveillance tech is not the primary activity of all these companies, they have all had, or still have some kind of connection to such technologies. The Norwegian Ministry of Finance has stated that it would not withdraw investments in these companies, nor would it discuss an eventual exclusion of surveillance industry companies from its investments.

On 19 January 2010 the Ministry of Finance announced that 17 tobacco companies had been excluded from the fund. The divestment from these companies totalled $2bn (NOK14.2bn). This is the largest divestment triggered by ethical recommendations in history.

6.8   European and other Scandinavian Jurisdictions

Traditions in Europe reveal a variety of alternatives to more traditional limited liability entities but again the predominant form is the limited liability company. There is another significant difference explored earlier. There are important differences in terms of corporate governance arrangements when compared with the Anglo American model. Not only are independent supervisory boards a common feature in these jurisdictions European and Nordic companies, large and small, use CSR to integrate social and environmental concerns in their business operations and in their interaction with their stakeholders. It is firmly viewed as a fundamental strategic aspect of corporate development and not a bolt-on determined by an external of threat and/or opportunity. The priorities focus on promoting best practices for lifelong learning, work organisation, equal opportunities, social inclusion and sustainable development.

Within the EU there is a public EU company. This is called a Societas Europaea, or "SE". An SE can register in any member state of the European Union and transfer to other member states. In January 2011, some 702 registrations have been reported. Examples of companies registered as a European Company are Allianz SE, BASF SE, Strabag SE, Gfk SE, and MAN SE. National law continues to supplement the basic rules in the regulation on formation and mergers.

European Company Regulation is complemented by an Employee Involvement Directive that sets rules for participation by employees on the company's board of directors. There is also a statute allowing European Cooperative Societies. There is no EU-wide register of SEs (an SE is registered on the national register of the member state in which it has its head office), but each registration is to be published in the Official Journal of the European Union.

The European Commission published a Green Paper on CSR in 2001[4]. The aims and objectives are set out well in the following quotation from the Executive Summary of the Report.

> *An increasing number of European companies are promoting their corporate social responsibility strategies as a response to a variety of social, environmental and economic pressures. They aim to send a signal to the various stakeholders with whom they interact: employees, shareholders, investors, consumers, public authorities and NGOs. In doing so, companies are investing in their future and they expect that the voluntary commitment they adopt will help to increase their profitability.*

CSR has gained significant importance across Europe, also as a new field of public policy debate. The Report describes how EU Member States aim to facilitate CSR by raising awareness, by advancing Sustainable Public Procurement, and by fostering Socially Responsible Investment. It provides a systematic description of CSR policies in Europe.

The main contribution of a European approach is to complement and add value to existing activities by:

- providing an overall European framework, aiming at promoting quality and coherence of corporate social responsibility practices, through developing broad principles, approaches and tools, and promoting best practice and innovative ideas

- supporting best practice approaches to cost-effective evaluation and independent verification of corporate social responsibility practices, ensuring thereby their effectiveness and credibility.

The Green Paper has launched a wide debate on corporate social responsibility at national, European and international level. This is attached as an Appendix.

6.9   Japan

Japan's limited liability industrial structures mirror those found in Anglo American and in Europe and Scandinavian jurisdictions. But there are significant differences. Japanese industrial organisation is characterised by the *keiretsu* which is unique to larger Japanese corporations. While not all larger Japanese businesses are *keiretsu* in design, most of Japan's major corporate entities are of this form. There are two types of *keiretsu*: the classical *keiretsu* and the vertically integrated *keiretsu*. The so-called Big Six Japanese business groups are all examples of classical form. These are the Fuyo/Fuji Group, Sumitomo, Sanwa, Mitsui, Mitsubishi, and Daiichi-Kangyo Ginko. They are bank-centred conglomerates.

Many major single-industry companies in Japan are increasingly viewed as vertical *keiritsu*. These include Hitachi, Toyota, Nissan, Toshiba, and Matsushita. These are more pyramid-shaped, with a single industry or company at the pinnacle of the pyramid and the member companies collected beneath. The *keiretsu* form a type of family of member companies, each connected to the others through cross-shareholdings. Each company within the *keiretsu* holds significant shares of stock in each of the other *keiretsu* members. The companies remain otherwise independent of each other, and are not subsidiaries of holding companies which were outlawed after World War II.

Classical *keiretsu* often have no single industry on which they focus. Yet it is their goal to create what is called a *one-set* principle. In this case, *keiretsu* members attempt to create a situation in which they would never have to rely on *non-keiretsu* firms to produce an end-product. Very large Japanese companies such as Toyota have begun to control enough subsidiary companies to attain the *one-set* principle. These large companies have assumed a form of vertically organised *keiretsu* having grown out of a central manufacturing company. Thus companies like Toyota can be viewed as a single-industry *keiretsu*. The Japanese state also plays a significant role in the affairs of industry

NPOs (not for profit organisations) are also numerous. They may be formed by any citizen group that serves the public interest and does not produce a profit for its members. NPOs are given corporate status to assist them in conducting business transactions. As of February 2011, 41,600 NPOs were registered across a wide spectrum of quasi commercial and non commercial activities.

Rather as in European and Scandinavian jurisdictions CSR in Japan is regarded as strategic business development tool reflecting full board-buy-in. Toyota is an extensively documented case which explains how the corporations addressed the twin challenges of developing a non-fossil fuel dependent at the same time acknowledging the imperatives of sustainability.

6.10   South Korea

South Korea like Japan has a particular type of corporate entity called the *chaebol*. These arose as a consequence of the South Korean government's emphasis on export-oriented economic policy. The new government in the 1960s under the leadership of President Park Chung Lee emphasized development and rapid growth of the South Korean economy. This policy encouraged the inflow of foreign capital to fund export oriented economic policy.

A *chaebol*can be defined as a business group consisting of large companies which are owned and managed by family members or relatives, in many diversified business areas. A single family usually referred to as the founding family, controls the entire web of companies woven around the core company. It has been recorded that the founding families control as much as 60 percent of the entire stake of these companies.

South Korean economic policy initially favoured the chemical industries and other heavy engineering. This was the period when the Korean government intervened in the allocation of resources and channelled resources to specific industry sectors to boost the economic growth. This period also saw the rebirth of Korean *chaebols*. As financial institutions (especially banks) were under quasi-government control, the government was able to ensure that these banks loaned money to these *chaebols*.

The top five *chaebols* (Samsung, Hyundai, LG, Daewoo and SK) at one stage accounted for more than 50 percent of Korean GDP and the top 30 *chaebols* for 75 percent of all economic activity in Korea. But this picture was to undergo fundamental of change. The Asian financial crisis in the 1990s acted as a catalyst for economic change. The South Korean economy faced rapid downsizing and restructuring of its industrial base. The intense pressure and stiff competition from China and India has further pushed Korean *chaebols* to become 'lean and mean' in the process.

Samsung and LG have become the exemplars of the post crisis South Korean economy. Both these companies faced massive down-sizing. They divested many business units that were not directly contributing to their core competence, invested heavily in research and development, and instilled a culture centred on building resonating brands. Also, the South Korean economy has allowed FDI (foreign direct investment) in many industry sectors and thereby facilitated an open economy that not only nurtures healthy competition but also fosters efficiency, productivity and profitability rather than mere size and sheer dominance on the economy by a handful of companies.

6.11   China

In China the state is never far away from its companies, according to a survey conducted by The Economist[5] Given the history of development this is not difficult to understand. Throughout the 1990s the rules of ownership were gradually changed. In 1995 the State Council endorsed a policy "retain the large, release the small". In 1997 it approved a huge transfer of ownership away from the state to municipalities with a view to promoting privatisations. This resulted in the closure of thousands of companies breaking the *iron rice bowl* guarantee of living standards for the masses.

On 27 October 2005 the People's Republic of China adopted a new Company Law[6]. This law became effective on 1 January, 2006. The new law replaces the old law which had been adopted in 1993. It represents a fundamental revision of the old law. Almost nothing of the old law has survived the revision. The new law governs two types of corporations: limited liability companies (*youxian gongsi*) and joint stock companies. It may be argued that changes to the laws governing limited liability companies are especially important to foreign investors in China. This is because the statutes governing foreign direct investment in China require foreign investors to operate through a Chinese limited liability company. But a word of caution is certainly appropriate[7].

For existing foreign invested limited liability companies, the rules on operation of such companies have substantially changed. Potential new investors must realise the old rules no longer apply and consider the new regime. Because foreign investors are currently prohibited from investing directly in China through joint stock companies, the following points will be limited to the changes regarding limited liability companies. The new law encourages the shareholders of limited liability companies to adapt the articles of association, previously rigidly fixed, to meet the purposes of their particular company. One striking change is that shareholders may elect to distribute profits or not as the case may be.

6.12   Russia

The Union of Soviet Socialist Republics (USSR) was formally dissolved on 26 December 1991 by declaration 142-H of the Soviet of the Republics of the Supreme Soviet of the Soviet Union. The conversion of the world's largest state-controlled economy into a market-oriented economy would have been extraordinarily difficult regardless of the policies chosen to bring it about. The policies chosen for this difficult transition emphasised liberalisation, stabilisation, and privatisation. These policies reflected the neoliberal *Washington Consensus* of the International Monetary Fund (IMF), World Bank, and US Department of the Treasury.

The programmes were designed by President Yeltsin's Deputy Prime Minister Yegor Gaidar, a liberal economist who favoured radical reform, and embraced the concept of "shock therapy". Shock therapy embraced massive privatisation of state owned industries. This was carried out by the State Committee for State Property Management of the Russian Federation under Anatoly Chubais. The primary goal was to transform former SOEs into profit-seeking businesses. These would be independent of government subsidies for their survival.

To distribute property quickly and to win over popular support, the reformers decided to rely mostly on the mechanism of free voucher privatisation. The Russian government took the view that the open sale of state-owned assets, as opposed to the voucher programme, would have likely resulted in the further concentration of ownership among the Russian *mafia* and the former Soviet political and industrial elites which they sought to avoid. Contrary to the intentions of the government, insiders managed to acquire control over most of the assets, which remained largely dependent on government support for some period thereafter.

Voucher privatisation took place between 1992 and 1994. Roughly 98 percent of the population participated. The vouchers, each corresponding to a share in the national wealth, were distributed equally among the population, including minors. They could be exchanged for shares in the enterprises to be privatised. Because most people were not well-informed about the nature of the programme or were very poor, they were quick to sell their vouchers for money. Most vouchers and most shares ended up being acquired by the management of the enterprises. The promise of the government to distribute the national wealth among the general public and ordinary employees of the privatised enterprises, eventually left the public deceived and disappointed.

Today the Russian economy is populated by a number of large privately owned companies, smaller formerly state-owned companies and a remaining backlog of state-owned industry. The role of SOEs in the Russian economy is still very important. About 30% of the industrial output in 2004 was to a varying extent under a corporate control of representatives of the Federal Government and regional authorities. Yet, due to specific peculiarities of the system of statistical observation in Russia this indicator is overestimated. Federal and regional unitary enterprises, joint-stock companies with a 100% Federal and regional government ownership, as well as State institutions account for only 7.9% of the volume of industrial output. No more than 40% of fixed assets in the national economy are registered on the books of these companies and organisations, which *inter alia* provide public services. However, in the banking sector the aggregate assets of the two State-owned banks alone account for close to 37% of the total assets of all banks in Russia.

Figure 11   Russian Voucher Privatisation Certificate

6.13   Brazil

Government-owned companies are divided into public enterprises (*empresa pública*) and mixed-economy companies (*sociedade de economia mista*). The public enterprises are subdivided into two categories: individual – with its own assets and capital owned by the Federal State – and plural companies. The latter entities' assets are owned by multiple government agencies and the Federal State, which have the majority of the voting interest. Caixa Econômica Federal, Correios, Embrapa, and BNDES are examples of public enterprises. Mixed-economy companies are enterprises with the majority of stocks owned by the government, but that also have shares owned by the private sector and usually have their shares traded on stock exchanges. Banco do Brasil, Petrobras, Sabesp, and Eletrobras are examples of mixed-economy companies.

Beginning in the 1990s, the federal government of Brazil launched a privatisation programme inspired by the Washington Consensus. Public-owned companies such as Vale do Rio Doce, Telebrás, CSN, and Usiminas (most of them mixed-economy companies) were transferred to the private sector as part of this policy.

6.14   South Africa

In South Africa the Department of Public Enterprises is the shareholder representative of the South African Government with oversight responsibility for state-owned enterprises in key sectors. These include: Defence, Energy, Forestry, ICT, Mining and Transport.

The corporate entities that this department is responsible for include:

Alexkor – Mining sector (diamond mining)
Broadband Infraco – ICT sector (national backbone and international connectivity)
Denel – Aerospace and Defence sector (armaments manufacturer)
Eskom – Energy sector (national electricity utility)
PBMR – Energy sector (development of Pebble Bed Modular Reactor nuclear energy technology)
South African Airways – Transport sector (international airline)
SA Express – Transport sector (regional and feeder airline)
SAFCOL – Forestry sector (manages forestry on state owned land)
Transnet – Transport and related infrastructure sector (railways, harbours, oil/fuel pipelines and terminals).
Telkom SA – Telecommunications sector (national fixed line telephone network (PSTN))
Other corporate entities not under the Department of Public Enterprises include the South African Post Office and the South African Broadcasting Corporation.

6.15   India

In India, an SOE is termed a *Public Sector Undertaking* (PSU). This term is used to refer to companies in which the government (either the Federal Union Government or the many state or territorial governments, or both) own a majority (51 percent or more) of the company's equity. There are currently around 250 PSU companies in India. Examples include:

Air India
Balmer Lawrie
Bharat Electronics Limited
Bharat Heavy Electricals Limited
Bharat Petroleum
Bharat Sanchar Nigam Limited
Bank of India

Biotech Consortium India Limited
Coal India Limited
Engineers India Limited
Cotton Corporation of India
Electronics Corporation of Tamil Nadu
Engineering Projects India Limited (EPIL)
Food Corporation of India
GAIL
Heavy Engineering Corporation
Hindustan Aeronautics Limited
Hindustan Cables
HMT Limited
Indian Oil Corporation
Indian Telephone Industries Limited
Jute Corporation of India Limited
State Bank of India
Mahanagar Telephone Nigam Limited
Mazagon Dock Limited
MECON Limited
Modern Food Industries
NTPC Limited
Nuclear Power Corporation of India Ltd
Oil and Natural Gas Corporation
PowerGrid Corporation of India
State Bank of India
Syndicate Bank
Steel Authority of India Limited
Tamil Nadu Electricity Board
Tamil Nadu State Transport Corporation
Kerala State Road Transport Corporation

6.16   Indonesia

SOEs are easy to recognise by their names. Company names with suffix PERSERO mean that the company is wholly/majority owned by the government. The government takes control of the state corporations under one single ministry, the Ministry of State Enterprises, which acts like the CEO of a holding company. Some of the government-owned corporations are;

Bank Mandiri, Bank Rakyat Indonesia and Bank Negara Indonesia – Banking sector
Pertamina – Energy, Oil/fuel, and gas sector
Garuda Indonesia – Transport sector (international airline)
Telkom Indonesia – Telecommunications sector
Perusahaan Listrik Negara – the Electric company, Energy sector (national electricity utility)
PT Kereta Api Indonesia – Transport sector (national railway)
Pos Indonesia – Postal service sector
TVRI – National television channel
PT Krakatau Steel – Steel producer
PT Dirgantara Indonesia – Manufacture (aircraft manufacture)
PT Industri Kereta Api – Manufacture (train manufacture)
PT Barata Indonesia – Manufacture
PT Boma Bisma Indra – Manufacture
Antara- News agency

During 2012, the Minister of State Enterprises decided to restructure various manufacturing companies and it was recommended that PT Barata should acquire PT Bisma to make an effective manufacturing sector.

Drawing conclusions from such a wide ranging assessment of corporate structures in so many different jurisdictions is difficult to make. But there are some general observations that can be made as follows.

Whilst the most common and most popular corporate form is the private limited liability company there are significant sectors of developing world economies that are populated by SOEs or state companies where there is private sector participation. The spectrum is wide. France and Italy, both advanced industrial economy still retain their attachment to SOEs or other forms of nationalised industry. These industries are unlikely to be privatised near term but are otherwise active as purchasers of privately owned businesses elsewhere.

Examples would include EDF (Electricite de France), the SNCF (French Railways) amongst others. Given the role of the State in these enterprises there is a special need to ensure that corporate governance is transparent and takes proper account of concerns that are sometimes directed at SWFs. These matters are fully explored in Appendix 3 of the OECD Guidance on Corporate Governance of State-owned Industries.

In other developing countries, India, Indonesia China and Brazil, amongst others, the sheer scale of SOEs will continue to raise fundamental concerns about the evenhandedness of government as an owner. The OECD's guidelines (as set out in Appendix 3) outline sensible proposals in respect of governance of these institutions. But there is a wider issue: how far will governments see SOEs and SWFs as vehicles for the realisation of wider macro-economic objectives? In this particular respect the exemplary performance of Norway is important.

Questions for Review

1. Why has the limited liability company structure grown in scale and importance over the past century and a half?

2. Why do unlimited liability entities and other co-operative structures continue to exist?

3. What is the difference between a publicly held limited liability company and a state-owned enterprise (SOE)?

4. What are the principal governance features of the limited liability company and how do they differ from *mutuals* and co-operatives?

5. Is there a case for co-determination in the work place?

6. Is there a case for having independent supervisory boards made to represent shareholders and stakeholders?

7. Why do corporate governance arrangements in Japan appear not to recognise the primacy of shareholders?

8. Is there a case for state intervention in commercial affairs and how best can this be brought about?

Learning Tasks

I   What sort of structure best serves enterprise development?

II   Design the optimal governance structure for a limited liability company?

III   How does supervision work as between unitary boards and with two-tier boards with independent supervision?

IV   Identify the ways in which Japanese and Korean development policies may seem to resemble those in the EU

V   Identify the key policy considerations the Chinese authorities should stress in terms of its future economic and commercial development?

Notes
[1] A *mutual* is an organisation (which is often, but not always, a company) is based on the principle of mutuality. A mutual organisation or society is often simply referred to as a mutual.
[2] The John Lewis Partnership is an employee-owned UK partnership. It operates John Lewis department stores, Waitrose supermarkets and some other services. The company is owned by a trust on behalf of all its employees. Employees are known as *Partners*. Partners have a full say in the running of the business and receive a share of annual profits, which is usually a significant addition to their salary. The group is the third largest UK private company in 2010.
[3] See: Sovereign Wealth Funds Generally Accepted Principles and Practices, October 2008.
[4] Commission of the European Communities Green Paper on CSR COM(2001) 366 final Brussels
[5] See Capitalism Confined pages 62 to 64 The Economist 3 September 2011
[6] Company Law of the People's Republic of China (promulgated by the Standing Committee of the National People's Congress, 27 October 2005 effective January 2006. Lawinchina
[7] The enforcement processes through the courts are yet untested but the greater clarity of the law may mean that courts will be able to deal more effectively with the new code.

Chapter 7

Corporate governance as a public concern issue

7.1   Summary

This chapter provides oversight into the development of thinking about corporate governance. Corporate governance as a major public policy concern is a relatively new phenomenon that has attracted enormous interest. This has brought about a widening and deepening of investigative journalism. The public interest in the affairs of the corporation has continued to rise. Other factors are also at work. Interest has risen dramatically as a direct consequence of the growing importance nationally and internationally of large scale enterprises and their *sustainability*.[1] This includes the increasing reliance on supply chains which involve different jurisdictions and the damaging events that have emerged from these relationships.

The footprint of the modern limited liability public company whose shares trade on stock markets is larger and more important than at any time in economic history. This has also occurred during a period of strong economic expansion and a sharp rise in competition nationally and internationally. Inevitably there are a wide number of controversial issues that compete for attention.

The attention of readers is drawn to the questions raised in the OECD/TUAC issues paper concerning corporate governance. This appears at the end of this chapter.

7.2   The historic backdrop

In the 18th and 19th centuries as explored earlier the business landscape was largely populated by unincorporated unlimited liability entities in which individual owner/partners controlled events. But this was to change. By the turn of the 19th century at least three factors were changing the institutional framework. First the accumulation of wealth of the middle classes meant they had a need to find different ways of investing their wealth. Second the passing of laws on limited liability encouraged larger scale investments offering safeguards to investors began to open up. Third very large scale investments in infrastructure (railways and telegraph notably) were in any event driving the separation of ownership from control.

To this we need to add that a managerial class also began to emerge along with the opening up of mass markets. The management corporation was thus born and became increasingly the dominant form of business organisation in Europe and the North America. By the 1920's as we have explored academics were debating the significance of the separation of ownership from control. Most notably Berle and Means (1932) had observed that shareholding was becoming increasingly dispersed with no shareholder having a large enough interest to exercise control over management. At the time of their research a large proportion of the largest US corporations of the day were effectively controlled by their managers.

These corporations continued to grow in importance alongside a further important structural development. Institutional investors (pension funds, investment funds and insurance companies) were funnelling more and more funds into publicly traded corporations. These investors preferred to remain passive in terms of the corporations in which they were invested. They favoured instead market mechanisms as a means of disciplining management.

With deregulation of capital markets in the 1980s and beyond institutional investors in Britain and the US became the dominant force. Against this backdrop concerns about both the accountability and the performance of management began to grow. Specific instances of scandal were to shape attitudes towards corporate governance in Britain and the United States. These brought about changes in the law and a raft of voluntary codes drawn up by industry aimed at strengthening corporate accountability and performance. These, as it will be seen, have fallen well short of curbing concerns about the entrenched power of directors.

7.3   Initiatives designed to improve corporate governance

Corporate governance has been sorely tested during this period. This is seen to be a direct consequence of the power that executive directors have upon reward systems including bonuses and share options. As a result this has caused directors and managers to take risks that have not been in the best interest of shareholders and have been damaging to the corporation. A number of high level committees have been spawned with the aim of making Corporate Governance more accountable and its practices more transparent. The Cadbury Committee (1992) was the first of a series of committees that examined and reported on aspects of British corporate governance. It recommended that company boardrooms should be constituted in such a way that they would feature appropriate sub-committees dealing with matters of remuneration, audit and nomination. Independent NEDs were to be increased in numbers with separation of the roles and functions of the CEO and Chairman of the Board.

After the Cadbury Report (1992), the Greenbury Report (1995) was published to address concerns about other aspects of corporate behaviour. Concerns focused on pay and benefits awarded by the board of directors to themselves. The report recommended that the remuneration committee should comprise NEDs, who would report annually on policy and disclose full details of the remuneration packages of the directors. The aim was to link remuneration to performance and to better align the interests of directors and managers with those of shareholders. The Greenbury Report now constitutes part of the Combined Code at section B. The Hampel Report (1998) was critical of the Cadbury Report. It affirmed that good governance should aim to ensure that stakeholders with relevant interests in the company were fully taken into account. It also went on to say that good governance might help to prevent malpractice and fraud but "it could not prevent them absolutely." [2]

The Combined Code (1998) consolidates the three previous codes in terms of the responsibilities of companies and institutional investors. All of the issues of remuneration, audit, and shareholder relations are covered. It was appended to the Listing Rules of the London Stock Exchange.[3] A year later, in 1999, the Turnbull Report was issued by the Institute of Chartered Accountants of England and Wales. It gave guidance specifically on issues of internal control highlighted in the Combined Code as being of particular importance. It sought to give guidance on how to establish and maintain robust systems of internal control. Later, in 2001 the Myners Report was published. This focused on the lack of interest from institutional investors to holdings in non-listed companies. It also registered particular concerns with regard to the behaviour of pension fund trustees and fund managers.

In 2002 the Sarbanes-Oxley Act was passed in the wake of the collapse of Enron and WorldCom in the US. The Act set new or enhanced reporting and compliance standards for all US public company boards, management and public accounting firms. The role being played by non-executive directors was judged to be not robust enough in terms of ensuring good practice and governance. Additionally, further criticism was levelled at the accountancy profession for what appeared to be a continuing inability to uncover, through the audit process, signals of underlying corporate problems and other fraudulent irregularities. This led to the creation of more committees to develop systems of governance that would be sufficient to prevent further scandals.

The Higgs Report (2003) resulted from the UK government extending the remit of its Company Law Review. It was a direct response to scale of fraud following the implosion and eventual liquidation of Enron. It focused closely on the responsibilities of NEDs. The report recommended that at least half the board should be constituted of non-executive directors. Companies were also urged to widen the *gene pool*[4] when recruiting NEDs.

The Smith Report (2003) was issued at the same time as the Higgs Committee and was appointed by the Financial Reporting Council. It reinforced the belief that accounting firms need to be careful in deciding which services to offer to a company if they were also conducting its audit. Its recommendations form part of the Revised Combined Code, applicable through the Listing Rules for the London Stock Exchange. Finally, the Revised Combined Code (2003) changed the combined code and added recommendations from the Higgs and Smith reports.

7.4   Some reactions to underlying governance concerns

In the face of growing public concerns about corporate governance CSR (corporate responsibility) activities conducted by corporations has expanded rapidly. CSR may very well be a response to wider public concern that corporation's in their activities do not pay attention to the real negative or unwanted aspects of their activities or otherwise fail to respond to social concerns in general and stakeholder concerns in particular. Who are the parties that speak for CSR and on whose behalf do they speak?

Why has CSR arisen as such an important socio political phenomenon? One way or another it has been around for a lengthy period of time. It emerges first as a coherent set of concerns in the 1970s though its real expansion took place in the 1990s. Some see this as reflecting the perception that directors and managers of corporations are less and less concerned about their failures to properly address what are properly seen as governance concerns. It follows from this assumption that companies and those who run them are more interested in using PR and other devices to portray their behaviour in a favourable light that addressing the underlying governance issues[5]. The cases presented for analysis in Chapter 10 explore these matters.

7.5   Defining CSR

We turn to another related question how can CSR be meaningfully and operationally-speaking defined? Mallen Baker provides an oft-cited example.

Different organisations have framed different definitions – although there is considerable common ground between them. My own definition is that CSR is about how companies manage the business processes to produce an overall positive impact on society.

This is illustrated in the following figure.

Figure 12

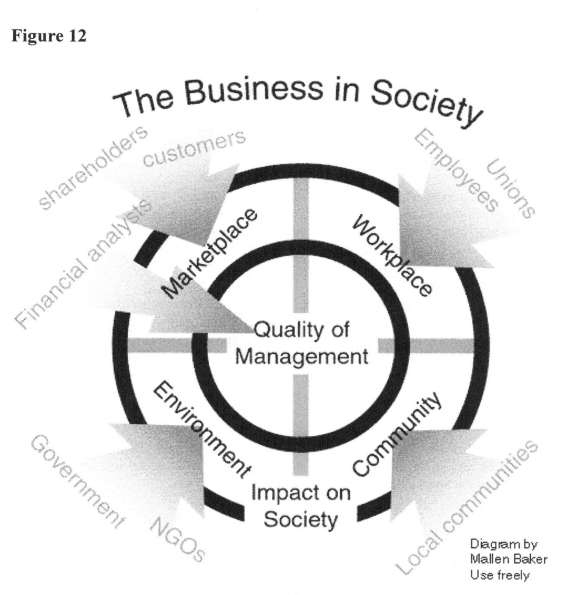

Companies need to answer to two aspects of their operations.
- The quality of their management – both in terms of people and processes (the inner circle).
- The nature of and quantity of their impact on society in the various areas.

The World Business Council for Sustainable Development[6] in its publication defines CSR as follows:

> *Corporate Social Responsibility is the continuing commitment by business to behave ethically and contribute to economic development while improving the quality of life of the workforce and their families as well as of the local community and society at large.*

The European model in contrast is more focused on operating the core business in a socially responsible way, complemented by investment in communities for solid business case reasons. The EU Green Paper on CSR defines CSR in the following way

> *[It is]A concept whereby companies decide voluntarily to contribute to a better society and a cleaner environment. Concept whereby companies integrate social and environmental concerns in their business operations and in their interaction with their stakeholders on a voluntary basis.*

The arguments in favour of this are:
- Social responsibility becomes an integral part of the wealth creation process – which if managed properly should enhance the competitiveness of business and maximise the value of wealth creation to society.

- When times get hard, there is the incentive to practice CSR more and better – if it is a philanthropic exercise which is peripheral to the main business, it will always be the first thing to go when *push* comes to *shove.*

But as with any process based on the collective activities of communities of human beings (as companies are) there is no *one size fits all'*. In different countries, there will be different priorities, and values that will shape how business act.

7.6   What has CSR achieved?

At a macro level it is hard to establish objectively whether things are worse today than they were because of CSR. Corporations as never before are investing heavily into telling the public at large that they are committed to responsibility in their behaviour and more specifically *sustainability*. Whether they are doing so in reality or not loses sight of the argument that it makes good business sense to be concerned about these matters. At a micro level accounting routines do not capture or portray this sort of information. Triple Bottom Line (TBL) accounting in particular is problematical because of the difficulty of moving from the "cardinal" (value related perceptions) to the "ordinal" (objectively measurable and comparable data sets). Without an objective base it is difficult to arrive at operational measures and indicators. Should be XYZ Plc be praised or penalised "*for only losing 25 lives in 2013*" when compared with some earlier period. Who can say?

7.7   Different approaches to CSR

The different approaches to CSR are linked for particular reasons to Anglo American debate and discussion. CSR is an English language invention. It comes in part from the environment within which listed corporations operate in Anglo American jurisdictions where shareholders (institutional investors) are the principal owners of company equity but are remote from the everyday management of those companies. The majority of all major corporations are stock market listed and shares are traded in public markets. They are also managed by unitary boards. Given the outsider controlled environment public debate about company affairs is much more developed in Anglo American jurisdictions.

How is CSR dealt with in other European languages and elsewhere? In Europe, especially *Rhineland* jurisdictions which are insider controlled, public scrutiny has been traditionally less intrusive. Stock markets play a lesser role in the trading of shares. Given the nature of two-tier boards in *Rhineland* jurisdictions some argue that such corporations are in any event more CSR-conscious than companies in Anglo American jurisdictions. Supervisory boards, which reflect wider interests than those of shareholders, are capable of exercising a restraining influence on the animal spirits of executive directors. This does not exist in Anglo American jurisdictions where unitary boards have total power in terms of decision taking and where shareholder influence is far less. In Japan and South Korea the "family" *keiritsu* and *chaebol* ownership structures appear historically to have been more responsive to wider social concerns even though stock markets are a widespread mechanism for trading shares.

CSR often appears to be linked to stakeholder-type concerns. If defining CSR raises difficulties trying to do the same in respect of stakeholders raises similar difficulties. It is easy to say that corporations should represent the interests of stakeholders but how can this ever be defined? If shareholders are viewed as stakeholders then that is straightforward. This can also easily be extended to employees. Much the same applies

101

to creditors. All these groups have rights reflected in law. But many issues in CSR affect other diverse stakeholder groups. This raises two main problems – how can corporations define those groups it should take into account; and what weighting should it attach to different stakeholder interests in arriving at an assessment of *costs and benefits*? This, as discussed earlier is, in part, a restatement of the TBL problem.

7.8   CSR and Stakeholders

How can the case for CSR and stakeholdership be advanced? Understanding that CSR has at least two faces may help us to make progress. One aspect of the CSR movement is NGO-driven, by people, who some argue have no in-depth knowledge or experience of how businesses in practice operate. On the other hand there is CSR driven by corporations seeking to shape public attitudes about their own commercial activities. This goes a long way to explaining the sharp differences that emerge in terms of outturns. Some will argue that the claims made by CSR have nothing to do with running businesses. Both Milton Friedman[7] and David Henderson[8] argue that the *business of business* is to make profit. As a hypothesis it cannot be easily challenged in a free enterprise economy in which primary wealth is generated by the business enterprise sector. As ever, however, this is only half the story. Profitability may very well be a central purpose of business endeavour but that says nothing about *what sort* of profit or *how* the profit is derived. A perhaps better way forward is to ask how best companies can become economically, socially and environmentally *sustainable*. The answer to this question is far from obvious. But just as turnover (from which profit is generated) is determined by social and citizen *tastes* as expressed in the market place through demand, so better standards in terms of *sustainability* need to be translated into market demand and ultimately company turnover.

Perhaps the most effective way of bringing this about is for companies to be required to *discover* these needs (as they discover other needs) and for all the participants in that process – employees, consumers, capital market players (banks and institutional investors) as well as NGOs to play their part. For corporations what is imperative is that they have the quality and strength of leadership to encourage this *awareness* to flourish within their own organisations. In short reform comes from the market place and not from edicts like companies *should be doing this rather than that*. Those companies that don't pursue sustainable agendas will face greater and more hostile scrutiny. Eventually they will be driven from the market.

7.8   **Some key unresolved questions**

Some important and persistent questions about corporate governance and CSR are set out in the following document

QUESTIONS FOR DISCUSSION

by Mr. Richard Tudway

Director, Centre for International Economics, (London, UK),

and an advisor to TUAC on corporate governance

September 2003

I.   THE ISSUES IN OVERVIEW

Public anxieties about governance

1. Anxieties across the OECD and beyond about the effectiveness of corporate governance are widely felt. Value measured in billions of dollars has been destroyed, not by commercial error alone, but also as a result of malfeasance. In addition, workers have lost their jobs, and in many instances their pensions and health care benefits, which in many cases represent their sole safety net. Meanwhile, public confidence in financial markets has been severely undermined. Recent corporate irregularities have not been confined to the United States. They have and continue to appear globally, even if differences exist around the extent of the problem. Trade unions have legitimate fears that these may in turn be symptomatic of a systemic failure in the framework of corporate governance.

2. In response a plethora of national level initiatives to reform corporate governance regimes have been introduced, or are being planned. Trade unions have welcomed these, but fear that they have not gone deep and wide enough, and that the emphasis on voluntary codes and standards, rather than a binding regulatory framework is an insufficient response to ensure effective implementation and enforcement of the new reforms.

3. The OECD Principles of Corporate Governance are the only multilaterally agreed benchmark to guide debates around reform efforts in this key area of public policy. They

include chapters on the following topics: The Rights of Shareholders; The Equitable Treatment of Shareholders; The Role of Stakeholders in Corporate Governance; Disclosure and Transparency; and The Responsibility of the Board. Upon their adoption, TUAC welcomed the Principles, in particular, the stakeholder chapter, which it saw not as the last word, but as a platform for further development.

4. Though non binding, the Principles are nevertheless emerging as the de-facto international comparative framework. For example, the World Bank and IMF use the Principles as a template to assess their members' corporate government environment, as part of the ROSC initiative (Reports on the Observance of Standards and Codes). The Principles are now being reviewed by the OECD. Views differ as regards the scope of the review. Some have argued to maintain the status quo, while others have suggested cosmetic changes. Trade unions have argued that the revisions should be deep and wide-ranging, with the addition of new chapters. They believe that the OECD has a unique opportunity to re-write the corporate mission for the 21st Century.

5. To set the stage for the OECD-TUAC Labour/Management Programme meeting the paper will discuss some of the underlying issues identified by trade unions as causing what they see as a systemic crisis in corporate governance. It then identifies reforms that they believe should be included in the review.

II   EMERGENT PROBLEMS IN CORPORATE GOVERNANCE

Collapse of accountability

6. Serious concerns have been raised concerning the collapse of corporate accountability, involving companies such as Enron and WorldCom in the US, and Marconi in Britain, and Ahold in the Netherlands. Though the corporations headlined are not alone - they are some of the best known. That raises disquieting concerns about the ownership and control mechanism of the corporation and its public accountability. One key issue surrounds the debate about the role and function of shareholders as owners, whether banks, pension funds or other institutional investors. The following questions have been raised as to whether:

- Shareholders lack the means of effective control; and
- They may be perceived as "absentee landlords" whose only wish is to receive regular   dividends and capital gains in a rising share market with no direct responsibility for the affairs of the corporation;

7. Complications in determining the duties and obligations of shareholders have it is felt left the corporation operating outside a credible framework of control and accountability, irrespective of jurisdiction. Overall there is the impression that many shareholders are in reality proxies and are in any case *conflicted* in acting straightforwardly as direct, interested, shareholders might otherwise do. These conclusions are difficult to avoid. The implications are far reaching for governance.

The issue of "tomorrows money today" – the new permissive-ism

8. A corrosive economics of greed is seen by much of the public, trade unions, and some opinion formers as being increasingly present in many corporations, resulting in a climate change in terms of managerial attitudes. They fear that corporations now pursue short-term commercial and financial goals with scant regard for whether such moves are strictly legal or are consistent with longer-term sustainable development. What could be termed a new corporate permissive-ism has been driven, it is argued by a combination of:

- An over-emphasis on stock options as a means of rewarding senior management that has fuelled a climate of greed;

- A corrosive, illegal insider trading culture within corporations;

- A pervasive copycat practice of bidding up executive remuneration;

- Chronic failures in the scope, composition, and regulatory framework governing the activities and the accountability of boards of directors; and

- An undue corporate influence on the global political process.

9. These influences have been compounded by a preoccupation with internal accounting devices that have the effect of overstating revenues and the real profitability of the corporation. *Off-balance sheet vehicles* have been widely abused in the pursuit of these ends with the collusion of financial and legal advisers, brokerage firms and other market makers. Though not in themselves illegal, these devices were used for example by Enron to deliberately conceal the true ownership of liabilities arising from these vehicles by methods of guarantee that were ultimately fraudulent. They were also used to siphon-off fees in underwriting and other service charges in a number of instances to benefit senior managers within Enron. Serious concerns have also been raised about the activities of external accounting and auditing firms – the gatekeepers. The collapse of Arthur Andersen was seen as graphic proof of a serious breakdown in the nature of the auditing profession. Widespread conflicts of interests arising as a largely self-regulated industry

were allowed to expand and to offer non-auditing services to their corporate clients. Similarly, questions remain over the role of other market makers such as rating agencies.

The issue of globalisation

10. Globalisation, especially financial market liberalisation and deregulation has impacted on corporate governance with unanticipated consequences. Though recognised regional corporate governance mechanisms are beginning to appear, for example at the level of the EU, and the trans-boundary aspects foreseen by Sarbanes Oxley, the dominant systems in terms of implementation and enforcement remain at the national level. The emergence of global corporations has encouraged management to exploit opportunities for regulatory arbitrage between different national jurisdictions[9]. In some well-publicised instances this has resulted in corporations relocating their headquarters to offshore tax havens to evade fiscal responsibilities, and other responsibilities, for example employee pension obligations. Veiling true beneficial ownership behind complex legal arrangements is used to hide the underlying intention. Globalisation has, furthermore created *grey areas* where national level regulatory bodies and other parties are uncertain as to which regulatory framework governs a corporation operating within their territories.

III   CORPORATE GOVERNANCE REGIMES ACROSS THE OECD

Diversity is the norm

11. While much is said about the convergence of corporate governance regimes across the OECD, key differences remain, for example, in the form and function of boards; the underlying philosophies of accounting practices, or to whom the board and corporation is legally accountable to. This is especially true as regards the way in which key stakeholders such as workers and trade unions are included, or excluded, from the governance process. In many European countries and Japan, law and practice is different when compared with Anglo American based jurisdictions. The former view these issues from a different perspective. Stakeholders often have established rights in law, or collective agreements, and direct representation in the governance of corporations. Here, for example, workers may appoint or recommend for appointment representatives from their own ranks to sit on the supervisory and executive boards of enterprises. Their rights and duties as directors are also clearly defined, including that they have a fiduciary duty to the company. In some instances trade unions also have that right. At the same time workers and trade unions often have institutionalised consultative rights at other levels of governance over key employment related issues. Similarly, pan-European legislation conferring rights to information and consultation on some issues, currently for workers

in multinational enterprises operating in the EU, will shortly be extended to all domestic enterprises, subject to certain thresholds. At the same time EU wide legislation on collective redundancies confers the right to information and consultation for workers.

12. However, this participatory approach to corporate governance should not be taken to infer that workers and unions have no voice in Anglo American based jurisdictions. In the United States workers have a voice and are represented as investors through their private retirement savings plans and ESOPS. This is increasingly the case in the UK as well. And, it is argued new and expected regulatory changes are widening and deepening these rights.

IV   SOME PROGRESS IN NATIONAL-LEVEL CORPORATE GOVERNANCE REFORMS

13. In response many governments are now enacting or in the process of enacting reforms to their national corporate governance regimes. The most high profile example is the Sarbanes Oxley Act of 2002 which has strengthened the scope for civil and criminal sanctions, including for gatekeepers. But reform efforts are underway across most of the OECD. The exact form of the reforms varies across countries, but includes: financial reporting and disclosure, the role of institutional investors, internal and external audit procedures, the form and composition of boards of directors, conflicts of interest, and implementation and enforcement. The UK has now released a consultative document on directors' remuneration. The reforms have enjoyed widespread support, though many, including trade unions are of the view that more can be done. Disquiet has also been expressed that an over-reliance on voluntary codes and standards for implementation and enforcement will be insufficient to overcome the failures of corporate governance.

V   THE REVIEW OF THE OECD PRINCIPLES OF CORPORATE GOVERNANCE

14. The paper has already touched upon the review of the OECD Principles of Corporate governance, which is being conducted by its Steering Group on Corporate Governance, to which TUAC and BIAC participate on an ad-hoc basis. The road map for the review was agreed at its meeting on 19-20 March 2003, and it is expected that the revisions will be presented for adoption to the Spring 2004 meeting of the OECD Council at Ministerial level. It has also been noted that views differ on the extent to which the Principles should be revised. The paper next indicates revisions that TUAC and its affiliates believe should be incorporated into the review.

Broadening stakeholder representation

15. TUAC believes that the case for broader stakeholder representation on the boards of corporations is compelling, and is underpinned by sound economic thinking. Within this paradigm workers like shareholders are investors in the corporation. Their investment, takes the form of human capital, for example in on and off the job training, where the returns are not captured in the wage. And, just as financial investors are now seen as having a right to a say in the governance process, so too are workers as investors. Similarly, current practices whereby workers are investors in corporations through their pension funds, or employees share option programmes (ESOPs) gives them a right to a voice in the governance process. At the same time, provisions are in place in a large number of OECD countries that give workers a right to be informed and consulted by the board about key issues surrounding the future direction of the enterprise.

16. As currently drafted however, the stakeholder chapter is limiting in that it focuses solely on the recognition of a stakeholder voice in the governance process as "established by law", while other performance enhancing mechanisms should be "permitted". To bring the Principles into conformity with current practices, the text should be revised to generalise a worker voice in the governance process.

Expanding the gene pool of directors

17. Any changes in the Principles might very well seek to reflect measures anticipated in new national initiatives – in particular those in America and Britain. The Sarbanes Oxley Act, 2002 is wide ranging. It covers board membership, the duties of board committees, accounting and auditing standards and conflicts of interest. Severe punishments are foreseen for breaches of law. Furthermore, changes have and continue to be introduced to the New York Stock Exchange and Nasdaq listing requirements (overseen by the SEC) for companies, that are seen by some as more far ranging. In Britain proposals for changes to company law have been advanced by the Company Law Reform Steering Group (CLRSG). Most recently the Higgs Enquiry has reported on the role of independent directors, as has the French Bouton Report.

18. Higgs recognises the need for strengthening the independence of non-executive directors. The appointment of a chairman should be independent from earlier allegiances or association with the corporation in question. Higgs also recommends a systematic widening and deepening of the gene pool from which directors are selected. The British CLRSG's report also places particular emphasis on the need for corporations and their boards to be responsive to changing stakeholder and societal expectations. This has

important institutional implications as well as implications for training and education in *directorship*. The Principles might wisely reflect these matters in any changes to the drafting of the Principles.

The responsibilities of shareholders

19. There needs to be a new chapter to cover the Responsibilities of Shareholders. This chapter needs to differentiate between institutions such as pension funds and Employee Share Associations (ESAs), and short term speculative institutions such as "hedge funds"[10]. Although both groups have fiduciary duties, pension funds are, however, providers of *patient capital*, with the implication that the investments they make are *long-term*. The option to 'exit' would normally in such cases be limited to *times of crisis*. In contrast hedge funds measure their investment over a much shorter time frame – sometimes one or a few days - and as such face different expectations over their responsibilities.

20. Pension funds have, in effect, a responsibility to the workers as stewards of the capital they are entrusted to manage. The Principles should set out clearly the need for institutional investors, including pension funds, to exercise the closest oversight of the corporations in whose firms they hold equity; how that can most effectively be achieved; and the necessary transparency and disclosure required to allow trustees to ascertain whether effective oversight is being discharged. Examples might include requiring such investors to vote in AGMs, and to disclose their voting patterns, and most importantly to allow them to nominate directors.

Disclosure and transparency

21. The existing chapter on Disclosure and Transparency chapter could benefit from revisions in key areas. A key issue for investors and worker alike is access to clear unambiguous and timely information on the exact geographical location of a corporation's particular operations, regardless as to whether this applies to a subsidiary or its supply chain. There is a similar need for transparency and disclosure on all aspects relating to ultimate beneficial ownership, including full details in respect of incorporation. There is a need to specify more clearly what is understood by foreseeable risk factors, what constitutes materiality and how these are expected to impact upon employees and other stakeholders.

The Board – roles, responsibilities and conflicts of interest

22. Against the background of recent corporate scandals, there is also a need now for a new chapter covering the Roles and Responsibilities of CEOs and Senior Management. It should cover issues such as the separation of roles of CEO and Chair; remuneration, especially the use of stock options, and full disclosure on ethical issues and conflicts of interest in respect of individual directors and employees.

23. The need to avoid conflicts of interests between for example the services offered by external auditors and the corporations that they audit, need also to be incorporated, along with those concerning credit rating agencies. Finally, implementation and enforcement were not included within the original Principles. Events demonstrate clearly that these twin issues should be included.

Implementation and enforcement

24. All OECD member countries have mechanisms to ensure the implementation and enforcement of their corporate governance regimes, but differences exist as to the mix of hard and soft law, and voluntary codes of practice that are utilised to ensure compliance. Yet, the current Principles could be termed "light" on implementation and enforcement. Developing and transition countries would certainly benefit from guidance in this area when contemplating reforms. There is therefore a need for the inclusion of a set of Principles and annotations that reflect the current practices in this area. Moreover, whilst the use of market mechanisms and incentives should be included as possible compliance mechanisms, so too should binding and soft law mechanisms, the latter including international arrangements.

Concluding remarks

25. In conclusion, governments in all jurisdictions face fundamental challenges in effectively addressing public concerns around corporate governance. Trade unions believe that the OECD Principles of Corporate Governance have a key role in informing and guiding the ongoing and future national level debates, as well as any emerging international framework required as part of the process of managing globalisation.

7.9   Conclusions

Corporate governance as an issue has grown steadily in the 4th quarter of the 20th Century and into the first decade or so of the 21st century - and along with it CSR. It will not abate. Evidence shows that governance issues are becoming ever more important. They are now complicated by evidence of corporations collaborating with state agencies in ways that may yet be proved to illegal. As we have seen corporations are now liable to meet far higher rules based standards in terms of financial reporting as evidenced by Sarbanes Oxley in the US, parallel developments in the UK and elsewhere. In the British context the emphasis on principles of sound governance have also been tightened as evidenced by the 2006 Companies Act and changes to the Combined Code.

But there remain many issues which are not adequately addressed as things stand. These have been explored in detail in the submissions to the OECD under the three main headings: Accountability, Permissive-ism and Globalisation. Concerns in respect of Accountability continue to focus on the ownership and *ex ante* supervisory arrangements. These are seen to be particular issues for concern in Anglo American jurisdictions. Board directors too frequently rely on the argument that they cannot be held responsible for delegated power in large complex organisations. There is also the continuing failure of institutional investors to take their responsibilities for corporate governance seriously and the failure to protect the interests of other stakeholders.

The global financial crisis which was triggered by events on Wall Street is a permanent reminder of the failings in this area. The same is true of *permissive-ism*. It confirms that standards of conduct have changed for the worse in a *race to the bottom* as corporations seek to exploit new untested ways of securing competitive advantage. Finally issues in the field of globalisation are persistent, recurrent problems. This includes the creation of elaborate tax avoidance schemes by multinational businesses which are designed to shield revenue from legitimate taxes. These developments are explored in the case studies in Chapter 10.

Questions for Review

1. What factors bring scandals about corporate governance to light?

2. Why is there the appearance that scandals have been mostly identified in Anglo American jurisdictions?

3. Are scandals just as frequent in other jurisdictions but simple less well reported than in Anglo American jurisdictions?

4. Why does the OECD continue to give *primacy* to shareholders in its Framework Report on corporate governance?

5. Why does the OECD ignore the need to separate execution from supervision in corporate governance?

6. Why are trade unions and employees not represented in the process of corporate governance in Anglo American jurisdictions?

7. Why is the definition of directors' duties in law left so vague?

8. Is there a case for modifying the business judgment rule and how would this be done?

9. Why are institutional investors referred in the OECD/TUAC document as *absentee landlords?*

10. Explain the reference to "tomorrow's money today"?

11. Why are off balance sheet vehicles identified as a regulatory concern?

12. Why does the OECD/TUAC paper lay such emphasis on stakeholder engagement?

13. Explain the importance of the reference to "expanding the gene pool of directors"?

14. Why does the OECD/TUAC report place such importance on increased shareholder responsibilities in good and effective governance?

15. What does the term *sustainability* mean?

16. 'The business of business is to make profit'. Is this statement consistent with the concept of sustainability?

Learning Tasks

I   Design the best and most effective structure for corporate governance?

II   Draw up a code in respect of directors' duties?

III   What qualifications would you deem as necessary for an effective NED?

Notes

[1] The economics of *sustainability* includes social cultural, health-related and monetary/financial aspects operating in harmony. Moving towards *sustainability* is a social challenge that entails international and national law, urban planning and transport, local and individual lifestyles and ethical consumerism.

[2] See: The Hampel Report 1988, page 17

[3] Now laid down by the UKLA (the UK Listing Authority)

[4] The *gene pool* is a reference to the backgrounds of the director class. Higgs was concerned to enlarge this.

[5] See: Tudway R & Pascal A-M *Corporate Governance, Shareholder Value and Societal Expectations* Corporate Governance, Vol. 6 Issue 3, pp.305 – 316, Emerald Group Publishing 2006.

[6] See: Holme Richard (Lord) and Watts Richard *Making Good Business Sense* World Business Council for Sustainable Development, 2000 - Business Ethics 2000

[7] See: Friedman, Milton (1970-09-13) *The Social Responsibility of Business is to Increase Profits* The New York Times Magazine.

[8] See: Henderson D *Misguided Virtue: False Notions of Social Corporate Social Responsibility*, New Zealand Business Roundtable, June 2001.

[9] Some large institutional investors are warning companies not to relocate or set up business in countries with weak corporate governance regimes. See "Funds warn companies favouring lax regimes". Financial Times Weekly Review of the Investment Industry, June 2 2003.

[10] The distinction between pension funds and hedge funds is merely used to illustrate the different functions, and responsibilities of financial investors.

Chapter 8

Different approaches to corporate governance

8.1   Summary

This is a factual and detailed chapter. Directors in all jurisdictions are subject to wide ranging *hard* and *soft* law imperatives. As a generalisation US jurisdictions favour strong *rules-based* enforcement a fact reflected in the proactive role of SEC (Securities and Exchange Commission) and the comprehensive nature of the Sarbanes Oxley Act 2002. In contrast British arrangements favour the setting out of *principles of best practice* with a reliance on the requirement to *comply or explain*. In other jurisdictions there is evidence of some mix of the two.

The chapter will critically examine the main provisions in the major jurisdictions identifying strengths and weaknesses based on experience with a statement of recommendations for improvement. It begins with an overview of US and British recommendations. It also examines the main approaches adopted by European, Nordic and other major OECD jurisdiction. Each section will conclude with an assessment of corporate governance.

8.2   The United States

The emergence of the US as the world's greatest industrial power explains the significance and the influence favouring Anglo American institutions. This has survived to the present day though as reported earlier it is increasingly challenged. The development of corporation law and corporate governance in the US is well described by Ira Millstein 2001[1]. His account offers a compelling apology for a system based on self regulation accompanied by strong disciplining forces of liquid capital markets, tempered from time to time by legislative intervention.

Other research supports the view that US corporate governance was also shaped by a legal framework which fostered the dispersal of ownership and had the effect of fragmenting financial institutions in turn, a consequence of the Glass Steagall Act (1933) and the Investment Company Act (1940). The effect of these developments strengthened the power of corporate managers. It has discouraged banks from playing a role in corporate governance when compared with Europe and Japan where banks have progressively built long term relationships with corporations.

8.3   Responding to crises in corporate governance

American history contains a well documented examination of corporate power in the late 19th and early 20th century As Tudway (2002) points out the racketeering tactics of railroad corporations is a 'chilling reminder of the impotence of government in the face of predatory corporate entities'.[2] In more recent times concerns regarding the viability of US corporate governance were triggered by the collapse of several large and successful companies. In the early 2000s there were several previously unparalleled events, notably the collapse of Enron, WorldCom, Tyco International, Adelphia Communications, amongst others. The crisis of confidence in corporate leadership and the *gate keeping* role of law firms and accounting firms alike and ultimately the effectiveness of capital markets as a disciplining influence triggered the Sarbanes Oxley Act.[3] This act also known as the 'Public Company Accounting Reform and Investor Protection Act' is commonly referred to as Sarbanes–Oxley, Sarbox or SOX.

Sarbox sets new or enhanced standards for all US public company boards, management and public accounting firms. The bill was enacted as a reaction to a number of major corporate and accounting scandals. It does not apply to privately held companies. The act contains 11 titles, or sections, ranging from additional corporate board responsibilities to criminal penalties, and requires the SEC to implement rulings on requirements to comply with the new law.

It also created a new, quasi-public agency, the PCAOB (Public Company Accounting Oversight Board) charged with overseeing, regulating, inspecting and disciplining accounting firms in their roles as auditors of public companies. The act also covers issues such as auditor independence, corporate governance, internal control assessment, and enhanced financial disclosure. It marks the most far-reaching reforms of American business practices since the time of Franklin D. Roosevelt.

Debate continues over the perceived benefits and costs of Sarbox. Opponents of the bill claim it has reduced America's international competitive edge against foreign financial service providers, saying Sarbox has introduced an overly complex regulatory environment into US financial markets. Proponents of the measure say that Sarbox has been a "godsend." It has improved the confidence of fund managers and other investors in the reliability of corporate financial statements.

8.4 An assessment of corporate governance in the US

There is an undoubted vigour about the approach of legislators and regulators to the on-going problems associated with corporate governance. Whether one takes the Enron crisis which triggered the Sarbanes Oxley Act or the Global Banking Crisis which triggered the Dodd Frank Act[4] the American response has been mostly positive and proactive. Unhappily it is only fair to say that some analysts see the more fundamental aspects of corporate governance is being side-stepped by legislative initiatives and the scale of reliance on regulatory intervention.

As a result far too little attention has focused on how power is used within corporate structures. The question turns on whether too much power lies in the hands of top executives, whether NEDs should have a more engaged role to play and, most importantly whether single unitary boards can fundamentally alter, for the better, the way corporations are governed.

8.5 British corporate governance

In contrast the evolution of British capitalism was on the face of things more restrained when compared with the red-blooded capitalism of the US throughout the 19th and 20th centuries. But serious problems began to surface in the late 1980s and 90s. Scandals, notably Polly Peck, the Maxwell Corporation and Marconi amongst others were the trigger for reforms of corporate governance. The collapse of three prominent public companies all of which had received clean bills of health from their auditors seriously undermined market confidence. Whilst the government vaguely threatened legislation industry, co-ordinated by the Bank of England, undertook a number of high profile investigations. The results of these different investigations were published in various reports.

The range and focus of the various enquiries stands as impressive testimony to the scale and importance of the many issues raised. Given the continued failure of major corporations to heed the recommendations of the many reports there are inevitably concerns that the light touch *comply or explain* regime is insufficiently robust.

8.6 Cadbury Report on Corporate Governance 1992

The City of London has a long history of self-regulation and so the first move on corporate governance took the form of the Cadbury Committee set up in May 1991 by the Financial Reporting Council, the London Stock Exchange and the accountancy profession to address the financial aspects of corporate governance. This committee was chaired by a prominent and respected British industrialist, Sir Adrian Cadbury. The following extract from the report captures the atmosphere of widespread concern:

Its sponsors were concerned at the perceived low level of confidence both in financial reporting and in the ability of auditors to provide the safeguards which the users of company reports sought and expected. The underlying factors were seen as the looseness of accounting standards, the absence of a clear framework for ensuring that directors kept under review the controls in their business, and competitive pressures both on companies and on auditors which made it difficult for auditors to stand up to demanding boards. (Cadbury, 1992, 2.1)

The committee's report was issued in December 1992. It looked into the performance and rewards of boards and recommended greater transparency and accountability in boardroom proceedings. It also recommended that the board should have three NEDS (non-executive directors) and the role of chairman and chief executive should be held by different people.

The report attached a code of best practice with guidelines for behaviour and disclosure. The main recommendations concern the appointment of NEDs and an audit committee to oversee greater control of financial reporting and the separation of the role of the chair and chief executive.

8.7   Greenbury Report on Director's Remuneration 1995

This study group was chaired by Sir Richard Greenbury, the then Chairman of Marks & Spencer Plc and reported in July 1995. It amended the section within the Cadbury report concerning executive pay. The main recommendations covered the appointment of a remuneration committee to determine directors' remuneration, and a nominations committee to oversee new appointments to the board.

8.8   Hampel Report on Corporate Governance 1998

The Hampel Committee was published in 1998. It reviewed the achievements of the Cadbury and Greenbury Reports. The Report consolidated the recommendations of the two previous reports and recommended the creation of a 'Combined Code' which was annexed to the London Stock Exchange Listing Rules. It also made recommendations on improving communication with shareholders and redressing the balance between implementing controls and allowing companies to find their own ways of applying corporate governance principles.

8.9　　　　　　　Turnbull Report　1999

A working party led by Nigel Turnbull was established to provide assistance for companies in reporting how they had applied the Combined Code (in particular section C2) and its principles. The report was published in late 1999. The report covers operational and financial controls based on high-level principles of good governance rather than rules or detailed checklists. The main recommendations were that:

- boards should be required to make an annual statement on the effectiveness of internal controls
- boards, not operational managers, were to be responsible for risk management and internal control
- guidance covers all internal controls, not just financial reporting, and takes a 'risk-based' approach
- guidance is to assist, not restrict, how a company operates
- boards should continue to review application of the guidance, to embed the controls in how a company operates, with procedures to identify and report weaknesses
- companies should not need to develop new processes
- external auditors' responsibility over internal controls should not increase.

8.10　　　　Myners Report on Institutional Investment in the UK

Paul Myners was commissioned by the British Treasury in March 2000 to review institutional investment in the UK. The report was published in March 2001. The report identified a series of distortions to effective decision-making by the institutions and made a number of proposals to tackle them. One of the proposals was that pension fund trustees voluntarily adopt on a *comply or explain* basis a series of principles codifying best practice for investment decision-making.

In December 2004 the Government published a review of the extent to which the principles codifying best practice for investment decision-making had brought about behavioural change. It found that the principles had been widely accepted as a benchmark of best practice in investment decision making. It also noted however that progress was lagging in some key areas. It put forward proposals to revise the principles to strengthen what they say in relation to the problems identified.

8.11 Sarbanes-Oxley Act 2002 - its impact on foreign listings in the US

The American SEC has stated that the Turnbull report complies with the US corporate government legislation, passed in the wake of the WorldCom, Enron and other financial scandals. The Act requires the CEO and the CFO to confirm that the financial statements fairly represent the financial position. They also need to test and document the effectiveness of controls against financial reporting fraud and to make a public statement on the effectiveness of internal controls.

All British companies listed in the US need to comply. This means that there is an impact on governance in the UK. The Financial Reporting Council published a guide for UK companies registered with the SEC in 2004 on the use of the Turnbull report for the purposes of the Act.

8.12   The Directors' Remuneration Report Regulations 2002

This regulation came into force on 31 December 2002. It introduced a requirement that directors of listed companies should produce for each financial year an annual remuneration report containing extensive disclosures about directors' remuneration.

The report must be put to shareholders for approval by ordinary resolution at the AGM. It is, however, an advisory vote only and is not enforceable.

8.13   Nolan Report on standards in public life

The Nolan Committee was established in October 1994 to review changes in how appointments to public bodies are made and to enquire into standards in British public life. Lord Nolan established the seven principles of public life. These principles were affirmed in 2001 during the five yearly review of the Committee. It was reaffirmed that the Committee should monitor ethical and environmental issues and report on areas of concern.

The Committee's First Report established The Seven Principles of Public Life, also known as the "Nolan principles" .They are also included in the Ministerial Code. They are:

- Selflessness – Holders of public office should act solely in terms of the public interest. They should not do so in order to gain financial or other benefits for themselves, their family or their friends.

- Integrity – Holders of public office should not place themselves under any financial or other obligation to outside individuals or organisations that might seek to influence them in the performance of their official duties.
- Objectivity – In carrying out public business, including making public appointments, awarding contracts, or recommending individuals for rewards and benefits, holders of public office should make choices on merit.
- Accountability – Holders of public office are accountable for their decisions and actions to the public and must submit themselves to whatever scrutiny is appropriate to their office.
- Openness – Holders of public office should be as open as possible about all the decisions and actions they take. They should give reasons for their decisions and restrict information only when the wider public interest clearly demands.
- Honesty – Holders of public office have a duty to declare any private interests relating to their public duties and to take steps to resolve any conflicts arising in a way that protects the public interest.
- Leadership – Holders of public office should promote and support these principles by leadership and example

8.14 Higgs Report on the role and effectiveness of non-executive directors

This review was led by Derek Higgs and begun in April 2002 with the final report published in January 2003. The main points were to amend the Combined Code (following the Hampel Report) for NEDs to take on a more demanding and important role on company boards. The primary recommendations involve:

- description of the role of the NED
- role of the chair and chief executive to be separate
- NEDs to be drawn from a wider pool of candidates
- a new definition of 'independent' directors
- improved recruitment, appointment, induction and development
- terms of engagement
- audit and remuneration committees
- audit and liability
- closer relationship between NEDS and major shareholders
- smaller listed companies
- making change happen.

The report also recommends that NEDs should:

- comprise half of the board
- be assessed annually
- not serve more than two three-year terms on the board
- meet as a group at least once a year without the chairman and the executive directors
- conduct a due diligence exercise before appointment to satisfy themselves that they can make a positive contribution.

8.15 Smith Review of Audit Committees

An independent group, chaired by Sir Robin Smith, convened in January 2003 to clarify the role and responsibilities of audit committees. The report was published in July 2003. The main recommendations were that:

- the audit committee should comprise of at least three members, all independent NEDs
- one audit committee member should have significant, recent and relevant financial experience
- suitable and timely training should be provided to committee members.

Recommendations on the role of the committee were to monitor the integrity of the financial statements, review the internal financial control systems, monitor the internal audit function, make recommendations to the board on external auditors, appointment, and monitor and review the performance and independence of external auditors. The recommendations are appended to the 2003 Combined Code.

8.16 Combined Code on Corporate Governance

Details were issued by the Financial Reporting Council (FRC) and came into effect on 1 November 2003 with reporting on its recommendations occurring after 1 November 2004.

The revised Combined Code builds upon the existing code and incorporates the recommendations of the Higgs and Smith Reports. The Code aims to foster more open and rigorous procedures for the appointment of directors and improved induction and development of NEDs. It recommends that half of the board members of the FT350 companies should be independent NEDs, that only NEDs should sit on the audit and remuneration committees and that if NEDs serve more than nine years they are no longer considered to be independent (unlisted companies should have two NEDs on the board).

The Code also calls for formal evaluation of boards, committees and individual directors. It takes a *comply or explain* approach to encourage best practice in corporate governance. Listed companies have to report on how they have applied the principles in the Code, confirm that they comply with the Code's provisions or provide an explanation in respect of any departures.

In July 2005 the FRC announced a review of the implementation of the Code which was published in January 2006. In July 2006 an updated Code superseding and replacing the 2003 Code was published.

8.17   An assessment of corporate governance in the UK

Britain has perhaps more than any other country explored the laws governing directors and their duties and obligations alongside the more behavioural aspects of management actions. This may explain the appearance of a better balance between rules and principles of behaviour which have shaped British thinking.

But as with the US there remains clear evidence that attempts to freshen and fundamentally alter the behaviour of management at board level and below have mostly failed. The Banking crisis of 2008 has revealed the extent to which the toxic combinations of the cult of *celebrity* in top management, unchallenged power and ineffective NEDs were key factors which explain the catastrophic failures in corporate governance and the unprecedented loss of wealth that this has caused. Despite every effort to exhort shareholders to play a more engaged and committed role in the management of those companies in which they are invested there has been no credible progress for reasons that are well known, well understood but not acted upon.[5]

8.18   The European Union

In May 2003 the European Commission issued an action plan on *Modernising company law and enhancing corporate governance in the European Union*.[6] The action plan contained twenty-four measures to be adopted before 2009 and was written to make it easier for companies and investors to operate across the EU borders. It was designed to promote enterprise, enhance competitiveness and stimulate investment and wealth creation. A review and consultation of the action plan was carried out by the European Commission in 2006. An important aspect of this work centres on corporate governance.

Corporate governance is traditionally defined as the system by which companies are directed and controlled and as a set of relationships between a company's management, its board, its shareholders and its other stakeholders. The corporate governance framework for listed companies in the EU is a combination of legislation and 'soft law', including recommendations and corporate governance codes. While corporate governance codes are adopted at national level, Directive 2006/46/EC promotes their application by requiring that listed companies refer in their corporate governance statement to a code and that they report on their application of that code on a *comply or explain* basis.

To identify the issues most relevant to good corporate governance within the EU the Commission conducted interviews with a sample of listed companies from different Member States and different economic sectors, with different levels of capitalisation and different shareholding structures. It also held meetings with corporate governance experts and with representatives of the investor community and civil society organisations.

Some relevant issues had already emerged in the context of the research undertaken in preparing the Green Paper on Corporate Governance in Financial Institutions and remuneration policies adopted in June 2010. However, financial institutions are viewed as a special case, because of the particular challenges faced in ensuring effective risk management and the systemic risks they may pose to the financial system.

8.19 An assessment of corporate governance in the EU

EU jurisdictions (which include European and Nordic jurisdictions) represent a wide spectrum of different arrangements in terms of the spread between single unitary boards and two-tier board structures based on independent supervision. A recent assessment made by the European Commission has highlighted the following areas.[7]

- The board of directors. High performing, effective boards are needed to challenge executive management. This means that boards need non-executive directors with diverse views, skills and appropriate professional experience. Such members must also be willing to invest sufficient time in the work of the board. The role of chairman of the board is particularly important, as are the board's responsibilities for risk management.

- Shareholders and their role. The corporate governance framework is built on the assumption that shareholders engage with companies and hold the management to account for its performance. However, there is evidence that the majority of shareholders are passive and are often only focused on short-term profits. It seems practical to explore ways in which shareholders can be encouraged to take an interest in sustainable returns and longer term performance, and how to encourage them to be more active on corporate governance issues. In different shareholding structures there are other issues, such as minority protection.

- The *comply or explain* approach which underpins the EU corporate governance framework is a source of weakness. The informative quality of explanations published by companies departing from the corporate governance code's recommendation is - in the majority of the cases - not satisfactory. In many Member States there is insufficient monitoring of the application of the codes. This needs to be addressed.

From these observations it is clear that similar problems are now surfacing within EU capital markets which are common in Anglo American capital markets. These include shareholder *detachment, short-termism* and the importance of high quality NEDs. The *comply or explain* observation is further evidence that reliance on directors to account for failures to comply to codes is unsatisfactory.

Figure 13   German Corporate Governance[8]

German Corporate Governance Code

This German Corporate Governance Code (the "Code") presents essential statutory regulations for the management and supervision (governance) of German listed companies and contains internationally and nationally recognized standards for good and responsible governance. The Code aims at making the German Corporate Governance system transparent and understandable. Its purpose is to promote the trust of international and national investors, customers, employees and the general public in the management and supervision of listed German stock corporations.

The Code clarifies the obligation of the Management Board and the Supervisory Board to ensure the continued existence of the enterprise and its sustainable creation of value in conformity with the principles of the social market economy (interest of the enterprise).

A dual board system is prescribed by law for German stock corporations: The Management Board is responsible for managing the enterprise. Its members are jointly accountable for the management of the enterprise. The Chairman of the Management Board coordinates the work of the Management Board. The Supervisory Board appoints, supervises and advises the members of the Management Board and is directly involved in decisions of fundamental importance to the enterprise. The chairman of the Supervisory Board coordinates the work of the Supervisory Board. The members of the Supervisory Board are elected by the shareholders at the General Meeting.

In enterprises having more than 500 or 2000 employees in Germany, employees are also represented in the Supervisory Board, which then is composed of employee representatives to one third or to one half respectively. For enterprises with more than 2000 employees, the Chairman of the Supervisory Board, who, for all practical purposes, is a representative of the shareholders, has the casting vote in the case of split resolutions. The representatives elected by the shareholders and the representatives of the employees are equally obliged to act in the enterprise's best interests. Alternatively the European Company (SE) gives enterprises in Germany the possibility of opting for the internationally widespread system of governance by a single body (board of directors).

The form that codetermination takes in the SE is established generally by agreement between the company management and the employee side. All employees in the EU member states are included. In practice the dual-board system, also established in other continental European countries, and the single-board system are converging because of the intensive interaction of the Management Board and the Supervisory Board in the dual-board system. Both systems are equally successful.

8.20   Japan

Japan is in many respects both different from other OECD corporate governance jurisdictions but has undoubtedly points of parallel with European jurisdictions notably Germany. Japanese corporations are historically oriented towards expansion. This suggests that motivations such as margins and profitability are viewed as being less important than growth. This appears to be aided by dispersed shareholding, rather as in the US and the UK. Most importantly there is high level of integration between managers and directors. Directors emerge from within the company.

8.21   The main influences

The main influences which have shaped policy and behaviour towards corporate governance are well rehearsed by Okabe (2009)[9] He identifies three main features as follows. First Japanese companies are historically oriented towards growth rather than the pursuit of earnings or profit in contrast with the assumed objectives of American and British firms. Second the "dispersion" of company ownership is widespread. This means that the company is not viewed as being owned by the shareholders. It is seen as being collectively owned by shareholders and stakeholders, notably employees. Shares are mostly held by financial institutions and other non bank corporations with individual shareholding fairly insignificant. In this respect the separation of *ownership* and *control* is similar to the situation in Anglo American jurisdictions.

Thirdly there is a high level of integration between company managers and directors. This arises because the majority of directors are drawn from the ranks of senior management. The traditional Anglo American concern about the *principal/ agent* problem is thus not seen in the same light. The director is not there to protect the interest of the shareholders as in Anglo American orthodoxy. The role of the director is to represent the interest of the employees. One perceived consequence is that company directors are not bothered by share performance as an end in itself: they are motivated by long term performance and continuity. Because of these features Japanese corporate governance remains problematical when judged by policy concerns elsewhere, but particularly in Anglo American jurisdictions. The Japanese are thus seen as being out of line with best practice elsewhere. The response of Japanese management to governance reform is lukewarm.

8.22   The Japanese Insider Model

The Japanese model is *insider* in orientation resembling corporate governance practices in some EU jurisdictions and most notably in Germany. The advantages that derive from this are that management can focus on long term development. In this way they represent the interests of future managers and the members of the work force. Financial transaction costs are also at a minimum given that banking relationships are close. The drawbacks with this are two-fold. First there is little transparency given the nature of implicit contracts in transactions. This can and does lead to abuses of power. These arrangements also hold back corporate restructuring where this is necessary. Finally the role of finance also plays an important role with Japanese corporations preferring to raise debt rather than equity further re-inforcing the disciplining role of banks.

The case of Olympus is a remarkable, though perhaps not typical example of corporate governance. This is investigated more fully elsewhere.[10] The newly appointed CEO (a long standing British employee and manager within Olympus) very soon unearths evidence of widespread financial irregularities. It is clear from the evidence that the Board were either unaware of these events or condoned what had happened. A non Japanese speaker it is hard to see how Mr Woodford would have been able to get to the bottom of these matters. Concerns have also been made about the governance of TEPCO (Tokyo Electric Power Company) following the nuclear disaster and serious management lapses in 2011 and Toyota in 2010 over quality problems which triggered a decline of $34bn in market capitalisation in two weeks to mention only two recent events. These are but three examples.

The Japanese corporate governance system is fundamentally different to governance systems in the US or Britain though there are parallels with arrangements in Rhineland jurisdictions. It is sometimes characterised as being a bank and insider related type of governance. This stands in contrast with the capital markets external disciplinary system common in the US and Britain. In reality two distinct systems appear to exist in Japan. One may be characterised as that common to independent firms: the other *keiretsu* in form.

The main bank system and the *keiretsu* are two different, yet overlapping and complementary, elements of the Japanese model.[11] Almost all Japanese corporations have a close relationship with a main bank. The bank provides its corporate client with loans as well as services related to bond issues, equity issues, settlement accounts, and related consulting services. The main bank is often a major shareholder in the corporation. It is noteworthy that US anti-monopoly legislation prohibits one bank from providing this multiplicity of services. Instead, these services are usually handled by different institutions.[12] These would include commercial bank loans; investment bank equity issuance; specialised advisory and other services.

Many Japanese corporations also have strong financial relationships with a network of affiliated companies. These networks are characterised by crossholdings of debt and equity, trading of goods and services, and informal business contacts. Government-directed industrial policy also plays a key role in Japanese corporate governance. Since the 1930s, the Japanese government has pursued an active industrial policy designed to promote Japanese corporations. This policy includes official and unofficial representation on corporate boards, especially when a corporation faces financial difficulty.

In the Japanese model, the four key players are: the main bank (a major inside shareholder), affiliated company or *keiretsu*(a major inside shareholder), management and the government. Note that the interaction among these players serves to link relationships rather than balance powers, as in the case in the Anglo American model. In contrast with the Anglo American model, non-affiliated shareholders have little or no voice in Japanese governance. As a result, there are few truly independent directors, that is, directors representing outside shareholders.

8.23   Share Ownership Patterns in the Japanese Model

In Japan, financial institutions and corporations firmly hold ownership of the equity market. Similar to the trend in the UK and US, the shift during the post war period has been away from individual ownership to institutional and corporate ownership. In 1990, financial institutions (insurance companies and banks) held approximately 43 percent of the Japanese equity market, and corporations (excluding financial institutions) held 25 percent. Foreigners currently own approximately three percent.

In both the Japanese and the German model, banks are key shareholders and develop strong relationships with corporations, due to overlapping roles and the multiple services provided. This distinguishes both models from Anglo American practice where such relationships are prohibited by antitrust legislation. Instead of relying on a single bank, US and British corporations obtain financing and other services from a wide range of sources, including well-developed capital markets.

Aoki and Okuno[13] (1996) explore the position of shareholders and employees in the so called *duel control* governance structure. Both shareholders and employees have control rights, and benefit from *contingent governance* where the control rights moves between inside stakeholders and outside stakeholders according to prevailing business conditions. The shareholder value model represents too narrow a view. It more fairly represents a *stakeholder value* model.[14]

This sort of *exceptionalism* where corporate governance in Japan is concerned is well summed up by Hiroshi Okuda, chairman of Toyota Motor Corporation and of the Japan Federation of Employers' Associations.[15] He makes the position clear in the following terms.

> *"It would be irresponsible to run Japanese companies primarily in the interests of shareholders. To be sustainable, children are told, corporations must nurture relationships with stakeholders such as suppliers, employees and the local*

128

community. So whatever the legal position, and the textbooks declare, the corporation does not belong to its owners. No matter that all the research shows that stock markets respond favourably to higher research and development spending. Nor that the audience consisted chiefly of long-term investors, such as pension funds. The chasm between Japanese and Anglo- American views on what companies are for and whose interests they serve could not have been clearer. It is not enough to serve shareholders."

8.24   South Korea

The history of the *chaebol* has been punctuated by claims of accounting fraud, poor corporate governance and illegal political donations. The system remains heavily dependent on founding families. The role of patronage is therefore crucial. There are also problems of succession in a number of industries. At another level it is sometimes argued that the *chaebol* stifles innovation and entrepreneurship. This, it is argued is exemplified by fewer start-up firms or cutting edge technology businesses, a claim made by the Korean Business School[16]. The larger conglomerates are accused of snapping up the best of the smaller companies and converting the most entrepreneurial into 'company men'. They are otherwise likened to light-hogging trees which prevent or otherwise discourage growth at lower levels beneath the canopy.

One of the most striking features of *chaebol* dominated development has been the very equal distribution of income between the upper and lower 10ths of population. Gini co-efficients, which measure income inequality, fell to an exceptionally low level of .28 between 1980 and 1997. It has since risen to 0.31 (on a par with Scandinavia) but is set to rise further. This is explained in part through substantial past subsidies to the SME sector. This however is changing. Subsidies are being withdrawn and the wage bills of *chaebols* are being reduced by recycling older and more expensive workers.

8.25   Conclusions

The approaches to corporate governance are strikingly different as between jurisdictions. The reliance on unitary boards appearing to represent exclusively shareholder interests stands in marked contrast with the approaches in Rhineland and other European jurisdiction including Nordic countries and Japan. These differences play a key role in determining corporate behaviour. The notion of *shareholder primacy* has something of a false ring about it.

Shareholders or institutional investors play little by way of an effective role in the governance of corporations in Anglo American jurisdictions. There is an air of make-believe about their claim for special treatment. In Rhineland and other related jurisdictions shareholders play an important and committed role in the governance through their representation, along with other stakeholders on independent supervisory boards. In Japan the same concerns about wider stakeholder interests are also in evidence.

The extent of scrutiny in respect of corporations in Anglo American jurisdictions has been wide ranging and constant in the wake of a stream of failures in terms of corporate governance. Despite these interventions the basic power structures with unitary boards and their sensitivity to wider stakeholder interests has not been positively affected.

Questions for review

1. Can you explain why there has been so much regulatory intervention in Anglo American jurisdictions when compared with elsewhere?

2. Why do the various reporting requirement in Britain (and elsewhere) rely upon *comply or expl*ain arrangements?

3. What accounts for the emphasis of *rules-based* regulation in the US when compared with the *principles-based* approach in Britain?

4. Why does it appear that in both Japan and South Korea stakeholder concerns have a higher priority than in Anglo American jurisdictions?

5. In what respects do corporate governance arrangements in Asia appear to resemble those in Rhineland jurisdictions? What explains this?

6. Does reliance on the external disciplining influence of capital markets provide a reliable safeguard against governance failures?

7. What are the essential differences in corporate governance arrangements within the EU and in Anglo American jurisdictions?

8. Does the heavy reliance on regulatory provisions within Anglo American jurisdictions make for better standards of corporate governance?

Learning Tasks

I   What features would you emphasise in an effective system of corporate governance?

II   If you believe that all executive boards of larger corporations need to be subject to independent supervision how would you see this happening?

III   How can the independence of NEDs be assured?

Notes

[1] See: Millstein I M, *The evolution of corporate governance in the United States* – Briefly Told Forum for US-EU Legal-Economic Affairs, Rome September 2001.

[2] See: Tudway R *op citThe Juridical Paradox of the Corporation* page 75.

[3] Sarbanes–Oxley, Sarbox or SOX, is a United States federal law that set new or enhanced standards for all U.S. public company boards, management and public accounting firms.

[4] The Dodd Frank Act makes wide ranging changes in the American financial regulatory environment that affect all federal financial regulatory agencies and almost every part of the nation's financial services industry.

[5] These matters have been explored fully elsewhere.

[6] European company law and corporate governance – 12.12.2012

[7] The EU corporate governance Green Paper, COM(2011)164 final Brussels, 5.4.2011

[8] See German Corporate Governance Code (as amended on May 13, 2013)

[9] See: Mitsuaki Okabe *Codes of Good Governance Around the World*, Chapter 20 New York Nova Science Publishers ISBN 978-1-60741-141-3 2009

[10] See: Chapter10, Case Study 3

[11] See Bergloef, Eric, 1993. *Corporate Governance in Transition Economies: The Theory and its Policy Implications* in Masahiko Aoki and Hyung-Ki Kim, editors, *Corporate Governance in Transitional Economies: Insider Control and the Role of Banks*. Washington, D.C.: The World Bank. EWMI/PFS Program /Lectures on Corporate Governance - Three Models of Corporate Governance – December 2005.doc 7

[12] This situation has changed with the end of the Glass Steagall era as banks have become universal banks.

[13] See: Aoki M and Okuno M *Comparative Institutional Analysis of Economic Systems* Tokyo University Press 1996

[14] Stakeholder theory suggests that the purpose of a business is to create as much value as possible for stakeholders. In order to succeed and be sustainable over time, executives must keep the interests of customers, suppliers, employees, communities and shareholders aligned and going in the same direction.

[15] This was made clear in a speech in September 2001 to the ICGN by Hiroshi Okuda, chairman of Toyota and of the Japan Federation of Employers' Associations.

[16] As reported in The Economist Briefing on the South Korean Economy dated 12 November 2011.

Figure 14   Two Financial systems and their functional properties:

Anglo-American model and Japanese-German model

	Anglo-American model	Japanese-German model
Main financial transaction	In the open market	By bilateral transaction
Main funding instrument	Securities	Loan
Dependence on banks	Low	High
Nature of bank loan	Short-term	Short-term and long-term
Importance of internal funds	High	Low
Shareholding by banks	Not important	Important
Major shareholders	Households Institutional investors	Banks Intercorporate shareholding
Block share trading	Frequent	Infrequent
Corporate control	Stock market	Banks (main banks)
Information acquisition and processing	Market acquire and distributes diversity of opinion and risk; Information cost is low	By continuous transaction, banks can acquire and share information with client firms; economies of scale works in formation acquisition
Allocation of risk	Risk is dispersed broadly to various economic units in financial markets	Risk is essentially concentrated in banks
Performance characteristics	More responsive to changes	Superior at implementing corporate policies that require agreements of various parties
Suitable economic activity	Developing new industries and new technologies (Product innovation)	Improving the efficiency of production process of existing products (Process innovation)
Industry examples	Railways, computers, and biotechnology	Automobiles and electronics

Source: Okabe M (2006; 2007: Table 5.3) *Codes of Good Governance Around the World*, Chapter 20 New York Nova Science

Chapter 9

The emergence of CSR – a step forward or a step back?

9.1   Summary

In Chapter eight the question what is CSR and why does it arise has been explored. CSR appears to reflect a collective sense of public concern that corporations in their everyday commercial activities do not pay attention to the negative and unwanted aspects of their activities or otherwise fail to respond to social concerns in general and stakeholder concerns in particular. This is not the same as saying that corporations are not very active in the CSR domain. They are: the output is huge.

We explore in Chapter 9 who the parties are that speak for CSR and on whose behalf they speak. In doing so we will consider how their claims are authenticated and verified. We will also explore how far the board identifies with CSR activities and what evidence there is of board *buy-in*.

We begin first by examining the drivers of CSR before moving to assess the relevance of ethics in these discussions. This will be done with particular reference to the public position taken by Barclays Bank and the publication of the Salz Review.

9.2   What does CSR really mean?

CSR concerns are undoubtedly a response to public anxieties about corporate behaviour. Since CSR is itself a response to a problem how can it be meaningfully and operationally-speaking defined? One major problem with relative values is the difficulty of establishing objectively the argument that things are worse today than they were, or that companies are less concerned about social and environmental concerns than they once were. Greenhouse gas emissions are higher. Other forms of environmental degradation and resource depletion are higher also. But so is aggregate economic growth and citizen welfare measured by benchmarks of general wellbeing and even poverty alleviation. What causes what? Can corporations be blamed for everything that goes wrong? Clearly they cannot.

The debate about CSR is linked for particular reasons to Anglo American debate and discussion. It is also a hotly debated matter. Remember what Milton Friedman once had to say about the matter:

> *I share Adam Smith's skepticism (sic) about the benefits that can be expected from "those who affect to trade for the public good" ... in a free society .... there is only one and only one social responsibility of business – to use its resources and engage in activities designed to increase profits.* [1]

CSR is an English language invention. It comes in part from the environment within which listed corporations operate in Anglo American jurisdictions. As we have seen it often arises where shareholders (institutional investors) are for whatever reason remote from the everyday management of the companies in which they are invested. All, or certainly most, major corporations are stock market listed. Shares are traded in public markets between institutional investors. In Anglo American jurisdictions corporations are also managed by unitary boards. Given the outsider controlled environment public debate about company affairs is more developed than insider controlled environments, those common in Rhineland and Nordic jurisdictions.

9.3   Approaches in Europe to CSR

How is CSR dealt with in other European languages and elsewhere? In Europe, especially *Rhineland* jurisdictions which are insider controlled, public information and public scrutiny of CSR claims appear to be less controversial. Stock markets also play a lesser role in terms of public expectations about corporate behaviour. Given the nature of two-tier boards in *Rhineland* and Nordic jurisdictions it is argued that corporations are in any event more genuinely and naturally CSR-conscious than companies in Anglo American jurisdictions.

Supervisory boards, which reflect wider interests than those of shareholders, are capable of exercising a restraining influence over executive directors. This appears not to exist in Anglo American jurisdictions where executive directors of unitary boards appear to exercise greater influence and power. Shareholder influence is also far less. In Japan and South Korea the "family" ownership structures whether *keiritsu* or *chaebol* also appear to be less focussed on shareholder interests and are more responsive to wider social and economic concerns.

Yet CSR even in Anglo American jurisdictions is closely linked to stakeholder-type concerns. This raises fundamental difficulties. It is easy to say that corporations should represent the interests of stakeholders but how can this be meaningfully defined? If shareholders are viewed as stakeholders then the task might be more straightforward. But the basic difference of interest between shareholders and other stakeholders retains a strong hold in the Anglo American context. The specific case of employees is a case in point. Their special claims are often denied the importance they merit. A wide range of stakeholder groups have rights reflected in law - so the counter argument runs. But many issues in CSR affect other even more diverse stakeholder groups. This raises two commonly cited difficulties: how can a corporation define the groups it should take into account; and what weighting should it attach to different stakeholder interests in arriving at an assessment of *costs and benefits*? This is in part the TBL problem, discussed earlier.

9.4   Promoting the Importance of Stakeholder Engagement

How can the case for CSR and stakeholdership be advanced? For the most part the CSR movement is NGO-driven by people who have no in-depth knowledge or experience of how businesses in practice operate. There is merit in the arguments of both Friedman and Henderson who argue that the business of business is to make profit. As a hypothesis it cannot be easily challenged in a free enterprise economy in which primary wealth is generated by the business enterprise sector. As ever, however, this is only half the story. Profitability may very well be as Friedman reminds us a central purpose of business endeavour but that says nothing about *what sort* of profit or *how* the profit is derived. A perhaps better way forward is to ask how best companies can become economically, socially and environmentally *sustainable*.

The answer to this question is again far from obvious. But just as turnover (from which profit is generated) is determined by social and citizen *tastes* as expressed in the market place through demand, so better standards in terms of sustainability need to gain expression in terms of turnover. Perhaps the most effective way of bringing this about is for companies to be required to *discover* these needs (as they discover other needs) and for all the participants in that process – consumers, capital market players (banks and institutional investors) as well as NGOs to play their part.

For corporations what is imperative is that they have the quality and strength of leadership to encourage this *awareness* to grow within their own organisations. In short reform comes from within the enterprise and not from empty edicts like companies should be doing this or that. But that process in itself is complex. The process has to be set up and managed properly. Those companies that don't adopt credible approaches in the quest for sustainability will not survive![2] But what is sustainability?

9.5   Different approaches to CSR in different jurisdictions

The EU Green Paper[3] on CSR is a significant document. It observes that an increasing number of European companies are promoting their CSR strategies in response to a variety of complex social, environmental and economic pressures. The aim of the Green Paper is to encourage corporations to connect with the various stakeholders with whom they naturally interact including employees, trade unions shareholders, investors, consumers, public authorities and NGOs. By so doing companies will be investing in their future. The presumption is that the commitments they embrace will enhance profitability and longevity.

As early as 1993, the appeal to European business by Jacques Delors[4] to take part in the fight against social exclusion resulted in a strong development of European business networks. At the turn of the millennium in March 2000, the European Council in Lisbon made a special appeal to companies' sense of social responsibility regarding best practices for lifelong learning, work organisation, equal opportunities, social inclusion and sustainable development.

9.6   Rising above the mundane

By setting out their social responsibilities and taking on commitments which go beyond common regulatory and conventional requirements companies will effectively raise the standards of social development, environmental protection and respect for fundamental citizen. The aim is to encourage companies to embrace open and transparent corporate governance. Reconciling the interests of various stakeholders in this holistic approach aims to promote the legitimacy of corporate endeavour and its sustainability. Management of corporations thus face significant demands if they are to meet these forward-looking challenges.

Addressing these challenges effectively must lead to the development of new partnership skills. This will involve exploring new spheres for existing relationships within the company regarding social dialogue. It will entail the generation of new skills at every level. These need to embrace equal opportunities and the effective management of change, at the plant and national level. There must be a commitment to the reinforcement of economic and social cohesion and on a global level a commitment to promoting environmental protection and respect of fundamental rights.

The EU CSR initiative will be driven mainly by large companies, even though socially responsible practices are being encouraged in all types of enterprises, public and private, including SMEs and co-operatives. The CSR case that has been selected for assessment is a medium sized German company with around 900 employees worldwide. It has been selected because of the rigour at every stage that has been shown in exploring what it seeks as a company to achieve in terms of it CSR initiatives. This case can be found in Appendix 3.[5]

It is worth remembering that the EU is concerned about CSR because it can be seen as a positive contribution to one of the most important strategic goals settled by the Lisbon[6] summit. This is described in the following terms:

> *to become the most competitive and dynamic knowledge-based economy in the world, capable of sustainable economic growth with more and better jobs and greater social cohesion*".

The Green Paper aims to promote the widest possible debate on CSR within Europe and internationally in a bid to foster the development of innovative practices, to bring greater transparency and to increase the reliability of evaluation and validation.

In Anglo American jurisdictions the same debate about the nature and purpose of CSR has not occurred in the same way. Corporations have played a key role in determining the debate. Business Schools have also contributed. Porter and Kramer (2006) have contributed one of the most influential papers. This seeks to set the case right for corporate CSR[7] The paper argues that prevailing approaches to CSR (in the US) are so disconnected from business as to obscure many of the greatest opportunities for companies to benefit society. Its conclusions are so obvious it is hard to see where on any learning curve US businesses find themselves. What the paper usefully does is to highlight many of the fallacies that have driven CSR in earlier times, notably the preoccupation with philanthropic acts, reactively addressing threatening stakeholder concerns and the compulsive drive for reputational enhancement. In the period since there has been little obvious change in the way in which corporations handle CSR despite rising public clamour over serious lapses in corporate ethical behaviour a matter to which we now turn.

9.7   The Issue of Ethics

The issue of ethics has become an increasingly important in the ongoing debate about corporate governance, corporate behaviour and CSR. The Barclays, Tesco and News Corp cases, in particular, explore some aspects of the challenges posed by exploring corporate behaviour through the lens of ethics. Specifically students are asked to assess the Salz Review of Barclays Bank. This is set out in Appendix 4.

As we shall see the two most important difficulties arise from setting out attainable ethical standards and then ensuring that in the context of business they are upheld in a meaningful and verifiable manner. The simple definition of 'business ethics' is that it is the study of proper business policies and practices regarding potentially controversial issues, such as corporate governance, insider trading, bribery, discrimination, corporate social responsibility and fiduciary responsibilities. Trying to apply ethics to commercial organisations creates however a wide range of challenges. Barclays commissioned the Salz Review[8] to examine how best they can address these matters. Surprising the word 'ethics' does not appear in the report yet this is what it must ultimately be addressing. They speak instead about 'culture' though in reality the report is addressing ethical issues

Every business organisation adopts an ethical posture of some sort. Individuals within the organisation will certainly have their own ethical principles. This may be different from that of the organisation or close to it. The challenge facing management is to create a culture within which there is a high degree of harmony between individually held ethical values and those of the organisation. This ultimately is the challenge Barclay's (and other organisations) face.

9.7　　　　　　　　The Salz Review

An extract from the Salz Review is published below:

> *Appendix B – What is Culture and How Can it Go Wrong*
>
> *In the body of this report we looked at the culture of Barclays and what we believe needs to change. We commissioned this appendix to provide greater context – beyond that of Barclays – of what culture is, why it matters, and how it can go wrong. The appendix draws more broadly on the body of research addressing cultural issues. We hope it provides useful background.*
>
> *The financial crisis of 2008 has rocked trust and confidence in the industry at all levels of society, including many of those who work within the industry itself. 'Culture' has been mooted by many as a root cause of the damage done and a programme of cultural change has been proposed as the course of action to aid recovery.*

The culture of banks, it is said, drove the wrong behaviours. The sector lost sight of its sense of purpose and lost sight of the values that are needed to run a successful global financial system. Leaders built banks that pursued profit at the expense of all else, failing to see the systemic risks and forgetting the fundamental principles of the profession of banking.

Leaders need a sense of purpose and integrity to redefine banking and restore trust with customers and employees. These leaders need to be people who see themselves and others as people first (not just employees or customers) and who recognise that creating organisations with 'good' cultures isn't a project or a short-term focus – rather it is the leaders' work. Work that requires a good grasp of people, culture and organisational development, as well as business, strategy and structure; the latter without the former is inadequate.

'Culture' and cultural change have become somewhat of buzz words amongst those faced with delivering change in banking. The reality of course is that changing culture should not be a goal. The goal should be to change the tangible things about what the service does for customers and how people will do their work; gradually, this will change the culture. Fundamentally changing how we work (beliefs, behaviours, structures and systems) is the more challenging part and takes time.

Yet elsewhere several important media commentators including the BBC and the Huffington Post refer to the Barclay's initiative in more explicit ethical terms:

New chief executive Antony Jenkins said in a memo sent to the bank's 140,000 employees that performance would be judged on a set of ethical standards in the wake of its Libor-rigging scandal.

He said: "We must never again be in a position of rewarding people for making the bank money in a way which is unethical or inconsistent with our values."

The banks' new code of conduct will centre on five values - respect, integrity, service, excellence and stewardship.

In his address[9] to the Barclay's global community in September 2012 Anthony Jenkins's address contained the following statement:

Barclays will operate to the highest ethical standards

We need to ask ourselves how this will be brought about? Talking about the ideals we associate with ethical behaviour does no harm. But will it do any good? Without actions to *live the words* nothing will happen. Directors, managers and employees will become progressively more cynical along with society at large. The gap between appearance and reality will widen further. There is a high risk that this is what may happen.

9.8   Why have Barclays decided to act?

Why Barclays has decided to act raises important question. One likely explanation is that top management in Barclays has taken the view that the reputational damage has already been so great that to redress the damage a very significant gesture has to be made. Simply admitting that things had gone wrong and the decision of the Board to terminate the bank's contact with Bob Diamond would not in itself be enough to stop further reputational damage. This may explain Anthony Jenkins' decision to launch a radically different initiative.

Looking at the performance of the bank as measured by share price movements it is evident that Barclays share price fell dramatically as the crisis broke from highs at around 350 (£3.50) to lows at around the 50p level before making gains throughout 2009. As the scandals began to engulf Barclays the share price fell, back steadily. With the ousting of Bob Diamond and the change of leadership the share price has shown some further modest recovery. It remains, however, significantly below pre crisis highs. Setting aside any higher minded ambitions on the part of Barclays new broom management it may be the case that the culture change initiative will continue to pay off. If true this has significant implications.

Reading the Salz Review two things emerge. First it is clear that Anthony Jenkins, as a conventional commercial banker, has little taste for the glitzier aspects of investment banking. His response stands in sharp contrast to the CEO of Goldman Sachs, Lloyd Blankein's view that his firm has no specific fiduciary duty since they view themselves purely as market makers. Second one gets a clear impression that the Review sees many of Barclay's problems resulting from long term cultural shifts within the bank. Anthony Jenkins makes clear his intention of restoring trust with customers and employees.

9.9 Utilitarianism

A major question for yet there is really no clear answer is how far and over what time scale can the sorts of changes that the Salz Review recommends be expected to bear fruit. There is a further connected question. How far are the stated objectives little more than a form of utilitarian ethics? Jeremy Bentham was a leading exponent and will be well remembered for his *felicific calculus* "the greatest happiness of the greatest number"[10] Happiness in this context is usually equated with personal satisfaction, the fulfilment of individual self interest. It is the maximisation of such self interest that is often regarded as the *good* to be maximised.

The problem ultimately with this position is that it does lead to a form of *moral relativism* or *tactical ethics* which has little to do with transcendental ethics as derived from moral philosophy. This is well illustrated by the so called *Prisoner's Dilemma* which ultimately weakens the old dictum *honesty is the best policy*. See Figure 14 *infra*. The impact of this in the context of the Salz Review may be to reduce its high reaching ambitions and address instead the pragmatic task of reputational rehabilitation on the part of Barclays Bank, its top management and employees.

9.10 Conclusions

The emergence of CSR rather like the proverbial *curate's egg* is only good in parts. It often represents a corporate response to things the Board sees going wrong around them. Barclay's response to a range of difficulties the bank has faced in recent years is an example. The aim is clearly to put matters right. But as actions unfold other problems will likely arise. The company may find itself overwhelmed by the challenge of recovering its reputation. This almost certainly explains the decision of NewsCorp to close down the discredited News of the World. The damage was viewed as irreparable.

The problem for the public at large is to know what to make of any claims that are made by corporations when they set about these exercises. How do they independently establish the truth? How do they get independent authentication and verification about progress as initiatives are rolled-out? These challenges have yet to be addressed.

But there are serious background problems with CSR which the public is left to make sense of. These arise where corporations go out of their way to present an image which masks the reality of actual behaviour. Enron might be seen as a classic example of organised duplicity but Enron is by no means alone in this respect.[11]Corporations frequently view CSR as a marketing or PR tool – a device for presenting CSR as if it were another product or market offering. One way to ensure that this does not happen is to require that there is full board *buy-in* and that the exercise does not degenerate into a PR battle for the minds. This problem, regrettably, is common. It is especially the case in Anglo American jurisdictions where independent supervision and *board buy-in* is weaker than in other jurisdictions.

Questions for Review

1. What influenced the directors of Eckes Gramini in setting out their approach to CSR?

2. Comment upon the level of board buy-in to the CSR project and the importance of this?

3. Why does the company place so much importance on the full engagement of its employee in the exercise?

4. How should we define a stakeholder?

5. Why does the EU Green Paper highlight the importance of *inward looking* and *outward looking* approaches?

6. Why is the approach in Anglo American jurisdictions so vaguely defined with ultimately an emphasis on external factors?

7. Why does the Salz Review never refer to the issue of ethics whilst in his address to Barclay's employees worldwide Anthony Jenkins is very specific in the use of this word?

8. What does moral relativism mean?

9. The Salz Review places specific emphasis on cultural change within Barclays. What do you understand by this?

10. How is the culture of an organisation determined?

Learning Tasks

I   Define a detailed approach you would propose for a CSR exercise?

II   Try to define a procedure for conducting a CSR initiative from the Porter and Kramer paper?

III   How best can commercial businesses address the challenge of ethical behaviour?

Figure 15   **The Prisoner's Dilemma**

	A Keeps Silent	**A Confesses**
B Keeps Silent	A imprisoned for one month	A Free
	B imprisoned for one month	B imprisoned for one year
	Total imprisonment two months	Total imprisonment one year
B Confesses	A imprisoned for one year	A imprisoned for six months
	B Free	B imprisoned for six months
	Total imprisonment one year	Total imprisonment one year

Notes

[1] See: Milton Friedman *The Social Responsibility of Business Is to Increase Profi*ts *op cit*

[2] Tesco is seen by some analysts as a company that needs to radically transform its business model. This raises huge challenges for a corporation that has previously relied on the simple dictum *source it cheap, extract the highest margin, damn the consequences!*

[3] The EU Green Paper on CSR COM(2001) final Brussels 18.7.2001

[4] Delors became the President of the European Commission in January 1985. During his presidency, he oversaw important budgetary reforms and laid the groundwork for the introduction of a single market within the European Community, which came into effect on 1 January 1993.

[5]Eckes Gramini is a medium sized German business. The exercise was completed by Ulrike Thiefelder an MBA student as part of her educational experience at Hult International Business School.

[6] A reference to the EU Lisbon Summit held in May 2000 to get to grips with the challenges of moving to the *knowledge economy* reflecting paradigm shifts in the global economy.

[7] See: Porter M E and Kramer M R *Strategy and Society – The Link Between Competitive Advantage and Corporate Social Responsibility.*

[8] The Salz Review – *An Independent Review of Barclay's Bank Practices*

[9] Barclays Global Financial Services Conference September 2012 (New York) Anthony Jenkins' opening remarks.

[10] Bentham J *The Principles of Morals and Legislation* (1789)

[11] The latest revelations involving confidential discussions between Rupert Murdoch and journalists at the Sun newspaper is an example of double standards and two-facedness. Whilst publicly expressing regret for the behaviour of his own journalists in private he completely dismisses the claims of unlawful behaviour.

Chapter 10

How firms reveal themselves through their behaviour

10.1   Summary

This chapter will attempt to establish a comprehensive procedure for assessing corporate claims in terms of the record of behaviour. The aim is to get beneath the words which appear to describe the positioning of the company in respect of important matters and to look at the reality in terms of documented history about behaviours.

Eight case studies are explored. They have been constructed on the basis of material available in the public domain. Each focuses on different aspects of corporate behaviour and how the company concerned has sought to portray its experience and its particular response to particular challenges. Each case contains a set of key questions related to the case.

10.2   Companies and their public image

The extraordinary growth in corporate responsibility reporting bears witness to the importance corporations attach to their public image. They spend a lot of time investigating these matters and how best they can portray themselves. There is a broad spectrum of CSR reporting judged in terms of the quality and authenticity of the claims made. There is also abundant evidence that much that is produced in terms of verification and authentication falls far short of what is acceptable.

The Enron report, not examined on this occasion, is an example of cynical systemic misrepresentation. It is worth recalling that as the chairman of Enron claimed in the company's annual CSR report that he and his board colleagues stood for the highest standards of propriety. As these words were being written, systematic fraud at the highest reaches of the company was being committed. Too frequently in the period since we have seen similar statements made which on closer inspection are discovered to be bogus.

Despite a huge growth in investigative journalism examples of corporate abuse of power, in some cases despite explicit mission statement proscribing certain activities, continue to surface. The eight specific case studies that are examined present a review of recent events which have impacted on the company's position in the market place. Examine them carefully. In each case an attempt has been made to fairly present the affairs of the company. Following each case a set of questions ask the student to examine more closely the particular events that have arisen in respect of the company.

10.3 Some comments on the cases

The following eight cases have been chosen because they have all in their different ways been the focus of keen public interest and comment. Seven of the companies chosen are limited liability public listed companies which have operated for many decades. They have grown from modest businesses driven by the entrepreneurial flair of their founding shareholders to very large global businesses. In each instance, with the possible exceptions of Goldman Sachs[1] and NewsCorp shareholding is highly diversified with little or no effective shareholder control over the business activities of the company in which they are invested. They are also companies that have unitary board structures.

The exceptions are Siemens and the John Lewis Partnership. Siemens is a German global engineering business with a two-tier board structure. John Lewis Plc is the principal trading subsidiary of the John Lewis Partnership plc ('the Partnership') and owns Waitrose Limited. There are no shareholders as such and no dividends are paid to shareholders. The Partnership consisting of around 84,000 employees has a complex governance structure which resembles closely the co-determination arrangements in *Rhineland* jurisdictions. The Council represents all members. It can discuss anything including the social and employment policies of the company. Its democratic control ensures that all members (from check out cashiers through to the most senior directors) have their say in the governance of the business and its commercial operations. All members are paid a basic salary plus pension and other benefits. They receive an annual bonus expressed as a percentage sum of their basic salary.

In the case of Siemens the company is in many respects a traditional *Rhineland* business with an independent Supervisory Board. What is singularly striking about the disclosures in the Siemens case is the scale of systemic corruption which eventually became part of the culture of the company. There are important lessons to be learnt.

10.3   Issues raised by the cases

The cases explore different aspects of corporate behaviour. They range from examples of corporate greed as expressed by executive behaviour and the corrosive influence this has upon corporate culture. It also explores the way in which corporations use their power and influence to lobby and otherwise exercise potentially damaging, undemocratic influence over public policy. Alternatively the problems of power and risk management are assessed in respect of companies that exploit opportunities where risks are at their very highest alongside the rewards to be gained and how trade-offs are settled. Finally in one instance the challenges of controlling and eradicating fraud are also explored.

Of the seven major publicly traded corporations that are examined there is clear evidence that the control of entrenched power is beyond the reach of the NEDs and/or the Supervisory Board (in the case of Siemens). The NEDs appear to be marginalised from any involvement in discussing key corporate decisions. Within the unitary board structures of these companies the problem of asymmetry of power as between executive directors and NEDs is clearly in evidence. In the case of Goldman Sachs there is no recognition of the importance of separating the position of CEO and Chair – a not uncommon event in American companies. There is also the matter of the public denial that Goldman's has any particular fiduciary duty – an astounding declaration for a corporation that has sought and secured registration as a Banking Trust Corporation under US law.

The case concerning BP reveals a pattern of failure to manage risk given the scale of its supposed commitment to environmental protection. There appears to be a lengthy history of failure on the part of BP to 'practice what it preaches'. These matters stretch from the Texas City oil refinery explosion in 2005, attributed to corporate cost-cutting in the face of known dangers, through to the Gulf of Mexico disaster which again focuses attention on inadequate on-going monitoring of high level risk. Many see the company's risk management failures as evidence of serious defects in BP's corporate culture which cannot easily be reversed. Much the same applies to Tesco whose culture nourishes unsustainable business practices with the pretence that it is not. Similar observations may apply to Olympus. In the cases concerning NewsCorp and Barclays it is evident that both have suffered as a consequence of a corrosive culture of securing business and competitive advantage at any costs and the failure of NEDs to secure any effective countervailing influence. This has resulted in deep seated indifference to the law and the public trust upon which their businesses depend.

CASE 1

The Tesco Case

Remember as you read this case that it represents as far as possible facts that have been reported. Nothing has been invented. Nothing has been intentionally distorted. The aim of the case is two-fold: to provide insight into the public affairs of a large and influential public company, and to enable readers to develop insights into the company's governance processes and draw defensible conclusions. The company concerned has not been consulted over the content and perspective the case provides.

10.1.1   The Background

Tesco PLC is a British multinational grocery and general merchandise retailer. It is the third-largest retailer in the world measured by revenues (after Wal-Mart (US) and Carrefour (France)). It is the second-largest measured by profits after Wal-Mart. It has stores in 14 countries across Asia, Europe and North America Malaysia, the Republic of Ireland and Thailand. It is the grocery market leader in the UK where it has a market share of around 30% of the total,

The company was founded in 1919 by Jack Cohen. The first Tesco store opened in 1929. The business expanded rapidly. By 1939 there were over 100 Tesco stores across the country. Since the early 1990s Tesco has increasingly diversified geographically and into areas such as the retailing of books, clothing, electronics, furniture, petrol and software; and more recently into financial services, telecoms and internet services, DVD rental and music downloads.

During the 1990s Tesco repositioned itself from a *pile 'em high, sell 'em cheap* downmarket retailer, to one with appeal across a wide social spectrum. This strategy has been highly successful though there have been serious recent trading setbacks. The chain grew from 500 stores in the mid-1990s to 2,500 stores by 2005. Tesco is listed on the LSE (London Stock Exchange) and is a constituent of the FTSE 100 Index. It had a recent market capitalisation of approximately £25bn.

10.1.2 Corporate Social Responsibility

Tesco claims it is deeply committed to CSR. It contributed 1.87% of its pre tax profits in 2006 to charities and local community organisations. This compares favourably with Marks & Spencer at 1.51% but not well with Sainsbury's 7.02%. Tesco has been praised in some quarters for leading the debate on CSR. In 1992, it launched a *computers for schools scheme*, offering computers in return for schools and hospitals financed by vouchers from people who shopped at Tesco. Up to 2004, £92 million of equipment had been supplied to these organisations. Recent turnover of around £50bn and profits before tax of around £3bn helps to put the *computers for schools scheme* into perspective. It represents around 0.2% of turnover.

In 2009 Tesco used the slogan *Change for Good* as advertising. This phrase is trade marked by UNICEF for charity usage but not for commercial or retail use. It prompted the UN agency to state,

> *It is the first time in UNICEF's history that a commercial entity has purposely set out to capitalise on one of our campaigns and subsequently damage an income stream which several of our programmes for children are dependent on."* UNICEF *went on to call on the public "...who have children's welfare at heart, to consider carefully who they support when making consumer choices".*

Tesco's also claims that it own labels for personal care and household products are *cruelty free*. This means that they are not tested on animals. These claims are widely disputed. There is no independent verification of the status of products from which Tesco's products are derived.

On the environmental responsibility front a 2011 Greenpeace report reveals that Tesco supermarkets in China were selling vegetables that contained illegal pesticides or at levels exceeding the legal limit. A green vegetable sample from Tesco revealed methamidophos and monocrotophos, the use of which has been prohibited in China since the beginning of 2007. How did that happen?

In May 2007, it was revealed that Tesco had moved the head office of its online operations to Switzerland. This allows it to sell CDs, DVDs and electronic games through its web site without charging VAT. The operation had previously been run from Jersey, but had been closed by the Jersey authorities who feared damage to the island's reputation. In June 2008, the British government announced that it was closing a tax loophole being used by Tesco. The scheme, identified by British magazine *Private Eye*, utilises offshore holding companies in Luxembourg and partnership agreements to reduce corporation tax liability by up to £50m annually. Another scheme involved depositing £1 billion in a Swiss partnership, and then loaning out that money to overseas Tesco stores, so that profit could be transferred covertly disguised as interest payments. This scheme is still in operation and is estimated to be costing the British exchequer up to £20 million a year in corporation tax. How can this be squared with their CSR claims elsewhere?

10.1.3   Influencing Government

According to Red Star Research, in the late 1990s Tesco executives featured on six government task forces, more than for any single company and far more than the other supermarket chains. John Longworth, group trading, law and technical director of Tesco PLC, sits on the Government Advisory Committee on Packaging Waste and Recycling. He is also one of nine commissioners of the Health and Safety Commission. Lucy Neville Rolfe, a former Treasury Official is Tesco's Director of Group Corporate Affairs, also sits on Government various committees. Her husband, during this time, was Permanent Secretary of Department of Agriculture.

Tesco was a £12m sponsor of the Millennium Dome. It was reported in The Observer newspaper, at the time, that a lobbying firm, LLM was involved in a campaign on behalf of Tesco to block plans for a tax on shopping centre car parks. It suggested 'that a £12 million Tesco donation to the Millennium Dome was part of a 'quid pro quo deal' for giving its support to the project'. The paper went on to say that there is no suggestion that Tesco made the Dome donation to help it get its way over the car park tax issue. But the plan to impose the tax was dropped from the subsequent White Paper on transport. The Sunday Times later stated that the estimated cost to Tesco of the car park tax, had it been approved, would have been £40m.

10.1.4   Cause Related Marketing

Tesco, along with most other supermarkets, is a member of the Freight Transport Association, a lobby group representing the interests of road hauliers. The FTA campaigns against restrictions on heavy vehicles travelling through residential areas at night, against restrictions on the size of heavy vehicles. It has also pressed for increases in the speed limit for large heavy vehicles on small country roads. In June 2004, Tesco co-signed a letter to the Chancellor calling on him to increase transport spending and 'fund the widening of the most congested parts of our key Trade Routes: the M1, M25, M4, M6, and M62'.

Tesco is a member of the British Retail Consortium (BRC), and regularly attends the BRC and the Scottish Retail Consortium (SRC) Summer Parliamentary receptions. Guests were given weighty going-home bags courtesy of Tesco and others. John Longworth, group trading, law and technical director of Tesco PLC, sits on several British Retail Consortium policy committees. Michael Wemms, a former Tesco director who went on to become chairman of House of Fraser, is the new chair of the British Retail Consortium.

Tesco is a high profile sponsor of Cancer Research UK (CRUK) Race for Life. It became a lead sponsor of the annual fundraising run in 2002, generating around 22% of the total £17m of funds. It undertook a large-scale recruitment campaign to encourage women to participate, supported through extensive TV, radio and in-store promotion. CRUK says the involvement gave the event a high street presence, with awareness among Tesco customers increasing from 14% in February 2002 to 39% in August. Funds raised by Tesco employees were topped up by 20% by the Tesco Charity Trust, resulting in a total contribution of £646,627. The company also delivered 55,055 of the 254,726 runners in 2002. 16,743 of these were staff members. This helped CRUK to exceed its participation targets.

10.1.5   Education and what the Educators think

Here's how one commentator views Tesco's involvement in education

> *'The school of the future will be franchised, branded and sponsored. To you [teachers at their annual conference] it is a nightmare prospect. To New Labour [the then British Labour Government] it represents progress, modernisation and the future.'*

> *'The prime minister wants schools to be run like Tesco stores. We'll have special offers. Two chemistry lessons for the price of one...'*

Doug McAvoy, General Secretary of the National Union of Teachers (2004)

Tesco began its Computers for Schools scheme in 1990. On a similar theme, to celebrate the Millennium, Tesco ran a project (now dropped) called Tesco SchoolNet 2000. It was billed as the world's biggest schools internet project. Thousands of children from more than 8,000 schools around the country created a unique record of the community life in the UK, 'a Doomsday Book for the 21st Century' based on the national curriculum. Tesco provided curriculum support materials, 52 advisory teachers, 340 internet centres in Tesco stores, 17 internet centres in libraries in areas where there are no Tesco stores and a help team. Schools booked into the internet centres where they could upload pupils' work onto the website. This work was showcased in the Learning Zone at the Millenium Dome.

Education Action Zones (EAZs) were initially local partnerships between groups of schools, businesses, parents, local education authorities and others designed to boost standards in challenging areas. These are now being transformed into Excellence in Cities Action Zones (EiCAZs) or Excellence Clusters. Tesco has been involved in these 'public private partnerships'. Sponsored projects included a school tour of the local supermarket in the Digby Granby and Toxteth (of Liverpool) EAZ.

10.1.6 Targeting Children and Influencing Education

Marketing experts reckon that if you start kids early on brand recognition you've got them hooked for life. In recent years, many corporations have moved into schools offering educational materials, events and competitions, as well as supplying schools with technology in exchange for high company visibility.

Since 1992 Tesco has been running the Computers for Schools scheme, whereby tokens on certain products (Walkers' crisps, Tetley tea and McVitie's biscuits) or with any purchase of over £10 at a Tesco store can be exchanged for computer equipment for local schools. Tesco is very proud of this scheme. In October 2000 it was awarded the Nestle Social Commitment prize at the Food and Industry Awards. However, parents and teachers have expressed concerns over the way the scheme encourages children to be brand-conscious consumers at an early age in order to get hold of the equipment their school needs.

A report by Which the British consumer magazine in 2001 showed that under the Tesco Computers for Schools scheme 21,990 vouchers were needed to buy a personal computer costing around £1,000. Parents would have to spend close on £250,000 to obtain the necessary vouchers.[2] Voucher schemes mean that pressure is put on parents to buy particular brands and shop in particular shops. This can cause additional financial difficulty for less well-off parents who might not normally shop there or choose to spend their income on junk food. It also puts pressure on pupils whose parents choose not to participate in a scheme. The provision of school equipment by corporations not only raises corporate brand awareness (the computers have Tesco's logos on them) but also lets the government off the hook, ultimately facilitating less spending on schools. The National Union of Teachers has voiced concerns about schools' creeping reliance on corporations for the provision of essential equipment.

There are also concerns that most of the products blessed with free computer vouchers come into the category of junk food. Children may learn about nutrition at school, but the next day in assembly they will be encouraged to buy as many crisps, biscuits and fizzy drinks as they can to enable them to get a computer. Tesco's statement on this is cynical:

> *All products are clearly labelled and if a shopper should have any health concerns they should directly contact the producer concerned*

Tesco also points out that customers do not have to buy the marked products to get tokens; rather than spending 35p on a packet of crisps, they can spend £10 on any purchase from Tesco and get a token worth the same amount.

10.1.7   Universities

Research Tesco sponsors the Tesco Centre for Organic Agriculture at the University of Newcastle on Tyne to provide research and development support for the UK organic food industry. A five year £450,000 sponsorship has been given to focus on a range of research, from organic crop rotation to livestock nutrition. Tesco works with a similar project at the University of Aberdeen.

Tesco provides core sponsorship for the 'Food Animal Initiative', based primarily at the University of Oxford, which develops new farming practices that are 'welfare friendly, food safe and environmentally sustainable'. Tesco also sponsored a Masters course in Strategic Communications at UMIST, along with Burson Marsteller and British American Tobacco. This course, the MSc in Corporate Communications and Reputation Management is now offered on a full time basis at Manchester Business School.

10.1.8   Training in Partnership

Since 1999, Tesco has run a Business Improvement Programme at Manchester Business School (MBS) for management staff. In October 2001, Tesco and the University of

Westminster pledged to work together over the only degree-recognised centre of excellence for Merchandise Planning. Tesco offers paid work placements and commercial rounding to 5 undergraduates in the second year of the course.

Tesco managers at distribution centres have the opportunity to study through the Institute of Logistics and Transport. Tesco has two Lifelong Learning Centres – at Welham Green Distribution Centre in Hertfordshire and Fennylock Distribution centre in Milton Keynes, where employees can sign up for e-learning through Learndirect.

10.1.9   Farming

Tesco has been accused of putting profit before people and the environment, despite the claims in its Annual Report and CSR report. It is claimed that Tesco continues to make huge profits at the expense of farmers, communities and the environment. Tesco is abusing the power that results from its huge market share (25.8%). Friends of the Earth and GAFF (Grassroots Action on Food and Farming) have called upon the government to:

- legislate to ensure that retailers trade fairly with their suppliers by imposing a new stricter Code of Practice on the biggest supermarkets, and appoint a watchdog with teeth to ensure it is being complied with
- stop any further consolidation of power.

Friends of the Earth is also seeking changes in Company Law so that communities can hold companies like Tesco to account for their impacts.

Tesco says:

> We have a long-standing commitment to source as much UK produce as possible". Tesco refers to its "commitment to UK farming" and claims that it has "consistently supported British farmers over recent years. As our business has grown, so has that of our suppliers. We have developed long term working relationships with our suppliers and by working together to meet customer needs we have both grown our market share.

Michael Hart chairman of the Small and Family Farm Alliance says that the increasing gap between farm gate and retail prices is in some cases down to "clear profiteering". For example, in 1991 the farm gate price of potatoes was 9p per Kg and the retail price was 30p; a 21 pence difference and a 233.5% mark up. In 2000 the farm gate price was 9p per

Kg but the retail price was 47p per Kg; the difference now being 38 pence – a huge mark-up of 425%. The same applies to the cauliflower farm gate price of 24p in both 1990 and 2000 with a retail price of 73p in 1990 and 98p in 2000; an extra 25p per cauliflower and a profit increase of 35%.

Michael Hart comments further:

> *Both of these products require no processing other than grading and packing, both of which are done by the farmers before being put on the supermarket shelf, so clearly the increase in the farm gate to retail difference is due to supermarkets wishing to increase profit margins at the farmers expense. This is a clear abuse of their power in the food chain and a practice which is and will cause severe damage to UK farming*

He argues that British farmers have delivered the higher and higher standards demanded by supermarkets but have been rewarded for doing so by supermarkets forcing down farm gate prices to levels which cause immense hardship among farming families, to the extent that agricultural charities are now paying out record levels of support for farming families and the number claiming state benefits are at previously unseen levels.

> *The low farm gate prices being paid to farmers by supermarkets he argues are destroying any chance we have of a sustainable farming system in Britain. Without profitable farming the environment, landscape and rural communities suffer. It is clear that supermarkets are using their near monopoly position in the food chain to make excess profits at the expense of both farmers and consumers*

Peter Lundgren is a Sussex dairy farmer's son and has a 95-acre arable farm in Lincolnshire. His farm is worked by contractors while Peter and his wife run a more profitable retail business. Peter was a founding member of the Family Farm Alliance. Responding to Tesco's claims about supporting UK farmers Lundgren comments:

> *Supermarkets are using their dominance of the food chain to fleece both the farmer and the consumer. And for what? Short term short-sighted profit. Tesco claims to care about its farmer suppliers but their pricing policy is not just damaging family farmers, it is also damaging the environment and rural communities as well. The farming industry is losing over 11 farmers a day; farmers who created and maintain the British countryside, and who support the rural economy and the rural communities. The loss of these farmers will mean the loss of so much more besides. It's time for Tesco to put its money where its mouth*

is and initiate policies that ensure UK farmers receive a fair farm gate price for producing safe wholesome food to the high welfare and high environmental standards demanded by the consumer

In the wake of the horsemeat food scandal where horsemeat has entered to the food chain without consumers being informed Tesco's response in a series of high profile adverts is set out below.

10.1.10   **Tesco's Poetic Public Response**

The problem we've had with some of our meat lately
Is about more than burgers and Bolognese.
It's about some of the ways we get meat to your dinner table.
It's about the whole food industry.
And it has made us realise, we really do need to make it better.
We've been working on it, but we need to
keep going, go further, move quicker.
We know that our supply chain is too complicated.
So we're making it simpler.
We know that the more we work with British farmers the better.
We've already made sure that all our beef is from the UK and Ireland.
And now we're moving on to our fresh chickens.
By July, they'll all be from UK farms too. No exceptions.
For farmers to do what they do best,
they need to know they've got our support.
We know this because of the work we've been doing
With our dairy farmers to make sure they always get paid
Above the market price.
We know that, no matter what you spend,
Everyone deserves to eat well.
We know that all this will only work if we are
Open about what we do.
And if you're not happy, tell us.
Seriously.
That is it.
We are changing

TESCO Evening Standard, London 28 February 2013

As a footnote in the affairs of Tesco - in September 2014 it was disclosed that profits in the corporation had been grossly overstated by around £400bn (£656m).

Tasks

1. 'Too often, corporate responsibility has existed at the level of rhetoric, while employers have struggled to spell out how it will change the way business is done. It has thus become easy to paint it as 'pure spin'. How does the statement help us to understand how Tesco positions itself in terms of its CSR?

2. Is it appropriate for a company like Tesco to assume that the way it operates and the cultural values it nurtures are appropriate for effective education?

3. Why does Tesco place such importance on lobbying government and ensuring that key employees have had experience of government?

4. What level of board *buy*-in is detectable from the conduct of Tesco's CSR activities?

5. Are you able to assess how much turnover from Tesco's customers is needed to support the computers in schools scheme?

6. What does the expression in the case "buy one get one free" mean exactly?

7. How would you characterise Tesco's relationship with the food industry that supplies its products?

8. How does the Tesco business model work in terms of its relationship with suppliers?

9. How do you view the farming industry's comments on Tesco?

10. What do you make of the response of Tesco to the latest food industry crisis in which traces of undeclared horsemeat has entered the food chain?

Key Concepts:

Board Buy-In; Authentication; Verification; Ethical Behaviour; Control of Public Institutions; Greenwash; Supply Chains; Public Accountability; Business Model

CASE 2

The Goldman Sachs Case

"The Great Vampire Squid"

Remember as you read this case that it represents, as far as possible, facts that have been reported. Nothing has been invented. Nothing has been intentionally distorted. The aim of the case is two-fold: to provide insight into the public affairs of a large and influential public company, and to enable readers to develop insights into the company's governance processes and draw defensible conclusions. The company concerned has not been consulted over the content and perspective the case provides.

10.2.1   The History

The Goldman Sachs Group, Inc. is an American multinational investment banking firm. It engages in global investment banking, securities, investment management, and other financial services primarily with institutional clients. It generated net revenues of around $34bn in 2012.

The firm was founded in 1869. It is headquartered at 200 West Street in the Lower Manhattan area of New York City, with additional offices in the major international financial centres including London. The firm provides mergers and acquisitions advice, underwriting services, asset management, and prime brokerage to its clients. Clients include corporations, governments and individuals.

The firm also engages in market making and private equity deals, and as a primary dealer in the United States Treasury security market. It is recognised as one of the premier investment banks in the world. It sparked controversy over its alleged improper practices, in the events leading up to the global financial crisis and since. These matters are explored below.

10.2.2 Goldman's influence and profile

Former Goldman executives have held high level government positions. Robert Rubin and Henry (Hank) Paulson both served as US Treasury Secretary under Presidents Bill Clinton and George W. Bush, respectively. Other former executives include Mark Carney, the former governor of the Bank of Canada who is now the Governor of the Bank of England. Mario Draghi a former Governor of the Banca D'Italia in Rome is now governor of the ECB (European Central Bank). Former Goldman employees have headed the New York Stock Exchange, the World Bank, and firms such as Citigroup and Merrill Lynch.

One of the most important events in the firm's history was its own IPO in 1999. The decision to go public was one that the partners debated for decades. In the end, Goldman decided to offer only a small portion of the company to the public, with some 48% still held by the partnership pool. A further 22% of the company was held by non-partner employees, and 18% was held by retired Goldman partners and two long time investors. This left around 12% of the company as being held by the public. Hank (Henry) Paulson became Chairman and CEO of the firm[3].

In 1999, Goldman acquired Hull Trading Company, one of the world's premier market-making firms, for $531m. More recently, the firm has been busy both in investment banking and in trading activities. It purchased Spear, Leeds, & Kellogg, one of the largest specialist firms on the New York Stock Exchange, for $6.3bn in September 2000. It also advised on a debt offering for the Government of China. In 2009 The Private Wealth Management arm of JBWere, a Goldman's earlier acquisition was sold into a joint venture with National Australia Bank. Goldman opened a full-service broker-dealer in Brazil in 2007, having set up an investment banking office in 1996. It expanded its investments into a wide number of companies. The firm is also heavily involved in energy trading, including oil, on both a principal and agent basis.

10.2.3   The global financial crisis

During the 2007 subprime mortgage crisis, Goldman was able to profit from the collapse in subprime mortgage bonds in the summer of 2007. It did so by short-selling subprime mortgage-backed securities. Two Goldman traders, Michael Swenson and Josh Birnbaum, are credited with bearing responsibility for the firm's large profits during America's sub-prime mortgage crisis. The pair, members of Goldman's structured products group in New York, made a profit of $4bn by "betting" on a collapse in the sub-prime market, and shorting mortgage-related securities. By summer of 2007, they persuaded colleagues to see their point of view and talked around sceptical risk management executives.

The firm initially avoided large subprime write-downs, and achieved a net profit due to significant losses on non-prime securitised loans being offset by gains on short mortgage positions. Its sizeable profits made during the initial subprime mortgage crisis led the New York Times to proclaim that Goldman Sachs is peerless in the world of finance. The firm's viability was later called into question as the crisis intensified in September 2008.

On 15 October 2007, as the crisis had begun to unravel, Allan Sloan, a senior editor for Fortune magazine, said:

> So let's reduce this macro story to human scale. Meet GSAMP Trust 2006-S3, a $494 million drop in the junk-mortgage bucket, part of the more than half-a-trillion dollars of mortgage-backed securities issued last year. We found this issue by asking mortgage mavens[4] to pick the worst deal they knew of that had been floated by a top-tier firm – and this one's pretty bad. It was sold by Goldman Sachs.

> This issue, which is backed by ultra-risky second-mortgage loans, contains all the elements that facilitated the housing bubble and bust. It's got speculators searching for quick gains in hot housing markets; it's got loans that seem to have been made with little or no serious analysis by lenders; and finally, it's got Wall Street, which churned out mortgage "product" because buyers wanted it. As they say on the Street, "When the ducks quack, feed 'em".

10.2.4   Consequences of the crisis on Wall Street

In September 2008, Goldman Sachs and Morgan Stanley, the last two major investment banks in the United States, both confirmed that they would become traditional bank holding companies, bringing an end to the era of investment banking on Wall Street. The Federal Reserve's approval of their bid to become banks ended the ascendancy of the securities firms, 75 years after Congress separated them[5] from deposit-taking lenders, and capped weeks of chaos that sent Lehman Brothers into bankruptcy and led to the rushed sale of Merrill Lynch & Co. To Bank of America Corporation.

In September 2008, Berkshire Hathaway agreed to purchase $5bn in Goldman's preferred stock, and also received warrants to buy another $5bn in Goldman's common stock, exercisable for a five-year term. Goldman also received a $10bn preferred stock investment from the US Treasury in October 2008, as part of the Troubled Asset Relief Program (TARP). Andrew Cuomo, then Attorney General of New York, questioned Goldman's decision to pay 953 employees bonuses of at least $1m each after it received TARP funds in 2008. In that same period, however, CEO Lloyd Blankfein and six other senior executives opted to forgo bonuses, stating they believed it was the right thing to do, in light of "the fact that we are part of an industry that's directly associated with the ongoing economic distress". Cuomo called the move "appropriate and prudent", and urged the executives of other banks to follow the firm's lead and refuse bonus payments.

In June 2009, Goldman Sachs repaid the US Treasury's TARP investment, with 23% interest (in the form of $318m in preferred dividend payments and $1.418bn in warrant redemptions). On 18 March 2011, Goldman Sachs acquired Federal Reserve approval to buy back Berkshire's preferred stock in Goldman. In December 2009, Goldman announced their top 30 executives will be paid year-end bonuses in restricted stock, with claw back provisions for five years.

10.2.5   Use of Federal Reserve's Emergency Liquidity Programmes

During the 2008 Financial Crisis, the Federal Reserve introduced a number of short-term credit and liquidity facilities to help stabilise markets. Some of the transactions under these facilities provided liquidity to institutions whose disorderly failure could have severely stressed an already fragile financial system. Goldman Sachs was one of the heaviest users of these loan facilities, taking out numerous loans between 18 March 2008 – 22 April 2009.

The Primary Dealer Credit Facility (PDCF), the first Fed facility ever to provide overnight loans to investment banks, loaned Goldman Sachs a total of $589bn against collateral such as corporate market instruments and mortgage-backed securities. The Term Securities Lending Facility (TSLF), which allows primary dealers to borrow liquid Treasury securities for one month in exchange for less liquid collateral, loaned Goldman Sachs a total of $193bn. Goldman Sachs's borrowings totalled $782bn in hundreds of transactions over these months. This number is a total of all transactions over time and not the outstanding loan balance. The loans have been fully repaid in accordance with the terms of the facilities.

10.2.6   Goldman's Financial Performance

In 2009, Goldman Sachs employed 31,701 people worldwide. The firm reported earnings of US$9.34bn and record earnings per share of $19.69. It was reported that the average total compensation per employee was $622,000. However, this number represents the arithmetic mean of total compensation and is highly skewed upwards as several hundred of the top recipients command the majority of the Bonus Pools, leaving the median that most employees receive well below this number.

In Business Week's recent release of the *Best Places to Launch a Career 2008*, Goldman Sachs was ranked No.4 out of 119 total companies on the list. The current Chief Executive Officer is Lloyd C. Blankfein. The company ranks No.1 in Annual Net Income when compared with 86 peers in the Investment Services sector. Blankfein received a $67.9m bonus in his first year. He chose to receive "some" cash unlike his predecessor, Paulson, who chose to take his bonus entirely in company stock. Investors have been complaining that the bank has near 11,000 more staffers than it did in 2005, but the performance of workers was drastically in decline.

In 2011, Goldman's 33,300 employees generated $28.8bn in revenue and $2.5bn in profit. This represents a 25 percent decline in revenue per worker and a 71 percent decline in profit per worker compared with 2005. The staff cuts in its trading and investment banking divisions are possible as the company continues to reduce costs to raise profitability. In 2011, the company cut 2,400 positions.

10.2.7   Corporate citizenship

Goldman Sachs has received favourable press coverage for conducting business and implementing internal policies related to reversing global climate change. According to the company website, the Goldman Sachs Foundation has given $114m in grants since 1999, with the goal of promoting youth education worldwide.

The company also has been on Fortune Magazine's 100 Best Companies to Work For list since the list was launched in 1998, with emphasis placed on its support for employee philanthropic efforts. The 2013 list cited the reason that the reported average annual compensation for an employee was more than $300,000. In November 2007, Goldman Sachs established a donor advised fund called *Goldman Sachs Gives* that donates to charitable organizations around the world, while increasing their maximum employee donation match to $20,000. The firm's Community TeamWorks is an annual, global volunteering initiative that in 2007 gave over 20,000 Goldman employees a day off work from May through August to volunteer in a team-based project organized with a local *not for profit* organisation. In March 2008, Goldman launched the 10,000 Women initiative to train 10,000 women from predominantly developing countries in business and management.

In November 2009, Goldman pledged $500 million to aid small businesses in their newly created 10,000 Small Businesses initiative. The initiative aims to provide 10,000 small businesses with assistance – ranging from business and management education and mentoring to lending and philanthropic support. The networking will be offered through partnerships with national and local business organizations, as well as employees of Goldman Sachs. In addition to Goldman CEO Lloyd Blankfein, Berkshire Hathaway's Warren Buffett and Harvard Business School professor Michael Porter will chair the programme's advisory council.

10.2.8   Lloyd Blankfein on fiduciary duty

In his testimony to the January 2012 FCIC (Federal Crisis Inquiry Commission) Lloyd Blankfein testified that in the firm's market making activities "we represent the other side of what people want to do. We are not a fiduciary. We are not an agent. Of course, we have an obligation to fully disclose what an instrument is and to be honest in our dealings, but we are not managing somebody else's money"

Goldman was dealing with institutional clients, not retail clients, in connection with the civil charges brought by the SEC. However, it has been argued that the caveat emptor (investor beware) principle does not sit well with the notion of Goldman as trusted advisor. It does threaten the basis of commonplace understandings about fiduciary duty.

Tasks

1. What conclusions can we draw from Blankfein's and the judiciary's comments on fiduciary duty?

2. What safeguards are there in place in terms of NEDs on the board of Goldman Sachs?

3. What are the principal cultural and ethical problems that arise with the events that attributed to Goldman Sachs in the run up to the global financial crisis?

4. Was it ethical or commercially efficient for Goldman Sachs to decide to pay $1m in bonuses to almost a thousand executives of the company following the injection of capital by Berkshire Hathaway?

5. Evaluate Goldman Sachs' claim in respect of its Corporate Citizenship initiatives?

6. What happens if the principles governing fiduciary duties are undermined the way they have been by Blankfein's declaration to the Congressional Committee?

7. How does the declaration of Blankfein's position regarding fiduciary duty fit alongside Goldman's use of the Federal Reserve's Emergency Liquidity Programmes?

8. How far were Goldman Sachs involved in the triggering of the global financial crisis?

Key Concepts:

Fiduciary Duties, Ethical Behaviour, Corporate Citizenship, Corporate Integrity; Public Influence and Control, Accountability

CASE 3

The Olympus Corporation

Remember as you read this case that it represents, as far as possible, facts that have been reported. Nothing has been invented. Nothing has been intentionally distorted. The aim of the case is two-fold: to provide insight into the public affairs of a large and influential public company, and to enable readers to develop insights into the company's governance processes and draw defensible conclusions. The company concerned has not been consulted over the content and perspective the case provides.

10.3.1   The History

The Olympus Corporation (*Orinpasu Kabushiki-gaisha*) is a Japan-based publicly traded company that manufactures optics and reprography products. Olympus was established in 1919, initially specialising in the microscope and thermometer businesses. Its global headquarters are in Shinjuku, Tokyo, Japan. Its US operations are based in Centre Valley, Pennsylvania. Its European operations are based in Hamburg, Germany.

The 2011 Annual Report states that, Olympus is governed by a 15-person board of directors. Tsuyoshi Kikukawa is its President and CEO with Tsuyoshi Kikukawa as

Chairman. The Board has three *outside directors*. It has a four-member 'Board of Auditors' which supervises and audits directors' performance. The company's executive committee consists of 28 members, responsible for day-to-day operations.

10.3.2   The Woodford controversy

Michael Woodford, an Olympus veteran of 30-years, was previously Executive Managing Director of Olympus Medical Systems Europe. After two weeks in his post of CEO, the board suddenly removed him as chief executive whilst allowing him to retain his board seat. Woodford alleged that his removal was linked to questions he raised in respect of several prior acquisitions. This included the $2.2bn deal in 2008 to acquire British medical equipment maker Gyrus. Thomson Reuters revealed that $687m was paid to a middle-man as a success fee – a sum equal to 31% of the purchase price - which ranks as the highest ever M&A fee.

Shareholding in Olympus is dispersed, and the company's key institutional investors are largely passive. As of end March 2011, investors included Nippon Life Insurance (8.4%), Bank of Tokyo-Mitsubishi (4.98%), Sumitomo Mitsui Banking (3.13%), and the Government of Singapore Investment Corporation (2.55%). Foreign institutions and individuals otherwise control 27.7% of Olympus shares.

Shareholders expressed concern, however, after Olympus share price almost halved in value following the Woodford revelations, and asked for "prompt action". Following his dismissal, Woodford passed on information to the British Serious Fraud Office, and requested police protection. He said the payments may have been linked to "forces behind" the Olympus board. The Japanese newspaper *Sankei* suggest that a total of $1.5bn in acquisition-related advisory payments could be linked to the Yakuza (a Japanese underworld organisation).

10.3.3   The problem with the board

The company responded on 19 October that "major differences had arisen between Mr. Woodford and other management regarding the direction and conduct of the company's business". On the Gyrus acquisition, it also declared the Audit Board's view that "no dishonesty or illegality is found in the transaction itself or any breach of obligation to good management or any systematic errors by the directors recognised." Mr Woodford was thereafter ousted.

He claims that there was a web of conspiracy to cover up certain transactions and fees paid in the acquisition of several businesses. The claim made is that Olympus paid $687m in advisory fees for the purchase of a British medical instruments company. The fees were paid to a firm incorporated in the Cayman Islands and another in New York neither of which can now be traced. Olympus also paid 100 times pre tax earnings for the purchase of the company in question. When the new CEO sought explanations for these transactions he was summarily dismissed by a unanimous decision of the board headed by the then Japanese Chairman.

Tasks

1. What role did the board of directors of Olympus play in monitoring and preventing the unlawful activities of other directors within the business? What sort of powers would they need to monitor these matters?

2. How far was the Board itself conflicted if the Chairman himself had authorised the unlawful payments.

3. Why did the Board decide to sack Mr Woodford after his appointment yet allowed him to remain on the Board?

4. What role did the shareholders play in challenging the actions of the Board once the scandal emerged?

5. Could this type of behaviour have continued unchallenged had there been an independent supervisory board? How do think a supervisory board would have handled the incident?

6. What is the significance of the bribe paid? What do we learn from the practice of bribing?

7. As a non Japanese speaker how could Mr Woodford possibly have played an effective role as CEO?

8. Why is there a reference to sums paid to a Japanese criminal organisation? Why would these payments have been made?

Key Concepts:

Fiduciary Duties; Ethical Behaviour; Independent Supervision; Audit, Independent Directors.

CASE 4

NewsCorp

Remember as you read this case that it represents, as far as possible, facts that have been reported. Nothing has been invented. Nothing has been intentionally distorted. The aim of the case is two-fold: to provide insight into the public affairs of a large and influential public company, and to enable readers to develop insights into the company's governance processes and draw defensible conclusions. The company concerned has not been consulted over the content and perspective the case provides.

10.4.1   The History

News Corp was created in 1979 by Rupert Murdoch as a holding company for News Limited. News Limited was created in 1923 in Adelaide; subsequently the controlling interest was bought by The Herald and Weekly Times. In 1949, Sir Keith Murdoch took control of The Adelaide News. When he died in 1952, his son Rupert inherited a controlling interest in an Adelaide afternoon tabloid, The News. From this his global empire was built.

10.4.2　　　　　　　　The Unfolding Scandal

The News Corporation scandal developed in mid year 2011. It did so out of a series of investigations following up the (British) News of the World royal phone hacking scandal between 2005 and 2007. Initially it seemed that the scandal was limited to a single journalist at News Corporation subsidiary the *News of the World*. Clive Goodman was jailed in 2007 for his actions. The then editor of the newspaper Andy Coulson also resigned though he denied any wrong-doing. He offered his resignation apparently on the grounds that the events had occurred on his watch. He was thereafter appointed head of Communications of the Conservative LibDem Coalition government in 2007 where he remained until he resigned in January 2011 given the scale of enquiries into the affairs of the News of the World being investigated.

Thereafter police and other enquiries revealed a much wider pattern of wrongdoing. This led to the resignation on 15 July 2011, of Rebekah Brooks. She was chief executive of News International and was widely criticised for her role in the controversy. On 17 July 2011, she was arrested on suspicion of conspiring to intercept communications and on suspicion of making corrupt payments to public officials. On 13 March 2012, she was again arrested on suspicion of conspiracy to pervert the course of justice.

On 15 May 2012, Brooks was charged with conspiracy to pervert the course of justice. Mrs Brooks said she was "baffled" by the decision to charge her. Mr Brooks, her husband, said he believed his wife had become "the subject of a witch-hunt". Rebekah Brooks and her husband appeared at Westminster Magistrates Court on 13 June 2012 on charges linked to the phone hacking scandal. The Judge told the defendants they would go on trial at a later date. The Brooks were remanded on bail.

The Crown Prosecution Service thereafter announced that Brooks would be charged, along with six other former members of the staff of the *News of the World*, with conspiring to intercept communications without lawful authority, from 3 October 2000 to 9 August 2006. Brooks was also charged with four specific counts of conspiracy to intercept communications without lawful authority. These include a charge relating to the hacking of the voicemail of a murdered schoolgirl Milly Dowler. The trial has been mostly settled. Coulson was found guilty of the main charges. Brooks, incredibly, was found not guilty of any criminal acts and acquitted.

10.4.3   Events in the US

Unlawful activities were not limited to Britain. News Corp owns a multitude of news outlets in the United States, including the *New York Post*, *The Wall Street Journal*, and the *Fox News Channel*. Several media critics have called for investigations into whether they too engaged in phone hacking activities. In addition to any possible illegal activities in the US News Corp and/or its executives might also face civil and criminal liability under the Foreign Corrupt Practices Act.

According to a former New York City police officer who spoke to the British newspaper *The Mirror* in 2009, the *News of the World* also attempted to retrieve private phone records of victims of the September 11 attack on the World Trade Centre in New York City In light of the suspected hacking, Senate Commerce Committee chairman Jay Rockefeller suggested that a US investigation of News Corporation should be launched. On 14 July, the Federal Bureau of Investigation announced it was launching an investigation into alleged hacking by News Corporation.

News Corp is also being investigated over claims that senior executives misled investors in 2011, causing the company's stock to be traded at an artificially high price. A US class action has been filed for investors who purchased News Corporation common stock between 3 March 2011, and 11 July 2011. On 11 July 2011, a group of shareholders led by Amalgamated Bank who were already suing News Corps over the purchase of Rupert Murdoch's daughter's media company, Shine Group, updated the lawsuit to include accusations that the board of News Corp failed to exercise proper oversight and take sufficient action since news of the hacking first surfaced at its subsidiary nearly six years ago.

On 13 September they added further charges concerning Floorgraphics a subsidiary of News Corp and the behaviour of another of News Corps subsidiary company NDS Group. The shareholders' attorney said that the phone hacking which took place in the UK was "part of a much broader, historic pattern of corruption at News Corp under the acquiescent eyes of a board that must have been fully aware of the wrongdoing, if not directly complicit in the actions.

In November 2012, it was reported that agents of News Corp had illegally bribed a member of the US military to obtain a photograph of an imprisoned Saddam Hussein wearing only his underwear. The photo was subsequently published in a News Corp outlet. Bribing public officials is a violation of the US law.

10.4.4   Events in Australia

In 2012 following a BBC Panorama report, allegations were made that News Corp subsidiary, News Datacom Systems (NDS) had used hackers to undermine pay TV rivals in Australia and elsewhere. Some of the victims of the alleged hacking, such as Austar were later taken over by News Corp. NDS had originally been set up to provide security to News Corp's pay TV interests but emails obtained by Fairfax Media revealed they had also pursued a wider agenda by distributing the keys to rival set top box operators and seeking to obtain phone records of suspected rivals. The emails were from the hard drive of NDS European chief, Ray Adams. In 2012 it was also revealed that Australian Federal police were working with UK police to investigate hacking by News Corp.

10.4.5   The case against NewsCorp

This is a story which carries with it profound implications for the governance arrangements. It is important to make clear that suspicions of wrong doing have risen to the very top of the News Corp, Rupert Murdoch, the Chairman. Whilst Mr Murdoch has not been charged there is ample circumstantial evidence that he was aware of what was going on in the *News of the World* and that he and his son James Murdoch almost certainly condoned if not encouraged the illegal activities. The Leveson Judicial Inquiry (chaired by Lord Leveson a Lord Justice of Appeal), was set up to explore the culture, practices and ethics of the British press following the News International phone hacking scandal. A series of public hearings were held throughout 2011 and 2012. The Inquiry heard evidence from Rupert Murdoch and his son James. They were evasive, forgetful and defensive throughout. The public perception was that they were untrustworthy and complicit in the events that had occurred.

Tasks

1. What role did the independent directors played in monitoring and preventing the unlawful activities of other managers and operatives within the business? What sort of powers would they need to monitor these matters? What evidence is there that they probed these issues at a time when there were many rumours about unlawful and corrupt behaviour within the group?

2. The Murdochs on several occasion in giving evidence have stated, inter alia, that their organisation was so large they could not possibly have been aware of all those matters of which the organisation has been accused. Whilst this is a standard defence in such

circumstances, given the close day-to-day personal relationship between Rupert Murdoch and Rebekah Brooks is it credible that he could have been aware of the culture of "doing business" within News International the British subsidiary? Were his actions in breach of his fiduciary duties to the company?

3. What role have shareholders had in their relationship with the Board of NewsCorp? Why did they ignore so many early suggestions that there was widespread wrongdoing within NewsCorp. They have lost value measured in $billions. How do they explain their own actions as institutional investors to the investors they in turn represent?

4. Could this type of behaviour have continued unchallenged had there been an independent supervisory board? How do think a supervisory board would have handled the incident?

Key Concepts:
Independent Directors; Board Supervision; Corruption; Unethical Behaviour; Accountability

CASE 5

The BP Case

Remember as you read this case that it represents, as far as possible, facts that have been reported. Nothing has been invented. Nothing has been intentionally distorted. The aim of the case is two-fold: to provide insight into the public affairs of a large and influential public company, and to enable readers to develop insights into the company's governance processes and draw defensible conclusions. The company concerned has not been consulted over the content and perspective the case provides.

10.5.1   The Background

BP Plc is a British multinational oil and gas company headquartered in London, England. It is the third-largest energy company and fifth-largest company in the world measured by 2012 revenues and is one of the six oil and gas *super majors*. It is vertically integrated and operates in all areas of the oil and gas industry, including exploration and production, refining, distribution and marketing, petrochemicals, power generation and trading. It also has renewable energy activities in biofuels and wind power.

As of December 2012, BP had operations in over 80 countries, produced around 3.3 million barrels per day of oil equivalent, had total proven commercial reserves of 17 billion barrels of oil equivalent and around 20,700 service stations. Its largest division is BP America, which is the second-largest producer of oil and gas in the United States. BP owns a 19.75% stake in the Russian oil major Rosneft, the world's largest publicly traded oil and gas company by hydrocarbon reserves and production. BP has a primary listing on the LSE (London Stock Exchange) and is a constituent of the FTSE 100 Index. It had a market capitalisation of £85.2bn in April 2013, the fourth-largest of any company listed on the exchange. It has secondary listings on the Frankfurt Stock Exchange and the New York Stock Exchange.

10.5.2   Environmental Record

BP has been involved in several major environmental and safety incidents, including the 2005 Texas City Refinery explosion which caused the death of 15 workers and resulted in a record-setting OSHA (Occupational Health and Safety Agency) fine and the 2006 Prudhoe Bay oil spill, the largest oil spill on Alaska's North Slope which resulted in a $25 million civil penalty, the largest per-barrel penalty at that time for an oil spill. In 2010 the Deepwater Horizon oil spill was the largest accidental release of oil into marine waters in the history of the petroleum industry, and resulted in severe environmental, health and economic consequences.

The company pleaded guilty to 11 counts of felony, manslaughter, two misdemeanours, and one felony count of lying to Congress and agreed to pay more than US$4.5bn in fines and penalties, the largest criminal resolution in US history. Further legal proceedings, which are not expected to conclude until 2014, are ongoing to determine payouts and fines under the Clean Water Act and the Natural Resources Damage Assessment. BP faces damages of up to $17.6bn.

10.5.3   Financial implications of the disaster

The Deepwater Horizon oil spill in April 2010 initiated a sharp decline in share prices, and BP's shares lost roughly 50% of their value in 50 days. BP's shares reached a low of $26.97 per share on 25 June 2010 totalling a $100 billion loss in market value before beginning to climb again. Shares value has declined steadily in the period since. In October 2014 they stood at 60% of their pre spill value.

On 22 March 2013, BP announced an $8 billion share repurchase programme. As of April 2013, $300 million was used, with a minimal impact to the share price. The buyback decision followed closure of the TNK-BP deal and it has to offset the dilution to earnings per share following the loss of dividends from TNK-BP. According to the company the buyback programme would provide shareholders near-term benefits from the reshaping of the company's Russian business. The buyback is also seen as a way to invest excess cash from the TNK-BP deal.

10.5.4   Extract from the Chairman's Report on the Incident

Investigation

Mark Bly–head of the Safety and Operations function–was asked by the then group chief executive to undertake an investigation aimed at analysing the chain of events surrounding the incident on the Deep water Horizon and to make recommendations to enable the prevention of a similar accident. The investigation team was tasked to work independently from other BP spill response activities and separately from any investigation conducted by other companies or investigation teams.

The Deepwater Horizon Accident Investigation Report (BP's Investigation Report) was published in September and outlined eight key findings relating to the causes of the accident.[6] The report did not identify any single action or in action that caused the accident and concluded that a complex and interlinked series of mechanical failures, human judgments, engineering design, operational implementation and team interfaces came together to allow the initiation and escalation of the accident. A series of 26 recommendations were developed to address each of the report's key findings and these have formed the basis of an action plan. The board tasked the group chief executive and senior management team to implement this action plan across BP and asked SEEAC (the Safety, Ethics and Environmental Assurance Committee) to oversee this process.

The board is monitoring the hearings of other, non-BP investigations and will consider how the conclusions from these investigations fit within the framework of findings and actions arising from BP's own report.

Internal initiatives

Following the accident, a number of internal initiatives have been commenced by executive management, with frequent reporting back to the board including examining what can be learnt to further improve BP's risk processes and the company's oversight of contractors. A number of these initiatives are still ongoing and will conclude in the course of 2011. As incoming chief executive, Bob Dudley announced that a new safety and risk division would be created (the Safety and Operational Risk Function) and that the Exploration and Production segment would be restructured from a single business into three functional divisions (Exploration, Developments and Production). Splitting the upstream business into separate functions is intended to foster the long-term development of specialist expertise and to reinforce accountability for risk management.

Reputation

During the crisis and afterwards, the board had extensive discussions about the reputational impact of the event, including how it might affect BP's licence to operate both in the US and elsewhere. This work continues to focus on BP's relationship with shareholders, governments, communities and indeed all those who come into contact with BP through its business operations. The chairman, the chief executive, the chairman of SEEAC and senior management have been actively involved in discussions with shareholders and other groups in an endeavour to address concerns and to start to rebuild trust.

Strategy

The events in the Gulf of Mexico led the board to undertake a review of strategy. Led by the Group chief executive and his team, the board attempted to address the key challenge of how to regain shareholder value and address core issues, including:

- Simplification (how to focus the company's operations across a wide geography).
- How the company could manage risk more tightly.
- How BP could focus on its core capabilities.
- The opportunity to reset the company's portfolio.

The board held three away-day discussions on strategy during the year; these were robust and explored a wide range of strategic options. The outcome of these deliberations on strategy was presented to the investor communityon1February2011.

Management and organisational changes

In late July 2011the board and Tony Hayward agreed that he would step down as group CEO on1 October, to be succeeded by Bob Dudley, and would leave the company and the board at the end of November. This decision was made following a series of extensive discussions by the board as to what strategic focus BP as a company should have in the longer term and what leadership was best equipped to embark on this next phase.

Through the nomination committee, the board engaged external advisers who identified an external candidate and existing executive director, Bob Dudley, for the position of group chief executive. After interviews and detailed consideration it was concluded that Bob Dudley had the strong industry, operational and geopolitical experience required for the role and, as a result, was appointed as group chief executive. Bob Dudley has handed over his duties as head of the Gulf Coast Restoration Organization to Lamar McKay, president and chairman of BP America.

In September the board agreed with Andy Inglis, executive director and head of the upstream business, that in order to facilitate the new organizational structure, he would relinquish his role and step down from the board at the end of October – leaving the company at the end of 2010. The executive vice presidents heading the three new upstream divisions report directly to Bob Dudley and the board decided that on the basis of this reporting line it would not replace Andy Inglis's position as an upstream executive director on the board. From 1 November 2010, executive director membership of the board has been reduced to three.

Tasks

1. What do we learn from the experience of BP in terms of its management of risk?

2. The Chairman's statement seems to present a picture of a company constantly recoiling from issues in the field of risk management which the Board does not appear to have full knowledge of. Is this a fair statement of the situation?

3. How do directors, including NEDs view their duty of care and their prime duty to protect the interests of the company?

4. How confident can we feel about the board's commitment to CSR? What evidence would we look for?

5. Is BP simply too big to effectively control it many diverse and high risk activities?

6. What can we learn from the events in BP about the company's culture?

Key Concepts:
Independent Directors; Board Supervision; Risk Management; Management Culture

CASE 6

Barclays Bank

Remember as you read this case that it represents, as far as possible, facts that have been reported. Nothing has been invented. Nothing has been intentionally distorted. The aim of the case is two-fold: to provide insight into the public affairs of a large and influential public company, and to enable readers to develop insights into the company's governance processes and draw defensible conclusions. The company concerned has not been consulted over the content and perspective the case provides.

10.6.1   The Background

Barclays PLC is a British multinational banking and financial services company headquartered in London, England. It is a universal bank with operations in retail, wholesale and investment banking, as well as wealth management, mortgage lending and credit cards. It has operations in over 50 countries and territories and has around 48 million customers. As of 31 December 2011 Barclays had total assets of US$2.42tr, the seventh-largest bank worldwide.

178

Barclays is organised within two business 'clusters', Corporate and Investment Banking, Wealth and Investment Management and Retail and Business Banking. The Corporate and Investment Banking, Wealth and Investment Management cluster comprises three business units: Corporate banking; Investment banking; and Wealth and investment management. The Retail and Business Banking cluster comprises four business units: Africa Retail and Business Banking (including the Absa Group); Barclaycard (credit card and loan provision); Europe Retail and Business Banking; and UK Retail and Business Banking. Barclays has a primary listing on the London Stock Exchange and is a constituent of the FTSE 100 Index.

10.6.2   The Libor Scandal

In June 2012, as a result of an international investigation, Barclays Bank was fined a total of £290m (US$450m) for attempting to manipulate the daily settings of the London Interbank Offered Rate (Libor) and the Euro Interbank Offered Rate (Euribor). The United States Department of Justice and Barclays officially agreed that "the manipulation of the submissions affected the fixed rates on some occasions". The bank was found to have made 'inappropriate submissions' of rates which formed part of the Libor and Euribor setting processes, sometimes to make a profit, and other times to make the bank look more secure during the financial crisis. This happened regularly between 2005 and 2009.

The BBC in London notes that the revelations concerning the fraud were "greeted with almost universal astonishment in the banking industry." The UK's Financial Services Authority (FSA), which levied a fine of £59.5m ($92.7m), gave Barclays the biggest fine it had ever imposed in its history. The FSA's director of enforcement described Barclays' behaviour as "completely unacceptable", adding "Libor is an incredibly important benchmark reference rate, and it is relied on for many, many hundreds of thousands of contracts all over the world." The bank's chief executive Bob Diamond decided to give up his bonus as a result of the fine. Liberal Democrat politician Lord Oakeshott criticised Diamond, saying: "If he had any shame he would go. If the Barclays board has any backbone, they'll sack him." The US Department of Justice has also been involved, with "other financial institutions and individuals" under investigation.

10.6.3   Lack of proper internal controls

The lack of specific internal controls, particularly in reviewing email communications, was one of the failures cited by a Commodity Futures Trading Commission regulatory order implementing its share of the Barclays settlement. The CFTC said Barclays lacked daily supervision and periodic reviews that could have detected the interest rate manipulation. "Appropriate daily supervision of the desk by the supervisors, as well as periodic review of the communications, should have discovered the conduct".

Barclays it is claimed by the CFTC lacked specific internal controls and procedures that would have enabled Barclays' management or compliance team to discover this conduct. Internal control is one of the principal means by which risk is managed. The Board should set appropriate policies on internal control and regularly assure itself that appropriate processes are functioning effectively to monitor the risks to which the company is exposed and that the system of internal control is effective in reducing those risks to an acceptable level. It is essential that the right tone is set at the top of the company. The Board should send out a clear message that control responsibilities must be taken seriously.

On 2 July 2012, Marcus Agius resigned from the chairman position following the interest rate scandal. On 3 July 2012, Bob Diamond resigned with immediate effect, leaving Marcus Agius to fill his post until a replacement is found. Within the space of a few hours, this was followed by the resignation of the Bank's Chief Operating Officer, Jerry del Missier. Barclays subsequently announced that Antony Jenkins, its existing Chief Executive of Global Retail & Business Banking, would become group chief executive on 30 August 2012.

10.6.4   Money Laundering

In March 2009, Barclays was accused of violating international anti-money laundering laws. According to the NGO Global Witness, the Paris branch of Barclays held the account of Equatorial Guinean President Teodoro Obiang's son, (Teodorin Obiang), even after evidence that Obiang had siphoned oil revenues from government funds emerged in 2004. According to Global Witness, Obiang purchased a Ferrari and maintains a mansion in Malibu with the funds from this account.

A 2010 report by the Wall Street Journal described how Credit Suisse, Barclays, Lloyds Banking Group, and other banks were involved in helping the Alavi Foundation, Bank Melli, the Iranian government, and/or others circumvent US laws banning financial transactions with certain states. They did this by 'stripping' information out of wire transfers, thereby concealing the source of funds. Barclays settled with the US authorities a fine of $298m.

10.6.5   Tax Avoidance

In March 2009, Barclays obtained an injunction against *The Guardian* to remove from its website confidential leaked documents describing how SCM, Barclays' structured capital markets division, planned to use more than £11bn of loans to create hundreds of millions of pounds of tax benefits, via an elaborate circuit of Cayman Islands companies, US partnerships and Luxembourg subsidiaries. In an editorial on the issue, *The Guardian* pointed out that, due to the mismatch of resources, tax-collectors (HMRC) have now to rely on websites such as WikiLeaks to obtain such documents, and indeed the documents in question have now appeared on WikiLeaks. Separately, another Barclay's whistleblower revealed several days later that the SCM transactions had produced between £900m and £1bn in tax avoidance in one year.

10.6.6   The Salz Review

In response to the widening and deepening crisis which has engulfed Barclays Bank the Board approved a fundamental review of its business practices. The review which has now been published was undertaken by Anthony Salz a lawyer. The Review was set up by Barclays as an independent review reporting to a non-executive committee of Barclays. The views, findings and recommendations included in this Report are entirely those of the Salz Review. Barclays will consider and decide for itself whether, and if so how, to act on the views, findings and recommendations contained in this Report.

The Salz Review's Terms of Reference are set out below.

> *The culture of the banking industry overall, and that of Barclays within it, needs to evolve. A number of events during and after the financial crisis demonstrated that banks need to revisit fundamentally the basis on which they operate, and how they add value to society. Trust has been decimated and needs to be rebuilt.*

> *Barclays acknowledged that need some time ago and has begun to put in place changes in the way in which it operates consistent with that need. However, recent events indicate clearly that Barclays, like other big UK banks, needs to redouble its efforts. That task may seem more daunting today than ever, but Barclays remains committed to it. As an institution, Barclays must move further and faster to demonstrate that banks, and those who work for them, consistently operate to the highest standards of probity, integrity and honesty. This requires clear evidence, not assertion.*

Culture is generally defined as "the instinctive behaviours and beliefs characteristic of a particular group". Changing a culture, therefore, requires at least three things:

• Affirming the key values and operative beliefs that guide the behaviour of everyone in an organisation – these are deep-seated and tend not to change without direct intervention.
• Ensuring that the actual behaviours of those who represent the organisation are consistent with those values (and are so regarded by those who come in contact with the bank); and
• Ensuring that vital reinforcing mechanisms, such as visible leadership examples, formal and informal systems and processes, policies and rewards, are aligned with those values, operative beliefs and behaviours.

The burden of proof required to demonstrate change in culture is now much higher. The Barclays Board is conducting this review (the Review) of Barclays business practices to assist in the bank's efforts to rebuild trust by making it a leader in business practice among not only its peer institutions, but also multinational corporates generally. The Review is independent, reporting to Sir Michael Rake and a sub-committee of Non-Executive Directors (the Committee) including David Booth; Alison Carnwath; and Sir John Sunderland. Anthony Salz has agreed to lead the Review (the Reviewer) in a personal capacity. Barclays Board and Executive Committee will consider the review's recommendations.

Tasks

1. Is there a problem with Barclays culture? Can you explain what the problem is?

2. One response to the difficulties engulfing the bank has been to highlight the difficulties associated with running such a large organisation? What light does this shed on directors' duties?

3. Is it credible for Barclay's directors to claim that they were unaware of the LIBOR scandal?

4. Why is it claimed that Barclay's lacked the appropriate internal controls to monitor and act upon the LIBOR scandal?

5. Would it be fair to say that Barclays has a problem in terms of its ethical behaviour. If true how do you think this can be addressed?

6. How would you define business ethics?

7. Is all business that is profitable and legal acceptable for corporations to exploit?

8. Why have criminal actions not been taken against managers and directors who allowed money laundering to take place within Barclays?

Key Concepts:

Risk Management Controls, Unethical Behaviour; Law Breaking; Directors' Duties.

CASE 7

Siemens AG

Remember as you read this case that it represents as far as possible facts that have been reported. Nothing has been invented. Nothing has been intentionally distorted. The aim of the case is two-fold: to provide insight into the public affairs of a large and influential public company, and to enable students to develop insights into the company's governance processes and draw defensible conclusions. The company concerned has not been consulted over the content and perspective the case provides.

10.7.1   The Background

Siemens AG is a German multinational engineering and electronics conglomerate headquartered in Munich and Berlin, Germany. It is the largest Europe-based electronics and electrical engineering company. Siemens' principal activities are in the fields of industry, energy, transportation and healthcare and finance. It is organized into five main divisions: Industry, Energy, Healthcare, Infrastructure & Cities, and Siemens Financial Services (SFS).

Siemens and its subsidiaries employ approximately 360,000 people across nearly 190 countries. It has reported global revenue of approx €73.5bn in of 2011. The company has been the focus of controversy in recent years concerning bribery and price fixing affecting a wide range of transactions. In resolving these problems Siemens has faced daunting challenges in terms of its corporate governance.

10.7.2   Price fixing within the EU

In January 2007 Siemens was fined €396 million by the EU (European Commission) for price fixing in EU electricity markets through a cartel involving 11 companies, among which were ABB, Alstom, Fuji, Hitachi, AE Power Systems, Mitsubishi Electric Corp, Schneider, Areva, Toshiba and VA Tech. According to the EC "between 1988 and 2004, the companies rigged bids for procurement contracts, fixed prices, allocated projects to each other, shared markets and exchanged commercially important and confidential information." Siemens was given the highest fine of €396 million, more than half of the total, for its alleged leadership role in the incident.

10.7.3   Bribery

Siemens agreed to pay a record $1.34bn in fines in December 2008 after being investigated for serious bribery. The investigation found questionable payments of roughly €1.3bn, from 2002 to 2006 that triggered a broad range of inquiries in Germany, the United States and many other countries.

In May 2007 a German court convicted two former executives of paying about €6 million in bribes from 1999 to 2002 to help Siemens win natural gas turbine supply contracts with Enel, an Italian energy company. The contracts were valued at about €450 million. Siemens was fined €38 million.

10.7.4   The network of bribery within the company

The network of bribery within Siemens was organised and managed by the Group Accountant Reinhard Siekaczek. The payments, he declared in evidence, were vital to maintaining the competitiveness of Siemens overseas, particularly in the telecommunications sector. What emerged in evidence was evidence of widespread payment of bribes, through a web of secret bank accounts and shadow consultants. Entrenched corruption had become endemic in this sprawling, sophisticated corporation. Siekaczek admitted in evidence that between 2002 and 2006 he oversaw an annual bribery budget of about $40m to $50m at Siemens. Company managers and sales staff used the slush fund to cosy up to corrupt government officials worldwide. There was no evidence of personal enrichment on the part of those involved in bribing including Mr Siekaczek.

German prosecutors initially opened the Siemens case in 2005. American authorities became involved in 2006 because the company's shares are traded on the New York Stock Exchange. In its settlement with the Justice Department and the Securities and Exchange Commission, Siemens pleaded guilty to violating accounting provisions of the Foreign Corrupt Practices Act, which outlaws bribery abroad. The US Justice Department allowed Siemens to plead to accounting violations because it cooperated with the investigation and because pleading to bribery violations would have barred Siemens from bidding on government contracts in the US. Siemens did not dispute the government's account of its actions.

The telecommunications business was awash in easy money. It paid $5 million in bribes to win a mobile phone contract in Bangladesh, to the son of the prime minister at the time and other senior officials, according to court documents. Mr. Siekaczek's group also made $12.7m in payments to senior officials in Nigeria for government contracts. In Argentina, a different Siemens subsidiary paid at least $40 million in bribes to win a $1bn contract to produce national identity cards. In Israel, the company provided $20m to senior government officials to build power plants. In Venezuela, it paid $16m for urban rail lines. In China, $14m was handed over for medical equipment. In Iraq, $1.7m was paid to Saddam Hussein and other senior members of the Iraqi government.

Nokia Siemens supplied telecommunications equipment to the Iranian telecom company that included the ability to intercept and monitor telecommunications, a facility known as "lawful intercept". The equipment was believed to have been used in the suppression of the 2009–2010 Iranian election protests, leading to criticism of the company, including the European Parliament. Nokia-Siemens later divested its call-monitoring business, and reduced its activities in Iran.

10.7.5 Greek controversy

Siemens has been accused of bribing Greek officials. In 2008, it was revealed that Siemens had bribed the two main political parties of Greece for approximately 10 years to be the sole provider of mechanical and electrical equipment of the Greek state. After the exposure the German authorities moved to arrest the representatives of Siemens in Greece, who had managed to escape from the Greek authorities. The German judicial system didn't allow the Greek authorities to cross-question the representatives. As a result, there wasn't any solid evidence against the corrupt politicians, who were not arrested and continue to be active in the Greek political system. Meanwhile, the Greek state cancelled the planned business deals. Since all spares were provided by Siemens, the equipment, like traffic lights eventually broke down, and projects like the metro expansion were abandoned

10.7.6   The Public Reaction

The bribes left behind angry competitors who were shut out of contracts and local residents in poor countries who, because of rigged deals, paid too much for necessities like roads, power plants and hospitals. Bribery leaves behind it a huge legacy of distrust.

Tasks

1. How could the scale of bribery within Siemens have been concealed if audit control had been effective? Why did the Supervisory Board allow this to happen? What responsibilities were placed at their door?

2. What was the role of the Management Board and the CEO in concealing these events?

3. The Group Accountant who oversaw the payment of bribes was anxious to ensure that funds never reached other employees of Siemens. Why was he so concerned about these matters?

4. Why did the US Justice Department accept that Siemens could plead violations of accountancy rules rather than defend charges of bribery and corruption?

5. Is there cause to defend the actions of the Chief Accountant in this case in that he claimed he was seeking only to protect jobs?

6. Siemens is one of the largest corporations in the world. Does its size tell us anything about the challenges of effective governance?

Key Concepts:

Transparency; Accountability; Auditing; Ethical Behaviour; Leadership; Joint and Several Responsibility; Business Model

CASE 8

The John Lewis Partnership

1Remember as you read this case that it represents, as far as possible, facts that have been reported. Nothing has been invented. Nothing has been intentionally distorted. The aim of the case is two-fold: to provide insight into the public affairs of a large and influential company, and to enable readers to develop insights into the company's governance processes and draw defensible conclusions. The company concerned has not been consulted over the content and perspective the case provides.

10.8.1   The Background

The business was founded in 1864 as a limited liability company. In 1920 the owners transferred the assets of the company into a trust owned by the employees. In later years the power sharing arrangements within the company were widened and deepened. In due time these were formalised within the John Lewis Partnership which is today an employee-owned UK partnership. The trade is conducted through John Lewis Plc. It operates John Lewis Department Stores (and Peter Jones), Waitrose supermarkets and a number of other services. All its employees - known as *partners* - have a say in the running of the business and receive a share of annual profits, which is usually a significant addition to their salary. The group is the third largest UK private company in the Sunday Times Top Track 100 for 2010.

Additionally, John Lewis also has the distinction of being UK's best high-street website after beating M&S in October 2010.[6] The chain's image is upmarket, and it appeals strongly to middle and upper class shoppers. Recently, however, John Lewis has broadened its marketing strategy towards all types of buyers, with the introduction of the 'Value' range to John Lewis and the 'Essential' range to Waitrose. The business has been significantly expanded.

10.8.2   The Partnership

Every employee is a partner in the John Lewis Partnership, and has a possibility to influence the business through branch forums, which discuss local issues at every store, and the divisional John Lewis, and Waitrose Councils. Above all these is the Partnership Council, to which the partners elect at least 80% of the 82 representatives, while the chairman appoints the remaining. The councils have the power to discuss 'any matter whatsoever', and are responsible for the non-commercial aspects of the business – the development of the social activities within the partnership and its charitable actions.

The Partnership Council also elects five of the directors on the partnership board (which is responsible for the commercial activities), while the chairman appoints another five. The two remaining board members are the chairman and the deputy chairman. These routes ensure that every non-management partner has an open channel for expressing his/her views to management and the chairman.

As well as this, the John Lewis Partnership publishes a weekly in-house magazine, called *The Gazette*. It is the oldest in-house magazine currently still being published in the UK. Each John Lewis branch also has its own weekly magazine, called *The Chronicle*.

The John Lewis Partnership has a very extensive programme of social activities for its partners, including two large country estates with parklands, playing fields and tennis courts; a golf club; a sailing club with five cruising yachts and two country hotels offering holiday accommodation for the partners. Partners are also enrolled in a very favourable pension scheme, receive a death in service insurance, and are given very generous holidays. In addition to this, upon completing 25 years of service for the company, partners are given a paid 6 month break.

Finally, every partner receives an Annual Bonus, which is a share of the profit. It is calculated as a percentage of the salary, with the same percentage for everyone, from top management down to the shop floor and the storage rooms. The bonus is dependent on the profitability of the partnership each year, varying between 9% and 20% of the partners' annual salaries since 2000. The Annual Partnership Bonus for 2007 was the top end 20%, this is before the recession started. The Annual Partnership Bonus for 2008 was 15% of a partner's gross earnings for the 2007/2008 financial year. The Annual Partnership Bonus for 2009 was 13% of a partner's gross earnings for the 2008/2009 financial year. The Annual Partnership Bonus for 2010 was 15% of a partner's gross earnings for the 2009/2010 financial year.

In the year 2007-2008, the managing director of John Lewis, Andy Street, who has worked since leaving university in 1985, was paid £500,000, plus a 20% bonus of £100,000. In the most recent financial year the John Lewis turnover was a shade above £8bn with profits a little below £500m

10.8.3   The Chairman's report

Everything we do – including our approach to sustainability – is aligned with our aims to increase the competitive advantage of our Partners, realise the full market potential of our brands and grow our business efficiently.

He went on: "In 2011/12, the Partnership achieved a good sales performance in a tough year for the economy. Profound changes are taking place in the retail sector and, importantly, this was a year when we upped the pace of innovation and investment. That came at the price of some short-term profit. Our good performance was the result of our 81,000 Partners' determination to give customers the best possible shopping experience. As always, the Partnership spirit is an intrinsic part of how we operate and is now, more than ever, crucial to our better and more sustainable way of doing business.

We were recognised as one of Britain's Top Employers by the Corporate Research Foundation, and retained our Workingmums.co.uk top overall employer award. Our Partners are key to this success. They embody our principles of respect, integrity and courtesy, and as owners of our business are actively involved in decision making.

A business like the John Lewis Partnership can set ambitious sustainability targets but it is only through successfully harnessing Partners' passion and energy that we can achieve engagement and participation across every aspect of our sustainability agenda. It also ensures that sustainability is placed at the heart of our decision making and informs a balanced approach to growth to achieve long-term commercial success.

10.8.4   Sustainable Growth

We are committed to growing efficiently and responsibly and demonstrated this during the year by opening new stores with significant sustainability features incorporated into the fabric of the buildings. Waitrose Stratford City (adjacent to the Olympic Park) was named Britain's 'greenest' shop within a shopping centre, and was awarded a BREEAM (Building Research Establishment Environmental Assessment Method) 'Outstanding' rating, the first post-construction outstanding rating for a retail building in the world. Refurbishment of John Lewis Cheadle achieved a BREEAM 'Excellent' rating.

Working closely with suppliers who share our values, our trusted brands are ensuring that the products we sell meet ever higher sustainability credentials and enable us to help our customers to make informed choices. In John Lewis, for example, we have introduced a Sustainable Product Identifier. Some 1,000 products currently carry the label and we'll extend its use further in 2012. As part of the Waitrose way, we have introduced environmental supplier targets for carbon, waste and water. This complements our work to increase the sustainability credentials of key product ingredients such as palm oil and soya.

10.8.5   Looking ahead

One of the key challenges that lie ahead is to achieve our target of a 15 per cent reduction (against our 2010/11 baseline) of operational carbon dioxide equivalent emissions by 2020/21. This task is significant, particularly for a growing business, but we have worked hard to put together a detailed carbon reduction plan focusing on areas where our carbon footprint is greatest. While achieving this is our main focus, we are also exploring how best we can influence carbon emission reductions in areas which extend beyond our direct control. For example, by building climate resilience into our supply chain, as well as considering broader environmental impacts such as water and biodiversity.

We continue to build on our award winning Community Matters scheme, looking to enhance the value we can bring to local communities, Partners and the business. In 2012 we have created new Partner volunteering opportunities and will look to build on these in 2013.

Everything we do – including our approach to sustainability – is aligned with our aims to increase the competitive advantage of our Partners, realise the full market potential of our brands and grow our business efficiently. Over the coming year we will be refining our strategy to ensure that our Partners, suppliers and customers are at the heart of our commitment to truly sustainable success".

10.8.6 Some extracts from the John Lewis Sustainability Report

Report assurance

Our co-ownership structure, built on the principles of openness and transparency, supports our commitment to open and honest disclosure and reporting. We do not currently seek formal external assurance for this report in its entirety. We have sought greater internal and external assurance for information included in this year's report. These assurance checks were conducted in March to include the information in the Partnership's Annual Report and Accounts so that combined internal and external assurance covers all numerical assertions in the Corporate Social Responsibility section of the Business Review. External assurance was used for the more specialist and complex datasets: our community investment and carbon emissions.

During 2012/13 we will continue to improve our data processes in light of these recommendations. We will also review the options for increasing our level of assurance for our 2013 sustainability report. We also believe that our involvement in external initiatives, benchmarks and awards and the best practice standards and independent certification schemes we use, add value and credibility to our programmes and reporting. Our performance is recognised by a number of independent organisations. Below we summarise the improvements we have made during 2011/12 in response to assurance conducted for last year's Corporate Social Responsibility report.

Response to Internal Audit report assurance process in 2011/12

During the production of last year's report our Internal Audit department provided a level of assurance by testing a number of the assertions we included. In response to points raised during this process we have made improvements in data processes. For example, we have worked with Partners throughout the business to increase our emphasis on ensuring that information provided for reporting is accurate and auditable. In addition, as part of our carbon reduction programme we have been implementing a new software system to house all emissions data: energy; transport; waste; water and refrigerants.

10.8.7   Relationships with suppliers

As a responsible retailer, the Partnership aims to source products from long- term sustainable supply chains, which minimise environmental impact and create trust and value for everyone involved. It makes business sense for us to trade responsibly with our suppliers – our business relies on their products and services. We appreciate that our suppliers face many challenges and we aim to take a balanced approach. Our strategy is to secure long-term relationships by working closely with them, involving them in our plans and treating them fairly and ethically. We share information openly and make suppliers aware of our goal to create a more sustainable supply chain. We encourage a sense of joint responsibility, helping our suppliers to grow alongside our own business.

We undertake joint business planning, and fair terms and conditions provide security for long-term investment decisions. This enables both parties to realise the benefits. Recognising that suppliers own trading arrangements, accreditations and status can change, we encourage a two way dialogue at all times. For example: Artko, a supplier based in the north of England, supplies some of John Lewis' wall art ranges We are working alongside Artko, providing the trading commitment needed to allow them to expand and develop new artists, such as British painter Sue Fenlon, who is now one of our best-selling artists. Our continuing commitment illustrates the value that we place on supporting businesses that strategically fit our own and enabling small businesses to grow by providing commercial assurances.

10.8.8 Responsible sourcing programmes

Our responsible sourcing programmes allow us to monitor the extent to which suppliers meet the requirements of our Responsible Sourcing Code. When we identify a shortfall, we work collaboratively with our suppliers to bring about improvements in labour standards and worker welfare. To assist us, we gather information from our suppliers using **Sedex** (Supplier Ethical Data Exchange, www.sedexglobal.com) and from that identify and prioritise risk factors within our supply chains. This informs the supplier sites that are prioritised for an independent audit.

The Partnership works collaboratively with peer organisations to find solutions and to encourage mutual understanding. For example, as a member of the Ethical Trading Initiative (ETI, www.ethicaltrade.org), the Partnership is working with other businesses, trade unions and NGOs to engage in projects that will deliver sustainable solutions to improve the lives of those working in global supply chains. The ETI vision is of a world where all workers are free from exploitation and work in conditions of freedom, security and equality.

This unique alliance enables the many common issues that cannot be easily addressed by individual companies to be tackled collectively. It also provides us with independent scrutiny which we believe will help us further develop and strengthen our Responsible Sourcing programmes. Since joining, both Waitrose and John Lewis have been able to engage in projects that will deliver sustainable solutions for our business, and for those working in the supply chains. We consider that our involvement in the ETI will help to build our knowledge of the issues.

Tasks

1. What difference does the partnership as distinct from typical limited liability governance arrangements make to the John Lewis business?

2. What do the extracts from the Sustainability Report tell us about a) the commitment and engagement of senior directors in all aspects of stated sustainability objectives, (b) the engagement of "partners" in this process and (c) the partnerships commitment to incremental progress and the collective monitoring of achievement?

3. How do directors and other partners give expression to their fiduciary duties?

4. How is the integrity of CSR in the Partnership maintained when they do not rely on external verification and authentication?

5. How does the Partnership reveal its commitment to co-determination in the workplace?

6. How does the company define its relationship with its suppliers?

Key Concepts:

Co-determination; Employees as Members; Democratic Participation; Fairness.

Notes
[1] The majority of shares in Goldman Sachs were held by senior members of the firm and employees at the time of the IPO in 1999. This picture has changed in the period since with institutional investors owning currently around 60% of the equity. The institutional investors include at least five of the largest hedge funds and asset management firms.
[2] This amounts 4/10ths of a percent per pound of revenue spent!
[3] This pattern of share holding has in the period since changed with institutional investors represented by hedge funds and other asset management firms the largest shareholder group.
[4] A maven is a trusted expert.
[5] Under the provisions of the Glass Steagall Act 1933.
[6] For further details on the Gulf of Mexico oil spill see page 34 of the Report.

Chapter 11

Conflicting Philosophical Paradigms

11.1   Summary

This is a difficult and challenging chapter as we try to pull together the different approaches in law to corporate governance and the different conclusions that appear to emerge in respect of different jurisdictions. As we have seen earlier the limited liability corporation, in its earliest stage of development, is an expression of unified purpose in which the corporation, its shareholders and directors fuse naturally. In legal terms and because of limited liability we have also seen that the corporation is separately defined in law from the shareholders. We have also seen that the directors, often at a very early stage, are the same parties as those who subscribe to the shares issued by the company. In commonsense simplicity, and as already stated, this might be likened, metaphorically, to the *Holy Trinity*: God the Father, the Son and the Holy Spirit.[1] This is the corporation or firm as we might informally describe it, at the earliest stage of its development.

As we have seen, this changes as the firm grows and develops. In reality little changes until the arrangements in respect of shareholding change. This occurs often as firms reach a point where they need to raise new capital from new shareholders. At its most fundamental, in Anglo American capital markets, this occurs when a corporation seeks public listing, often by way of an IPO (Initial Public Offering). At this point very often the founding shareholders are replaced by institutional investors or at the very least the holdings of the founders are significantly reduced depending on the scale of new equity raised. The nature of this change is fundamental in Anglo American jurisdictions though markedly different, as we have seen, elsewhere. These differences are in turn the drivers of *path dependency*. They explain in large measure why there are so many striking differences between jurisdictions and why it is important for us to understand these differences.

11.2   The Corporate Actor

Though generalisations are difficult to make it is fair to say that the behaviour of the different corporate actors is ultimately transformed as firms grow and develop. The first major change is that the concept of the *Holy Trinity* is for all practical purposes destroyed in the Anglo American model. The Directors are frequently quite different from the shareholders (or institutional investors). Directors may hold shares, and are often incentivised to do so, but these are likely to represent a very small percentage of total issuance. The institutional investors are in reality *disconnected* from the corporation in which they are invested. This is the first stage in Ireland's *cleansing* process which we explored earlier.

Shareholders cease to be engaged in any meaningful *ex ante* manner with the affairs of the corporation. Like most of the community they rely on *ex post* discovery of what *has* happened. In this situation the directors play a dominant role in the affairs of the corporation subject to *hard* and *soft* regulation an arrangement whose effectiveness depends critically on the provisions of the Memorandum and Articles of Association and the AGM (Annual General Meeting). The situation in *Rhineland* jurisdictions and others is, as we have seen, fundamentally different. Most markedly this is because of the existence of two-tier boards where the supervisory board which represents the shareholders and other stakeholders supervises the actions of the executive board. The metaphor of the *Holy Trinity* is preserved. Through the supervisory board the different, complex interests of the different corporate actors is worked through. This is a vitally important observation and must be a key consideration as we try to define the directions of reform.

11.3   Confusions and contradictions in the law

We need also to explore more closely how the role of the director is determined. To the lay reader of the law, to policy makers in the field of the company and its governance and to the public at large the arrangements which address the key issue of directors' duties are confused and seemingly contradictory. One assumes that the aim of the law should be to establish clear principles which can, with some high level of certainty, be consistently applied in particular circumstances. This is illusive when it applies to directors' duties in Anglo American jurisdictions. There are many examples. We should remember also the Siemens case. We may also fairly draw the conclusion that German law enforcement in the case examined appeared to fall short of dealing decisively with the failure of directors to address the bribery issues within the corporation – though there may well have been other factors at play notably the fact that the frauds were initiated outside Germany.

In the Anglo American context it has been earlier demonstrated that the law of limited liability in 1856 severed the historical link between the company and the members (or shareholders). This has left a number of unresolved conundrums. There was initially a period of confusion about the significance of limited liability. This was finally, if controversially, settled by the Salomon judgment in 1897. That ruling made clear that the company was an entity in law separate from the shareholders and owned its own assets. This re-enforced the significance of the earlier Foss Harbottle judgement (1843) which conferred in law the right of directors to manage the affairs of the company effectively to the exclusion of, *ex ante*, shareholder involvement. The effect of these different judgments has resulted in four main paradoxes in Anglo American jurisdictions as follows.

11.4 The Corporation, the Directors and the Corporators

First the duty of care of the directors is to the company, (apart from the duty of honesty and fair dealing which is a duty to shareholders). It excludes any specific requirement on the directors to take account of shareholder interests. Second this legal *oddity* is resolved by relying on the claim in law that the company and the shareholders are in a contractual relationship which is expressed in the Articles of Association and the specific provisions of section 14 of the British Companies Act 1985. This legal fudge, as we have explored, generates doubt and speculation. Strictly speaking it entails that the company's constitution is 'signed and sealed by each member' but as already stated the documentation fails to identify the company in that contract. The company, as we have seen, is a separate legal entity in law. It is not, except by sleight of hand, a party to this transaction.[2]

This creates doubt and uncertainty not only as to the true status of the company, but most importantly to the meaning of directors' duties. The legal response to this confusion is the claim that the company is not just the legal entity or *the business* but is effectively the sum of the *corporators*– a totally confusing rationalisation. Third this portrayal suffers from a very clear difficulty. It appears to gainsay the distinction elsewhere in law that the company is an entity separate in law from the shareholders. This muddle leads to the inevitable question – why has the judiciary encouraged a remedy which ultimately fosters further confusion and uncertainty? At one level the portrayal appeals to an intuitive, commonsense view[3] about the relationship between the company and the shareholders. But in law the position is different. This confusion is well exemplified in the baffling remarks of David Mackie QC sitting as a deputy judge in Platt v Platt (1999). He reasoned as follows:

> *Whilst the directors have a fiduciary duty to the company (rather than the shareholder), in some circumstances it would be perfectly proper for the directors to be seen to have a duty to the shareholders.*

How, why and when this would be the case is never explained. In fairness it needs to be noted that the case of Platt versus Platt involved a small company. As we have explored above the fact is that small companies and their shareholding arrangements and relationships with directors are very different to public companies where shares are, for example, quoted in a public market. But the judge's comments must leave lay persons with the fear that where directors' duties are concerned judges live in a strange parallel universe.

11.5 The Company's Interest

The fourth and final difficulty arises in the identification of the company's interests by the directors. It is clear from the Report of the Second Savoy Hotel Investigation, discussed earlier, that even if the interests of the company can be construed as being the same as the shareholders interests a question arises as to whether the interests of prospective shareholders (who are not known at the time) should be weighed alongside those of existing shareholders. This formulation may very well lead to a situation where directors' recommendations may not be in the interest of current or future shareholders. In reality that is a common outturn. Directors take decisions which are not in the interests of current or incoming shareholders.

This is a view which runs counter to the practicalities of commercial life, especially in take-over situations, where the directors are required to choose between competing bidders with the interests of the current shareholders uppermost. This seemingly commonsense view is further evidence that the law in these critical areas remains ambiguous and unclear. It must be concluded that the law fails to provide a clear framework within which directors' duties can be effectively monitored or redress achieved.

11.6 The evolution of directors' duties

The concept of directors' duties is grounded in ambiguity and controversy. There are two main reasons that account for this. The first reason is that directors' duties continue, as Penner (2000) explains, to be influenced by the historical overhang of trusteeship and the fiduciary duties flowing from that[4]. They remain tempered by considerations of equity as well as common law.[5] Some view this as subjecting directors, in litigation, to lesser standards than would normally apply under common law. Directors' duties, even in the contemporary setting where they are expected to be business *risk takers*, is still influenced by the overriding principle that he should be a *clean handed* fiduciary, and must not seek to benefit from his position of trust.

Because of the seemingly high standard expected of directors, courts are judged to be more tolerant of lapses especially where matters of commercial judgment are concerned - provided there is no evidence of dishonesty.[6] Whilst it is understandable that directors should be expected to observe the very highest standards of integrity, given the enormous economic power they exercise, reliance on principles relevant to the operation of trusts and reflecting the behaviour expected of trustees seems curiously misplaced in the contemporary world. Parkinson (1993) comments upon this seeming paradox as follows:

> 'Once it is accepted that management involves technical expertise, the court could without departing from the existing but anomalous principle that the standard of care is linked to the attributes of the director impose an appropriately higher standard, given that most executive directors of large companies do have considerable business experience.'[7]

Addressing the strictly legal issues raised by Parkinson (1993), the balance of common law and equity in so far as it applies to directors' duties is articulated in section 170 of the Companies Act 2006:[8]

> The general duties are based on certain common law rules and equitable principles as they apply in relation to directors and have effect in place of those rules and principles as regards the duties owed to a company by a director.

> The general duties shall be interpreted and applied in the same way as common law rules or equitable principles, and regard shall be had to the corresponding common law rules and equitable principles in interpreting and applying the general duties.

The same historic balance, between common law and equity, is explicitly preserved. The opportunity to change the legal balance, underpinned by sound arguments in favour of establishing objective standards for judging directors' skill and care, and by so doing reflecting contemporary commercial reality, was consciously avoided. The unhelpful historic overhang of equity continues to taint the new statutory provisions.

11.7   Trying to fix the disconnect between shareholders and the company

The second reason derives from the fact that the directors owe their duty to the company and not the shareholders. This anomaly, as discussed earlier, is only in appearance resolved by using the argument that the company and the shareholders are effectively bound together contractually by section 14 of the Companies Act 1985. The Companies Act 2006 appears to acknowledge this anomaly. The wording of section 172 has been changed to the extent that the director's duty to the company is *for the benefit of the members, as a whole*.[9]

The problem with this caveat is that it takes no account of the two matters of substance. First it ignores that the company is a separate entity in law from the shareholders, a direct consequence of the 1856 act of limited liability, and a matter well established in common law. Second, as already stated, the company is not a signatory to the provisions of section 14 of the Companies Act 1985 an anomaly that is not resolved satisfactorily in section 172 of the Companies Act 2006.[10] The erroneous presumption that each member signs and seals the agreement with the company as an independent entity is sidetracked.

As a consequence the relationship between the company and the shareholder remains anomalous. This anomaly is compounded further remembering that directors' duties are explicitly to the company, and not the shareholders. This creates difficulties and uncertainties where shareholders are seeking legal redress against errant directors. Under the rule of Foss v Harbottle the true plaintiff in any action is the company, and not the shareholders - who mostly do not have status to sue.[11]

Even if shareholders succeed in being allowed to progress an action against directors on behalf of the company there are a least two further hurdles ahead. First directorship has never been regarded as a profession defined, for example, in terms of technical expertise. Hence the standards for judging directors are unlike those imposed upon persons performing professional services, such as medical practitioners, who are required to satisfy the standard of 'the ordinary skilled man exercising and professing to have' the relevant skill.[12] Second, because of the overhang of equity, directors are treated as being in a position similar to that of a trustee or agent. The significance of this is that far lower standards of performance are expected in common law though this may be slowly changing.

In Norman v Theodore Goddard 1991,[13] Judge Hoffman argued that the Insolvency Act section 214 (4), which links the standard of skill to the function performed, contained an accurate statement of the test in common law. This has the implication that someone possessing knowledge and experience in some particular area of technical expertise will be required to satisfy a higher standard than that of the ordinary man. This interpretation, unhappily, runs alongside the more pervasive interpretation that directors are not generally expected to display the level of professionalism one might reasonably expect from a professional person. These matters are considered in the following section.

11.8   The skills of the director

Whilst historically this might well have been a reasonable conclusion to draw, in the modern world the continued portrayal of the director as the 'well intentioned amateur' rather than a properly qualified professional brings the law into disrepute. Parkinson (1993) addresses a range of landmark judgments which amply support the claim that the standards by which directors' actions are judged are less onerous that those that might otherwise bear on an ordinary individual under common law, untempered by equity, in cases of civil tort. There are various factors which explain the low standards expected of directors.

First directorship, as already stated, is not classified as a profession, even though executive directors, (as distinct from non executive directors), in particular will often have been appointed from the senior ranks of general management in the company concerned presumably because of their outstanding top management and commercial prowess. It is instructive that the British Institute of Directors has reported in the past that 9 out of 10 directors received no formal preparation for becoming a director and that fewer than a quarter had any professional qualification.[14] Perhaps significantly the British Higgs Review of Non Executive Directors which reported in January 2003 stressed amongst other matters the importance of companies providing in-house training for upcoming executive directors. The Report also recommended that the chairman of the board and the chief executive should be responsible for providing a comprehensive induction programme for non executive directors.[15] There is no evidence that these recommendations have been taken seriously.

A second factor is that the courts strenuously avoid second-guessing business judgments at least in Anglo American jurisdictions. This is commented upon by the French jurist Tunc (1986) who contrasts and compares the Anglo American approach to the court's assessing the soundness or otherwise of business decisions, to the approach followed in France. Under French law directors are held responsible for the actions of the company under Art 1382 C.Civ. As a point of jurisprudential principle Tunc argues that it would be a denial of justice if the judiciary were to regard these matters otherwise.[16] It is viewed as being unthinkable under French law that a judge would state that business decisions are the sole province of the board and its directors. Yet Anglo American jurisdictions still have to develop fair and acceptable tests that can be applied in the objective assessment of directors' business skills.

11.9   The director as a risk taker

In reality directors of commercial businesses are expected to take risks if they are to generate profit. This suggests that a different approach to the assessment of risk taking in the case of directors of commercial companies is warranted. In practice, however, the courts maintain that that it is not their task to evaluate management decisions where commercial judgment applies. The justification for this is that even if management produced a detailed assessment of the risks associated with a particular action, the court could not reasonably assess whether the projected profits from the scheme justified the risk involved. This is surely mistaken.

A late 19th century judgment captures the essences of the dilemma. In Re Faure Electric Accumulator Company, Judge Kay argued that to fetter directors of commercial companies with the strict rules of the Court of Chancery where matters of risk and reward were concerned 'would be exceedingly disadvantageous to the companies they represent',[17] a view which may explain the low standards of competence imposed by the courts in cases of litigation and 'judicial reticence' where matters of commercial judgment are concerned.[18]

There is another view which argues that mismanagement by directors should be controlled by way of shareholder supervision.[19] This observation and its credibility goes to the heart of corporate governance and the structure which governs the rules and institutions of the corporation, and the statutory, common law (or elective origin) by which the processes of supervision and control are established. The effectiveness of shareholder supervision will depend critically on three factors. First the availability of relevant *ex ante* information provided by the board of directors as to the performance of the company. Second the capacity of shareholders at the AGM to take informed decisions about the performance of directors. Third the commitment of shareholders to monitor the performance of board directors, where other remedies may offer a more convenient solution.

The verdict on the effectiveness of shareholder supervision has been mostly sceptical though the rise in shareholder activism may result in improvements. Scepticism derives from the fact that for shareholder democracy to operate effectively shareholders need to be motivated to cause this to happen. Given the scale of institutional investment in Anglo American publicly quoted companies, the outlook is not promising. But changes are afoot as evidenced firstly by increased shareholder activism and secondly by the growth of hedge fund involvement in the corporate equity market and private equity investors.

11.10   To whom do directors owe their fiduciary duty?

A final consideration centres on the ambiguity which surrounds to whom directors owe their fiduciary duty. Though it is mostly clear that the duty is owed to the company, it appears, by implication, in the Companies Act 2006[20] that this duty extends also to the shareholders.   This inference stands notwithstanding the underlying opinion in International Plc v Coats Paton Plc (1989), that directors do not have a particular fiduciary duty to shareholders except in the requirement that they act 'in good faith and not fraudulently, and not to mislead whether deliberately or carelessly' them. In the same case Lord Cullen went on to say that the 'directors have but one master, the company'[21]. This needs in turn to be set against the view that directors should take account of both the short term and the longer term interests of the company which complicates the straightforward account that the interests of the company are the same as the current shareholders – a matter returned to below.

The notion, however, that the directors have a duty to the company is not without problems. Since the company, as we have seen, is an inanimate legal fiction how are its interests identified and acted upon? The contractarian view, as we have seen, relies on the argument that the company and the shareholders are contracting parties through the provisions of the Articles of Association and section 14 of the Companies Act 1985. Contractarians will reason that because of these provisions the company's interests and the shareholders' interests are, in practice, coterminous. This is a well established position in law.[22] Justifying this proposition relies, however, on a conflation of the terms "company" and "shareholder"[23] and invites the criticism that it is, at base, a tautology.[24]

Giving practical effect to its meaning may, in practice, be either impossible or even undesirable for directors' to attempt. On the other hand a realist approach[25] points in yet another direction. According to this view the company's interest can also be construed and supported as being wider, embracing shareholders, (current and prospective) employees, creditors and other constituencies.   These contrasting views raise complications in the context of directors' duties and the courts' understanding of how these duties should be exercised. It inevitably leaves directors' duties grounded in ambiguity and uncertainty as the following examples portray.

In the Savoy Hotel and Berkeley Hotel Report of the (then) Board of Trade, initiated under section 165 of the Companies Act 1948, the contractarian bias was further complicated. What is telling about the report of the inspector is that it was not enough for the directors to act in the short term interest of the company, (by trying to remove an asset from the company's control, so as to take it beyond the reach of a take-over bidder); the directors must have regard also for the longer term interests of the company and should therefore take account of the interests of future shareholders. This very greatly complicates, in certain circumstances, the choices facing directors.

11.12   How directors' duties are currently defined in law

Directors' duties under the Companies Act 2006[26] are defined under seven broad headings as follows.

- Duty 1 requires that the director's act within the powers laid down by the company's constitution. This is reflected in the 'proper purpose' doctrine. It draws its authority from the judgment of Lord Greene who stated that directors must not exercise their power for any collateral purpose – meaning parallel or even ulterior.[27] An obvious example would be the issuance of shares which may result in the voting rights of an existing majority being adversely affected – where there is an intention on the part of the directors to bring this about.

- Duty 2 – the duty to act in the interest of the company and promote its success [section 172] contains some of the most challenging and controversial difficulties in terms of legal practice and common law precedent. Directors are, for example, precluded from furthering their own interests or of the interests of some other third party,[28] The duty specifically requires directors to take into account of short term and long term consequences of their actions; the interests of the company's employees[29] and other stakeholders and the impact of the company's operations on the community and the environment.[30] Settling the issue of whether the duty has been fulfilled will rest with the courts to settle in disputed cases.

- The duty to exercise independent judgment, Duty 3 is, again, problematical.[31] There is no straightforward means of establishing whether directors' exercise independent judgment since board decisions are for the most part collective, or portrayed in that manner, and their deliberations are in any case viewed as confidential. The only basis on which judgments about 'independence' might be conclusively settled is in cases where board members do not agree and make public their dissent. For obvious reasons there is little in the way of public information about how internal disputes are settled[32] though the duty to promote the success of the company may result in better public awareness of how directors' settle complex controversial issues of judgment.

- Duty 4 which concerns the exercise of reasonable care, skill and diligence continues to be blighted by the generally low standards of performance that are expected of directors. Section 174 of the Companies Act 2006 does make clear that the duty will be judged against that of the diligent person. This brings into prominence again the conclusions reached in Norman v Theodore Goddard[33] in which Hoffman J used the "diligent person" criteria as established under section 214 of the Insolvency Act 1986 in settling objective criteria.

- Duty 5 concerns the avoidance of conflicts of interest, a requirement which sits awkwardly alongside the view expressed by the CLSRG in its recommendation that 'the law should only prevent the exploitation of business opportunities where there is a clear case for doing so.'[34] Duty 6 forbids the acceptance of benefits from third parties such as bribes. Duty 7 requires directors to declare an interest in any proposed transaction or arrangement.[35]

Duty 2 was widely debated by the CLRSG because of its perceived importance in terms of corporate governance. The eventual legal provisions as set out in section 172 of the Companies Act 2006 changes less than many had hoped for. The provisions are set out in full.

Figure 16   British Directors Duties

172 Duty to promote the success of the company
(1) A director of a company must act in the way he considers, in good faith, would be most likely to promote the success of the company for the benefit of its members as a whole, and in doing so have regard (amongst other matters) to

(a) the likely consequences of any decision in the long term,
(b) the interests of the company's employees,
(c) the need to foster the company's business relationships with suppliers, customers and others,
(d) the impact of the company's operations on the community and the environment,
(e) the desirability of the company maintaining a reputation for high standards of business conduct, and
(f) the need to act fairly as between members of the company.

(2) Where or to the extent that the purposes of the company consist of or include purposes other than the benefit of its members, subsection (1) has effect as if

the reference to promoting the success of the company for the benefit of its members were to achieving those purposes.

(3) The duty imposed by this section has effect subject to any enactment or rule of
law requiring directors, in certain circumstances, to consider or act in the interests of creditors of the company.

One significant development is that shareholder interest[36] is now viewed as central and explicit in the legal provisions. Whilst this is to be welcomed in as far as it might appear to strengthen corporate governance it is seen by some critics as weakening the former provisions of section 309 of the Companies Act 1985 which required directors to 'have regard in the performance of their functions the interests of the company's employees in general as well as interests of its members'. The provisions of section 309 have been removed from the Companies Act 2006.

11.13   Shareholder redress through the Companies Acts

In examining how the law that governs the action of directors in the discharge of their duties the provisions of section 303 of the Companies Act 1985 (s 168 of the CA 2006) need to be assessed. The aim of the provision is to enable shareholders who feel that directors are not, by their actions, promoting shareholder value, to make appropriate changes. The provision permits an ordinary majority of shareholders to dismiss any or all of the directors. No reason is required, regardless of any contrary provisions in the company's articles or particular provisions in director's service contracts. The provision is subject only to the obligation to pay compensation to any director whose contract is wrongfully terminated. This provision is supported by the section 368 of the Companies Act 1985 which empowers the holders of 10% of voting shares to requisition an early meeting of the company.

Evidence of past use of section 303 provisions is scanty. This might be explained because compensation for breach of contract may be substantial. This, in turn, has encouraged corporate governance best practice to recommend limiting the length of directors' service contracts. These recommendations are now supported by statutory provisions. The provisions may be seen to benefit shareholders under British arrangements when compared with arrangements in the US. According to Kahan (1998) the opportunity to dismiss directors in the US only arises annually, (or at an even longer interval in the case of staggered boards).[37] The fact remains, however, that British section 303 provisions are not widely used. This, in turn, may well be a consequence of the collective action constraint which arises where shareholdings are widely dispersed.

11.14 Balancing interests of company, shareholders and stakeholders

The issue that there are constituencies other than shareholders that should be consulted by companies as part of best practice corporate governance continues to attract controversy. The classic view as expressed by Parkinson (1993) is that under British company law a company should be run for the benefit of owners of the company, namely the shareholders though as he points out this has been modified by statute and case law in the UK.[38] As Padfield (1995) reminds, one of the many competing and alternative views is that other constituencies affected by corporate activity deserve recognition.[39] Plender (1997) argues that employees, suppliers, customers and local communities have a legitimate interest in and stake in the affairs of the company.[40]

In the grand British debate on corporate governance[41] in the 1990's little sustained attention was paid to the stakeholder model of the company. The presumption throughout was that the company's interests were coterminous with those of the shareholder and the official debate faithfully reflected this view.[42] As Cheffins[43] (2000) points out there was a feeling of disappointment with the failure of the DTI (Department of Trade and Industry) to address, fundamentally, the issue of stakeholdership. This was at first 'adopted' as a popular, vote winning concern by the incoming labour government. In 1998 the DTI launched a comprehensive review of corporate law. Part of the intention was to open up discussion on the issue of the model of the company society might choose to adopt. At an early stage in the deliberations of the CLRSG (Company Law Reform Steering Group) a "pluralist" approach[44] was explored.

This was seen as an alternative to one predicated exclusively on ownership by shareholders. The "pluralist" approach[45] would have required directors to have regard for social and ethical objectives. It would also have involved altering the composition of company boards to ensure that stakeholders had suitable representation and requiring companies to report on relations with employees, suppliers, customers and the community'.[46] The "pluralist" approach was eventually quietly abandoned in favour of the 'enlightened shareholder approach'.[47]

Davies (2005)[48] expresses the view that to have continued to pursue the stakeholder or pluralist approach would have produced an unenforceable formula without extensive reconstruction of the composition of the board so as to reflect stakeholder interests. What he might have considered is that if Pareto efficiency[49] is an accepted economic goal –

where improvements to at least one participant's well being can be made without reducing other participant's well being - there may be definite benefits to be obtained from constituency reporting. Statutes that enable directors to mitigate or eliminate losses to other constituencies, where market forces alone do not resolve these conflicts satisfactorily, may result in such transactions producing net gains in social wealth.[50]

Whilst recognising worker interests as stakeholders, Davies argues that German co-determination arrangements have never embraced the notion that the company board can or should try to act as a 'sort of representative Parliament of all of those affected by the company's actions'. In doing so he fails to point out that German Company Law, from the mid 19th century Weimar period, recognised the representation of a broad range of stakeholders in the corporation. This is enshrined in article 14(2) of the Federal Constitution. This states simply and clearly: 'Property imposes duties. Its uses should also serve the public good'.[51]

Section 172 of the Companies Act 2006 requires that directors take into account a range of stakeholder interests. This, in theory, leaves open new avenues where directors can be challenged if they fail in their duty to take account of these interests. Progress on this front will depend on how far the judiciary will use the opportunity to establish new objective standards against which to judge performance. Davies (2005)[52] expresses strong doubts that this will happen, leaving stakeholders to make what they will of disclosure requirements under the Business Review requirements. These requirements replaced the OFR (Operating and Financial Review) provisions which were repealed in November 2005

11.15   Conclusions

In this chapter we have tried to unravel some of the fundamental differences in the way in which the law has sought to portray the corporation in different jurisdictions and how this has shaped directors' duties. The corporation as we have seen is portrayed differently in different jurisdictions. The portrayal in respect of the corporation under English and American law portrays the company at some stage in its limited liability existence as an aggregate real entity but as a result of developments in common law and the Salomon judgement emerges as a fictional entity with an identity separate from the shareholders.

The European, *Rhineland* and Nordic tradition sees this development differently. The corporation emerges as an *aggregate* real entity because the laws in those jurisdictions had the foresight to realise that under limited liability the detachment of the shareholders from the ownership of the company would have to be compensated for. This explains the emergence of the independent supervisory board put in place to protect shareholder and stakeholder interests. The same general effect can be detected in Japanese and South Korean jurisdictions through the *keiritsu* and the *chaebol* respectively. This development did not occur in Anglo American jurisdictions.

The analysis supports conclusively the need for a radical overhaul of the laws governing both the role of the board in Anglo American jurisdictions and directors duties if a better balanced relationship between the corporation, the directors and the various stakeholders is to be promoted.

Questions for review

1. Is the business judgement rule and its parallels in other Anglo American jurisdictions appropriate in contemporary circumstances?

2. If judges should be expected to assess business decisions taken by directors on what basis should this be undertaken?

3. How can shareholders obtain redress where the competence of directors is challenged?

4. Are directors duties under English law defined clearly enough and can they be enforced?

5. Do common law notions of directors' duties conflict with expecting directors to take commercial risks?

6. 'Property imposes duties. Its uses should also serve the public good' Explain why you agree or disagree with this statement?

Learning Tasks

I   Define the objectives that directors should be judged against?

II   Define what should count as evidence of competence in assessing directors?

III   Define what you would regard as incompetence where directors' actions are concerned?

Figure 17

Letter to the Financial Times

Dismal failure of efforts at reform
From Mr Richard Tudway.

I refer to your general comments on the published findings of the Financial Services Authority on the stewardship of the Royal Bank of Scotland (Editorial, December 4) and those of your Lombard columnist ("FSA ensures lessons of RBS boardroom stay unlearnt", December 4).

It is truly astounding that the lessons of the RBS boardroom stay both unlearnt and unstated. The major events associated with the triggering of the global financial crisis serve to show, beyond any reasonable doubt, that unitary corporate board structures in Anglo-American jurisdictions, as a matter of urgency, need overhauling.

The mixing of execution and supervision as foreseen in these structures in the case of RBS and in a number of other instances in recent times has led to a failure to rein in or otherwise challenge the power of dominant executive directors. Can it possibly, ever, be otherwise?

The evidence is blindingly clear. The efforts dating back to the Cadbury recommendations in the 1990s through to Higgs and beyond, aimed at establishing a better balance of power at board level and more effective supervision by non-executive directors, have mostly failed. Institutional investors, as ever, are impotent shareholders in driving forward reform. Without fundamental reform events such as this will continue to destroy wealth.

Richard Tudway, Centre for International Economics, London

Notes

[1] As already cited the Holy Trinity implies that the existence of three distinct entities: God the Father, God the Son and God the Holy Spirit are also a single unity.

[2] This problem arises because of unresolved tensions and conflicts between the aims of the 1844 Joint Stock Companies Act and the 1856 Law of Limited Liability. The 1844 Act was aimed at creating a constitutional default document by using an artificial contract which would bind all members of the company. Limited Liability results in the creation of an entity in law which is separate from its shareholders.

[3] See: Re Chez Nico (Restaurants) Ltd (1992) and Coleman v Myers (1977). Deputy Judge Mackie in his summing up in Platt v Platt (1999) spoke about these judgements being 'plainly right'. Others might take the view that problems in the law and its application in particular cases arise from the fact that no two limited liability entities, and the relationship between directors and shareholder that exists within them, is always going to be the same. The obsession with "one size fits all" simply doesn't work.

[4] See: Penner J E *The Law of Trusts* (2nd edition) 2000. Penner explains in sections 1.9 – 1.11 and 2.9 – 2.12 in particular the manner in which equity, as a manifestation of common law, could provide relief to suitors on grounds where matters of fairness in relation to trust and property were concerned, as distinct from actions at common law.

[5] See: Penner J E *op cit* and his discussion of the 'fusion of law and equity' and the unalterable 'clean hands' principle [a reference to honesty] that equitable relief is discretionary and may compromise remedies originally granted at common law. See para 1.13 page 8.

[6] See: Penner J E *op cit* who explains that 'equity's imposition of stringent personal obligations upon a legal owner to hold property for the benefit of another, with the result that he is no longer able to treat the property as his own may be regarded as the paradigm case of equity's interference with common law rights in pursuit of justice' para 1.14 page 9.

[7] See: Parkinson J *op cit* page 106

[8] See: Section 170 Scope and nature of general duties: subsections (3) and (4) page 78 Companies Act 2006

[9] See: The Companies Act 2006 (c. 46) Part 10 – A company's directors, Chapter 2 General Duties of Directors.

[10] The wording of section 14 reflects accurately the wording of the [unlimited liability] Companies Act 1844 in which the owners were indistinguishable from the undertaking in law. The provision therefore took no account of the company's status as a separate entity following limited liability in 1856.

[11] Shareholders holding shares of a nominal value of 10% of issued share capital may under the Fifth Directive on Company Law (OJ, C240, 9.9. 1983,2 initiate a derivative action to be brought on behalf of the company against the directors.

[12] See: Bolam v Friern Hospital Committee [1957] 2 All ER 118

[13] See: Norman v Theodore Goddard [1991] BCLC 1028 at 1030-31.

[14] See: Professional Development of and for the Board, I O D 1990.

[15] See: The Higgs Report on Non Executive Directors, January 2003. Note in particular the Summary of Recommendations, page 4.

[16] See: Tunc A LQR 1986 Vol 102 p 549

[17] See: Re Faure Electric Accumulator Company (1888) 40 Ch D 141 at 151

[18] It is relevant to note that the danger of discouraging enterprise is a key justification the American courts use to justify the 'business judgement rule'

[19] See: Parkinson J *op cit* page 101 - 105.

[20] Section 172 of the CA 2006 states that the goal for directors should be to 'promote the success of the company for the benefit its shareholders'. See para 4.2 below.

[21] See: Dawson International Plc v Coats Patons Plc (1989) comments by Lord Cullen

[22] See: Greenhalgh v Arderne Cinemas Ltd (1951) and the comments of Evershed MR in that dispute.

[23] Sometimes referred as "corporators"

[24] To argue that the company and corporators are the same rests on a definition of expedience. Whilst decisions by directors' can be taken on behalf of corporation and may thereby be construed as reflecting the interests of shareholders the converse cannot be established without empirical proof.

[25] The realist approach recognizes the independent existence of the corporation. See: Stokes M *op cit* footnote 99

[26] As set out in the CA 2006 General Duties of Directors, Chapter 2

[27] See: Re Smith & Fawcett Ltd [1942] Ch 304 CA. See also: Regentcrest plc v Cohen (2001) which demonstrates well the subjective nature of the 'good faith' formulation in proving breach of duty.

[28] In Re Smith and Fawcett Ltd (1942) Lord Green stated that directors must exercise their discretion *bona fide* in what they consider – not what the court may consider – is in the best interest of the company.

[29] This more explicit statutory formulation in respect of duties to employees has replaced s 309 of the CA 1985 which it has been argued expanded the meaning of the company as a whole [as stated in the legislation] to include employees in general, though this has never been tested.

[30] These highly debatable matters, where *enlightened shareholder value* is concerned, will be judged against common law rules and equitable principles that currently exist, a development which will require the court to reconsider its philosophy of 'judicial non intervention'.

[31] Emphasising the decision in Fulham Football Club v Cabra Estates Plc [1994] 1 BCLC 363, CA it re-inforces the point that directors collectively run the company and have a collective responsibility for their decisions.

[32] The decision of the board of Marks & Spencer to act against the Cadbury recommendations hints that there may have been dissension between board members on the issue. See: http//business.timesonline.co.uk/tol/business/industry_sectors/retailing/article360803:

[33] See: Norman v Theodore Goddard (a firm) [1991] BCLC 1028 *op cit*

[34] See: *Completing the Structure*. The Report of the CLRSG (2001) *op cit* para 3.26.

[35] The no conflict rule introduces a substantive change by allowing other directors to authorise the conflict where one was thought to arise.

[36] The concept of *enlightened shareholder value* defines the company's interests in terms of the shareholders. In doing so it removes the ambiguity associated with the original section 309 provisions of Companies Act 1985 which appeared to require directors in promoting the interests of the company, to balance the interests of employees in general alongside those of shareholders.

[37] See: Kahan M 'Jurisprudential and Transactional Developments in Takeovers' in Hopt et al (eds) Comparative Corporate Governance (Clarenden Press, Oxford 1998) page 691

[38] See: Parkinson J *op cit* pages 81 – 87. Parkinson's earlier view is also affected by the CA 2006. This explicitly states that directors must take into account wider constituencies in meeting their duty to promote the success of the company, for the benefit of the shareholders. The earlier controversial stakeholder oriented provisions of section 309 of the Companies Act of 1985 have been removed.

[39] See: Padfield F M, *Challenges for Company Law in Perspectives on Company Law* 1, 10 – 14, 1995.

[40] See: Plender J *A Stake in the Future – the Stakeholding Solution* Nicholas Brearley Publishing, 1997. Plender portrays the stakeholder case in accessible language.

[41] The Cadbury, Greenbury and Hampel Committees respectively.

[42] See Dignam A *A Principled Approach to Self Regulation? The Report of the Hampel Committee on Corporate Governance* 19 Co Law 140, 141 – 142 (1998)

[43] See: Cheffins B *Current Ends in Corporate Governance: Going to London, to Milan via Toronto* Duke Journal of Comparative and International Law Vol 10,5

44 The concept of pluralism in corporate governance debated by the CLRSG was aimed at enhancing the inputs of various stakeholders and lessening the control of managers in corporate governance. See also: Molz R *The theory of pluralism in corporate governance. A conceptual framework and empirical test.* Journal of Business Ethics Vol 14 No 10 1995

45 The pluralist approach has its counterpart in American jurisdictions which is expressed in terms of non-shareholder constituency statutes which are commonplace. See Macey J R   Stetson Law Review Vol 21 p 31. He sums up the dilemma, from a US perspective in the following terms. Such statutes 'simply confuse the legal landscape by forcing directors to attempt an impossible task – pleasing a multitude of masters with competing and conflicting interests. These are described in detail in: *Other Constituency Statutes: Potential for Confusion.* AmericanBar Association Committee (1990) 45 Business Lawyer 2253, 2261.

46 See; Cheffins B *op cit* page 30. See also: *Modern Law for a Competitive Economy,* Report of the CLRSG paras 5.1.30 – 5.1.33, 5.146 – 5.1.47 and 5.1.50.

47 This wording requires directors to 'promote the success of the company for the benefit of its members while having regard to the interests of others (see Appendix 1). This was viewed by some as a definite step backwards,

48 See Davies P *Enlightened shareholder value and the new responsibilities of directors*. A lecture delivered at the University of Melbourne (the inaugural W E Hearn lecture) 4 October 2005.Downloadable at: 144.140.79.140/camac/camac.nsf/byHeadline/PDFSubmissions_2/$file/AMPCapital_CSR.pdf

49 See: Kwang Ng Yew (1983) *Welfare Economics*, Macmillan for an analysis of the Pareto efficiency argument.

50 An example of this might include the decision of Marks and Spencer Plc to adopt a voluntary carbon emissions offset scheme as its contribution to global Climate Change objectives.

51 See: Charkham J   *Keeping good company* OUP 1994, Chapter 2.

52 See: Davies P (2005) *op cit* p 9

Chapter 12

Tomorrows Corporation

12.1   Summary

In this chapter we will seek answers to a fundamental question: what shape should the corporation of tomorrow take? This is central to the task we have addressed throughout in this book. Corporations play a fundamental, irreplaceable role in the generation of wealth, the opening up of new market possibilities and the welfare of those who work for the corporation and society more broadly.

In meeting these challenges it is clear that fundamental reforms need to be undertaken. These should aim to strengthen corporations in their quest for wealth creation whilst ensuring that corporations are well and effectively governed to ensure that they firmly reflect the wider concerns of society in realising those ambitions. Our proposals are aimed at strengthening the legitimacy and standing of corporations.

12.2   The provenance of the corporation

In the preceding chapters we have explored the following principal aspects of the corporation. We have examined its medieval origins in an unlimited liability European world. We have examined the impact off limited liability and the confusions that this created in Anglo American jurisdictions and the differences elsewhere. We have examined the different portrayals of the corporation in different jurisdictions and the divide between its interpretive portrayal as a *legal person* and an *aggregate entity*. Finally we have examined the *path dependent* way in which corporate governance arrangements have evolved.

In doing these things we have investigated in some depth the legal provisions mainly in Britain but also elsewhere which both govern and create the climate within which business is conducted. We have seen through a wide number of examples how failures continue to arise despite our best efforts to tighten up and make it more difficult for serious lapses to occur. We will now examine under various headings where fundamental changes to need to be addressed if the corporation of tomorrow is to better address the challenges of legitimacy.

12.3   The role of directors

In the British context a full discussion of the role of the director is provided in Chapter 5. Reference has been made to the Report of the CLRSG (Company Law Review Steering Group). Whilst emphasising that directors need to have a clear statement of what is required of them this as already argued has never materialised. In general terms case law already provides guidance on such matters as obedience to the company's constitution; loyalty to the purposes of the company in securing the interests of its members; independence of judgement; avoidance of conflicts of interest; care skill and diligence in the discharge of their duties. The CLRSG nevertheless argued that there is a need for a clear accessible statement setting out *what is expected* of directors.[1]

Perhaps the most significant and controversial specification centres on the director's obligations to be cognisant of broader stakeholder interests and the environment. These matters are controversial because they will formalise responsibilities for complex issues which some will argue are not part of the remit of good and effective corporate governance. This will take directors into new areas by requiring that they provide a "review of the business, its performance, plans and prospects" including an assessment of social and environmental impacts.[2] In short the skills and attributes required to run tomorrow's company and to seriously address these challenges will make significantly different demands in terms of skills and experience when compared with the past. Recycling of former senior level executive directors can no longer be relied upon to meet the challenges of the future.

12.4   The knowledge, skills and attributes needed for the job

As we have seen The *Higgs Report*[3] focused a good deal of useful light on the functions of boards in British public companies and on the particular role of the non executive director (NED). Interest in the NED in the terms of reference for his report arose out of concerns that failures in corporate governance may, at root, amount to a failure on the part of NEDs to perform their important function effectively. There will be those reading the Higgs Report who will end up feeling that it is, in many respects, a side show -- a distraction from other more fundamental questions. But it is important to understand why the government felt it had to address this matter. Central to the evolution of the Combined Code in Britain and parallel codes in the American jurisdictions, the NED, or independent director, is seen to play a crucial "ring keeping" role. This flows from the designation of the directors as being *non executive* - not part of the everyday running of the business - meaning independent from other corporate or organisational obligations and commitments.[4]

It was always foreseen that NEDs would be experienced enough, strong minded enough, and independent enough to challenge board decisions if this proved necessary in a bid to protect the interest of shareholders and other stakeholders. In practice there is plenty of evidence to show that this is not the case. This is drawn from examples where NEDs have claimed they were simply unaware of the implications of certain issueson which the board took decisions[5]or were otherwise not fully informed, or perhaps worse did nothing.

There are, however, more serious considerations. NEDs are expected to put in a very small amount of time for which they receive commensurate remuneration. Typically NEDs in Britain are paid in the region of £30,000 - £40,000 per annum for providing support and attending meetings of two or three days a month. Some argue that this means NEDs can never be on top of complex matters because the amount of time they are able to invest is very limited. The idea of increasing the number of days and the remuneration meets with the objections that this might begin to place the NED in the same category as a full time executive director and compromise his or her independence. There is a further behavioural question that is often ignored. NEDs are frequently kept at arm's length by other key executive board directors. Some see this as evidence that NEDs are seen, at best, as a "necessary evil", at worst a potential source of trouble.[6]

Two matters have emerged that are noteworthy. First – it is argued that NEDs are too often not what they appear to be. NEDs, so the critics argue, are drawn from a very narrow pool of talent. In some instances they sit together on different boards, or board committees. This creates a network of interests likely to promote just about anything other than "independence" of view and a commitment to good corporate governance. Higgs recognised this problem. He famously refers to the need to widen the *gene pool* of directors. This, it should be noted, was not only a response to the narrowness of background and interests within the current pool of talent. It was also recognition that changing perceptions in the field of corporate governance and CSR were creating new challenges that the current *gene pool* was not well equipped to address.

Second it might be argued that too little attention has been given to the need to ensure that NEDs have the necessary vocational qualifications to effectively address the task. There is no systematic attempt to ensure that directors and/or NEDs have undertaken any substantial training in the practice of good governance. As with so much else there is an unhealthy reliance on corporate *connections* and past corporate experience, to the neglect of the wider skills that are evidently required.

12.5   The role of the board

Few matters are as controversial and as vexed as the role of the board. The first difficulty is that the board in Anglo American jurisdictions lacks a strong and effective constitutional underpinning. The relationship between the board and the corporation is not set out clearly in law. In practice the board is seen as being a creature of the corporation. Traditions elsewhere, but particularly in *Rhineland* and Nordic jurisdictions, make this constitutional difference very clear. There is a need in British and American company law to clarify these matters. In doing so the constitutional status of the board will need to be clearly defined.

There is a strong case for arguing that the board should be an entity separate from the corporation. It needs to have duties and obligations in law that ensure that it represents the interests of shareholders and other stakeholders - as well as those of the corporation. As things stand the board is inseparable from the corporation – a role which prevents the board from representing the interests of shareholders and other stakeholders in any meaningful way. In short neither the board nor its directors can act as a countervailing influence over the corporation. In practice it confers still greater powers to the corporation.[7]

Within the *Rhineland* model the structure of governance is differently designed. Central to the design is the two-tier board system – the executive board and the supervisory board. The executive board is responsible for the day to day running of the company. The supervisory board is there to oversee the activities of the executive board and to respond to the interests of shareholders and other stakeholders including workers representatives who sit as directors. Critics of the two-tier system of governance – mainly those in Anglo American jurisdictions - complain that it creates an interminably complex system of management and governance that in Anglo American jurisdictions would simply not work.

Critics argue that the appearance of such structures in Anglo American jurisdictions would make it impossible for corporations to access capital markets. Investors would never feel comfortable about a structure of governance which weakened capacity to take effective and timely commercial decisions.[8] There is also a powerful aversion in Anglo American jurisdictions to the concept of worker directors and other forms of trade union or stakeholder representation at board level. There is no appetite to share power. Without doubt, however, there is a compelling case for examining how far the dynamic of the two-tier board structure might add to or otherwise improve corporate governance in Anglo American corporations. This needs to be fully explored.

12.6 The role of the board in driving forward the corporation

The role of the board in driving forward the corporation is of course of central importance. The effectiveness of the corporation almost certainly mirrors the effectiveness and the leadership of the board in any particular situation. Again, however, the question arises - do unitary board structures offer the best prospect for viable commercial development and corporate governance? The evidence is, surprisingly, mostly anecdotal. Anglo American world class businesses like Apple, Microsoft, Boeing, Bank America (all from America) and perhaps Rolls Royce, GSK, BAE and HSBC (from Britain) mostly offer evidence of effective, corporate commercial development based on unitary board structures. Those same companies also aspire to high standards (or mostly high standards!) of corporate governance.[9]

When these are compared with their homologues in *Rhineland* Europe and the Nordic countries any observer is bound to pause. The *Rhineland* includes companies like BMW, VW, Bayer, Siemens, Deutsche Bank, in Germany and Philips and ING Bank, the Netherlands, and EADS, (a European Company registered in the Netherlands)which includes Airbus Industrie. In the Nordic countries companies like, Novo Nordik (Danish) Statoil, (Norwegian), SKF, Skanska, Sandvik (Swedish) and Nokia (Finland). These names, chosen casually, raise a vital question. How have these *Rhineland,* Nordic and wider European companies survived and competed if the two-tier system of monitoring and accountability is so fundamentally flawed? The provisional conclusion must be that many of the objections to two-tier corporate governance structures come from those whose natural preference supports the unitary structure. This matter urgently needs to be independently examined and evaluated.

*Rhineland*and Nordic structures may, in the end, provide a more effective democratic control structure for the corporation, though not without reservation. They are often viewed as being opaque when compared with their Anglo American counterparts. By tradition less is made public about internal company deliberations. Public pressure for greater transparency is less. But some facts are hard to challenge. Two-tier structures provide a better representation of the diverse interests impacted by the corporation. They also offer a longer term commitment to sustained investment and development.

12.7 The relationship between board and management

What is management and what is directorship? This question raises vital issues which need to be better understood. In turn this raises questions concerning the relationship

218

between the board of directors and the corporation. In the unitary board model the corporation is for all practical purposes coterminous with management and direction. As observed earlier this presents a serious constitutional issue. Boards are not distinguished clearly enough in law or practice from the corporation. The same issue arises between the *board* and management. The reality is that the board is part of a hierarchical corporate continuum with independent directors bolted-on to offer the appearance of effective governance.

As employees moves higher up the management structure of the corporation the best may eventually be appointed to the board. The most respected managers within the ranks of senior management will eventually succeed to become members of the board. This arrangement is both meritocratic and anomalous. Management is the voice and actions of the corporation. Management's relationship with the board therefore needs to be carefully defined. Only in this way can the board represent effectively the wider interests which are affected by the actions of the corporation.

In the overall architecture there has to be recognition that the board is a key organ of the corporation. The board needs to be able, in its role, to represent the collective expression of energy of which the corporation is a manifestation. The board needs to be able to ensure that it can reasonably, and in an even-handed manner, protect the interests of shareholders and other stakeholders and meet changes in societal expectations of the corporation in relation to CSR and environmental best practice.

12.8   Democracy in the workplace

Democracy in the workplace is a contentious matter. The process for selecting board members falls far short of meeting any serious standards of democratic scrutiny. The appointment of board members is for the most part a firmly closed business. This is a preserve of the board. The board initiates its own searches either from within the corporation or outside. For executive directors it is common practice for the board to select from their midst whoever appears to best meet the needs. For external or independent appointments *head-hunters* are frequently used but this is again closely controlled by senior directors if not the CEO.

Only when the *chosen* candidate has been identified are the shareholders then consulted and invited to approve the board candidates. It is rare for shareholders to raise strong or serious objections.[10]Though the shareholders have the right to be consulted over nominations, views and opinions expressed by them are often ignored. Resolutions, as reported elsewhere, are not legally binding.[11]This raises a further issue. Without knowing in detail the key professional attributes expected of directors it is an impossible to decide who is likely to be best person to discharge those duties. We know that successful directorship must encompass proven commercial experience. People seeking to direct companies must meet these requirements. For the most part this stipulation tends to translate into knowledge and understanding of how key commercial and financial reports are put together and interpreted. There is an understandable emphasis on financial and commercial literacy. It is, however, only part of the skill and knowledge base that a director needs to have when accepting the responsibility of directorship. There is little public debate about these matters.

With NEDs the skill profile is in many respects more challenging. NEDs need to know and understand what is required of them as independent directors. This, as already stated, may very well be quite different to what is required of executive directors. NEDs have to demonstrate understanding of how to manage their responsibilities. This will always entail a rigorous process of research verification and authentication of important corporate claims. NEDs are seldom involved directly in the origination of documents presented at board meetings. The best safeguard against dishonest, exaggerated or misleading claims is for the NED to seek and exact full answers to key questions regarding authenticity. This will entail the provision of adequate resources to enable the NED to discharge his or her duties. This would assure that NEDs can effectively discharge their tasks. It will otherwise counter the concern that without sufficient knowledge they will be unable to take informed decisions.[12]

We are bound also to consider the ultimate significance of co-determination in the workplace. In doing so we see the corporation not just as Eisenberg (1989) defines it: 'aprofit seeking enterprise of persons and assets organised by rules.'[13] It is, in reality, the embodiment of collective and associative action. This is compellingly illustrated in the John Lewis Case where we have seen the directors, managers, members[14] and other stakeholders in a commercially successful relationship of co-operative endeavour. Ultimately, to quote Teubner (1994)[15] this gives *autopoietic* expression to the aims and purposes of corporate endeavour.

12.9   The "he is one of us" mentality

By far the most important single barrier to selecting the best people has already been acknowledging in the *Higgs Review* in Britain and in parallel reviews in the US.[16] The processes of selection and appointment inevitably replicate existing peer group qualities and values. It is an outstanding example of the pervasive and destructive influence the self-like selection process from a network of potential equals. Whilst this phenomenon is by no means limited to the selection of directors to serve on company boards it is one of the most urgent problems that need to be addressed if the evils of *crony capitalism*[17] are to be effectively addressed.

One possible way to address this problem is to ensure that shareholders and other key stakeholders such as trade unions have a right in law to select and recommend for appointment directors who they judge to have the appropriate skills and experience.[18] This requires, however, a clear statement on what constitutes evidence of those skills and aptitudes along with the rights, duties and loyalties of directors. There are, however, other barriers to entry. Potential candidates may be discouraged from being nominated because they fear that there will be overwhelming hostility to their appointment from existing vested interests. This problem will not easily be resolved until the constitutional status of the board has been satisfactorily resolved. As noted earlier, the board is constitutionally indistinguishable from the corporation as things stand. This is wrong. The board needs to be seen as an organ of the corporation but otherwise independent from the corporation. In this way the board would negotiate its own budget, funded by the corporation, to realise the task of proper effective supervision of the corporation's activities.

The aim is that directors, but independent directors in particular, would be resourced to discharge the burden of responsibility upon them. This might take the form of support staff appointed by the board (not the management or the corporation) to provide independent professional advice on issues concerning the corporation on which the board has to take a robust view if the best interests of the corporation the shareholders and stakeholders, alike are to be protected. [19]

12.10   Managing the relationship with members and stakeholders

It is sometimes argued that the only responsibility the board has is to shareholders, (or members as they are sometimes referred to). This is because they are commonly, if mistakenly, referred to as the owners of the corporation. As a corollary of this it is also argued that stakeholders have no rights beyond those that are established elsewhere in law. This has the effect of producing a phoney *them and us* conflict. The reality is that corporations and their boards are rapidly realising that good and effective corporate governance must ensure that stakeholders as well as shareholders are properly considered in the formulation of corporate strategy. This is now seen increasingly as a key factor determining success and longevity. This is not, however, the same as saying those corporations (and their boards) that address the concerns of stakeholders other than shareholders inevitably enjoy better quality profits. Research in this area falls short of establishing any clear correlation between these different situations.

Opinion surveys, however, increasingly point out that corporations (and their boards) that show respect for stakeholder concerns are certainly well regarded by society at large. This may mean that employees are better disposed to work for well respected corporations or that consumers will be better disposed to buy the products of such corporations. This data has certainly awakened corporate awareness that public concerns and public opinion needs to studied carefully.[20] The implication is that stakeholder concerns do have to be properly internalised into board decision taking. It is now accepted wisdom that there is no irreconcilable conflict between the interest of shareholders and other stakeholders. It also appears to follow that shareholder interest will be better protected when there is proper and effective stakeholder engagement.

Managing this relationship effectively remains, however, problematical. In a bid to claim the high ground many corporations conduct exercises in CSR. Sadly much, perhaps the most, of what is undertaken in the name of CSR turns out to be little more than self serving PR-driven propaganda. As we have explored earlier, too many corporations see CSR as a type of marketing exercise in which brand image building is the exclusive concern. One consequence of this is that claims made by corporations are often not independently verified nor is there evidence that stakeholders have been systematically consulted in determining whatever it is the corporation is claiming. There are also other examples. Enron was audacious in the self serving claims it made about CSR during the period the corporation was being pillaged by some of its most senior board directors. NEDs were silent, or unaware, or both, throughout.

Moves to establish a sounder footing to CSR are now everywhere in evidence. This is an encouraging sign. But it will take time before corporations will be willing to open up these processes to full public scrutiny in assessing the merit, the accuracy and the relevance of the claims made.[21] Fundamental shifts in the way in which boards operate will certainly determine the rate of progress we can expect.

12.11 The importance of governance in promoting success of the enterprise

Motivation is a key factor in successful development. There can be little doubt that good governance is highly advantageous. At workplace level there is overwhelming evidence that employees in organisations which have been criticised for their governance standards are often unhappy and dismotivated. The case of the decline and eventual fall of Marconi Plc in 2005 is a prime example. Board level incompetence, greed and indifference led to huge job losses with those employees who remained left facing a bleak, unpromising future. The directors who were eventually deposed were rewarded with hefty benefits resulting from unexpired contracts and generous pension funds - when many others were left with nothing. There can be few more telling examples of the long term damage that poor governance fosters at every level but most importantly at the level of industrial relations. Marconi is only one of a number of high profile cases where working people and their families have suffered from the gross and unpunished incompetence of senior directors and NEDs.

There is little doubt that good and effective corporate governance is also a key determinant in sustainable commercial development. Good and effective governance ensures that strategic decisions regarding the corporation's development are fully debated – not decided by dominant personalities. In the case of Marconi there is clear evidence that key strategic policy decisions about the future thrust of the corporation were inadequately assessed in terms of prospective commercial risk. The board failed to assess thoroughly enough the fundamental nature of the switch of business focus that the Chairman and chief executive (both Marconi insiders) were determined to pursue.

12.12   Conclusions

In trying to sketch out the shape of the corporation of tomorrow we have pulled together the conclusions that have emerged in different stages of our research. The most important conclusion reached is that the corporation, in order to maintain and strengthen its legitimacy has to be seen to be governed in the interest a wide range of stakeholders and not simply shareholders. As we have discovered the Anglo American model falls well short of what is required to address the challenges of the future. The most effective way of realising this ambition is for all corporations to ensure that there is in place a proper independent supervisory board which will faithfully represent those broader interests.

The supervisory board will also be responsible for overseeing the activities of the executive board of management. Getting the institutional structures in place will also make possible a proper examination of directors' duties. Only in this way can public confidence in the management of large scale corporate entities is to be strengthened. Only in this way will the corporation emerge as an effective, inclusive economic and social entity capable of responding to the challenges of the future.

Questions for review

1. Why is important for directors and NEDs to have a clear enforceable statement of what is expected of them in discharging their tasks?

2. The knowledge and skills of the director remains unresolved. What sort of vocation qualifications might best meet the need?

3. Increasing the numbers of NEDs on unitary boards may do little to fundamentally change board behaviour. Is there a case for separating execution from supervision as foreseen in *Rhineland* two-tier structures?

4. How best can we address the challenge of widening the *gene pool* of directors?

5. How best can the constitutional independence of the board be established?

6. Would you agree that the constitutional arrangements governing the corporation should protect the democratic fabric of society?

7. Should boards recognise and internalise the interests of important stakeholders such as employee?

8. How do we raise CSR above self serving PR hype?

Learning Tasks

I   Construct a constitution for a publicly held corporation.

II   Define the key vocational skills directors should have.

III   How should stakeholder interests be taken into account in decision taking?

Notes

[1] See Annex C Vol 1, pages 344 to 348 of the CLRSG Final Report *op cit*

[2] See para 3.34 Volume 1 of the Final Report *op cit*

[3] The Higgs Report *op cit*

[4] This too is not without serious controversy since the law does not in either British or American jurisdictions admit the existence of non executive or independent directors. In law they are all directors. No distinction is made between different types.

[5] This argument was used by Lord Wakenham an NED (or independent director) of Enron at the time the scandal first broke. He claimed that he did ask for clarification of certain key issues appearing in documents at board meetings on which decisions were subsequently taken. He argued that he did not receive satisfactory clarifications on those matters but did not resign from the board or otherwise make public his misgivings.

[6] Interestingly a recent upheaval within the governance structure of the BBC - a British corporation established by Royal Charter – has revealed that much energy was spent by the executive directors in trying to avoid involving the governors [the equivalent of NEDs in public companies] in the operations of the BBC.

[7] The 1990 landmark judgement of the British House of Lords underscores this problem. In the case Caparo Industries versus Dickmanit was ruled that there is effectively no scope for tortious action by shareholders against auditors since the auditors owe a duty of care to the corporation not the shareholder. This confers further power on the corporation and its organ, the board, at the expense of other stakeholders.

[8] Needless to say critics of the *Rhineland* and Nordic models are unable to explain the number of world class global businesses that operate in these jurisdictions and under these arrangements.

[9] Remembering however that BAE, as major global arms supplier, has been at the centre of serious accusations of bribery.

[10] Attempts by Sainsbury Plc to appoint an independent chairman, Sir Ian Prosser resulted in a strong and effective campaign from shareholders. Sainsbury Plc felt unable or unwilling to fight the opposed shareholders and by mutual consent with the board the chosen member was rejected.

[11] Matt Barrett was appointed to the Chair of Barclays Bank Plc in 1999. In contradiction of the recommendations of the British Combined Code and the Higgs Review his former deputy John Varley was eventually "accepted" as Chairman in 2004 despite shareholder concerns.

[12] The spate of examples where NEDs have failed to restrain entrenched management power has fostered unfounded fears that the supply of suitable NEDs would dry up in response to widespread criticism.

[13] See: Eisenberg M A *op citThe Structure of Corporation Law* (1989) 89 Colum L Rev 1461 at 1471.

[14] Members, whether they are members of a company not limited by shares or as shareholders in a company limited by shares.

[15] See: Teubner G *Enterprise Corporatism: New Industrial Policy and the Essence of the Legal Person.* Wheeler S ed. 1994. His analysis puts the evolution of legal doctrine in America and Britain on its head. It starts with the corporation because it exists in reality, not as some fiction but as a real entity. This enables one to then identify the organs through which the different corporate actors give expression to the corporation. This is the essence of *autopoiesis.*

[16] The Sarbanes Oxley Act of 2002 in the US embodies many of the concerns about the independence of directors, the untrammelled power of executive directors and the need to ensure the selection and recruitment of strong independent directors.

[17]*Crony capitalism* it should not be overlooked was a term coined by Anglo American commentators on the "corruption" within the governance of Asian corporations which lead to the 1987 collapse of corporations and banks in South Korea, Thailand, Indonesia and elsewhere in the region. These developments triggered the publication by the OECD of the first set of Principles of Corporate Governance

in a bid to promote best practice internationally. The Principles were very largely inspired by the Anglo American model of governance which, it was argued, provided the best tested safeguards against cronyism. [18] Dangers, however, abound! It will never be a safe or satisfactory solution for other shareholder and or stakeholder groups to be invited to nominate until such time as there is a clear consensus on the skills and aptitudes needed for success. It is important to realise, for example, that corporations are commercial entities and have to operate within the confines of economics and commerce. They are not like Companies Limited By Guarantee, NGOs, charities, voluntary sector organisations or trade unions. It would be wrong to assume that the sorts of qualities found in successful managers and directors of such entities would necessarily be appropriate to the commercial boardroom situation.

[19] This will inevitably face deep opposition on the grounds that it will weaken the capacity of the board to take effective and timely decisions. This objection needs however to be assessed against experience in the two-tier *Rhineland or* Nordic systems of governance where the supervisory board oversees the activities of the executive board.

[20] The classic example is the failure of Shell in the Brent Spar episode to gauge the level of public anger to the corporation's failure to find an environmentally responsible solution to the disposal of an unwanted North Sea oil rig. Shell, believing that it could weather the storm, was eventually obliged to abandon the decision to bury the rig in Atlantic deep water.

[21] This process will also benefit, in the long term, by moves to establish Socially Responsible Investment (SRI) with the Footsie4Good and the Dow Jones Corporate Responsibility Index being examples of this

Chapter 13

The case for fundamental reform of corporate governance

13.1   Summary

'If it ain't broken why mend it', a familiar American aphorism. When applied to the corporation and its governance it's difficult to resist. Whatever problems from time to time arise with the corporation and its governance we are assured that they can be addressed and remedied - within the existing framework. Can we continue to rely on such assurances? When we look closely at the law governing the largest publicly traded corporations and their behaviour we can see that nothing can be taken at face value. There are some serious underlying problems. These have to be addressed if genuine and pressing public concerns about the corporation are to be effectively remedied.

To understand the nature of the problem we have looked at the historical evolution of the corporation. The reason for this is important. The corporation, as we have seen, is a social and political creation. It is rooted in *concession*. It is an entity that has been *accorded* legal status. It is not, in contrast, a natural person like a wealth creating individual whose rights and duties are grounded in natural law. Sociologically and legally speaking the corporation is different. It is a device created in recognition of the fact that the vehicle of individual endeavour is sometimes inadequate for the attainment of certain economic objectives. In identifying the right reforms we need to take into account these matters if the legitimacy of the corporation is to be restored.

13.2   The role of enterprise in economic development

As a legal entity the corporation has a long and mostly illustrious history. Its origins as we have seen date back several centuries in Europe. The corporation exists because of the awareness that certain types of social and economic undertaking cannot be sustained by individual effort alone. For good and obvious reasons certain objectives can be better by individuals working in combination over generations. Individuals cannot alone achieve these objectives. As an enterprise the corporation is the embodiment of this perception and purpose.

Let us again remind ourselves of what enterprise-related activities involve. The efforts of Adam Smith's 'butcher, baker and candlestick maker' form part of long list of activities which have evolved over time. Individuals acting as economic agents generate goods and services for households and producers - the staples of all societies. Adam Smith in his Wealth of Nations explored the nature and causes of these activities in the wealth creation process. He was a prime mover in explaining the critical role of enterprise in driving sustainable economic development. These activities existed well before the arrival of money as a medium of exchange. Individuals bartered their own effort in terms of output for the output they needed from others. They literally exchanged grain for cloth – hand implements for other producers' goods and so forth. As we have seen, however, not all economic activity is exclusively individual in nature.

The medieval manorial system, which pre-dated the market economy so vividly described by Adam Smith, was organised on a similar basis of individual exchange. But there were already some significant differences. Within this system there was recognition that some things were beyond the reach of any one individual. The system itself had to be maintained. This was achieved by *contributions* and other *dues* to the lord of the manor for the maintenance of all aspects of the system and its continuity. Such terms as *boon harvests* and other imposts describe these collective dues. Today we would recognise these as taxes levied to support collective goods such as defence, education, justice, health and social security.

There was recognition within these ancient arrangements that certain activities of a collective nature could not be maintained or sustained on an individual basis. The manorial system is thus an informal example of corporate expression. The system could not operate without this collective underpinning. The system declined as these underpinnings were weakened. As we move forward in history these underlying collective perceptions continuously re-assert themselves. With the passage of time they too adapt to changing circumstances.

13.3   The growth of corporate activities

Throughout Europe and elsewhere, monarchs, princes and the Church as we have seen allowed for the creation of corporate entities. Such initiatives entailed forms of public sponsorship and public accountability. Hence in Europe townships were granted charter status along with universities and other expressions of corporate effort such as merchant and craft gilds. All of these activities had at least two features in common. They reflected permanence and continuity in terms of time. Because they are concessionary in nature they also provided a basis for accountability and control. Individuals working alone could not be expected to meet these standards. A number of *incorporated* individuals, with new members replenishing retiring or dying members, could with more certainty sustain this throughout different generations.

At the time Adam Smith was writing in 1776[1] corporations were firmly established as institutional vehicles. International trading opportunities in European countries including Britain were being exploited by chartered companies and other partnership forms. They supplied the capital and the management. They shared in the profits and losses. The liability of such undertakings was effectively unlimited though, as we have seen, this was circumvented in England through *deed of settlement* companies. The full rigour of unlimited liability was thus avoided. This was to become an important factor in the debate which led to the passing of the Joint Stock Companies Act in 1844.

We need also to remember what was happening during the economic and technological change we now refer to as the industrial revolution. As with the Internet of today, contemporary observers in the early 19th century were pondering the significance of changes taking place around them. They had witnessed what are commonly described as agrarian revolutions in the 17th 18th and 19th centuries. Agricultural activity was fundamentally reshaped during these revolutions. Population pressure was transforming farming from a localised, small scale open-field activity, into an organised market-driven undertaking. Crop yields and more effective forms of cultivation and harvesting were uppermost considerations driving innovation and technological change. The growth of larger towns and later the emergence of industrial conurbations and railways created new pressures for change. The same processes were affecting all aspects of economic life. The era of sponsored technology-driven industrialisation was about to break.

13.4   The impact of industrialisation

As industrialisation advanced, so too did the need for capital to support technological and market innovation. Attention also focused on institutional reforms. These were needed if new opportunities were to be opened up. One matter, which attracted close attention, was the role of capital in industrial and commercial development. Whereas in earlier periods organised investment capital had played a more informal role in development the awareness was growing that capital would play a pivotal role in future developments. This could only happen if savings, the counterpart of investment, was effectively organised and controlled. If savings were to be mobilised on a sufficient scale to meet this need an effective bridgehead between savings and investment had to be established.

This is a critical social and economic turning point. It caused attention to focus on how best savings could be transformed into capital to sustain industrial development. Observers began to realise that the flow of capital for industrial development depended on three crucial considerations: a market for the new output had to be created: technology to enable production to meet the needs of the market had to be developed, and specialist capital market skills were needed to orchestrate events.

These new paradigms were radically different from those which characterised commercial activity in earlier periods. Single proprietors mostly undertook this activity. Access to capital was much less important. Capital support for activity carried out by partnerships and other corporate endeavours was mostly informal. Most importantly these activities all carried unlimited liability for commercial risk – a discipline judged to be essential to the functioning of a stable market economy.

13.5   The arrival of limited liability and its implications

Those looking at the new possibilities for industrial development spotted the weakness in the existing institutional and legal arrangements. They realised that a market for capital could not be effectively exploited without redefining the ownership obligations for such entities as partnerships and corporations. There was, significantly, little interest in single proprietors. A new status would be needed for a new style corporation. The new style corporation would, by its nature, need to be able to access equity investment. From a presentational standpoint it would ideally be a business run by a successful entrepreneur who would then bring the necessary capital and management talent into the business. This was a fundamental transforming event.

This design, for it to succeed, had to address the issue of shareholder risk. An ingenious solution was identified. Shareholders within the new architecture would be enabled to act purely and simply as investors. They would have no active role to play in running the business. Though they would play a crucial role as a source of equity funding they would have no role to play in the everyday management of the corporation. This was a major development. For this to happen one final incentive was required.

13.6   A sweetener for shareholders

Since shareholders would no longer have any responsible for the commercial affairs of the company in terms of everyday management – they would be rewarded with an exemption in respect of corporate liability. The law of limited liability was thus born. Despite the confusions over the nature of limited liability that followed its enactment effectively established a new relationship between ownership, management and capital. The law as we have seen was to have a fundamental impact upon the subsequent evolution of the corporation and commercial and corporate law.

The effect of the law was the transformation of a concession-based institution, originally designed to make possible a collective expression of effort – commercial or otherwise. Because capital had grown in importance and was critical to the development of new technologies and new markets a specific mechanism had to be created. These new arrangements would enable larger scale equity to be put into businesses with shareholders being detached or *cleansed* from management process.

13.7   Shareholding and question of ownership

As we have seen shareholders under these new arrangements became *detached* downstream claimants on the stream of profits generated by the corporation with managers employed by the corporation as agents supposedly of the shareholders. Though under these arrangements shareholders were technically the owners of the corporation, ownership in any meaningful sense of the term was effectively denied. This fact became more evident as corporations grew larger and eventually became stock exchange listed. Because shareholders don't *own* they cannot in any real sense control – something that has been steadily reinforced in common law judgments. The role of the shareholder as an owner of the corporation was thus effectively brought to an end.

But we should not forget the shareholder is a key player in a properly functioning capital market. Unless, at the outset, the shareholder buys an equity stake in the corporation the corporation will remain without capital. Once the shareholder parts with his investment his role begins to change. As time advances and founding shareholders are replaced by institutional investors the shareholding function is transformed. The institutional investor becomes a passive player whose prime concern is that a dividend is paid to him out of the profits generated by the corporation. The responsibility of management is to ensure that the corporation remains a viable going concern and can generate profits sufficient to meet investor expectations in terms of dividends, capital growth and the on-going investment needs of the business.

13.8　　　　　　　　　　　The paradox of the corporation

We have asked and explored the question - wherein does the ownership of the corporation lie. Do the shareholders actually own? Does the corporation have an existence of its own? As we have seen the corporation enjoys an independent legal status. Its legal existence is however a personification of an individual not an actual or real individual. We should recall that the chartered or unlimited liability corporation, in much the same way, was an individual expression of something essentially collective in nature. It too was in every sense a personification of an individual – but not an actual individual. It is, as we have seen earlier, a device of convenience.

In formulating limited liability laws this underlying concept remained intact. It had to. Under pre-limited liability laws individual members of the corporation were jointly and severally responsible for its affairs. Though the corporation might be referred to as if it was a singular entity, in reality and law the ownership lay with the individual members or owners who had unlimited joint and several liability. Though ownership relationships change as a result of limited liability, liability remains. The new corporate entity effectively assumes the unlimited liability, which has been lifted from the shoulders of shareholders. The corporation thus emerges as a legal entity — a personification of a legal person with, effectively, unlimited liability. This creates a paradox. The corporation is termed as being limited liability. In reality it is that the shareholders enjoy limited liability - not the corporation.

Herein lies a difficulty. If the corporation is a legal person then what is the liability status of that person, how is it assessed, how is it controlled and by whom is it controlled? In their efforts to resolve this paradox jurists have at times chosen to try and eliminate the ambiguity that surrounds the status of the corporation. They have chosen two fundamentally different though interconnected routes in doing so. First they have systematically undermined the reality of the corporation's existence as a legal person. This has been achieved by portraying the corporation to a comprehensive network of contracts, the so called *nexus of contracts*. This process of reduction effectively negates any notion of existence, real or personified, for the corporation. It also helps to justify the argument that corporations should not be separately regulated. The second route they have chosen is to rely on the existence of the corporation as a legal person by endowing it with citizen status and by this way distinguishing the corporation and what it is from the directors who must act on its behalf.

13.9   The magician's sleight of hand

Understandably the man in the street is baffled by what appears as a magician's sleight of hand. A real entity that we could formerly recognise by its members and owners has been spirited away as a result of limited liability. Does this mean that the corporation no longer exists — except as a *nexus of contracts* or as a fictional person? Whilst on face of things this appears to be true reality of course informs us differently. Corporations are powerful entities. They exist, materially. They straddle, in many instances, the globe. The scope of their activities cannot possibly be defined by known and existing contracts. They may be and often are subject to myriad liabilities, some concealed, some latent, some yet to be expressed. This must be a powerful counter to the argument that the corporation is but the summation of its contracts. In the alternative we are left with Bob Diamond's portrayal of the corporation as some sort of errant child which management has the responsibility for *disciplining*. It is a baffling sleight of hand.

There is only one credible answer to the question - what is the corporation? It is the people it employs, the managers who run it, the products and services it generates and the shareholders. We can easily identify the party that speaks the mind and does the deeds of the corporation. This party is the management of the corporation. What, we may then ask, is the response of management to that claim?

The response of management is clear. They point out that legally they are servants or employees of the corporation. They do not own the corporation. They only act for the corporation. Misleadingly as we have seen, the shareholders are portrayed as owners of the corporation. In reality the shareholders neither own nor determine the actions of the corporation. So who in fact owns the corporation and who is legally accountable for its actions? To that fundamental question there remains no satisfactory answer. We are left only with the knowledge that managers act and speak for it. The corporation can do nothing without management action. The corporation has no power and no voice – except when management speaks and acts for it. And so the mystery deepens and the fog thickens. The corporation remains in a strange limbo yet wielding immense power that is exercised only when management takes a decision to do something in its name.

13.10   The ambiguous status of management

In practice one might fairly conclude that the managers effectively own and certainly control the corporation. As we have seen they maintain that as employees of the corporation they act for the corporation as agents for the shareholders who are the owners. Managers in this circular argument claim that whatever actions they take are taken *for and on behalf of the corporation.* As if in justification there is another frequently concealed argument which takes the form: "what we did was without prior knowledge of tortious implications". It is increasingly common for managers to protect themselves against commercial liability or tort action arising from the corporation's management-determined activities. The instinct of management to protect itself from exposure is powerful. Liability is thus pushed back onto the unthinking, unknowing corporation. The corporation in the end carries the liability with shareholders and other stakeholders bearing the losses.

Apart from issues of difficult-to-secure criminal liability, management is effectively ring-fenced from any actions that arise from the commercial and market operations of the corporation, which it determines. This ensures that the corporation is the natural focus of legal attention – not management. Management responding on the part of the corporation, but not answerable or accountable for its collective deeds, defend actions taken against the corporation in law. An activity reminiscent of the favourite childhood games: pass the parcel!

13.11 An unsatisfactory basis on which to build corporate governance

The situation is as unclear as it is unsatisfactory. The corporation's existence in any form other than contract has been systematically dismembered. Yet common sense tells us that the corporation exists in reality, beyond contract. This raises a number of fundamental problems associated with governance. Under English and American law it means that management is the only meaningful focus in determining governance.

Whilst this is, in practice, where power and responsibility lies it is unacceptable to have to address management on matters for which management is not legally accountable. Because of the legal portrayal of the corporation, management speaks and acts on behalf of it. Since no approach to the corporation will realise a practical result without management's involvement it must therefore be assumed that management is effectively the corporation. But as we have seen the response of management is to contest any legal interpretation which would hold them individually or collectively responsible for the actions of the corporation they take on its behalf and in its name.

13.12   A hindrance to progress and accountability

This is a wholly satisfactory solution. The problem is that the nature of the corporation and its status as a legal person has been mishandled in law. The corporation should, if its proper legal status is to be admitted, be responsible to the different parties of which it is constituted. Under such arrangements the corporation would then be the genuine expression of the interests of managers, shareholders, workers, creditors and other stakeholders. The evolution of corporate law effectively denies this reality. It leaves management as the proxy-respondent to legal actions against the corporation and other wider concerns which centre on corporate governance. This is clearly wrong. It denies access to a much wider group which should rightly represent the corporation but in practice are denied access. It is also wrong because it distorts and deforms management behaviour and undermines the legitimacy of the corporation.

The remedies for this state of affairs lie first in recognising the legal contradictions that have arisen in the interpretation of the legal status of the corporation. If the corporation assumes its rightful legal responsibilities under the law then it is obliged to create appropriate institutions, which reflect the collective nature of those responsibilities. This opens up afresh the importance of co-determination through which the corporation can play a full, effective and accountable role in national and international economic development and in so doing recognise the true underlying *concessionist* expression of its creation. In failing to do so, and with eyes and minds firmly closed, we risk perpetuating the illusion that viable corporate governance can be achieved without a fundamental reappraisal of its underpinnings.

13.13   Conclusions

The case for reform is a compelling one. Large corporations exercise huge power. They also shape our common culture. This power has to be properly and effectively supervised and controlled. In Anglo American jurisdictions there is incontrovertible evidence that the power exercised is not appropriately supervised and controlled. Whatever form measures to improve matters take they must reflect recognition of this reality.

Large listed corporations must be subject to regulatory arrangements which fit the power they wield. Not all limited liability companies are the same as we have seen. They change in a radical way as they expand and develop especially when they seeking listing and raise new capital. Proper institutional arrangements have to be put in place to ensure that shareholders and other vitally important stakeholders are represented in all decisions taken by the corporation. Leaving this to executive directors on unitary boards fleshed out with NEDs selected by the executive directors can no longer be accepted as the most important ingredient in effective and sustainable corporate governance.

Questions for review

1. What are the fundamental problems with corporate governance in Anglo American corporations?

2. Is the corporation in your understanding an *aggregate entity* or simply a *legal person*?

3. Why does the problem of unaccountable power arise where corporations are concerned?

4. How in your view should the corporation law be framed to address the challenges?

5. Why is it argued that the corporation is grounded in concession?

6. Why is it suggested the laws of limited liability as they were framed under English law and elsewhere in Anglo American jurisdictions may be at fault?

7. Are you clear why shareholders do not own the corporation?

8. Is there a credible case for independent supervision and co-determination in the workplace?

Learning Tasks

I   Design a governance structure which will meet the needs of tomorrow

II   Design the terms and conditions of an independent supervisory board

III   Describe the legally enforceable obligations would you place on company directors?

Figure 18

Letter to The Economist

Who owns the company?

SIR – Schumpeter's column on outsourcing company boards talked of "the relationship between shareholders who own companies and managers who run them" (August 16th). The notion that shareholders "own" the corporation is in most important respects wrong and needs careful qualification. Institutional investors (commonly referred to as shareholders) in publicly traded corporations under Anglo-American jurisdictions are in many fundamental respects different from the shareholders of private and untraded corporations.

They do not and cannot, because of limited liability, own the assets of the corporation. Schumpeter could do worse than read the judgment of the House of Lords in Salomon v Salomon (1897) which starts the ball rolling. The corporation owns its assets and the board manages these assets. The only thing the shareholders own is a conditional claim on the profits of the corporation, depending ultimately on the board as to what dividend, if any, the corporation declares. The only ultimate sanction they have is to sell and buy elsewhere.

The problem with the boards of publicly traded corporations is that they have too much unaccountable power. Because the boards are unitary in structure there is no proper or effective independent governance. The scale of cronyism is both wider and deeper than Schumpeter cares to admit. Neither Sarbanes-Oxley nor the Cadbury code of best practices addresses this matter in a fundamental way.

Governance arrangements are not the same elsewhere. In Rhineland and Nordic jurisdictions there are important lessons to be learnt about "inclusivity" which Schumpeter sensibly supports.

Richard Tudway

London

Notes

[1] Adam Smith in his Wealth of Nations, (1776) *op cit* saw with remarkable prescience, that shareholders in limited liability companies would eventually become completely detached from the companies in which they were invested. This, as we have seen, he did not favour arguing that it would foster irresponsible behaviour.

Chapter 14

Conclusions

14.1　　　　　　　　　Summary

In exploring the principal question posed in this book, concerning the ownership of the corporation and laws governing directors' duties, a number of detailed conclusions can be drawn. These are set out under the following five headings:

- Rebuilding larger corporations to reflect a wider legal, economic and social reality

- Requiring and enforcing higher standards of company stewardship from directors

- Promoting more active stakeholder and shareholder participation

- Re-crafting the law governing the corporation

- Re-crafting the law governing directors' duties

14.2　　　　The wider legal, economic and social reality

Portraying historically the company as a separate legal person and a legal fiction has created an enduring paradox about the nature of the corporation. As we have explored common sense informs us that large mature corporations have histories and distinctive cultures which arise from their past and on-going existence. In Anglo American jurisdictions a wider debate about the broader social, economic and cultural role of the corporation has been discouraged.

This debate has been eclipsed by the false inference that shareholders, as owners, should continue to enjoy an exclusivity of treatment. This myth retains sway despite the fact that in Anglo American jurisdictions the act of shareholding has been radically transformed. This false inference continues to undermine efforts to strengthen corporate governance and accountability. This feature serves only to favour management entrenchment, undermines the legitimacy of the corporation and fuel social disquiet. This must change.

It will be best addressed by requiring all larger, publicly traded corporation at least being required in law to separate, independent supervisory boards whose task it will be to provide independent oversight of the actions performed by the executive directors. The new boards will represent the wider *aggregate* interests of the corporation including stakeholders and shareholders. The board of supervisors will be responsible in law for ensuring the proper and effective *ex ante* accountability of the corporation and the contractual terms and conditions of top executive management.

- **See the corporation as an aggregate entity reflecting the plurality of interests it comprises**
- **Strengthen the legitimacy of the corporation**
- **Address the false inference that shareholders are owners of the corporation and should enjoy an exclusivity in governance**
- **Require all publicly traded corporations to create separate, independent supervisory boards whose task it will be to provide independent ex ante oversight of the actions performed by the board of management**

14.3   Securing higher standards of stewardship

It has been amply demonstrated throughout that serious failures in the governance of corporations persist particularly in Anglo American jurisdictions. The debate about corporate governance has been at centre stage for over thirty years in the UK following the abandonment of co-determination proposals in the late seventies. The proposals anticipated the introduction of a two-tier board structure and the appointment of worker directors. These were abandoned in favour of a more *business friendly* assessment of how best to address the challenge of effective governance. Since then efforts to widen out the debate on corporate governance have been stifled.

The Higgs Report, on the role of NEDs, following the collapse of Enron in the US, and the history of Marconi Plc in Britain, contained some potentially radical proposals for encouraging a change in the *gene pool* of directors. As with so much else in this field, the proposals took the form of non statutory recommendations. Developments in the post-Higgs period provide little evidence of any fundamental change in board composition though the number of independent NEDs has increased, as a proportion of executive directors.

Following several years of intense deliberation about the structure and content of company law, Section 172 of the British Companies Act 2006 as we have seen earlier now contains a more explicit statutory requirement on directors to take account of employee, environmental and social interests and that these should form the basis of an annual report to shareholders. Attempts to adopt a *pluralist* stakeholder approach were abandoned in favour of the *enlightened shareholder value* approach. This requires that the directors act in ways that will promote the success of the company for the benefit of shareholders.

It will be for the courts to establish objective criteria, having regard to common law precedent and equity, where litigation arises. Disappointingly, the prevailing philosophy of judicial restraint, where matters of commercial judgment are concerned is unlikely to drive the pace of progressive or constructive change. These difficulties are compounded by the history of confusion and ambiguity that has coloured common law.

As we have seen from the various case studies that have been explored there is a common thread throughout where failures in corporate governance are allowed to take hold. The common cause is the failure of NEDs to supervise independently within single unitary board structures. Execution has to be separated from supervision if we are to move forward.

- **Separate execution from supervision in corporate governance**
- **Introduce co-determination in the workplace which will follow naturally from independent supervision in which all stakeholders including shareholders are represented**
- **Foster changes in the *gene pool* of directors as foreseen in the British Higgs Report**
- **Strengthen the statutory requirement that boards will take full account of employee, environmental and social interests in all decisions taken**
- **Withdraw the default preference for judicial constraint as evidenced by the Business Judgement Rule**
- **Protect shareholder and stakeholder wealth**

14.4   Promoting active stakeholder engagement

The underlying goal in effecting a more proactive style of corporate governance turns on encouraging shareholders to use their powers to discipline directors of underperforming companies. For all the arguments that have been recited there is little scope for much in the way of fundamental change. Institutional investors (and other types of equity investors including hedge funds) behave irredeemably as short-termist *absentee landlords.*

This is explained in part by the inherent difficulties of enforcing any of the legal provisions in a situation where shareholders are mostly impotent when management underperformance arises. They are more likely to sell their stake in the erring enterprise than fight for change. Changes in the laws governing limited liability, which might expose shareholders to liability in tort, might stimulate a constructive change in stance though this remains a distant prospect at best. Failures in this area continue to undermine the legitimacy of the corporation. These failures can only be effectively addressed through the adoption of co-determination in the work place.

- **Promote higher standards of professionalism from direction by objective tests of competence**
- **Incentivise shareholders and stakeholders to ensure that such competence tests are employed by the courts in cases where directors are accused of negligence**

14.5   Re-crafting the law of the corporation

The problem in progressing the debate in Anglo American jurisdictions about the role or corporations is two-pronged. First the decision to offer universal access to limited liability. Second the conclusions flowing from the Salomon judgment. With the wisdom of hindsight limited liability was probably not an appropriate regime for all companies. For the vast bulk of enterprises a form of incorporation falling short of full limited liability might have been preferable. But the British obsession with *one size fits all* was irresistible.

Limited liability would then have been limited to companies seeking to raise significant capital with commensurate risk to shareholders and other creditors. In exchange such companies would have been required, through their governance structures, to reflect the greater scale of social and economic importance flowing from full limited liability incorporation. In this way at least two very different types of corporate entity would have evolved in Anglo American jurisdictions. Instead, under British law, limited liability is common in its application for all types and sizes of company, a quite inappropriate solution. Many such businesses remain undercapitalized a situation which will not change. But the more serious problem exists with the larger corporate entities which are simply regarded as small companies *writ-large* when clearly they are not.

The failure to make this distinction limits the scope to treat larger, publicly quoted companies, in a fundamentally different way in terms of governance to their smaller counterparts. The failure to have anticipated a time when substantial corporations would have grown into much larger corporations has robbed British law of the chance to examine how such corporations, through their governance structures, might have been encouraged to play a more responsive role in terms of changing social and economic expectations. There is a powerful case for addressing this jurisprudential shortfall.

- **Tighten the conditions governing limited liability to encourage greater engagement by institutional investors in the governance of publicly traded corporations**
- **Review whether the existence of one-size-fits-all unconditional limited liability for smaller companies is a handicap in raising capital**

14.6   Re-crafting the laws governing directors' duties

Directors' duties also have to be realistically enforceable. The laws often in Anglo American jurisdictions are weak and ineffective. Directorship should require a much higher level of professionalism. Directors cannot be condemned for making bad business decisions. The risk of failure can never be removed. That misses the point. Directors must be required to show an acceptably high level of professional competence in their approach to the assessment of risk and decision-taking. Proper and effective benchmarks for assessing competence must be developed. Why should a company director be viewed any differently to a neuro surgeon in terms of his or her qualifications and professionalism in assessing risk? The double standard that currently exists can no longer be accepted as the norm.

- **Redefine directors' duties to promote higher enforceable standards of professionalism**
- **Create a public corporation fit for purpose**

Orthodoxy means not thinking - not needing to think. Orthodoxy is unconsciousness

(George Orwell *1984* written in 1949)

243

Questions for review

1. How can we change the *gene pool* of directors in any fundamental way?

2. How would you describe the crisis of legitimacy in the governance of Anglo American corporations?

3. How will stakeholder representation be protected?

4. How will the proposals for change put forward impact upon global governance and supply chains?

5. Should larger publicly held corporations be obliged to meet higher standards of public accountability and engagement?

6. Will upgrading corporate governance standards simply lead to a race to the bottom?

Group Tasks

I   Specify the ideal background experience the independent director should have?

II   Define the legal requirements of the corporation of tomorrow?

III   How should rules governing institutional investors be changed?

Figure 19

How Sir Victor put state ownership in its place

Published: November 5 2008

Sir, Your report (November 4) on the reactions of Sir Victor Blank, chairman of Lloyds TSB, to the impact of state participation in the ownership of Lloyds/HBOS reveals a gravely important truth.

It is that the British government, as a shareholder in the new entity, will simply fail in its efforts to foster stronger corporate oversight. Sir Victor informs us that the state, as a shareholder, has the power to veto but not to nominate potential non-executive directors. The new entity's board will settle that matter. The fact that the government has invested taxpayers' money in that business in reality changes nothing.

The common law position as he states it is true. His comments have the merit of warning the public that the idea of thoroughgoing shareholder oversight of board actions is all but illusory. Shareholders – whether they happen to be the state, institutional investors or the ordinary man in the street – have limited leverage over boards (and management) of publicly quoted corporations, including banks. His comments reveal explicitly the true value of shareholder oversight. We should take heed.

More widely, "shareholder democracy" – under arrangements in Anglo-American capital markets, dominated by dispersed institutional shareholders, unitary board structures and reliant on board-selected and appointed independent directors to keep the ring – scores low on the credibility scale.

The idea that board-appointed, part-time independent directors can exercise the required degree of constructive influence over full-time executive directors is, mostly, make-believe. This must prompt the question: where does that leave the state (and the taxpayers) as shareholders in the new entity. The honest answer has to be quite some distance away from the position indicated by both the prime minister and the chancellor in their various public statements.

Unitary board structures, supported by Britain's much-vaunted Combined Code, offer few credible checks where corporate power is concerned. The "gene pool" alchemy, on which the late Sir Derek Higgs relied in his post-Enron assessment of how to improve the Combined Code, will never bear fruit. Lipstick on the pig, as the Americans say, only changes the *appearance* of things. A pig is, after all, a pig.

Time now for an honest and fundamental public debate about these matters.

Richard Tudway

Centre for International Economics
London WC1, UK

Bibliography

Aoki M Corporations in Evolving Diversity OUP (2010)

Aoki M and Okuno M Comparative Institutional Analysis of Economic Systems Tokyo University Press (1996)

Allen F and Gale D Comparing Financial Systems (2000) MIT Press

Alchian A and Demsetz H Production, Information Costs and Economic Organisation (1972) American Economic Review

Beck Stefan and Scherrer Christoph, The German Economic Model Emerges Reinforced from the Crisis Global Labour Column (2010).

Bentham J The Principles of Morals and Legislation (1789)

Bergloef, Eric, 1993. Corporate Governance in Transition Economies: The Theory and its Policy Implications inAoki M and Kim H K editors, Corporate Governance in Transitional Economies: Insider Control and the Role of Banks. Washington, D.C (2005)

Berle A and Means G The Modern Corporation and Private Property (1932) Policy Implications

Bratton W W The New Economic Theory of the Firm The Law of the Business Enterprise ed Sally Wheeler (1994)

Bryer R A Accounting for the Railway Mania of 1845 – A Great Railway Swindle (1991) 16 Accounting, Organisation and Society, 437

Cadbury Code of Corporate Governance (1992)

Calomiris C The Costs of Rejecting Universal Banking: American Finance in the German Mirror 1870 – 1914 (1995)

Charkham J Keeping good company OUP (1994), Chapter 2

Cheffins B Company Law Theory Structure and Operation (1997)

Cheffins B Current Ends in Corporate Governance: Going to London, to Milan via Toronto Duke Journal of Comparative and International Law Vol 10,5 (1999)

Coase R H The Nature of the Firm Economica (1937)

Combined Code (British Code of Corporate Governance)

Commission of the European Communities Green Paper on CSR, Brussels (2001)

Corporate governance, board diversity and firm performance Working Paper (2002)

Corey L The House of Morgan (New York) G Howard Watt (1930)

Davies P Principles of Modern Company Law (1997)

Davies P Enlightened shareholder value and the new responsibilities of directors (2008)

Dewey J The Historic Background of Corporate Legal Personality (1926)

Dignam A A Principled Approach to Self Regulation? The Report of the Hampel Committee on Corporate Governance (1998)

Dodd E M For Whom Are Corporate Managers Trustees? (1932)

Drucker P The Concept of the Corporation (1948)

Dubois A B The English Business Company after the Bubble Act 1720 – 1800 , New York, (1938)

Eisenberg M A The Structure of Corporate Law (1989)

EU Green Paper Promoting a European Framework for Corporate Social Responsibility (COM (2001)

EU corporate governance Green Paper Brussels (2011)

Farrar J Corporate Governance Theory, Principle and Practice (1998).

Franks J, Mayer C & Wagner H, 2006. The Origins of the German Corporation, (2006)

Freund-Kahn Sir O Some Reflections on Company Law Reform (1944)

Friedman M The Social Responsibility of Business Is to Increase Profits. New York Times Magazine (1970)

Geldart W Legal Personality (1911)

German Corporate Governance Code (2013)

Getzler J and Macnair M   The Firm as an Entity before the Companies Acts: AssetPartitioning by Private Law. (2005)

Grantham R The doctrinal basis of the rights of company shareholders (1998)

Hall P and Soskice D (2002) and Amable B Varieties of Capitalism (2003).

Jensen M C and Meckling M Theory of the Firm: Management Behaviour Agency Costs and Ownership Structures (1976)

Goncalves J R B and Madi M A C Private Equity Investments and Labour: Current trends and challenges of trade unions (2010)

Hall Stuart The neoliberal victory must be challenged. We start today. The Guardian 24 April 2013

Halsbury's Laws of England (4th edition) Vol 9 (1973)

Hansmann H and Kraakman R The end of history for corporate law (2000)

Higgs D (The) Review of the Effectiveness of Non Executive Directors (2003)

Henderson D Misguided Virtue: False Notions of Social Corporate Social Responsibility, New Zealand Business Roundtable (2001)

Holme R (Lord) and Watts R Making Good Business Sense (2000)

Honore A M Ownership, in A G Guest, ed. Oxford Essays in Jurisprudence (First Series) (Oxford Clarendon Press (1961)

Ikegami E The Taming of the Samurai. Honorific Individualism and the Meaning of Modern Japan (1995)

Ireland P Corporate Governance, Stakeholding and the Company: Towards a Less Degenerate Capitalism. (1996)

Ireland P The Triumph of the Company Legal Form 1856-1914 in Adams (ed) Essays for Clive Schmitthof (1985)

Ireland P The Myth of Shareholder Ownership (1999)

Jensen M C and Meckling M Theory of the Firm: Management Behaviour Agency Costs and Ownership Structures (1976)

Kahan M Jurisprudential and Transactional Developments in Takeovers (1998)

Kuran T The absence of the corporation in Islamic law. Origins and persistence (2005)

Kwang Ng Yew Welfare Economics (1983)

List Frederich Das Nationale System der Politischen Ökonomie (1841)

Lobban, M. (1996). Corporate identity and limited liability in France and England 1825-67

(1996)

Lobban M Nineteenth Century Frauds in Company Formations – Derry v Peek in Context (1991)

Lowry J & Dignam A Company Law (2005)

Mackay C Extraordinary Popular Delusions and the Madness of Crowds (1841)

Marsh P Short-termism on trial (1990).

May Brown Rowe and Maw Hedge Funds and Institutional Shareholder Activism (2006)

Mitsuaki Okabe Codes of Good Governance Around the World (2009)

Millstein I M The evolution of corporate governance in the United States – Briefly Told Forum for US-EU Legal-Economic Affairs, Rome September (2001)

Micklethwait J and Wooldridge A   A Future Perfect The Challenge of Hidden Promise of Globalisation (2000)

Modernising Corporate Law, London Department of Trade and Industry (2002)

Meisel N   Lessons from France's Corporate-Governance Experience for Developing Countries and Emerging Economies OECD Development Centre, Les Trente Glorieuse (2002)

OECD Principle of Corporate Governance (2004)

Okabe M Codes of Good Governance Around the World (2009)

ONS (Office of National Statistics) Share Holding: A Report on the Ownership of Shares

Ottolenghi S   From peeping behind the veil to ignoring it completely (1999)

Padfield F M Challenges for Company Law (1995)

Parkinson J Corporate Power and Responsibility (1993)

Penner J E The Law of Trusts (2000)

Phillips and Drew 'Pension fund indicators, a long term perspective on pension fund investment (2000)

Plender J A Stake in the Future – the Stakeholding Solution (1997)

Pollock Frederick (Sir) Has the Common Law Received the Fictions Theory of Corporations? (1911)

Porter M E and Kramer M R Strategy and Society – The Link Between Competitive Advantage and Corporate Social Responsibility. (2006)

Rathenau W Vom Aktienwesen (1917)

Rixon F Competing interests and conflicting principles: an examination of the power of alteration of articles of association (1986)

Salz Review (2013)

Sarbanes Oxley Act (2002)

Sealy L The Director as Trustee (1967)

Sealy L S Perception and Policy in Company Law Reform (1996)

Stokes M Company Law and Legal Theory The Law of Business Enterprise ed Sally Wheeler (1994)

Teubner G Enterprise Corporatism: New Industrial Policy and the 'Essence' of the Legal Person (1994).

Tudway R The Juridical Paradox of the Corporation (2002)

Tudway R and Pascal A-M Corporate governance, shareholder value and societal expectations (2006)

Tudway R and Pascal A-M Beyond the ivory tower: from business aims to policy making. (2006)

Tudway R Corporate Governance in a radically changed world – a fresh look at the Rhineland model (2010)

Tunc A The Judge and the Businessman (1986)

Williamson, Oliver EMarkets and Hierarchies: Analysis and Antitrust Implications (1975)

Laws and Legal Judgements

British Law
Joint Stock Companies Act of 1844
Companies Clauses Consolidation Act 1845
Limited Liability (Consolidation Act 1856
Companies Act 1985
Companies Act 2006

American Law
Sarbanes Oxley Act (2002)
Dodd Frank Act (2009)

British Legal Judgements
Ashby Rly Carriage & Iron Co v Riche [1875] LR 7 HL 653
Automatic Self Cleaning Filter Co v Cuninghame [1906] 2 Ch 24 CA
Bligh versus Brent (1836) Y & C 268
Bartlett v Barclays Bank Trust Co Ltd (1980) CH155
Bolam v Friern Hospital Committee [1957] 2 All ER 118
Borland's Trustees v Steel Brothers & Co Ltd [1901] Ch 279,288
Brady v Brady [1988] BCLC 20, CA
Caparo Industries v Dickman HL 1990
Re Chez Nico (Restaurants) Ltd (1992)
Coleman v Myers (1977)
Dawson International Plc v Coats Patons Plc (1989)
Re Faure Electric Accumulator Company (1888) 40 Ch D 141 at 151
Foss v Harbottle (1843) 2 Hare 461
Fulham Football Club v Cabra Estates Plc [1994] 1 BCLC 363, CA
Gramophone and Typewriter Ltd v Stanley (1908)
Greenhalgh v Arderne Cinemas Ltd (1951)
Isle of Wight Rly Co v Tahourdin (1883) 25 ChD 320 CA.
Lennard's Carrying Co v Asiatic Petroleum Co Ltd [1915] AC
Norman v Theodore Goddard [1991] BCLC 1028 at 1030-31.
Regentcrest plc v Cohen (2001)
Re Smith & Fawcett Ltd [1942] Ch 304 CA
Short v Treasury Commissioners [1948] 1 K. B. 122 C. A
Salomon v Salomon & Co Ltd [1897] AC 22 , HL
Re Stanley [1906] 1 Ch. 1
Watson v Spratley (10 Ex 222) 1854

Glossary of Terms

A

Absentee Landlords

Shareholder or institutional investors are sometimes referred to as absentee landlords a reference to the fact that they own shares in companies in which they are invested but play no role in the affairs of those companies.

Activist Investors

Investors who try to use an ownership position to actively pursue governance changes at a corporation. The objectives of the activist investor might differ from those of other shareholders. Examples of activist investors might include the following:

- Pension funds that manage assets on behalf of union employees
- Institutional funds with a social mission, such as environmental, religious, or humanitarian causes.
- Hedge fund managers driven by a desire for short-term gain.
- Individual investors with outspoken personal beliefs

Agency (Issues)

A situation of misaligned incentives which arises when a third-party agent is hired to act on one's behalf describes the agency problem. In a corporate setting, agency problems occur when a manager who is hired to run a company in the interest of shareholders and stakeholders takes actions which benefit him/her with the costs borne by corporation and by extension, shareholders and other stakeholders. For example, an executive might manipulate accounting results to increase the size of his or her bonus, or might pursue an expensive acquisition, even though these actions are value destroying. Agency problems can be mitigated through corporate governance features which restrict or discourage these actions or through incentives which align the interest of management and the corporation.

Aggregate Concept of the Corporation

The corporation may be defined as a collection of particular persons or items, formed into one body. The corporate aggregate is one formed of a number of natural persons.

AGM

The AGM is a mandatory, public yearly gathering of a publicly traded company's executives, directors and interested shareholders

Anglo- American Model

A term used to describe governance models prevalent in the United Kingdom and United State and other English speaking countries. The Anglo American model is portrayed as being shareholder-centric (meaning that the primary purpose of the corporation is considered to be the maximization of shareholder value), with a single board of directors, management participation on the board (particularly the CEO), and an emphasis on transparency and disclosure through audited financial reports.

Articles of Association

In corporate governance, a company's articles of association is a document which, along with the memorandum of association form the company's constitution, defines the responsibilities of the directors, the kind of business to be undertaken, and the means by which the shareholders exert control over the board.

Audit Committee

The audit committee is responsible for overseeing the company's external audit and is the primary contact between the auditor and the company. This reporting relationship is intended to prevent management manipulation of the audit. Under Sarbanes-Oxley, the audit committee must have at least three members, all of whom are financially literate; the chair also must be a financial expert. The obligations of the audit committee include:

- Overseeing the financial reporting and disclosure process
- Monitoring the choice of accounting policies and principles
- Overseeing the hiring, performance, and independence of the external auditor
- Overseeing regulatory compliance, ethics, and whistleblower hotlines
- Monitoring internal control processes
- Overseeing the performance of the internal audit function
- Discussing risk-management policies and practices with management

Autopoiesis

This derives from Greek αὐτο- *(auto-)*, meaning "self", and ποίησις *(poiesis)*, meaning "creation, production". It refers to a system capable of reproducing and maintaining itself. The term was introduced in 1972 by Chilean biologists Humberto Maturana and Francisco Varela to define the self-maintaining chemistry of living cells. Since then the concept has been also applied to the fields of systems theory, sociology and the business enterprise

B
Bankruptcy
Bankruptcy is a situation in which a corporation becomes insolvent (i.e., the value of its liabilities exceeds the value of its assets). In bankruptcy, the legal obligation of the corporation is to preserve and maximize the financial claims of creditors (rather than shareholders).

Benchmarking Compensation
Compensation benchmarking is the process by which a company's senior executive compensation levels and practices are compared to those of other companies (may be in same market, industry or sector). Compensation benchmarking is one of the tools that compensation committees use.

Board Buy-In
This is a reference to the extent to which the main board is fully identified with the CSR exercises conducted by the company

Board Diversity
The degree to which individual directors on a board represent a wide range of personal or professional backgrounds, experiences, or viewpoints.

Board of Directors
A group of individuals elected to represent the interests of shareholders and monitor the corporation and its management. Generally speaking, a board serves two roles: an advisory role and an oversight role. In its advisory capacity, the board consults with management regarding the strategic and operational direction of the company. Attention is paid to decisions that balance risk and reward. Board members are selected based on the skill and expertise they offer for this purpose, including previous experience in a relevant industry or function. In its oversight capacity, the board is expected to monitor management and ensure that it is acting diligently in the interests of shareholders.

Board Structure
A description of a board based on its prominent structural attributes, such as size, professional and demographic information about the directors serving on it, their independence from management, number of committees, director compensation, etc. Although much attention is paid to board structure, most research evidence finds little relation between board structure and a company's performance or governance quality.

Business Ethics

Business ethics is the study of proper business policies and practices regarding potentially controversial issues, such as corporate governance, insider trading, bribery, discrimination, corporate social responsibility and fiduciary responsibilities.

Business Judgment Rule

This rule is used in British and American jurisdictions. Under the business judgment rule, a court will not second guess a board's decision (even if, in retrospect, it was proved to be seriously deficient) if the board followed a reasonable process by which it informed itself of key, relevant facts and then made a decision in good faith. Good faith requires that the board act without conflicting interests and that it not turn a blind eye to issues within its responsibility. If the board can demonstrate that it satisfied these criteria, the courts will not intervene.

Business Model

A business model links specific financial and nonfinancial measures in a logical chain to delineate how a company's strategy translates into the accomplishment of stated financial goals. The board evaluates the business model for logical consistency, realism of targets, and statistical evidence that the relationships between performance metrics and stated goals are valid.

C
Capital Market Efficiency

The degree to which markets set correct prices for labour, natural resources, and capital, based on the information available to both parties in a transaction. Accurate pricing is necessary for firms and individuals to make rational decisions about allocating capital to its most efficient uses. When capital markets are inefficient, prices are subject to distortion and corporate decision making suffers. Efficient capital markets can act as a disciplining mechanism on corporations. Companies are held to a "market standard" of performance, and those that fail to meet these standards are punished with a decrease in share price or increase in borrowing costs. Companies that do not perform well over time risk going out of business or becoming an acquisition target.

Capitalisation

This refers to the value of the equity of a quoted corporation normally equal to the value of ordinary shares multiplied by the number of shares in issue.

Chaebol (Korea)
The conglomerate organisations that dominate the Korean economy are referred to as the chaebol. Chaebol which means "financial house," are not single corporations but groups of affiliated companies that operate under the strategic and financial direction of a central or headquarter organisation rather as a Holding Company. A powerful group chairman holds ultimate decision-making authority on all investments and leads the headquarters organisation. The chaebol has features in common with the Japanese keiretsu, (see below).

Chairman of the Board
The Chairman is the director who presides over meetings of the full board of directors. The chairman is responsible for setting the agenda, scheduling meetings, and coordinating actions of board committees. Because of his or her prominent position, the chairman is considered the most powerful board member and also the public "face" of the board. Traditionally, the CEO has served as the chairman of the board. In recent years, however, it has become more common for a nonexecutive director to serve as chair as laid down in the British Cadbury Code.

Civil Law
A system of law, mostly European in origin, that relies on comprehensive legal codes or statutes written by legislative bodies. The judiciary bases decisions on strict interpretation of the law instead of legal precedent. Civil law is also known as "statute law."

Codes of best practice
These comprise recommendations by experts and others on corporate governance strategy, structure, model and other related dimensions that companies should incorporate to achieve "good governance". This includes the splitting of the powers of the Chair and CEO. Benchmarks include The Cadbury Committee (1992), The Greenbury Report (1995); The Hampel Report (1998) and the Higgs Report (2003).

Codetermination
This is a system of corporate governanced under which the interests of shareholders and employees are expected to be balanced in corporate decision-making. The philosophy of codetermination notably underlies German corporate law and laws in other jurisdictions.

Common Law

A system of law under which judicial precedent shapes the interpretation and application of laws is referred to as common law. Common law emerged first in England and was adopted by all other English-speaking countries. Judges consider previous court rulings on similar matters and use this information as the basis for settling current claims.

Compensation Committee

The committee of the board that is responsible for setting the compensation of the CEO and for advising the CEO on the compensation of other senior executives. The responsibilities of the compensation committee are as follows:

- Set the compensation of the CEO
- Set and review performance-related goals for the CEO
- Determine appropriate compensation structure for the CEO, given performance expectations
- Monitor CEO performance relative to targets
- Set or advise the CEO on other officers' compensation
- Advise the CEO and oversee compensation of nonexecutive employees
- Set board compensation
- Hire consultants to assist in the compensation process, as appropriate

Concession

The concessionary interpretation of the corporation is that its existence arises from legal concessions granted by supreme legislative authorities such as parliaments in Europe and Congress in the US.

Contractarian

Contractarians posit that a corporation is little more than a nexus of contracts. They argue that because corporations involve nothing more than private contractual orderings among various parties, there should be little or no meaningful regulation to impinge on those parties' liberty to contract as they see fit.

Corporate Citizen

The corporation, because of its status in law as a legal, if fictional entity, is now increasingly referred to as a corporate citizen. By extension it is increasingly portrayed as an entity, like a real person, that has rights and duties. It is also often portrayed to behave like a real person when it cannot.

Corporate social responsibility (CSR)

CSR is often referred to as corporate conscience, corporate philanthropy, corporate citizenship, corporate social performance, or sustainable responsible business. Responsible business is judged to be a form of corporate self-regulation integrated into a business model.

Corporators

A corporator has a narrow and a wider meaning. The narrower meaning refers to the members or shareholders of a corporation. A broader and more common understanding of the term corporator includes all of those directly associated with the corporation including employees, suppliers and customers.

Creditworthiness

Creditworthiness reflects the ability and willingness of a borrower to repay debt obligations. Creditworthiness is determined based on a combination of quantitative and qualitative factors, including availability of collateral, leverage ratios, interest coverage, and diversity and stability of revenue streams, among other factors. Institutional investors that invest in corporate debt use credit ratings to determine the likelihood that they will be paid the full principal and interest owed to them over the life of the bond. In some cases, investors such as money market funds are only allowed to invest in debt with a sufficiently high rating. Companies with higher credit ratings are generally rewarded in the market with lower interest rates on their borrowings, while companies with lower credit ratings are generally charged higher rates.

D

Deed of Settlement Companies

Deed of Settlement companies were designed to circumvent the basic intention of partnership prior to the passing of laws on limited liability in Britain. They were a socio-economic reflection of the growing distance of some equity partners from the everyday running of the business, a factor which ultimately led to the introduction in Britain of limited liability in the mid 19th century

Directors and Officers (D&O) Liability Insurance

D & O refers to an insurance contract purchased by a corporation on behalf of directors and officers to protect them from certain costs associated with litigation. These policies cover litigation expenses, settlement payments, and, in rare cases, amounts paid in damages (up to a limit specified in the policy). Most companies purchase D&O insurance on behalf of their board.

Dirigiste
A reference to the French post war system of state-led industrial development

Dodd–Frank Wall Street Reform and Consumer Protection Act 2010
This bill was introduced following the global financial crisis in 2008 to promote the financial stability of the United States by improving accountability and transparency in the financial system. Important governance-related provisions of Dodd-Frank include the following:

- Proxy access—Shareholders or groups of shareholders are eligible to nominate directors on the company proxy.
- Say-on-pay—Shareholders are given a nonbinding vote on executive compensation.
- Disclosure—Companies must provide expanded disclosure on executive compensation, hedging of company equity by executives and directors, the independence of compensation committee members, and the decision of whether to have an independent chairman.

On January 25, 2011, the US Securities and Exchange Commission adopted amendments to its disclosure rules and forms to implement Section 951 of the Dodd-Frank Wall Street Reform and Consumer Protection Act, which added Section 14A to the Exchange Act. These amendments took effect on April 4, 2011.This section requires public companies subject to the US Federal proxy rules to:

- provide their shareholders with an advisory vote on executive compensation, generally known as "Say-on-Pay" votes
- provide their shareholders with an advisory vote on the desired frequency of say-on-pay votes; and
- provide their shareholders with an advisory vote on compensation arrangements and understandings in connection with merger transactions, known as "golden parachute" arrangements. Such golden parachute arrangements would need to be disclosed in merger proxy statements.

Duel Boards
This is a reference to the separation of the executive board and the supervisory board common in Rhineland and Nordic jurisdictions. Under these arrangements the Supervisory Board is the upper level board and supervises the activities of the executive board which reports to it.

Dual-Class Shares

A company with dual-class shares has more than one class of common stock. In general, each class has equal economic interest in the company but unequal voting rights. For example, Class A shares might be afforded one vote per share, whereas Class B shares might have ten votes per share. Typically, an insider, founding family member, or other shareholder friendly to management holds the class of shares with preferential voting rights, which gives that person significant (if not outright) influence over board elections. Dual-class stock thus tends to weaken the influence of public shareholders and is often considered an effective antitakeover defense.

Duty of Care

A fiduciary duty is a duty of care under corporate law. The duty of care requires that a director make decisions with due deliberation. In the United States, courts enforce the duty of care through the rubric of the "business judgment rule." Much the same applies under English law. This rule provides that the judgment of a board will not be overridden by a court unless a plaintiff can show that the board failed to inform itself regarding the decision at issue or that the board was infected with a conflict of interest, in which case there may have been a violation of the duty of loyalty. Courts have rarely ruled against a board for a violation of the duty of care. Even if a board decision was clearly wrong, if the board can show that it engaged in some consideration of information related to the decision, the courts will adopt a hands-off posture. The business judgment rule is most protective of outside directors. In the absence of "red flags" regarding what management is telling them, they are permitted to rely on what they hear from management to inform their decision. Moreover, companies are permitted to include exculpatory provisions in the charters that protect an outside director from suits for monetary damages for breach of the duty of care, so long as the director has not acted intentionally or in bad faith.

Duty of Loyalty

Fiduciary duty also includes the duty of loyalty under corporate law. The duty of loyalty addresses conflicts of interest. For example, if management is considering a transaction with a company in which a director has a significant financial interest, the duty of loyalty requires that the terms of the transaction promote the interests of the shareholders over those of the director. As another example, if a director discovers a business opportunity in the course of his or her service to the company, the duty of loyalty requires that the director refrain from taking the opportunity before first determining whether the company will take it. The law lays out procedures for a board to follow in situations when a potential conflict of interest may exist.

E

Executive Compensation

The total set of cash and noncash incentives offered to attract, retain, and motivate an executive to achieve corporate objectives.

Efficient Market Hypothesis

The Efficient Markets Hypothesis asserts that financial markets are "informationally efficient" when it involves decisions to invest in securities in publicly traded markets.

Externalities

In economic theory an externality is a cost (or benefit) which affects a party(s) who did not choose to incur that cost or benefit.

Ex Ante

This is a reference to business matters that are discussed and debated before the event with supervising directors and before action is taken.

Ex Post

This is a reference to business matters that are not discussed and debated with supervising directors before action is taken.

F

Fictional concept of the Corporation

The artificial creation of the company in law has led to the description of the corporation as fictional concept. This is well summed up in Chief Justice Marshall's famous definition in the Dartmouth College case in 1819, wherein he spoke of the corporation as "an artificial being, invisible, intangible, and existing only in contemplation of the law."

Fiduciary Duties

Fiduciary duties represent a legal or ethical relationship of trust between two or more parties. Typically, a fiduciary prudently takes care of money for another person. One party, for example a corporate trust company or the trust department of a bank, acts in a fiduciary capacity to the other one, who for example has entrusted funds to the fiduciary for safekeeping or investment. In the case of board directors this is a reference to various duties they have to shareholders in the discharge of their tasks.

Financial Risk

Financial risk is the degree to which a company relies on external financing (including capital markets and private lenders) to support its ongoing operations. Financial risk is reflected in such factors as balance sheet leverage, off-balance sheet vehicles, contractual obligations, maturity, schedule of debt obligations, liquidity, and other restrictions that reduce financial flexibility. Companies that rely on external parties for financing are judged to be at greater risk than those that finance operations using internally generated funds.

G

Glass Steagall

This act was passed by the US Congress in 1933 following the collapse of Wall Street in 1929. The act insisted upon the separation of investment banking from commercial banking until its eventual repeal in 1999.

Gini- Co-efficient

The Gini coefficient is a measure of statistical dispersion intended to represent the income distribution of a nation's residents.

Golden Shares

Golden shares are a special category of shares issued and bought often by governments who invest in private companies. The shares provide special rights to the holders and can be used to block change of ownership. The British government holds a golden share in Rolls Royce Plc which confers rights to veto any undesirable takeover.

Greenwash

This is a term used to describe the underlying intention of claims made by corporations, often in CSR reports, that are untrue or misleading in terms of the activities of the corporation.

H

Hard and Soft law

This is a reference to laws that are on the statute book and enforceable by the courts and other "laws" that are not enforceable. They are mostly "comply or explain" in nature.

Holy Trinity

The *holy trinity* is a metaphor for the corporation describing the relationship between God the Father, the Son and the Holy Spirit. It describes the relationship of unity or "oneness" between the Shareholder, the Director and the Company at the outset of its existence.

I

Incorporation

Incorporation is the forming of a new corporation (a corporation being a legal entity that is effectively recognized as a person under the law). The corporation may be a business, a non-profit organization, sports club, or a government of a new city or town or a university.

Independent Directors

Independent directors are expected to be free from conflicts of interest that impair objectivity. Companies that trade publicly in the United States and Britain are required to have a majority of independent directors. The main stock markets in both countries define independence as having no material relationship with the listed company (either directly or as a partner, shareholder, or officer of an organization that has a relationship with the company). A director is not considered independent if the director or a family member:

• Has been employed as an executive officer at the company within the last three years.
• Has earned direct six figure compensation (Pounds, dollars or Euros) from the company in the last three years.
• Has been employed as an internal or external auditor of the company in the last three years.
• Is an executive officer at another company where the listed company's present executive have served on the compensation committee in the last three years.
• Is an executive officer at a company whose business with the listed company has been the greater of 2 percent of gross revenues within the last three years.

Insider Trading

The US SEC uses the term "insider" to identify individuals—corporate officers, directors, employees, and certain professional advisors—who have access to material financial and operational information about a company that has not yet been made public. Similar arrangements exist elsewhere. Insiders are restricted in their ability to engage in transactions involving company securities (both purchases and sales) and may trade only when they are not in possession of material non public information. Trades made on the basis of such information are considered "illegal insider trading" and are punishable with jail and financial penalties.

Internal Controls

These are the processes and procedures that a company puts in place to ensure that account balances are accurately recorded, financial statements reliably produced, and assets adequately protected from loss or theft. Effectively, internal controls act as the "cash register" of the corporation, a system that confirms that the level of assets inside the company is consistent with the level that should be there, given revenue and disbursement data recorded through the accounting system.

J

Jurisdiction

Jurisdiction is a reference to the particular legal system operating in any specific country.

K

Keiretsu (Japan)

The keiretsu is a system of interrelationships between companies that is prevalent in Japan. Under the keiretsu, companies maintain small but not insignificant ownership positions among suppliers, customers, and other business affiliates. These ownership positions cement business relations along the supply chain and encourage firms to work together toward an objective of shared financial success. Bank financiers own minority stakes in industrial firms and are key partners in the keiretsu. Their investments indicate that capital for financing is available as needed. The keiretsu is similar to the Korean chaebol.

Key Performance Indicators (KPIs)

Key performance indicators (KPIs), or key performance measures, include both financial and nonfinancial metrics that validly reflect the current and future performance of a company. The board uses key performance measures to evaluate management performance and award compensation. Financial KPIs include measures such as total return; revenue growth; earnings per share; earnings before interest, taxes, depreciation, and amortization (EBITDA); return on capital; economic value added (EVA); and free cash flow. Nonfinancial KPIs include measures such as customer satisfaction, employee satisfaction, defects and rework, on-time delivery, worker safety, environmental safety, and research and development (R&D) pipeline productivity. Although each company should develop a set of KPIs that is relevant for its own business, in practice certain KPIs are broadly used by many companies.

L
Laissez Faire
The(French by origin) political philosophy of "leaving things alone" as in the French language "leave it alone."

License to Operate
Corporations by taking substantive voluntary steps can persuade governments and the wider public that they are taking issues such as health and safety, diversity, or the environment seriously as good corporate citizens with respect to labour standards and impacts on the environment.

Lipstick on the Pig
This is a slang term used by operators in the investment banking industry to describe something that is not a very attractive deal for investors but can be made more attractive by applying lipstick.

Long-Term Incentives
Cash or noncash compensation (such as stock options, restricted stock, or performance units) that vests over multiple years and therefore rewards an executive for long-term performance. Long-term incentives extend the time horizon of the executive and are intended to counteract the natural tendency of a risk-averse executive to focus on short-term rewards at the expense of long-term investment.

M
Malfeasance
Knowingly exceeding authority involving dishonest, fraudulent and improper actions or behaviour.

Management and Supervisory Boards (Rhineland and Nordic Countries)
Two-tier board structures are required under various jurisdictions including Rhineland and Nordic countries. The management board is responsible for the day to management of the company and its strategy. The supervisory board oversees, ex ante, the management board and its planned actions.

N
Net Asset Value
Net asset value (NAV) is the value of an entity's assets less the value of its liabilities. Net asset value may represent the value of the total equity, or it may be divided by the number of shares outstanding held by investors and, thereby, represent the net asset value per share.

Nexus of Contracts

The nexus of contracts represents a theory put forward by a number of economists and legal theorists. The theory asserts that corporations are nothing more than a collection of contracts between different parties - primarily shareholders, directors, employees, suppliers, and customers and that the nature of the corporation is essentially contractarian in nature meaning that its existence flows in turn from enacted legislation.

Non Executive Director

A non executive director or NED is a director who is appointed to the board of a company to ensure that the executive directors meet faithfully their broader obligations.

O

One Size Fits All

This is a reference to bureaucratic necessity of trying to reduce all legislative provisions to one generalised description – a tendency that can sometimes lead to misunderstanding and confusion.

P

Path Dependence

Path dependence is a metaphor from the physical sciences. In its narrow conception it explains why specific institutions and behaviour are influenced by specific historical events. The behaviour of capital markets and their organisation and the shaping on corporate governance to meet those requirements would be an example.

Peer Group

A peer group is a group of companies that are similar in industry, size, complexity, and/or geography. Peer groups are used to evaluate the relative financial and operating performance of a given company. They are also used for benchmarking the size and structure of executive compensation programmes. Because the choice of participants in a peer group can influence relative comparisons, peer groups can be subject to manipulation (for example a company that is not relevant might be included in the peer group to create a favourable comparison, or a company that is relevant might be excluded to obscure an unfavourable comparison).

Personification

This is a figure of speech in which inanimate objects or abstractions are endowed with human qualities or are represented as possessing human form

Publicly Traded

This refers to shares that are issued and traded on a stock market.

Q No examples

R
Realist Concept of the Corporation
The realist theory sees a legal person as a real personality in an extra juridical and pre-juridical sense of the word. It also assumes that the subjects of rights need not belong merely to human beings but to every being which possesses a will and life of its own. As such, being a juristic person and as 'alive' as the human being, a corporation is also subjected to rights. Under the realist theory, a corporation exists as an objectively real entity and the law merely recognizes and gives effect to its existence. The realist theory also contends that the law has no power to create an entity but merely having the right to recognise or not to recognise an entity. A corporation from the realist perspective is a social organism while a human is regarded as a physical organism. A corporation from the realist perspective is a social organism.

Reification
Reification arises in the treatment of an analytic or abstract relationship as though it were a concrete entity. As an example take an association of individuals who make up the "company" (typically a partnership) and then separate the "company" from those individuals (as occurred following the passing of the law granting limited liability to shareholders). This has the effect of creating a fictional legal entity called a "company" – and stands as an example of reification.

Rhineland (Jurisdictions)
This a reference to the countries that border the River Rhine in Europe. The River Rhine rises in Switzerland and empties into the North Sea through Holland. Within the jurisdictions that border the River Rhine there are common systems of corporate governance which require corporations to have two-tier systems of board management with the supervisory board overseeing the actions of the executive board.

Rules of the Game
This is an expression which undergirds path dependence. It entails that the rules that are fashioned in different jurisdictions are done to facilitate *the game*.

S
Short-termism
Short-termism may be defined as an excessive focus on short-term results at the expense of long-term interests. It is often associated with the behaviour of Anglo American capital markets.

Severable

Severable is defined in law as something that is capable of being separated from other things to which it is joined and maintaining nonetheless a complete and independent existence. This suggests that shares cannot be viewed as real estate.

Shareholders

Shareholders are the holders of the corporations ordinary shares or stock.

Social Market Economy

This refers to arrangements, mostly in Europe and Scandinavia, which aim to provide countervailing influence to the operations of the free market in determining economic outcomes.

Sovereign Wealth Funds.

A SWF is a state-owned investment fund investing in real and financial assets such as stocks, bonds, real estate, precious metals, or in alternative investments such as private equity fund or hedge funds.

Stakeholders

Stakeholders is a terms used to describe those parties which are judged to be a key importance to the success of the business. These terms vary in meaning between different jurisdictions. Often this includes employees as well as customers of the company and its suppliers.

State Owned Enterprises (SOEs)

These corporations often start their lives as limited liability companies but for some reasons are then "nationalised" by governments. Sometimes they are created by governments. This is the case with Sovereign Wealth Funds.

Supply Chain

This refers to the contractual arrangements that corporations frequently make with other suppliers in other different jurisdiction to supply goods and services to the lead corporation

T

The Cadbury Committee (1992)

The Cadbury committee was the result of an initiative by the accountancy profession and its sponsors (the Financial Reporting Council, the London Stock Exchange and the Bank of England) "to help raise the standards of corporate governance and the level of confidence in financial reporting and auditing." The committee's final report, published in 1992, provided a benchmark set of recommendations on governance widely considered to be best practices. These include:

- Separation of the chairman and chief executive officer titles.
- The appointment of independent directors to the board.
- Reduced conflicts of interest at the board level because of business or other relationships.
- The creation of an independent audit committee.
- A review of the effectiveness of the company's internal controls.
  The recommendations of the Cadbury Committee formed the basis of London Stock Exchange listing requirements and have influenced governance standards in the US and several other countries. They have subsequently been revised by later committees.

The Greenbury Report (1995)
The Greenbury Committee was commissioned to review executive compensation in the Britain. The committee recommended establishing an independent remuneration committee entirely comprised of nonexecutive directors.

The Hampel Report (1998)
The Hampel Committee was established to review the effectiveness of the Cadbury and Greenbury reports. The committee recommended no substantive changes and consolidated the Cadbury and Greenbury 40 Corporate Governance Matters reports into the "Combined Code of Best Practices," which the London Stock Exchange subsequently adopted.

The Higgs Report (2003)
A British report produced by Sir Derek Higgs who was asked to evaluate the role, quality, and effectiveness of nonexecutive directors among British companies. The Higgs report recommended the following:

- At least half of the board should be nonexecutive directors.
- The board appoint a lead independent director to serve as a liaison with shareholders.
- The nomination committee should be headed by a nonexecutive director.
- Executive directors should not serve more than six years on the board.
- Boards should "undertake a formal and rigorous annual evaluation of its own performance and that of its committees and individual directors."
- The recommendations of the Higgs Report were combined with those of the Turnbull Report and the Combined Code to create the Revised Combined Code of Best Practices.

Higgs believed that the elevated status of nonexecutive directors on the board would be "pivotal in creating conditions for board effectiveness."

Transparency
The degree to which a company provides details that supplement and explain accounts, items, and events reported in its financial statements and other public filings. Transparency is important for shareholders to properly understand a company's strategy, operations, risk, and performance of management. It is also necessary when shareholders make decisions about the value of company securities. As such, transparent disclosure plays a key role in the efficient functioning of capital markets.

U
Ultra Vires
This means in Latin *beyond the powers*. This doctrine which is found in the law of corporations states that if a corporation enters into a contract that is beyond the scope of its corporate powers, the contract is illegal.

V
Verification
This is a reference to the processes and procedures followed by corporations in validating and authenticating the CSR claims they make.

W
Works Council
A works council is a "shop-floor" organisation representing workers, which functions as local/firm-level complement to national labour negotiations. Works councils exist with different names in a variety of related forms in a number of European countries, including Germany and Austria (Betriebsrat); Luxembourg (Comité Mixte, Délégation du

Personel); the Netherlands and Flanders in Belgium (Ondernemingsraad); France (Comité d'entreprise); Wallonia in Belgium (Délégués du Personnel); and Spain (Comité de empresa).

X
No examples

Y
No examples

Z
No examples

Author Index

Subject Index

Appendix 1

On Line Public Consultation on Corporate Governance and the Financial Crisis

Proposal for discussion

Preamble

1.   Following the Corporate Governance Steering Group's Roundtable discussion on corporate governance and the financial crisis on 18 March, the OECD secretariat has invited further on line comments in determining its next steps. The **Issues for Consultation** are set out in an OECD document downloaded from the OECD web site.[1]

2.   The matters set out below address two of the four headings - **Board Practices** and the **Exercise of Shareholder Rights.** The two remaining Issues for Consultation focus on Board Remuneration and Risk Management. These are matters of key importance but cannot be addressed until the other two main issues identified are fundamentally investigated.[2] The proposals are submitted as independent evidence to the Steering Group together with a list of strategic study objectives.

Board Practices

3.   During the Roundtable difficulties may have arisen from the use of the same term with subtly different meanings in languages different to English. Discussants spoke about "boards" and "board practices" as if all board structures are more or less the same everywhere, when they are not, and relate to shareholders in much the same sort of way, when they don't. This may conceal significant misunderstandings. These matters need to be systematically explored and clarified.

4.   Misunderstandings may also have arisen where different types of board structures, (unitary and dual executive-supervisory) were being discussed, and the different ways in which they operate. These differences have, possibly, a critical bearing on access to *ex ante* information, and the effective exercise of shareholder rights. Nobody knows for certain the scale and importance of these differences, except that they are significant.

5.   The term "information" was frequently used "generically" and without particular qualification. This too may have resulted in misunderstandings. The difference between *ex ante* and *ex post* information is of crucial importance. Within Anglo American unitary board arrangements, shareholders depend mostly on *ex post* information or fairly loose forecasts about what *might* be the case, in the future.[3] Supervisory board structures in other jurisdictions appear to obtain, as a matter of course, vital *ex ante* information upon which effective supervision critically depends. Nobody knows for certain the scale and importance of these differences, except that they exist.

---

[1] http://www.oecd.org/document/18/0,3343,en_2469_32813_42229906_1_1_1_1,0.html 13/04/2009

[2] Governance Remuneration and the Implementation of Risk Management are matters clearly related closely to the proper functioning of the board and the exercise of shareholder supervision. They cannot realistically be addressed outside an examination of first order matters of concern.

[3] As foreseen in the now defunct British OFR (Operating and Financial Review) and under the Sarbanes Oxley Act 2002 in the US.

1

The Exerciser of Shareholder Rights

6.   This goes to the heart of current difficulties in Anglo American jurisdictions. It has most recently been brought to centre-stage as a result of the British government taking a very large equity stake in Lloyds/HBOS and discovering that, as shareholders, they have no clear mechanism for calling the board to account, *ex ante*, for its actions.[4]

7.   Current arrangements supporting shareholder rights are embedded in "soft" comply or explain rules, and *statute* and common *law* in Anglo American jurisdictions. The directors of publicly held corporations (bank and non bank) often do not (and cannot easily[5]) share *ex ante* information with shareholders. More to the point the shareholders have no powers to insist upon this. They also have no standing in law to sue for perceived wrongs against the company committed, for example, by directors,[6] who do not owe them a duty of care. The duty is owed to the company, a separate legal entity).[7] Hence where serious disputes with directors are concerned, over negligence for example, (including the duty of care and skill), shareholders are obliged to rely on a *derivative action* where the corporation[8] (as the lawful plaintiff), sues the directors a process which is complicated, risky and costly to initiate.

8.   Though it is common practice in Anglo American jurisdictions to speak colloquially about shareholders being the "owners" of the corporation, and thereby being entitled, as such, to be "informed" about its affairs, this is not straightforwardly the case. The shareholders are not, strictly speaking, the owners of the corporation.[9] The corporation, in the post limited liability world, is a separate legal entity which owns its own assets.[10] Shareholders own shares, but shares, as landmark common law judgments support, do not represent a claim on the company's assets.[11] The implications of these findings are frequently misunderstood.

9.   The use of the word "shareholder" is also a cause of confusion. Founder "shareholders" (who invest original equity into the company) are, for example, very different to "shareholders" who are simply investors in shares, as in the case of

---

[4] This has generated a good deal of debate in the UK. The essences of the argument are set out in a letter *How Sir Victor put state ownership in its place* published in the FT on 5 November 2008. The issues raised remain unresolved. Similar difficulties are being experienced by the US authorities.

[5] Regulations concerning *shadow directors* are an impediment to information sharing with particular institutional investors; insider trading rules also pose a potential danger to institutional investors who may accidentally become aware of price sensitive information about other companies in which they hold investments.

[6] As foreseen in *Foss v Harbottle* 1843, except in cases of fraud on a minority or other related offences.

[7] The legal "fiction" of provisions under *section 14* of the British Companies Act of 1985 portrays the shareholders as enjoined in a contract with the corporation. The reality is that neither party is a signatory. *Section 14* resolves none of these long dated underlying legal problems.

[8] An inanimate legal fiction in law whose actions can only be given expression by its directors.

[9] They cannot be, because of limited liability, which separates in law the company from the shareholders and confers limited liability on the shareholders.

[10] There may be case for removing limited liability from the largest publicly held corporations given the "too big to fail" mantra popular in recent policy decisions. This would have the effect of forcing institutional shareholders to establish credible mechanism of control over executive management.

[11] Except in the case of liquidation though not necessarily in acquisition as evidenced in *Short versus Treasury Commissioners* (1948), which makes clear this vital point in law.

2

institutional investors who buy and sell shares in third party transactions. Yet it is commonplace for people to speak of them as if they were broadly the same when they are not. This leads to misunderstandings. European shareholding which, broadly speaking, is patient, long term and often "founding" in nature, is quite different to shareholding in Anglo American jurisdictions which is institutional and short term, where shares are bought and sold in third party transactions. This results in very different forms of behaviour – the most important of which is that, generally, European shareholders take a longer term view on shareholder value, when compared with Anglo American institutional shareholders who are, inevitably, shorter term in perspective.[12]

Board Structures

10.   The behaviour of shareholders and boards, alike, cannot be separated from board structures. Sweden provides an example where unitary board structures exist for certain types of company in which independent directors, <u>alone, sit.</u> In the Swedish model the unitary board is <u>independent from</u> the executive directors whose actions they are there to supervise.[13] This sort of "countervailing influence" does not exit within the Anglo American unitary framework. The absence of this imperils accountability and from recent past experience confirms the serious threat that it poses to shareholder value.

11.   Concerns about these matters, following the Enron scandal in the US, prompted the British Government to initiate a thoroughgoing review of the role of NEDs (non executive directors) in 2002[14] The resulting Higgs Report placed great importance on a very significant expansion of NEDs on the boards of publicly held companies, with the independent chairman being responsible for organising the NEDs. Unfortunately there is little evidence that these aspects of Higgs have been taken, seriously, into account. Anglo American boards remain strongly "executive" in orientation, with NEDs generally regarded as an unavoidable *Combined Code*[15] requirement.[16]

12.   Most recently the British Financial Services Minister, Lord Myners[17], in the face of mounting criticism of the failure of NEDs, and institutional investors to ensure better and more effective disclosure in the context of the global financial crisis, has proposed a further strengthening of the role of NEDs.[18] He has specifically suggested that NEDs should be funded by the corporation, if necessary, to support independent research into

---

[12] The research by Peter Marsh in the 1980s on *short-termism* in Anglo American capital markets helps to provide an English-speaking take on this, though it provides no insight into European habits and practices.

[13] A glance at the website of Tomorrows Company, a British research outfit reveals some interesting insights into the importance of independent supervision and the need for the board to be independent of the company.

[14] The Higgs Report on Non Executive Directors, January 2003.

[15] The British *comply or explain* code of good corporate governance.

[16] The shocking revelations in the serious British press about NEDs being intimidated in the case of RBS Bank may very well, as the facts are revealed, confirm the asymmetry of power in British and American board structures which undermines independent scrutiny.

[17] As a former fund manager one supposes that Lord Myners speaks with an insider's understanding of how institutional investors, in practice, operate.

[18] See The FT 6 April 2009 "Myners urges radical shake-up of boards" in which the Financial Services Minister urges a number of fundamental changes which can only be realised if equally far reaching changes are made to board structures.

3

the affairs of the corporation on whose board they sit, as NEDs. This can only be taken as recognition that existing arrangements do not provide an adequate countervailing power over the actions of executive directors.[19]

Conclusions

13.   A significant though little quoted contribution to the theory of corporate finance appeared in the Journal of the Wharton Business School, in 2002. The article argues that too little is known or understood about the differences between different board control models and the role of the shareholders and their rights in protecting shareholder value in different OECD countries.[20] The research supports the conclusions that models in jurisdictions other than Anglo American achieve better performance ratings in terms of a number of key performance measures used as proxies for shareholder value.

14.   The reasons which might explain these matters need, urgently, to be explored and the results of the research published in full. Only in this way will trust in the capacity of the corporation to generate and protect shareholder wealth, and report credibly on its actions to society, be restored.   Some of the key objectives of the research are set out below:

- What limitations exist in Anglo American board structures which prevent institutional shareholders from obtaining relevant *ex ante* information vital to the exercise of effective supervision?

- What legal changes would be required to enable institutional shareholders from obtaining ex ante information vital to the exercise of effective supervision?

- Can countervailing influence be achieved within board structures that are executive in composition, culture and orientation?

- Should all boards be organised as supervisory entities separate from the executive functions of managing the corporation?

- What evidence is there that supervisory board structures are better at protecting shareholder value than unitary executive-oriented board structures?

Richard Tudway
Centre for International Economics
London   14 April 2009
Tel (44) (0) 11 444 811078
richardtudway@compuserve.com

END

---

[19] Some see this as a further step towards the creation of supervisory boards independent of executive boards representing shareholder and other stakeholder interests.

[20] See Allen and Gale *A Comparative Theory of Corporate Governance*, Wharton Business School 2002

4

Appendix 2

Organisation de Coopération et de Développement Economiques
Organisation for Economic Co-operation and Development

22-Sep-200

English - Or. Engl

PUBLIC AFFAIRS AND COMMUNICATIONS DIRECTORATE
PUBLIC AFFAIRS DIVISION

Labour/Management Programme

THE REVIEW OF THE OECD PRINCIPLES OF CORPORATE GOVERNANCE

Report on a meeting of trade union experts held under the OECD Labour/Management Programme

Contact: Mr. Jeremy Maddison, BIAC/TUAC relations, Public Affairs Division, Tel: 33.1.45.24.90.9
Fax: 33.1.44.30.63.46, Email: jeremy.maddison@oecd.org

JT00149724

Document complet disponible sur OLIS dans son format d'origine
Complete document available on OLIS in its original format

OECD LABOUR/MANAGEMENT PROGRAMME

THE REVIEW OF THE OECD PRINCIPLES OF CORPORATE GOVERNANCE

Report on a meeting of trade union experts
held under the OECD Labour/Management Programme

(Paris, 19 June 2003)

Formal relations between the OECD and representatives of trade unions and of business and industry in Member countries are conducted through two organisations officially recognised by the OECD Council. These are the Trade Union Advisory Committee to the OECD (TUAC) and the Business and Industry Advisory Committee to the OECD (BIAC). In addition to various forms of policy discussion throughout the year, arrangements provide for meetings at the technical level, which do not engage the responsibility of the organisations. Such meetings are held either in the form of ad hoc discussions with the Secretariat, or under the Labour/Management Programme for which a series of meetings devoted to specific themes is established at the beginning of each year.

After meetings held under the Programme, a rapporteur draws up a report of the discussion on his own responsibility, for distribution to the social partners and to the relevant OECD Committees. The opinions expressed in such reports are those of the rapporteur, except where they are specifically attributed to individual participants, and do not necessarily reflect the views of other participants or of the OECD.

TABLE OF CONTENTS

FOREWORD

Under the OECD Labour/Management Programme for 2003, a meeting of trade union experts on "The Review of the OECD Principles of Corporate Governance" was held in Paris on 19 June 2003. The meeting was prepared in collaboration with the Trade Union Advisory Committee to the OECD (TUAC).

Below, you will find the Agenda of this meeting, along with the overall report of the discussions of the meeting of experts, which was prepared by Ms. Sue Kendall-Bilicki, designated as General Rapporteur for this activity.

**THE OPINIONS EXPRESSED AND ARGUMENTS EMPLOYED IN THIS REPORT
ARE THE RESPONSIBILITY OF THE AUTHOR
AND DO NOT NECESSARILY REPRESENT THOSE OF THE OECD**

AGENDA

Opening session

- Introductory remarks by the Deputy Secretary-General, Mr. Richard Hecklinger
- Discussion

Setting the Stage

- Presentation of the Issues Paper by Mr. Richard Tudway
- Tour de Table: The challenges at national level based on comments from Trade Union Representatives
- Discussion

Second Session: Work of the OECD Steering Group and Role of Stakeholders

- Presentation by the OECD Directorate for Financial, Fiscal, and Enterprises Affairs
- Trade Union Presentation
- Discussion

Third session: Discussion on Key Issues: The Rights and Responsibilities of Shareholders, Executive Remuneration and the Board

Brief Presentations on each topic to be made by:
- The OECD Secretariat
- Trade Union Experts

Fourth Session: Discussion on Key Issues (continued): Transparency, Disclosure, Accounting Standards, Implementation and Enforcement

- Brief Presentations on each topic to be made by the OECD Secretariat and Trade Union Experts
- Other Issues

Closing Discussion

5

QUESTIONS FOR DISCUSSION

by Mr. Richard Tudway
Director, Centre for International Economics, (London, UK),
and an advisor to TUAC on corporate governance

I.   THE ISSUES IN OVERVIEW

Public anxieties about governance

1.   Anxieties across the OECD and beyond about the effectiveness of corporate governance are widely felt. Value measured in billions of dollars has been destroyed, not by commercial error alone, but also as a result of malfeasance. In addition, workers have lost their jobs, and in many instances their pensions and health care benefits, which in many cases represent their sole safety net. Meanwhile, public confidence in financial markets has been severely undermined. Recent corporate irregularities have not been confined to the United States. They have and continue to appear globally, even if differences exist around the extent of the problem. Trade unions have legitimate fears that these may in turn be symptomatic of a systemic failure in the framework of corporate governance.

2.   In response a plethora of national level initiatives to reform corporate governance regimes have been introduced, or are being planned. Trade unions have welcomed these, but fear that they have not gone deep and wide enough, and that the emphasis on voluntary codes and standards, rather than a binding regulatory framework is an insufficient response to ensure effective implementation and enforcement of the new reforms.

3.   The OECD Principles of Corporate Governance are the only multilaterally agreed benchmark to guide debates around reform efforts in this key area of public policy. They include chapters on the following topics: The Rights of Shareholders; The Equitable Treatment of Shareholders; The Role of Stakeholders in Corporate Governance; Disclosure and Transparency; and The Responsibility of the Board. Upon their adoption, TUAC welcomed the Principles, in particular, the stakeholder chapter, which it saw not as the last word, but as a platform for further development.

4.   Though non binding, the Principles are nevertheless emerging as the de-facto international comparative framework. For example, the World Bank and IMF use the Principles as a template to assess their members' corporate government environment, as part of the ROSC initiative (Reports on the Observance of Standards and Codes). The Principles are now being reviewed by the OECD. Views differ as regards the scope of the review. Some have argued to maintain the status quo, while others have suggested cosmetic changes. Trade unions have argued that the revisions should be deep and wide-ranging, with the addition of new chapters. They believe that the OECD has a unique opportunity to re-write the corporate mission for the 21st Century.

5.   To set the stage for the OECD-TUAC Labour/Management Programme meeting the paper will discuss some of the underlying issues identified by trade unions as causing what they see as a systemic crisis in corporate governance. It then identifies reforms that they believe should be included in the review.

II   EMERGENT PROBLEMS IN CORPORATE GOVERNANCE

Collapse of accountability

6.   Serious concerns have been raised concerning the collapse of corporate accountability, involving companies such as Enron and WorldCom in the US, and Marconi in Britain, and Ahold in the Netherlands. Though the corporations headlined are not alone - they are some of the best known. That raises disquieting concerns about the ownership and control mechanism of the corporation and its public accountability. One key issue surrounds the debate about the role and function of shareholders as owners, whether banks, pension funds or other institutional investors. The following questions have been raised as to whether:

- Shareholders lack the means of effective control; and
- They may be perceived as "absentee landlords" whose only wish is to receive regular dividends and capital gains in a rising share market with no direct responsibility for the affairs of the corporation;

7.   Complications in determining the duties and obligations of shareholders have it is felt left the corporation operating outside a credible framework of control and accountability, irrespective of jurisdiction. Overall there is the impression that many shareholders are in reality proxies and are in any case *conflicted* in acting straightforwardly as direct, interested, shareholders might otherwise do. These conclusions are difficult to avoid. The implications are far reaching for governance.

The issue of "tomorrows money today" – the new permissive-ism

8.   A corrosive economics of greed is seen by much of the public, trade unions, and some opinion formers as being increasingly present in many corporations, resulting in a climate change in terms of managerial attitudes. They fear that corporations now pursue short-term commercial and financial goals with scant regard for whether such moves are strictly legal or are consistent with longer-term sustainable development. What could be termed a new corporate permissive-ism has been driven, it is argued by a combination of:

- An over-emphasis on stock options as a means of rewarding senior management that has fuelled a climate of greed;
- A corrosive, illegal insider trading culture within corporations;
- A pervasive copycat practice of bidding up executive remuneration;
- Chronic failures in the scope, composition, and regulatory framework governing the activities and the accountability of boards of directors; and
- An undue corporate influence on the global political process.

9.   These influences have been compounded by a preoccupation with internal accounting devices that have the effect of overstating revenues and the real profitability of the corporation. *Off-balance sheet vehicles* have been widely abused in the pursuit of these ends with the collusion of financial and legal advisers, brokerage firms and other market makers. Though not in themselves illegal, these devices were used for example by Enron to deliberately conceal the true ownership of liabilities arising from these vehicles by methods of guarantee that were ultimately fraudulent. They were also used to siphon-off fees in underwriting and other service charges in a number of instances to benefit senior managers within Enron. Serious concerns have also been raised about the activities of external accounting and auditing firms – the gatekeepers. The collapse of Arthur Andersen was seen as graphic proof of a serious breakdown in the

nature of the auditing profession. Widespread conflicts of interests arising as a largely self-regulated industry were allowed to expand and to offer non-auditing services to their corporate clients. Similarly, questions remain over the role of other market makers such as rating agencies, etc.

The issue of globalisation

10.   Globalisation, especially financial market liberalisation and deregulation has impacted on corporate governance with unanticipated consequences. Though recognised regional corporate governance mechanisms are beginning to appear, for example at the level of the EU, and the trans-boundary aspects foreseen by Sarbanes Oxley, the dominant systems in terms of implementation and enforcement remain at the national level. The emergence of global corporations has encouraged management to exploit opportunities for regulatory arbitrage between different national jurisdictions[1]. In some well-publicised instances this has resulted in corporations relocating their headquarters to offshore tax havens to evade fiscal responsibilities, and other responsibilities, for example employee pension obligations. Veiling true beneficial ownership behind complex legal arrangements is used to hide the underlying intention. Globalisation has, furthermore created *grey areas* where national level regulatory bodies and other parties are uncertain as to which regulatory framework governs a corporation operating within their territories.

III   CORPORATE GOVERNANCE REGIMES ACROSS THE OECD

Diversity is the norm

11.   While much is said about the convergence of corporate governance regimes across the OECD, key differences remain, for example, in the form and function of boards; the underlying philosophies of accounting practices, or to whom the board and corporation is legally accountable to. This is especially true as regards the way in which key stakeholders such as workers and trade unions are included, or excluded, from the governance process. In many European countries and Japan, law and practice is different when compared with Anglo American based jurisdictions. The former view these issues from a different perspective. Stakeholders often have established rights in law, or collective agreements, and direct representation in the governance of corporations. Here, for example, workers may appoint or recommend for appointment representatives from their own ranks to sit on the supervisory and executive boards of enterprises. Their rights and duties as directors are also clearly defined, including that they have a fiduciary duty to the company. In some instances trade unions also have that right. At the same time workers and trade unions often have institutionalised consultative rights at other levels of governance over key employment related issues. Similarly, pan-European legislation conferring rights to information and consultation on some issues, currently for workers in multinational enterprises operating in the EU, will shortly be extended to all domestic enterprises, subject to certain thresholds. At the same time EU wide legislation on collective redundancies confers the right to information and consultation for workers.

12.   However, this participatory approach to corporate governance should not be taken to infer that workers and unions have no voice in Anglo American based jurisdictions. In the United States workers have a voice and are represented as investors through their private retirement savings plans and ESOPS. This is increasingly the case in the UK as well. And, it is argued new and expected regulatory changes are widening and deepening these rights.

---

[1]   Some large institutional investors are warning companies not to relocate or set up business in countries with weak corporate governance regimes. See "Funds warn companies favouring lax regimes". Financial Times Weekly Review of the Investment Industry, June 2 2003.

IV   SOME PROGRESS IN NATIONAL-LEVEL CORPORATE GOVERNANCE REFORMS

13.   In response many government are now enacting or in the process of enacting reforms to their national corporate governance regimes. The most high profile example is the Sarbanes Oxley Act of 2002 which has strengthened the scope for civil and criminal sanctions, including for gatekeepers. But reform efforts are underway across most of the OECD. The exact form of the reforms varies across countries, but includes: financial reporting and disclosure, the role of institutional investors, internal and external audit procedures, the form and composition of boards of directors, conflicts of interest, and implementation and enforcement. The UK has now released a consultative document on directors' remuneration. The reforms have enjoyed widespread support, though many, including trade unions are of the view that more can be done. Disquiet has also been expressed that an over-reliance on voluntary codes and standards for implementation and enforcement will be insufficient to overcome the failures of corporate governance.

V   THE REVIEW OF THE OECD PRINCIPLES OF CORPORATE GOVERNANCE

14.   The paper has already touched upon the review of the OECD Principles of Corporate governance, which is being conducted by its Steering Group on Corporate Governance, to which TUAC and BIAC participate on an ad-hocbasis. The road map for the review was agreed at its meeting on 19-20 March 2003, and it is expected that the revisions will be presented for adoption to the Spring 2004 meeting of the OECD Council at Ministerial level. It has also been noted that views differ on the extent to which the Principles should be revised. The paper next indicates revisions that TUAC and its affiliates believe should be incorporated into the review.

Broadening stakeholder representation

15.   TUAC believes that the case for broader stakeholder representation on the boards of corporations is compelling, and is underpinned by sound economic thinking. Within this paradigm workers like shareholders are investors in the corporation. Their investment, takes the form of human capital, for example in on and off the job training, where the returns are not captured in the wage. And, just as financial investors are now seen as having a right to a say in the governance process, so too are workers as investors. Similarly, current practices whereby workers are investors in corporations through their pension funds, or employees share option programmes (ESOPs) gives them a right to a voice in the governance process. At the same time, provisions are in place in a large number of OECD countries that give workers a right to be informed and consulted by the board about key issues surrounding the future direction of the enterprise.

16.   As currently drafted however, the stakeholder chapter is limiting in that it focuses solely on the recognition of a stakeholder voice in the governance process as "established by law", while other performance enhancing mechanisms should be "permitted". To bring the Principles into conformity with current practices, the text should be revised to generalise a worker voice in the governance process.

Expanding the gene pool of directors

17.   Any changes in the Principles might very well seek to reflect measures anticipated in new national initiatives – in particular those in America and Britain. The Sarbanes Oxley Act, 2002 is wide ranging. It covers board membership, the duties of board committees, accounting and auditing standards and conflicts of interest. Severe punishments are foreseen for breaches of law. Furthermore, changes have and continue to be introduced to the New York Stock Exchange and Nasdaq listing requirements (overseen

by the SEC) for companies, that are seen by some as more far ranging. In Britain proposals for changes to company law have been advanced by the Company Law Reform Steering Group (CLRSG). Most recently the Higgs Enquiry has reported on the role of independent directors, as has the French Bouton Report.

18.   Higgs recognises the need for strengthening the independence of non-executive directors. The appointment of a chairman should be independent from earlier allegiances or association with the corporation in question. Higgs also recommends a systematic widening and deepening of the gene pool from which directors are selected. The British CLRSG's report also places particular emphasis on the need for corporations and their boards to be responsive to changing stakeholder and societal expectations. This has important institutional implications as well as implications for training and education in *directorship*. The Principles might wisely reflect these matters in any changes to the drafting of the Principles.

The responsibilities of shareholders

19.   There need to be a new chapter to cover the Responsibilities of Shareholders. This chapter needs to differentiate between institutions such as pension funds and Employee Share Associations (ESAs), and short term speculative institutions such as "hedge funds"[2]. Although both groups have fiduciary duties, pension funds are, however, providers of *patient capital*, with the implication that the investments they make are *long-term*. The option to 'exit' would normally in such cases be limited to *times of crisis*. In contrast hedge funds measure their investment over a much shorter time frame – sometimes one or a few days - and as such face different expectations over their responsibilities.

20.   Pension funds have, in effect, a responsibility to the workers as stewards of the capital they are entrusted to manage. The Principles should set out clearly the need for institutional investors, including pension funds, to exercise the closest oversight of the corporations in whose firms they hold equity; how that can most effectively be achieved; and the necessary transparency and disclosure required to allow trustees to ascertain whether effective oversight is being discharged. Examples might include requiring such investors to vote in AGMs, and to disclose their voting patterns, and most importantly to allow them to nominate directors.

Disclosure and transparency

21.   The existing chapter on Disclosure and Transparency chapter could benefit from revisions in key areas. A key issue for investors and worker alike is access to clear unambiguous and timely information on the exact geographical location of a corporation's particular operations, regardless as to whether this applies to a subsidiary or its supply chain. There is a similar need for transparency and disclosure on all aspects relating to ultimate beneficial ownership, including full details in respect of incorporation. There is a need to specify more clearly what is understood by foreseeable risk factors, what constitutes materiality and how these are expected to impact upon employees and other stakeholders.

The Board – roles, responsibilities and conflicts of interest

22.   Against the background of recent corporate scandals, there is also a need now for a new chapter covering the Roles and Responsibilities of CEOs and Senior Management. It should cover issues such as the separation of roles of CEO and Chair; remuneration, especially the use of stock options, and full disclosure on ethical issues and conflicts of interest in respect of individual directors and employees.

---

[2]   The distinction between pension funds and hedge funds is merely used to illustrate the different functions, and responsibilities of financial investors.

23.   The need to avoid conflicts of interests between for example the services offered by external auditors and the corporations that they audit need also to be incorporated, along with those concerning credit rating agencies. Finally, implementation and enforcement were not included within the original Principles. Events demonstrate clearly that these twin issues should be included.

Implementation and enforcement

24.   All OECD member countries have mechanisms to ensure the implementation and enforcement of their corporate governance regimes, but differences exist as to the mix of hard and soft law, and voluntary codes of practice that are utilised to ensure compliance. Yet, the current Principles could be termed "light" on implementation and enforcement. Developing and transition countries would certainly benefit from guidance in this area when contemplating reforms. There is therefore a need for the inclusion of a set of Principles and annotations that reflect the current practices in this area. Moreover, whilst the use of market mechanisms and incentives should be included as possible compliance mechanisms, so too should binding and soft law mechanisms, the latter including international arrangements.

Concluding remarks

25.   In conclusion, governments in all jurisdictions face fundamental challenges in effectively addressing public concerns around corporate governance. Trade unions believe that the OECD Principles of Corporate Governance have a key role in informing and guiding the ongoing and future national level debates, as well as any emerging international framework required as part of the process of managing globalisation.

FINAL REPORT

by
Sue Kendall-Bilicki
Senior Editor, OECD Observer
Public Affairs and Communications Directorate
OECD

BACKGROUND AND INTRODUCTION

Corporate governance emerged as a major issue of public concern in the wake of the Asian financial crisis of the late 1990s. The OECD Principles of Corporate Governance were adopted in 1999 as part of broader multilateral efforts to improve global financial stability in reaction to that crisis.

The Principles consist of five chapters: The Rights of Shareholders; Equitable Treatment of Shareholders; The Role of Stakeholders in Corporate Governance; Disclosure and Transparency; and The Responsibilities of the Board. In 2000 the Principles became one of 12 key standards of global financial stability and are now used as a benchmark by international financial institutions.

Corporate governance hit the headlines again in late 2001 in the wake of Enron and other financial scandals in the U.S. and elsewhere, coupled with steep falls in stock markets. These raised concerns not only about measures to limit fraud but also the effect on shareholders, pension funds and jobs of collapsing share prices, as well as rising public criticism of compensation packages for some top executives.

OECD ministers decided at their annual meeting in May 2002 in light of these developments that a review of the Principles scheduled for 2005 should be brought forward for delivery to ministers in 2004.

The Trade Union Advisory Committee to the OECD (TUAC) has been involved in the work on the Principles of Corporate Governance since its inception, and participates on an ad hoc basis in the OECD Steering Group on Corporate Governance which is carrying out the current review.

As part of the review process, TUAC requested a meeting under the auspices of the OECD's Labour/Management Programme (LMP) to discuss the major failures, weaknesses and challenges, and policy responses that have arisen in corporate governance. TUAC was responsible for setting the list of participants and for an issues paper to guide the discussion. This meeting followed a two-day session of the steering group the same week.

CONTEXT OF THE REVIEW AND ISSUES AT STAKE

1. Objectives of the review

There was a clear commitment from all participants to the need for such a review and to achieving the best possible outcome, although there were diverging views on how far the principles should be changed and in what way.

The secretariat said that the recent corporate scandals had in fact shocked industrial governments out of what may have been complacency that what had happened in Asia could not happen to them because they had strong and credible corporate governance systems. That is what had spurred them into calling for an accelerated review.

Participants noted that the 1999 Principles have been instrumental in attracting foreign direct investment (FDI) and more importantly in boosting domestic investment in developing and transition countries. It was argued that had the Principles been followed strictly in the past, corporate collapses and scandals would not have occurred. Participants said that how the Principles could be strengthened, provide guidance on legal constraints, and help prevent conflicts of interest were key considerations.

The secretariat said that the review would increase awareness by all sides of what issues need to be addressed; to enable countries to learn from each other's experience of what has been done at national level and to produce an even more effective tool for countries that want to improve their practices. There were also suggestions that the Principles should offer guidance to help countries not just to implement an improved governance regime but also to effectively enforce it.

For TUAC participants, the overarching question for the review was whether the revised text will pass the "post-Enron test" and provide a way to restore legitimacy to corporations. TUAC participants argued that the principles should provide an international "standard of reference" for corporate governance in both the industrial and the developing world as well as a point of reference for national reforms. Many felt that to achieve this, the principles require radical rethinking and redrafting. Some warned that the changes proposed so far are not enough and do not pass the "post-Enron" test.

Several participants expressed concern that the sense of urgency from governments and business immediately after the scandals, which had led to the review being accelerated, had apparently evaporated. There were now signs of complacency, both from some governments and from business, and of reluctance to change anything. Some TUAC participants said this is short-sighted, arguing that it is in the interest of all parties to improve the environment for investment and confidence in businesses. For that to happen, measures need to be put in place that will restore confidence and credibility. One TUAC participant questioned whether the goal of the review was to react to past crises or to prevent future ones. The secretariat replied that the review would target both, by being "proactive in preventing".

2. Coherence of the review with other global actions

Participants generally agreed that the OECD is the best place to deal with corporate governance since it groups the major industrial countries which are the home base of many of the world's large multinationals. Several TUAC participants stressed that the purpose of the principles is not corporate governance per se and to prevent future corporate collapses but corporate governance to achieve economic and social development worldwide. They said the principles should also be linked to the development agenda laid out in such forums as Monterrey and Johannesburg, the IMF/World Bank Poverty Reduction Strategy Paper agenda, the promotion of the ILO 1998 Declaration on core labour standards, the work of the UN and the OECD on prevention of money laundering, as well as issues such as auditing and accounting standards. If the various frameworks are to work well, they need to be compatible. Several

TUAC participants also said the principles should be better integrated into the OECD's work as a whole, particularly the OECD Guidelines for multinational enterprises (MNE Guidelines) and the OECD's work on public governance

These links were supported by the OECD Development Centre representative, who highlighted the important relationship between corporate and public governance, competition policy and regulatory governance in a developing country perspective.

The secretariat agreed that coherence with the rest of the OECD's work was important, particularly for developing countries, since they are often trying to bring various elements of OECD work together into a single package to create a climate that encourages growth and investment.

3. Review process and consultation

The secretariat said that following the two meetings of the steering group it was clear that there was a commitment from all participants to the need for such a review and to achieving the best possible outcome, although there were diverging views on how far the principles should be changed and in what way.

The secretariat noted that differences of culture, history and views as to the role of social partners between OECD members make it difficult to reach agreement on how to make the principles of corporate governance more specific. However, there was a consensus that the principles should remain aspirational and outcome-oriented, leaving flexibility as to how a particular principle might be achieved. In these circumstances there is a lot that the OECD and other international organisations can do to lay out best principles and good practice that can form the basis of legal and regulatory frameworks for OECD countries and beyond. The OECD seeks to guide the development of corporate governance regimes that will encourage investment and give confidence to investors and stakeholders.

The secretariat stressed the open and transparent nature of the process, which involves not just the steering group and interlocutors such as BIAC and TUAC but also meetings with other stakeholders, and a public invitation to comment from any interested party. The secretariat said it would try to take comments from all these into account when drafting texts for submission to the Steering Group.

Several participants agreed that it was important not to become bogged down in detail and lose sight of the fundamental point of the review: to look at what a good company is and how to make it work.

Several TUAC participants noted that one problem in reaching agreement on difficult issues such as stakeholder participation was that the steering group is made up of representatives of a broad range of ministries from different countries, with very different concerns. It was suggested that this problem could be resolved by giving the steering group more status and resources, by converting it into a fully fledged committee.

4. Review issues

The role of the company was taken up by several participants as fundamental to the review. Some TUAC participants said the current principles implicitly share the business view of the company as an entity owned by shareholders. But, they said, there is now a broader social awareness that the company is not simply a private institution but has wider responsibilities and duties. The wealth of society, in short, is not just a matter of private property or private institutions. The corporate entity is a major driver of growth and development in all economies, and must be allowed to grow and prosper. But it follows from the TUAC position that it is critical to have principles that respect the role of trades unions and other stakeholders in the governance of the corporation if its legitimacy is to be restored and enhanced.

TUAC participants called for the principles to be made broader and deeper, with a greater emphasis on the role of stakeholders, particularly workers, and how this should be given expression at board level; the duties and obligations, as well as the rights, of shareholders; and the role of the board, particularly the chief executive officer (CEO). TUAC called for a new chapter to be added covering the CEO and for the chapters on stakeholders, the board and its functioning to be developed further. Conflict of interest and the role of institutional investors were also included as topics missing from the current Principles that need to be addressed.

The secretariat agreed that the role of corporations in growth creation in our societies has become increasingly important. As a result, the company, how it is governed, its influence on society and the way it accommodates demands from society are increasingly a policy issue and the OECD is well-placed to serve that policy dialogue.

The secretariat noted fundamental changes in ownership structure, including the shift from large individual investors to institutional investors and the increased reliance on capital markets. Two cross-cutting issues could be singled out following the consultations of March, the steering group meeting that followed, and the non-OECD roundtables over the past three years, participants said: conflicts of interest and the role of institutional investors. TUAC said the existing language on conflict of interest was short of what is required to ensure an independent board and effective enforcement of the Principles. Concerning institutional investors, it was argued that the Principles should be more explicit on the right incentives to use their voting rights in an intelligent and cost-effective way.

5. Assessment of national differences and implementation

The secretariat said that a key element in reviewing the Principles is the fact that there is no "one size fits all" solution. Cultural and social differences between countries, such as differences in board structure between the Anglo-American and continental European models, have to be recognized and taken into account if the Principles are to be useful. This meant looking at the actual situation in individual countries and creating practical, workable solutions that could work for everyone, rather than crafting regulations for an ideal corporation in an ideal world that does not exist. The secretariat said its survey of current practice in participating countries had revealed differences between perception and practice in several areas, for instance showing that in many cases shareholder rights existed on paper but in practice were ineffective.

Several participants raised the question of how companies, whatever structural system they follow, go about putting the principles into practice and how to find a way to avoid simple "box-ticking" by directors. They cited examples of companies which had put audit committees or executive pay monitoring committees in place essentially to be able to say they had set them up rather than to perform a real function. There are also differences of perception between countries as to what such committees' functions are.

Several TUAC participants highlighted the differences in the way different countries deal with corporate governance. The extent of formal union involvement varies, with participants from continental Europe detailing methods of regulation in which labour is formally involved in drawing up corporate codes while the Anglo-American model tended to favour a mixture of laws and rules set by regulatory bodies, with boards being left with wide discretionary powers under "comply or explain" provisions. In some cases, codes were backed up with government threats of legislation if they were not strict enough. Both types of system can be rendered more complex in the case of federal systems where regulatory responsibilities are divided between national and federal authorities.

THE ROLE OF STAKEHOLDERS

6. The role and definition of stakeholders

Several stressed that the principles needed to define more clearly what a "stakeholder" is, and their role, responsibilities and rights, in order to avoid national systems that paid lip-service to the idea of stakeholder involvement without spelling out just who they meant.

One TUAC participant said a stakeholder could be defined as anyone who affects or is affected by the company, such as society in general or people living around a plant. This begs the question of how such a general concept of stakeholdership can ever be effectively extended to involvement in governance. But stakeholders who are clearly "constituents"— meaning someone who adds to the corporation's productive resource and needs to be protected – would also have rights and responsibilities. By this definition, shareholders and workers should have the same level of rights and responsibilities since they have the same kind of relationship to the corporation. The case for a worker voice in corporate governance was also made in a developing country perspective, where contractual arrangements may not be the norm and labour rights may not be guaranteed by law.

The secretariat cautioned that pushing the worker as stakeholder argument too far and over-estimating the firm-specific capital carried by individuals could backfire and be used as a basis to create a "free agent" category of worker responsible for their own unique contribution to the process, which is happening in some hi-tech companies. This is then reflected in the wage structure and can be used to divide the workforce into types of firm-specific knowledge, which could cut out a large part of workforce who are not work-specific and can easily be replaced.

7. Worker participation as a contribution to corporate performance

TUAC participants noted that there is a literature showing that higher employee involvement in decision-making makes for a more flexible, successful business. This would support the case for a clear statement of these benefits in the stakeholder section of the principles. Since workers participate in creating the products that in turn generate the wealth, they are as much a stakeholder as a shareholder in the company.

A World Bank survey of 1,000 studies on the economic effects of unions and collective bargaining, for example, found that high unionisation rates were linked to improved economic performance. It should be possible to draw at least a passive analogy from this on the effect of employee participation in corporate governance. Looking at the question from the reverse perspective, if employees do not play a major role in strategic decisions affecting them it leads to conflict, lack of loyalty, grievances, and ultimately a less stable business environment for the company.

The secretariat said that one problem with arguments for stakeholder representation and involvement in board decisions is the lack of a large body of evidence to demonstrate the outcome and benefits. A lot of studies have been done on labour-related questions such as wage-setting, but relatively little work has been done specifically on the contribution of stakeholders.

TUAC participants acknowledged that there may not be an extensive literature specifically linking employee involvement and better corporate governance, but said that in many countries where worker involvement and social partnership have been the practice for many years, little research work has been done because there is a general consensus that this is clearly the best way to get results. A recent ILO study of several European countries found that in times of rapid change, countries with extensive social dialogue and stakeholder involvement cope much better with challenges and suffer less friction and unemployment than those without.

Several TUAC participants also said that the economic argument in support of worker involvement was far from new, and asked why the secretariat wanted unions to produce proof of their argument when companies and governments operating systems based on shareholder control without worker involvement were not being asked to prove their benefits.

8. Workers as bearers of corporate risk

Several TUAC participants said that the argument for stronger worker involvement in corporate governance was not only motivated by their contribution to corporate performance, but also because they bear risks equal to or higher than shareholders. Shareholders do not "own" the company in any real sense – they cannot sell it or use its assets, but they do bear the residual risk, as do stakeholders and constituents. Workers also have a stake in the firm, in the shape of firm-specific knowledge which is of value to the company and they bear a risk since that value is lost if the company fails. Employees are in fact more exposed to risk than shareholders because they are not fully in control of the contractual relationship: shareholders always have a choice whether to sell but a worker can be forced to leave even if he wants to stay. Furthermore, the worker's risk is undiversified as he has only one job whereas a shareholder generally spreads ownership of shares across several companies. The case was said to be even stronger for transnational corporations, because these workers face higher risks of unemployment due to jobs going abroad following internal restructuring. TUAC participants were therefore of the view that workers should have a voice in board decisions since they cover items with a direct impact on workers, such as restructuring or foreign direct investment allocation, that directly affect the livelihood of workers and their families.

The secretariat said that if the benefits to all were straightforwardly obvious, corporations would want to take action. But it is not easy to convince everyone that employees bear the same kind of risk as shareholders or creditors. They are paid, and are thus the first beneficiaries of profit, and can walk away when they want without finding someone else to do their job, whereas shareholders have to find a buyer for their shares to replace them.

9. Worker representation on company boards

The meeting spent some time discussing the case of worker and trade union representation on company boards. One TUAC participant cited the case of a European company that chose to have trades unionists seated on the board of directors in the one-tier system to ensure quality of the social dialogue within the company as it was facing major restructuring.

However, TUAC said, worker representation on the board was not necessarily a guarantee of full access to the decision-making process. One TUAC participant cited the case of union representatives on the board of a European company who had been excluded from discussions about an upcoming takeover bid although it would affect jobs. Another pointed out that in the Anglo-American single-tier board model even when workers are shareholders, either directly or via worker pension funds, they still may have no power over the board.

The secretariat raised the question of conflict of interest arising for workers as stakeholders, or worker pension funds on the board: who do they represent – their own constituency which put them on the board, or the company as a whole? Similar issues also arose with special representation for minority shareholders.

TUAC participants replied that the risk of conflict of interest was low because the bottom line was that both need long-term sustainable growth in the corporation to be successful. Another said that when it came to worker representatives on the board, how they were chosen could affect the role they were expected to play. In countries with two-tier boards, union representatives can be chosen by a union or a federation and the further away from the shop floor they were, the more likely they were to represent general interests.

For TUAC, the question of conflict of interest was not only a concern for worker representation on boards; the same question could be applied to any board member, and the answer from national company laws is ambiguous: are they responsible to shareholders or to the company, or both? In a sense it is both, and in any case if the board is responsible to the company then it is responsible to all its constituents. One problem when talking about corporate governance and conflict of interest is that the view about appropriate responsibilities has changed. In the 1950s and 1960s there was a prevailing view that the board was responsible to all the constituents of the company, but in the 1980s the equation shifted in almost all countries to become one of responsibility to shareholders only. Worker shareholders and worker representation on boards were widespread already. The answer in regard to their role was that they should be seen as shareholders when dealing with issues of the company as a whole, and employees when dealing with issues such as wages.

10. The review of the stakeholder chapter

TUAC participants expressed disappointment that the steering group had shown reluctance to change the existing chapter on stakeholders. TUAC is particularly interested in ensuring that the role of stakeholders is clearly articulated in the principles.

Some TUAC participants stressed that in looking at the role of stakeholders, and particularly workers, the principles must take account of other ways of doing business than the Anglo-American model, and recognize that other countries have a strong social dialogue culture, notably through works councils and worker representation on boards.

Some TUAC participants said the principles should state that corporations are bound to justify and explain their actions to stakeholders and involve them in the decision-making process.

The secretariat said it was quite clear to all that consensus about the stakeholder section was going to be difficult to find. To inform the discussion the secretariat for its part had sought to inform the debate with the results of recent research. The corporate governance principles certainly put the issue of stakeholders on the table, the secretariat said, noting that when they were first issued these principles were the only multilateral document with any clout to have any significant section on stakeholders. But most participants in the steering group had said they felt fairly comfortable with the way stakeholders are currently dealt with.

The secretariat also cautioned against getting too bogged down in detail of wording and definitions, noting that experience to date in working with the principles, particularly in non-OECD countries, had shown that what is really important is that the principles provide an underlying rationale to discuss the issue.

SHAREHOLDER RIGHTS AND RESPONSIBILITIES

11. The role of institutional shareholders

TUAC participants said it was clear that, in many cases, shareholders lack effective control of corporations and this has to be addressed. Shareholders are reacting, but in many cases companies are still resisting control either by shareholders or other outside regulators. Some noted that despite corporate mantras about shareholder control in the US, in many cases they had no voice in selecting the board, and even when they could bring a vote it was not binding.

TUAC participants supported the idea of giving shareholders more power over the board, including by being able to nominate directors. Business has raised the problem of the extra burden that will be imposed on companies if shareholders have the right to raise proposals at annual general meetings (AGMs). But the mere ability to make such proposals may not in itself be enough to achieve change. Cases were cited where shareholders had put a resolution to the AGM which were noted but not acted upon. Others stressed that any such resolutions from shareholders must be binding or there was little point in having them.

The secretariat noted that the survey of actual practice in countries had been able to make clear the difference between perception and practice, and how ineffective shareholder rights actually were in some cases. There are wide differences in current practice between countries when it comes to shareholder rights, and transparency, in terms of executive remuneration. Some countries allow shareholders to vote, but only in an advisory capacity, others have a binding vote but only on an overall package and in some cases shareholders can determine what an individual package will look like.

Several TUAC participants said the principles should state that active ownership is better than passive ownership. The secretariat agreed that active ownership is better than passive ownership, but said what is really important is to have "informed ownership". It also cautioned that mandatory voting by major shareholders, as suggested by some TUAC participants, is not the best incentive to active, informed, ownership as it could simply lead to lots of proxy voting.

TUAC participants said they wanted the revised principles to include not just the rights but the responsibilities of shareholders. This should include making institutional investors responsible for exercising close oversight of companies in which they hold equity. There was a suggestion that institutional investors could be given tax breaks for example, to keep their holding in a particular company for a longer period than is now the case with some institutional investors.

Some participants said it is clear from the evidence of the past few years that however many rights you give investors, without the right cost-effective incentives they will not invest. This means making the decision-making process accessible to shareholders. So the principles should cover not only the rights of investors but also seek to ensure that the regulatory framework facilitates participation. There was a view that in this case it should be clear that "facilitating" meant making it easier for investors to fulfil their responsibilities, rather than just exercising their rights. But shareholders and proxy shareholders also have to be able to act in an effective way in controlling the activities of the corporation and bringing it to account.

12. Governance and engagement of pension funds

Some TUAC participants said there was a need to give pension fund investors incentives, such as tax breaks, to be active in the companies where they held shares and to stay to sort out problems rather than selling up. Worker pension funds have to have a voice, they said, citing losses to worker pension funds due to falling stock markets, in some cases linked to financial scandals within companies, and lack of worker involvement in managing these funds. However, pension funds often choose to be passive to increase their efficiency and the rate of return on their investment, and do not have any exit strategy when problems of corporate governance arise. More transparent financial markets were needed, TUAC said, but the review also had a role to play in facilitating the transparency of proxy voting. Although institutional investors require greater transparency from corporations, they refuse to disclose their own voting policy and many trustees hire financial intermediaries with serious conflicts of interest. One TUAC participant recalled the distinction between pension funds and mutual funds managed by banks, as well as within pension funds, between large public pension funds that manage their investments internally (with low risk of conflict of interest) and smaller ones that appoint trustees to manage their investments.

One TUAC participant said workers must have representatives on their own pension funds. These are more the workers' property than that of the company but workers are often not represented. US pension funds have lost three trillion dollars, a gap that now has to be bargained back from employers; if workers were on the pension fund boards in the first place they would be handled with a more responsible attitude. It is important to get elected worker representatives on pension funds in the revised principles.

The secretariat said there is good support from member countries on the importance of having the need to deal with conflict of interest in the principles and this might well be strengthened as part of the review.

THE RESPONSIBILITIES OF THE BOARD

13. Remuneration of the Board and executives

Several TUAC participants said it was clear that current systems of checks and balances, and systems of self-regulation, were not working, citing changes in style and ways of working that have led to over-remuneration and unhealthy levels of payment via stock options etc, resulting in cases where directors and other executives brought corporations to their knees and still walked away with million-dollar packages.

The secretariat noted that the move toward more disclosure of executive, and especially director, remuneration had met resistance on the grounds that this would break solidarity between members of the board. However more and more countries were calling for individual executive and board remuneration to be declared.

TUAC participants said shareholder votes for remuneration should be binding and on an individual basis, as a global sum covering several people was not sufficiently transparent to enable shareholders to make a proper judgement. They also said that there were myriad ways of organizing this in detail, but the bottom line was that the principles should be able to state that the board must have a way to determine compensation in relation to performance of the company as measured against standards set by the board. One TUAC participant suggested that stock options should be replaced by actual shares, and that executives should be forced to keep them for a minimum period after leaving the company to ensure they acted in the best long-term interests of the enterprise.

14. Composition of the Board

There were also several calls for broader participation in boards, because too many boards are self-perpetuating and drawn from a narrow group of people. TUAC participants said the revised principles should give a clearer idea of how to widen board participation. Adding worker and minority shareholder representation, some said, would immediately broaden the perspective of the board as a whole. It was important to achieve an expanded gene pool of directors, to enable the boards to respond effectively to society's changing expectations in terms of corporate social responsibility and "environmental governance" issues. TUAC participants also said there are too many examples of the same people sitting on multiple boards with little time to devote to any of them.

The secretariat noted that several countries have expressed concern that a narrow "gene pool" can affect the quality of the board and are trying to improve it. But one crucial question comes back to the issue of whether the members of the board would feel that they were representing a certain electorate rather than working for the company as a whole. In some two-tier boards, for example, there is a need for more members not representing narrow interests but representing all the interests of the company.

15. Independence of the board and separation of functions

TUAC participants wanted a new chapter in the principles dealing specifically with the CEO and senior management that would cover separation of roles between the CEO and chair, remuneration packages, and full disclosure of conflicts of interest, especially when it came to outside auditors.

Some TUAC participants said the current principles do not give a satisfactory delineation of the purpose, role and responsibility of different members of the board or of different tiers in multi-tier boards. There may be different ways of organizing things, but the bottom line is that whatever board model is being followed, all corporations need an executive and supervisory function and to allocate responsibility. Therefore it would make sense for the principles to go into more detail about the division of responsibility between the CEO and chairman and their functions. Furthermore, separating the role of chair and chief executive in the one-tier system should be given in the principles not as best practice but as a minimum standard.

The secretariat said that one way to help with this would be to facilitate effective shareholder influence on the composition of the board, and indeed some countries are moving in this direction.

The secretariat said that the principles already state that the board should be able to exercise objective judgement on corporate affairs independent, in particular, from management. But it warned that some formulae being put forward by TUAC participants for governing "independent" shareholder representation on the board could be too prescriptive in terms of defining independence. At the same time, the secretariat said, perhaps there is a need to talk more about the requirements to ensure independence – which in a number of countries also means independence from a block shareholder -- and how to implement this aspect of the principles. For instance, in some countries there are proposals that companies should specify their corporate governance arrangements, and identify who their independent directors are, detailing their area of expertise and how many board meetings they have attended. In any case, the question of who is "independent" or not, and how many are on the board, cannot be sorted out until you resolve how the board is chosen. And, the secretariat noted, if shareholders were choosing the board, rather than say a CEO, the problem would no longer be the same.

OTHER ISSUES: TRANSPARENCY AND ENFORCEMENT

16. Disclosure and transparency

TUAC participants said that the chapter on disclosure and transparency needed to be more detailed to pass the "post-Enron test" and should shift from good practices to minimum standards. The review should cover disclosure and transparency not just in financial terms but also covering a number of other elements, including geographical location, foreseeable risks such as potential site cleanup bills in future, and "sustainability" factors such as training and development. Geographical location in particular should be seen as an issue for everybody, especially in developing countries, as it was an element in risk management for institutional investors.

Several TUAC participants raised the problem of transparency of internal procedures and safeguards in accounting/auditing systems and elsewhere, as well as transparency of proxy voting. This would favour shareholder activism. At least one survey showed that once proxy voting became transparent in a country, proxies had to be much more careful about how they voted and not blindly supporting management to serve just one client. Such moves can help protect workers' savings.

TUAC participants also stressed that shareholders need full transparency and disclosure when it comes to beneficial ownership. Some said the transparency section should delineate what kind of information shareholders should have.

The secretariat said the principles are clear about disclosure requirements but that in practice disclosure was not often the same thing as transparency. There has been an enormous proliferation of ways to improve board functioning and in many countries this has led to the creation of a large number of committees but often their actual function is not understood by anyone. A Swedish report found that major companies there had "audit committees" that were nothing like audit committees in the US, for example, which could be misleading for shareholders unless clearly explained.

17. Enforcement of the Principles

Often corporations say they are owned by shareholders but it is difficult for them to make their voices heard, and most importantly to have their views respected, TUAC participants said.

TUAC participants said that the principles should also deal more with the types of legal mechanism countries can use to enforce the principles. Self-regulation clearly is not an option, one said, citing the fact that the Enron board voted three times to suspend its own corporate governance code in the run-up to the 2001 scandal. A lot remains to be done to enforce independence of directors, auditors and disclosure of compensation, as well as to prevent insider trading and corporate malfeasance.

Several TUAC participants said that the corporate governance principles should take the revised MNE guidelines as an example on enforcement. The review of this part of the MNE guidelines may have been a painful process, but it did result in a crucial strengthening of the enforcement part and this is a lesson for the corporate governance principles. One TUAC participant said that if the current review deals with implementation and enforcement of laws at national level, future discussion should look at the possibility of international rules and regulations.

The secretariat noted that enforcement differs widely between countries. In at least one country now, for example, there is personal responsibility for directors who make decisions that adversely impact pensions.

CONCLUSION

TUAC participants welcomed the efforts of the steering group in pushing for a substantial review of the Principles and looked forward to continuing work on the review. TUAC suggested the OECD secretariat could elaborate in a concept paper on "what is a good company?" and propose to the member states to reflect on it. Several TUAC participants mentioned the Peterson report as a good example of a report on corporate governance reform that the steering group could take aim at.

The secretariat said that the meeting was beneficial in getting at length the analytical and factual arguments underpinning TUAC positions. This will enable the secretariat to give the maximum amount of "intelligence" to the steering group to enable them to make an informed decision.

It also said, in response to comments about the challenge of finding a solution acceptable to all in the steering group as well as BIAC, TUAC and other groups that having diverging views on the table was an asset, not a liability, as it meant ideas would be tested and this would help improve the quality of the final product. There are real conflicts and if participants try to deny that, the process will never move forward.

ANNEX -- LIST OF PARTICIPANTS

TRADE UNION EXPERTS

Ms. Eva BELABED	Member EESC (European Economic and Social Committee) belabed.e@ak-ooe.at	AUSTRIA
Mr. Ronald JANSSEN	Service d'Études Confédération des Syndicats Chrétiens de Belgique (CSC) RJanssen@acv-csc.be	BELGIUM
Mr. Marcel PEPIN	Confédération des Syndicats Nationaux (CSN) marcel.pepin@csn.qc.ca	CANADA
Mr. Peter CHAPMAN	SHARE pchapman@web.ca	CANADA
Mr. Vladimir MATOUSEK	Senior Advisor Macroeconomic Department Czech-Moravian Confederation of Trade Unions (CMKOS) Matousek.Vladimir@cmkos.cz	CZECH REPUBLIC
Mr. Ole PRASZ	Salaried Employees' & Civil Servants' Confederation (FTF) ole.prasz@ftf.dk / hanne.beck@ftf.dk	DENMARK
Mr. Marc DELUZET	Secrétaire confédéral Confédération Française Démocratique du Travail (CFDT) mdeluzet@cfdt.fr	FRANCE
Mr. Bernard SAINCY	Secrétaire national - UGICT - Union Générale des Ingénieurs, Cadres & Techniciens Confédération Générale du Travail (CGT) b.saincy@ugict.cgt.fr	FRANCE
Mr. Benoît ROBIN	Assistant confédéral Secteur économique Force Ouvrière (CGT-FO) brobin@force-ouvriere.fr	FRANCE

Mr. Roland KÖSTLER	Referat Recht Hans Böckler Stiftung (HBS) Roland-koestler@Boeckler.de	GERMANY
Ms. Marina RICCIARDELLI	Confédération Italienne des Syndicats des Travailleurs (CISL) marina.ricciardelli@cisl.it	ITALY
Mr. Giuseppe DE NARDO	Fondi Pensione Union Italienne du Travail (UIL) fondi@uil.it	ITALY
Mr. David COATS	Head Economic & Social Department Trades Union Congress (TUC) dcoats@tuc.org.uk	UNITED KINGDOM
Mr. Jon ROBINSON	Trades Union Congress (TUC) Congress House jrobinson@tuc.org.uk	UNITED KINGDOM
Mr. Richard TUDWAY	Advisor to TUAC on Corporate Governance Centre for International Economics RichardTudway@compuserve.com	UNITED KINGDOM
Mr. Ron BLACKWELL	**Chair of the meeting** Director Corporate Affairs Department American Federation of Labor & Congress of Industrial Organizations (AFL-CIO) rblackwe@aflcio.org	UNITED STATES
Mr. Norbert KLUGE	Research Officer European Trade Union Institute (ETUI) nkluge@etuc.org	E.U.
Ms. Carla COLETTI	International Metalworkers' Federation (IMF) ccoletti@imfmetal.org	

TRADE UNION ADVISORY COMMITTEE TO THE OECD (TUAC)

Mr. John EVANS	General Secretary Email: evans@tuac.org
Mr. Roy JONES	Senior Policy Advisor Email: Schneider@tuac.org
Mr. Pierre HABBARD	Consultant Email: habbard@tuac.org

RAPPORTEUR

Ms. Sue KENDALL-BILICKI

Senior Editor
OECD Observer
Public Affairs Division
Email : sue.kendall-bilicki@oecd.org

OBSERVERS

Mr. Klaus-Jochen GÜHLCKE

Counsellor
Permanent Delegation to the OECD
Email: klaus.guehlcke@germany-oecd.org

His Excellency Mr. Francesco OLIVIERI

Ambassador
Head of Delegation
Permanent Delegation to the OECD
Email : olivieri@rappocse.org

Mr. Kjell ANDERSEN

Special Counsellor
Permanent Delegation to the OECD
Email: kjell.andersen@mfa.no

Mr. Lukas BEGLINGER

Deputy Permanent Representative
Permanent Delegation to the OECD
Email: lukas.beglinger@pao.rep.admin.ch

Mr. Dharamdeo RAMKISSOON

Office Manager
Permanent Delegation to the OECD
Email: Dharamdeo.Ramkissoon@fco.gov.uk

Ms. Tania D. TESCHKE

Acting Advisor for Science and Social Policy
Email: teschketd@state.gov

OECD SECRETARIAT

General Secretariat

Mr. Richard HECKLINGER

Deputy Secretary-General
Email: Richard.hecklinger@oecd.org

Directorate for Financial, Fiscal, and Enterprise Affairs

Mr. Mats ISAKSSON

Head of Division
Corporate Affairs Division
Email: mats.isaksson@oecd.org

Mr. Grant KIRKPATRICK

Principal Administrator
Corporate Affairs Division
Email: grant.kirkpatrick@oecd.org

Development Centre

Mr. Charles OMAN
Principal Administrator (Corporate Governance)
Economic Analysis and Development Policy Dialogue,
Division I
Email: charles.oman@oecd.org

Public Affairs and Communications Directorate

Mr. John WEST
Head of Division
Public Affairs Division
Email: john.west@oecd.org

Ms. Meggan DISSLY
Principal Administrator
Civil Society Liaison Manager
Email: meggan.dissly@oecd.org

Ms. Margaret-Anne PHILLIPS
Coordination Officer
Email: margaret-anne.phillips@oecd.org

Mr. Jeremy MADDISON
BIAC/TUAC Relations
Email: jeremy.maddison@oecd.org

Appendix 3

HULT International Business School

CORPORATE SOCIAL RESPONSIBILITY

* * * * *

The "Eckes-Granini Deutschland GmbH" & CSR

Ulrike Ch. Thierfelder

Table of Contents

I.   Introduction

This paper will be looking at how one particular company, the Eckes-Granini Group GmbH, treats CSR[1] within the juridical system of Germany[2]. For the analysis of this aspect, I will be looking in particular why the company started a CSR initiative, how the history and nature of the corporation has influenced its approach to CSR, how this approach is implemented within its corporate governance structure and how sustainable the CSR approach is on a long-term scale.

II.   Eckes-Granini & CSR

The Company's Core Business

Eckes-Granini today[3], is a producer of fruit juices and non-alcoholic, fruit-based beverages. Over the course of its existence the company has expanded from Germany into other European countries and the rest of the world. It now, owns subsidiaries in 15 countries[4]. The company employs approximately 1500 people worldwide of which 600 work for the German subsidiary[5]. Eckes-Granini is the market leader within its core area and has been very successful in terms of profitability even in the recent years of economic and financial crisis.

It has also gained a good, long-lasting reputation among its consumers as well as business partners which adds to the high brand value of Eckes-Granini. (Eckes-Granini Deutschland GmbH, 2011)

[1] See Appendix 8 for a definition of CSR
[2] This analysis cannot look at the entire Eckes-Granini Group GmbH as the group is present in several juridical systems, but will focus on the approach taken by its headquarter in Germany and the two other German sites in Bröl and Bad Fallingbostel which form together the Eckes-Granini Deutschland GmbH.
[3] See Appendix 1 for a brief history of Eckes-Granini
[4] See Appendix 4 for details about the existing subsidiaries
[5] See Appendix 2 for some quick facts

Why CSR?

Ludwig Eckes, the owner of the company at the time, started the company's CSR initiatives already in the 1960's. His underlying reasoning was based on three things: first the nature of his company as a family-enterprise which was handed from one generation to the next, second his understanding of entrepreneurship and the importance he attaches to employees, and thirdly that he "owed" something to the community in which the company had been started and run since 1857[6]. This approach to CSR which was formalised during the 1980's with regard to HR (Human Resource Management) and in the 1990's with regard to environmental issues. It has been maintained as family and company tradition until today.

The Company's Corporate Governance Structure

Even at the time when Eckes-Granini was still a fully family-controlled company it had an advisory council in place which would supervise the actions of the executive board of the company. In 1991 it was transformed into a corporation with limited liability. The management intended to list the company on the stock exchange, and the corporate structure was changed to meet the official legal requirements of the German stock exchange. In the end, the public issuing of stocks did not take place. Nevertheless since then, Eckes-Granini has an official executive board on the level of the Eckes-Granini Group GmbH as well as an official supervisory board on the level of the financial holding "Eckes AG"[7].

With regards to CSR, the executive board is required to present all projects to the

supervisory board once a year for approval. The Eckes-family as founder and owner

---

[6] See Appendix 1 and 5 for an introduction to Eckes-Granini's history and its summarised history of CSR
[7] See Appendix 3 for an overview of the two boards

Ulrike Ch. Thierfelder

Page 5

remains represented on the supervisory board in person or indirectly and still takes a large influence on all aspects of the corporation as well as its CSR projects.

The individual CSR projects are handled on various levels, but the main responsibility lies with the CEO of Eckes-Granini. (Eckes-Granini Deutschland GmbH, 2011) To him report two project-responsible managers: the managing director of HR for all people-related CSR projects and the managing director of supply chain management for all environment-related projects. However, in general Eckes-Granini has implemented a people and environment strategy within its corporate culture in which every single employee is responsible for CSR and needs to commit to the corporate goals when entering the company as well as on a daily basis.

Stakeholders & Validation of CSR

The identification of relevant stakeholders for the CSR projects of Eckes-Granini is done through its executive board and outlined in the company vision and mission. The main stakeholders, following the tradition of Ludwig Eckes, are Eckes-Granini's employees and consumers. The company invests a lot of time and funds in its personal and organisational development programs and in market research to support these two stakeholder groups. (Thierfelder, 2012) Also, the company places a high importance on its suppliers and partners which need to equally adhere to all CSR initiatives. This adherence is secured in the supply chain management processes within the supplier selection as well as in the purchasing procedures.

The validation of all CSR projects since its formal introduction in 1992 is done through EMAS, the official European Eco-Management and Audit Scheme and re-evaluated every three years. Since its introduction, Eckes-Granini has received the EMAS validation in every valuation period. Also, it has received various recognition awards through the state for exceeding regulatory compliance factors by large.

III. CSR Sustainability & Conclusion

In my opinion, the fact that CSR was introduced as a vision of the owner-family and passed on through the generations has had a large impact on its sustainability. The company structure, with the owner-family still taking influence on the advisory board level, also helps in maintaining this vision. They ensure that the tradition of the company remains regardless on how the company is structured today.

For Eckes-Granini CSR is a "matter of honour, tradition and of the heart" rather than a matter of PR and image enhancement or merely adhering to regulations. Due to this, all projects are started with a long-term strategy and, thus, maintained. The employees who work for Eckes-Granini highly identify with the company and, thus, take pride in making their working environment as well as their products sustainable.

In conclusion, it can be said that the history of the company shows that this approach has been well-implemented into the core of the company culture and will remain there. Over the course of the years, Eckes-Granini has successfully proven to be a benchmark setting and exemplary company with regards to CSR and sustainability.

Appendices

Appendix 1 - Brief History of the Eckes-Granini Group GmbH

The Eckes-Granini Group GmbH was founded by Peter Eckes as "Eckes Group" in 1857 as a manufacturing and distribution company for spirits. From 1933 onwards it also entered the fruit juice market in Germany and expanded this branch later internationally. In 1991 it was turned into a corporation with limited liability: the Eckes AG. In 1994 Eckes acquired the competitor Granini and merged it with its fruit juice sector into one business line: the Eckes-Granini Group GmbH, which has held, since, all fruit juice business related operations. The group is made up of several regional subsidiaries of which Eckes-Granini Deutschland GmbH is headquartering from Germany. The spirits business line of Eckes, originally the core business, was sold off to other companies in the years 2006/2007. The Eckes AG remains the financial holding of the Eckes-Granini Group GmbH until today.

Appendix 2 - Eckes-Granini Deutschland GmbH: Quick Facts

Headquarter: Nieder-Olm, Germany (Rhineland-Palatinate)

Sites in Germany: Nieder-Olm, Bröl. Bad Fallingbostel

Sales Germany (2010):   420 Mio. Litres

Market share Germany (2010):   17%

Employees Germany (2010):   approx. 600

Strategic brands: granini, hohes C, FruchtTiger

Appendix 3 - Eckes-Granini Group GmbH: Corporate Governance Structure

| Organe |

Aufsichtsrat der Eckes AG

Axel Hamm	Vorsitzender
Dr. Karl Brings	Stellv. Vorsitzender
Thomas Hübner	
Stefan Kobold	
Christian Köhler	
Thierry Paternot	

Geschäftsführung der Eckes-Granini Group GmbH

Thomas Hinderer	Vorsitzender der Geschäftsführung
Ulrich Bunk	Geschäftsführer Supply Chain
Sidney Coffeng	Geschäftsführer Controlling & Finanzen, IT
Heribert Gathof	Geschäftsführer Eckes-Granini Deutschland
Albert Grätz	Geschäftsführer International Business Development
Sabine Holtkamp	Geschäftsführerin Human Resources & Organisationsentwicklung
José Marti Cos	Geschäftsführer Marketing, R&D
N. N.	Geschäftsführer Eckes-Granini France

Glossary

Aufsichtsrat =
supervisory board

Geschäftsführung =
executive board

Vorsitzender =
President

Vorsitzender der
Geschäftsführung =
CEO

Geschäftsführer =
Managing Director

Appendix 4 – Eckes-Granini Subsidiaries[8]

Landesgesellschaften		
Deutschland	Eckes-Granini Deutschland GmbH	Nieder-Olm, Deutschland
Dänemark	Valsølille Most Aps	Glostrup, Dänemark
Estland	Eckes-Granini Eesti AS	Tallinn, Estland
Finnland	Eckes-Granini Finland Oy Ab	Turku, Finnland
Frankreich	Eckes-Granini France SNC	Macon, Frankreich
Lettland	SIA Eckes-Granini Latvija	Riga, Lettland
Litauen	UAB Eckes-Granini Lietuva	Vilnius, Litauen
Norwegen	Brämhults AS	Oslo, Norwegen
Österreich	Eckes-Granini Austria GmbH	St. Florian, Österreich
Rumänien	Eckes-Granini Romania S.R.L.	Bukarest, Rumänien
Schweden	Brämhults Juice AB	Brämhult, Schweden
Schweiz	Eckes-Granini Suisse S.A.	Henniez, Schweiz 51%
Spanien	Eckes-Granini Iberica S.A.U.	Barcelona, Spanien
Ungarn	Sió-Eckes Kft.	Siófok, Ungarn
Türkei	Yıldız Granini Meyve Suyu Sanayi Ve Ticaret A.Ş	Istanbul, Türkei 50%

100 % Geschäftsanteile, wenn nicht anders angegeben

Glossary

Deutschland = Germany
Dänemark = Denmark
Estland = Estonia
Frankreich = France
Lettland = Latvia
Litauen = Lithuania
Norwegen = Norway
Österreich = Austria
Rumänien = Romania
Schweden = Sweden
Schweiz = Switzerland
Spanien = Spain
Ungarn = Hungary
Türkei = Turkey

[8] 100% owned subsidiaries if not stated otherwise

Appendix 5 – Eckes-Granini's History of CSR & Approach

The story of CSR within Eckes-Granini essentially already starts in the 1960's at a time when the company was still called "Eckes Group" [9]. The owner at that time, Ludwig Eckes, believed that employees are the biggest asset of a company and that, hence, his employees needed to be respected and developed.[10] He also considered value preservation and enhancement to be more important than profit maximisation – a company doctrine which has remained in place until today. (Thierfelder, 2012) As a consequence, he started investing in his employees in terms of training and development and also initiated several philanthropic projects in Nieder-Olm and the nearby bigger city Mainz to return some of the benefits these two communities had contributed to his business[11]. This initially philanthropic approach became more formalised in the beginning of the 1980's when Eckes introduced first concepts and measures of human resource management[12] and organisational development with regards to internal personal development and leadership trainee programs[13]. Also at the same time, Eckes started thinking about environmental issues. Being mainly a distillery and, hence, producing a lot of waste as well as using a lot of natural resources, he and his family felt that investing in environmental programs would be essential in making the

---

[9] See Appendix 1 for a brief introduction to the history of Eckes-Granini
[10] Until today it remains part of Eckes-Granini's vision to live an open and entrepreneurial company culture which motivates, engages and develops people.
[11] For example: infrastructure, security, education and social systems
[12] See Appendix 6 for an example of Eckes-Granini's "Human Resource Policy" and "Leadership and "Guidelines for Leadership and Co-operation" from the year 1999/2000
[13] Today's deputy president of the Eckes AG's supervisory board started as leadership-trainee at that time and, also, two members of the Eckes-Granini Executive Committee started their career within Eckes as trainees and were developed up to the top management.

company sustainable and also something valuable to pass on to his heirs.[14] In the beginning of the 1990's (Thierfelder, 2012) Eckes initiated a formalised environmental program which would adhere to – and even exceed – the regulatory compliance it had to meet in order to turn into a corporation. This formalisation was successfully implemented in 1992 when Eckes was validated from the EMAS[15] for the first time. This validation has been renewed until today in every validation period (3 years) and, additionally, Eckes(-Granini) has received several recognitions from the state Rhineland-Palatinate as well as Germany on the whole for its exemplary approach to environmental protection and business practices.

Over the past 20 years, Eckes-Granini has implemented and maintained various CSR initiatives. Some examples are (Eckes-Granini Deutschland GmbH, 2011):

- Human Resource Policy and Guidelines to Leadership and Co-operation:
- Supply Chain Management initiatives:
    - o Distribution management in terms of truck load policies: precise planning in order to avoid half-loaded or empty trucks to reduce emissions.
    - o Supplier selection: suppliers are required to adhere to the same EMAS guidelines as Eckes-Granini itself.
    - o Constant technology updates with regards to efficiency and environmental impact

---

[14] The fact that the company has been handed on from one generation to the next has always influenced the Eckes-family to secure traditions and also to constantly ensure that the company is a valuable thing to be proud of.
[15] See Appendix 7 – EMAS for a brief overview of the concept

- Environmental Initiatives:

    o "Every employee is an environmental issues manager" policy

    o Reduction of water and energy usage throughout its entire supply chain

    o Reduction of waste through advanced purification plant technologies

    o First German company to introduce tetra pack and PET to reduce chemical usage with regards to cleansing of glass bottles.

- Consumer Intimacy, Quality Management and EHS Initiatives:

    o Label transparency: clear, simple and complete labelling on all products with regards to their target audience (kids' products are labelled in a language that is also understandable to kids)

    o Regional "raw material" to support local agriculture and also ensure quality

    o Highly stringent quality control measurements with regards to health and safety.

    o Health and Safety initiatives on all sites – whether administration or production (f.ex. every site has a dedicated site-doctor that is available on site in his own office at least once a week).

Appendix 6 - Eckes AG's "Human Resource Policy" and "Guidelines for Leadership and Co-operation" (1999/2000)

Preface

Herbert Verse   *Gottfried Thierfelder*

Ladies and Gentlemen,

our group lives from the people, who work here. Their work and co-operation determines our success.

To facilitate this contribution to the company performance it is vital for all employees, to know where we want to go and what we can expect from each other.

This small booklet on the "Principles of the Human Resources Policy" and "Guidelines for Leadership and Co-operation" shall give this orientation. It answers general questions about Human Resources (HR) Policy in general and about Leadership and Co-operation.

About 100 Managers from all levels and regions formulated these guidelines and discussed them within their organizations. Thus, what you hold in your hand is the result of European teamwork. We trust, that the guidelines can be supported by all our employees, so by you.

But words only are not enough. We have to live what we request from us and others in the reality of our group's day to day business. We would like to encourage you to check with your superior and colleagues whether we fulfil our demands and to give mutual feedback. It's only if we speak about it we have a chance to improve. This applies to all levels – also to us in the Board.

Let us all together do a further step into an even more successful future. Let us bring the Principles and Guidelines into life.

Yours

Herbert Verse   *Gottfried Thierfelder*

4

Objectives of the Human Resources Policy

The Eckes group is to establish a framework

- for personal responsibility und future-orientation of the employees

- for performance and result orientation

- for internationality

- for the personal development of the employees

- for equality of opportunities, regardless of sex and origin

- for openness to continuously changing processes and constructive participation – also if personally concerned

so that "employees enjoy working in the Eckes group" (vision)

6

Principles of the Human Resources Policy

Qualified and motivated employees guarantee our success.
With our aim towards a successful, long-term co-operation for mutual benefit we offer a great variety of perspectives.

We expect from our employees independence in thinking and action as well as a sense of responsibility and self-initiative in the pursuit of common goals.

Each employee is responsible for his professional qualification and further development while obtaining the support of his superiors. We attach high priority to constant learning processes and continuous development and thus support the employees within the scope of the operational feasibility and the company goals.

We expect our employees to have the required flexibility and the necessary will for change.

8

Principles of the Human Resources Policy

We are unable to guarantee full job security in our fast-moving times with rapid innovations and permanent changes in our accustomed markets. However, we offer opportunities for further education and development. This means solid grounds for a professional future of our employees within the company or outside via the rise of modern and future-oriented technologies, concepts, organizational structures, operational procedures and processes.

We demand and promote the constant learning-process and know-how transfer of our employees in the company and among all of its parts, countries, sites and organizations. We give manoeuvrability and opportunities to personal development within the framework of our objectives and abilities.

We expect, practice and encourage open communication and critical dialogue among all employees in the company.

10

Principles of the Human Resources Policy

We offer attractive working conditions via
- flexible job organization with high personal responsibility
- performance-oriented compensation-systems, open for diverse, variable requirements
- leeway and support for further education activities
- respect the private life of our employees under consideration of the operational requirements.

We expect from our employees performance-orientation and full dedication in respect of the goals and objectives of the company as well as the readiness for transfer to all companies, facilities and departments at home and abroad.

We provide a creative atmosphere and enrichment of thinking by generating diversity and cultural open-mindedness. We support this by actively utilizing the European labor market and by promoting cultural interests and activities of our employees.

From our managers we expect leadership and social competence in the co-operation with employees, colleagues, business-partners and customers. This will be the standard for appointing executive positions.

12

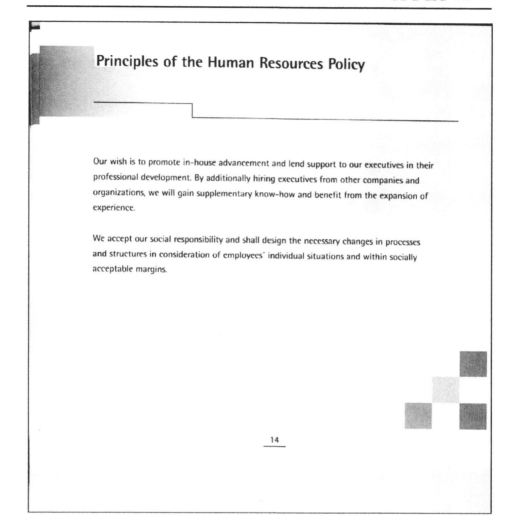

Principles of the Human Resources Policy

Our wish is to promote in-house advancement and lend support to our executives in their professional development. By additionally hiring executives from other companies and organizations, we will gain supplementary know-how and benefit from the expansion of experience.

We accept our social responsibility and shall design the necessary changes in processes and structures in consideration of employees' individual situations and within socially acceptable margins.

14

Eckes Guidelines for Leadership & Co-operation

- We treat each other with respect and set examples of what we expect from each other.

- We transmit visions, agree on clear objectives and permit leeway for their realization. Where needed - we provide guidance and support.

- We tolerate mistakes and learn from them.

- We communicate openly, supply quick and concise information and encourage the dialogue.

- We demand and support performance - which we reward.

- We offer opportunities for individual development and invest in training and further education.

- Our goal is a corporate culture full of creativity, enjoyment and pride.

16

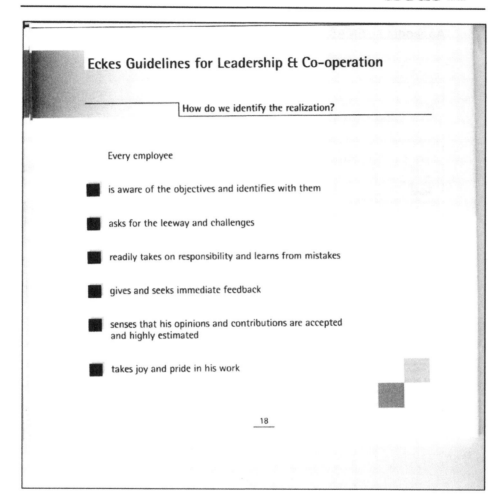

Eckes Guidelines for Leadership & Co-operation

How do we identify the realization?

Every employee

- is aware of the objectives and identifies with them

- asks for the leeway and challenges

- readily takes on responsibility and learns from mistakes

- gives and seeks immediate feedback

- senses that his opinions and contributions are accepted and highly estimated

- takes joy and pride in his work

18

Appendix 7 - EMAS (Eco-Management and Audit Scheme)

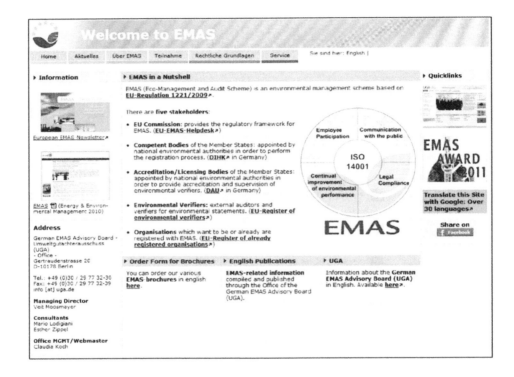

Appendix 8 – Definition of CSR

For the term *corporate social responsibility* (CSR) there is no one, generally accepted definition. However, in Germany, the interpretation of the term according to the *Green Paper of the European Commission* (European Commission, 2011) has been largely accepted. According to this interpretation, CSR is defined as a voluntary contribution of economy to a sustainable development that exceeds compliance to regulations. (Wikipedia, 2012) This definition refers to what is also called the *"Triple Bottom Line"*: a responsible, entrepreneurial behaviour within the core business (profit), the adherence to ecologically relevant aspects (planet), and the creation of a sustainable relationship with employees and other relevant stakeholders (people). (Wikipedia, 2012)

References & Bibliography

Eckes-Granini Deutschland GmbH, 2011. Eckes-Granini Deutschland GmbH - Geschäftsbericht 2010. [Online]
Available at: http://eckes-granini.de/pdf/Geschaeftsbericht_2010.pdf
[Accessed 31 03 2012].

Eckes-Granini Deutschland GmbH, 2011. Eckes-Granini Deutschland GmbH - Umwelterklärung. [Online]
Available at: http://eckes-granini.de/pdf/umwelterklaerung_2011.pdf
[Accessed 31 03 2012].

European Commission, 2011. Green Paper - The EU Corporate Governance Framework. [Online]
Available at: http://ec.europa.eu/internal_market/company/docs/modern/com2011-164_en.pdf
[Accessed 31 03 2012].

Thierfelder, G., 2012. Managing Director HR & Environmental Issues (rtd.) for Eckes-Granini [Interview] (02 04 2012).

Wikipedia, 2012. Wikipedia - Corporate Social Responsibility. [Online]
Available at: http://de.wikipedia.org/wiki/Corporate_Social_Responsibility
[Accessed 02 04 2012].

Wikipedia, 2012. Wikipedia - Triple Bottom Line. [Online]
Available at: http://en.wikipedia.org/wiki/Triple_bottom_line
[Accessed 31 03 2012].

Appendix 4

Context

The culture of the banking industry overall, and that of Barclays within it, needs to evolve. A number of events during and after the financial crisis demonstrated that banks need to revisit fundamentally the basis on which they operate, and how they add value to society. Trust has been decimated and needs to be rebuilt.

Barclays acknowledged that need some time ago and has begun to put in place changes in the way in which it operates consistent with that need. However, recent events indicate clearly that Barclays, like other big UK banks, needs to redouble its efforts. That task may seem more daunting today than ever, but Barclays remains committed to it. As an institution, Barclays must move further and faster to demonstrate that banks, and those who work for them, consistently operate to the highest standards of probity, integrity and honesty. This requires clear evidence, not assertion.

Culture is generally defined as "the instinctive behaviours and beliefs characteristic of a particular group". Changing a culture, therefore, requires at least three things:

- Affirming the key values and operative beliefs that guide the behaviour of everyone in an organisation – these are deep-seated and tend not to change without direct intervention.
- Ensuring that the actual behaviours of those who represent the organisation are consistent with those values (and are so regarded by those who come in contact with the bank); and
- Ensuring that vital reinforcing mechanisms, such as visible leadership examples, formal and informal systems and processes, policies and rewards, are aligned with those values, operative beliefs and behaviours.

The burden of proof required to demonstrate change in culture is now much higher. The Barclays Board is conducting this review (the Review) of Barclays business practices to assist in the bank's efforts to rebuild trust by making it a leader in businesses practices among not only its peer institutions, but also multinational corporates generally. The Review is independent, reporting to Sir Michael Rake and a sub-committee of Non-Executive Directors (the Committee) including David Booth; Alison Carnwath; and Sir John Sunderland. Anthony Salz has agreed to lead the Review (the Reviewer) in a personal capacity.

Barclays Board and Executive Committee will consider the review's recommendations carefully, with the intention of implementing them in full. Barclays will publish an account of how it specifically intends to implement them a short time after the conclusion of the Review. The broader work at Barclays oriented at changing the bank's culture will be particularly informed by the Review's recommendations.

The Programme of Work

Given the nature of what banks do, customers and clients must be at the heart of everything that Barclays does and, therefore, at the heart of the bank's values. The nature of what Barclays does also gives rise to responsibilities to counterparties. These responsibilities include the indirect impact the bank has through its activities, including through its role in promoting and protecting the integrity of the public and private markets in which it participates.

To rebuild trust, Barclays must start with an open and honest assessment of the bank's current values, principles and standards of operation; determine to what extent they need to change; test how well decision-making processes currently incorporate those values, principles and standards, and outline how those processes need to change; and determine whether or not the appropriate training, development, incentives and disciplinary processes are in place to reinforce them.

The Review will analyse past events that have had a particularly negative impact on the bank's reputation. The purpose is not to determine the truth or otherwise of any allegations surrounding those events. The analysis in those areas will rather focus on understanding whether there was a gap between the bank's articulated values and behaviours and the way in which the bank operated in practice and to identify if there are actions that need to be taken to reduce the likelihood of similarly negative events occurring in the future. The Review will also analyse current practices to understand how current behaviours and reinforcing mechanisms fit with the bank's stated values and operative beliefs. It is not, though, an investigation or audit of those activities.

The Reviewer will undertake extensive, independent analysis to build a fact base; identify priority areas for change; develop a set of recommendations for change; and prepare and publish, after consultation with the Committee, a report (the Report) on the findings and recommendations of the Review. The scope of the Review's recommendations will be global and span all businesses within Barclays without exception.

One of the principal recommendations in the Report will concern changes to the mandatory code of conduct (the Code) that is applied across Barclays. The Code should establish clear standards of behaviour, in plain language; provide the framework for a zero-tolerance policy regarding compliance with the Code; and be flexible to evolve with stakeholder expectations. The Report will also include recommendations for improvements to key policies and procedures to make them more consistent with the Code, and mechanisms to create assurance for the Board and the Executive Committee that the Code has been implemented.

The Report may make any further recommendations as the Reviewer deems relevant to Barclays based on the evidence studied and conclusions drawn.

Approach to the Review

The Reviewer will ultimately have the responsibility for agreeing how the Review will progress with the Committee. It is anticipated that the workplan will have six streams of work.
1. Create familiarity with Barclays principal business segments, including the key competitors and historical, contemporary and prospective challenges within each segment;
2. Conduct detailed review of past events identified as having caused material reputational damage for Barclays and the industry, with particular emphasis on events since the start of the financial crisis;
3. Review Barclays current global values, principles and standards;
4. Analyse key policies and procedures to identify potential weaknesses in reinforcing mechanisms;
5. Develop new global, mandatory code of conduct and recommendations for its implementation and ongoing assurance; and
6. Prepare a public report on findings and recommendations.

With respect to the fourth workstream, the Reviewer has discretion to identify the policies and procedures to test through the Review. Those may include some or all of: customer, client and counterparty focus; market integrity requirements; conflicts of interest; product and pricing suitability; reputational risk management; governance standards, including internal controls; leadership behaviours; whistleblowing; induction, training and assurance; performance management and development; and incentives.

The Review will be evidence-based. Any conclusions drawn and recommendations set out in the Report will be linked directly back to analysis completed during the Review.

To build that evidence, the Review will rely on access to a wide range of stakeholders (including, for example, customers, clients, shareholders, regulators, government officials, staff (current and former) and other interested parties) and any internal and external data (including relevant papers, reports, minutes, etc.) pertinent to the scope of the Review, subject only to legal privilege. Barclays will ensure that any current or former staff involved in the process receive full indemnity and are able to provide input on a non-attributable basis, so that they may participate without any fear of potential consequences. To facilitate broad input into the Review, any interested stakeholder will be able to submit a perspective or evidence via queries@salzreview.com. The bank will conduct any bespoke customer and client research required by the Reviewer. It will also arrange any interviews required by the Reviewer.

According to specifications agreed with the Reviewer, the bank will fund the external Review team. It is anticipated that will include the support of a senior, independent individual to act as deputy reviewer and an appropriately sized team from a well-regarded professional services firm (or firms) with skills and experience appropriate to a review of this nature. Both will be selected in consultation with the Reviewer. Barclays will also make available appropriate internal staff to support the Review.

Expected Timeline

The Review is expected to publish its Report in the Spring of 2013, in advance of Barclays 2013 Annual General Meeting.

Appendix 5

The inaugural Today Business Lecture.
Bod Diamond CEO Barclays Plc

Soon after the financial crisis of 2008 I was at a meeting in Washington with a group of US senators. They had invited me to provide a point of view on new regulation; regulation aimed at ensuring we never have to go through the events of 2008 ever again.

I had recently attended similar discussions with regulators and policy makers here in the UK and in Europe. While I was there, a senior economic adviser at the White House put a question to me.

"Do you think banks can be good citizens?" he said.

I wanted to answer yes, but before I could reply he said: "If the answer is "yes", think about the fact that no-one will believe you."

I did think about that - I have thought about it quite a bit over the past three years.

I want to use this opportunity tonight to share with you my views on why the answer to that question must be "yes"; it's because the single most important thing for banks and for businesses now is to focus on helping to create jobs and economic growth; and being able to do that requires us - banks in particular - to rebuild the trust that has been decimated by events of the past three years; and that rebuilding trust requires banks to be better citizens.

I believe in this passionately.

That is why since I became chief executive of Barclays, at the beginning of this year, the management team has focused on four strategic priorities - one of which is citizenship.

Would I have chosen citizenship as a key priority five years ago? I doubt it. Events of the past few years have caused me to change my mind. Let me try to explain why.

We stand today at the end of a long cycle of excess borrowing - borrowing by financial institutions, by governments, by consumers, and by businesses.

Developed economies now face the twin challenge of reducing both public spending and government deficits while at the same time stimulating economic recovery.

There is no better example than Greece.

We now know that government debt as a proportion of GDP in Greece was unsustainable at 150%, but we also have to recognise that the ratio is 100% in the US and 83% in the UK. Ten years ago those ratios would have been roughly half that.

With such high debt levels, government deficits have to be reduced - they're simply too big to be managed by increasing taxes alone.

The solution has to include a reduction in public spending.

It's no surprise then that the UK government has started doing just that, in order to avoid higher costs of borrowing.

As a result, the UK can still borrow at a rate of 2.5% while Italy, Spain Portugal and Ireland have to pay between 6% and 12%.

Think about this. This is simplified, but it's important. If the UK government had to pay 6%

1

interest on its current outstanding debt, it would cost all of us in the UK another £40 billion a year.

That's about half the annual budget for the National Health Service.

Governments in the UK, US and Europe are working to reduce spending, with varying degrees of success and varying degrees of public acceptance.

We've seen violent protests in Greece, public sector strikes across Europe, anti-capitalist demonstrations that started on Wall Street have spread to other places around the world, including St Paul's Cathedral here in London.

Young people have been especially hard hit by high levels of unemployment.

The threat of further social unrest remains if we don't work together to generate stronger economic growth and more jobs.

In these circumstances the private sector has an obligation to generate growth and banks have a vital role to play in spurring that growth.

But for banks to play their role effectively, they need a much more constructive relationship with customers, with the public, with governments and with regulators, so that the focus can be on the future.

To have that shared focus, trust must be rebuilt.

And to rebuild trust, in my view, three things must happen.

First, we have to build a better understanding of how businesses and banks work together to generate economic growth; second, we have to accept responsibility for what has gone wrong; finally, most importantly, we have to use the lessons learned to become better and more effective citizens.

I'll talk about each one of these in turn.

I'm under no illusion that this will be easy.

Let me tell you a very quick story.

Earlier this year a national newspaper posted anonymous interviews on the internet with people working in financial services.

The interviews were carried out by an academic, an academic who persuaded bankers to talk about their life at work so that readers might come to "a more nuanced and realistic view" of what bankers are all about.

I looked on the internet to see how people reacted to these interviews. One blogger wrote to an investment banker who advises companies:

"You have neither a clue nor a care about the impact of your activity on the rest of the world. You're thoroughly self-absorbed... and utterly vacuous."

Another one said: "Does this have social value? Undoubtedly. Check the ingredients list on your bag of groceries. Find out how many companies produce them. Would they be able to do that without access to capital, without access to risk management, without reducing costs by merging with their competitors?"

I didn't say that, I want you to know that. I don't even know how to blog.

I'm talking about this now because when people have such polarised opinions it's not easy to have a meaningful exchange, so you can understand why I was anxious when I was invited to speak this evening.

My hope is that this evening's discussion can make a contribution to creating a more helpful dialogue.

I believe it is in all of our interests to achieve that because the growth of the economy - and the job creation that will come with that - depends on it.

So let me turn to my first theme: winning back trust calls for a much better understanding of the role that businesses and banks play in generating economic growth.

One recent survey revealed that 90% of people think big business is essential for the UK's economic prosperity. Yet 60% said that businesses have not done enough to convince people that they are a force for good.

Twice as many people said that investment banks do harm to the UK economy as those that said they benefit it.

With such a breakdown of trust and understanding it's difficult to know where to begin. But I'd like to start with what banks do at their most basic, because we've done a very poor job of explaining how we contribute to society.

Banks hold deposits and savings entrusted to them by individuals, by businesses, by governments and by central banks.

They put that money to work, helping people to buy homes for example or lending to businesses to invest in expansion.

They make it easy for people to use their money - imagine for a second a world without cash machines, without credit and debit cards, without currency for foreign travel.

Banks also help governments and central banks around the world to finance their spending. They enable people and businesses to transfer money and make payments, both here in the UK and internationally - 768m payments around the world each day.

They allow companies, governments and pension funds to better manage their risks and as a result keep money flowing to where it's most productive.

This is what's important - banks do these things by taking risk.

I know it sounds controversial to suggest banks must take risk, in the wake of a near collapse of the financial system, but banks serve little economic or social purpose unless they do so.

Every time a bank lends money on a mortgage they're taking risk: Liquidity risk - what if the depositor wants their money back before the borrower repays it? Credit risk - will the person be able to pay it back? Interest rate risk - what will happen to interest rates over the life of the mortgage? Market risk - will the property maintain its value?

Every time a bank gives someone a credit card they're taking risk. Every time a bank lends to a small business that needs capital to grow, they're taking risk.

It's by taking these risks, and by managing them well, that banks support customers and encourage business innovation.

When I was in Yorkshire earlier this year, I met R&R Ice Cream. R&R Ice Cream started as a small family business. Today they're the second largest ice cream manufacturer in Europe employing almost 2000 people.

They have grown by acquiring businesses in Germany, France and Poland and by investing in scalable and sophisticated manufacturing.

Their plant is one of the most amazing facilities I have ever seen.

Banks were able to support this growth by helping them invest in plant and machinery, by helping them finance acquisitions, by helping them facilitate cross border trade and by helping them manage risk.

I also met with Swann Morton in Sheffield, the home of steel manufacturing. They began in the 1930s making razor blades for the UK.

Today they import steel from all over Europe: their real expertise is precision manufacturing. The precision with which they control production is astounding.

They are now the largest European manufacturer of surgical blades, exporting to over 100 countries around the world.

They were able to invest in plant, acquire new property, import and export with the support of banks.

Sukhpal Singh is an entrepreneur I met in Cambridge who came here as a refugee from Uganda in the 1970s.

At the age of 18 he borrowed £5000 - from his father and from a local bank - to buy a car parts shop in North London.

His business is now the largest supplier of car parts in the UK with 90 branches across the country and with plans for expansion across Europe.

I've lived in England for many years but I've spent most of that time working with large international companies.

This year, in my new role, I have had a great opportunity. I have had the opportunity to visit small businesses like these all around the UK.

I've learned from these visits that the UK has strong successful businesses that are very good at accessing international markets. International trade is a large part of their business - a large part of their plans for growth.

They have shown me that the needs of small and large business are surprisingly similar. Small companies today want to be big companies tomorrow.

Tesco is a terrific example of just that. Tesco started out as a small UK business, supported by UK banks, here in its domestic market.

Today Tesco employs almost half a million people in 5000 stores across 13 different markets in Europe, in Asia and in North America.

As a result of its ability to trade and invest globally, Tesco is now the third largest retailer in the world.

They need a bank to facilitate international payments - but that's not enough.

When supermarkets buy coffee from Kenya and sell it to consumers in another country they're exposed to risk; the risk of fluctuating exchange rates - the risk, in this example, of fluctuating coffee prices.

Supermarkets manage these risks with the help of an investment bank.

I share these stories because I believe they illustrate the contribution that banks can make by working closely with businesses.

But the principle also applies to other organisations.

Let's shift, let's talk about a pension fund: Pension funds need returns on their investments of about 7% in order to honour their liabilities; in other words to pay savers their pensions.

At a time when interest rates are close to zero in developed economies and equity markets continue to be volatile, pension funds need some alternative way to deliver those returns.

Investment banks help them to access a broad range of investments in order to do just that.

Interestingly, it's not really much different with governments: When the UK or US government issues bonds to fund a deficit, the buyers are not solely in the UK or the US - they're in Asia, Europe, Latin America and the Middle East.

Investment banks provide direct access to these buyers. They make markets to auction these bonds so that governments obtain them for the best price and investors will only buy if they know they can sell these securities back when they want to.

So banks make sure that is easy by establishing a large consistent market of buyers and sellers. To do this they put capital at risk in order to discover what the market is willing to pay.

When banks do this well, interest rates are lower. If interest rates are lower, government and business borrowing costs less.

Without this, the result is clear - an increased cost of borrowing, higher taxes, lower public spending, slower economic growth and higher unemployment.

Providing this kind of support to clients requires banks to take risk but this is not speculative trading, so it bothers me when these activities are caricatured as gambling.

These activities serve a social purpose and meet a real client need whether they are carried out on behalf of governments, pension funds businesses or individuals.

Why is all this important? Why are we talking about this? Because at a time when governments are reducing spending, banks have an especially critical role to play in supporting businesses: Businesses that show real ingenuity and entrepreneurship.

Businesses that can deliver growth.

Businesses that hold the key to creating more jobs and generating economic activity.

The opportunity is here. It is our responsibility to seize it.

At the same time we have to accept that the financial crisis in 2008 resulted in a widespread loss of trust in banks in particular, and in the workings of the market economy more broadly.

So let me turn to my second theme.

The second thing we have to do to restore trust is to accept responsibility for what went wrong.

A lot has been written about the causes of the crisis, there have been many thoughtful contributions to help us understand what happened and I could not do justice to the topic in the time I have today, so I'm not going to dwell on this.

What is important is to learn from what went wrong.

In very simple terms, it's important to demonstrate that we get it.

A lot of that learning has already been included in new financial regulation - regulation that I personally welcome.

Let's make no mistake about it - strong banks want strong regulation.

No taxpayer money should ever again be put at risk to rescue a failed or failing bank.

I understand why many people wonder if anything has really changed. But the reality is - much has changed.

Today banks are not borrowing as much, they have significantly more capital, and they have far more stable and liquid sources of funds to lend.

Pay structures are changing, so risk and pay are better aligned to ensure there are not rewards for failure though clearly levels of pay within the industry are a real cause of real concern and ongoing debate.

There's greater understanding of where assets are held in the financial system. Banks today are safer and sounder.

But that alone is not enough.

I knew that day I went to Washington to talk about regulation that, just as banks had a role to play in the crisis in 2008, they also had a critical role to play in putting things right.

That day I came to the firm conclusion that banks - and the private sector - would have to adopt a broader set of objectives and responsibilities in order to truly restore trust. They would have to become better citizens, my third and final theme.

For me becoming a better citizen means three things:

First, it's about how we behave, especially with our customers and clients; second, it's about what we do, and in particular how we help those customers and clients create jobs and economic growth; and third, it's about how we contribute to the communities we serve in many other ways.

I know how angry customers are about issues such as Payment Protection Insurance. That's why we are working hard to clear claims as quickly as possible.

We want to put things right. But we know it's not enough just to apologise. We have to try to make sure that things like that don't happen again.

In part that comes down to culture.

It's a very personal thing, but throughout my career - from my time as a teacher, to my time as a banker - I have seen just how important culture is to successful organisations.

Culture is difficult to define, I think it's even more difficult to mandate - but for me the evidence of culture is how people behave when no-one is watching.

Our culture must be one where the interests of customers and clients are at the very heart of every decision we make; where we all act with trust and integrity.

But it's not just about how we behave towards our customers and clients. It's also about how we work together with our colleagues, because if you have to deliver for customers with 150,000 colleagues around the world, as we do, you better be able to work as a team.

As far as I'm concerned, if you can't work well with your colleagues, with trust and integrity, you can't be on the team.

Culture truly helps define an organisation.

I talked about my views on citizenship and culture recently at an international conference. This led to an interesting discussion with Michael Porter, who is a professor at Harvard.

We talked about the connection between my views and what he terms shared value where businesses create economic value and profit in a way that also creates value for society.

Let me give you some examples of shared value from the world that I know best, which is banking.

Nowhere is this more vivid than in sub-Saharan Africa. Barclays has banks in 12 countries across the continent and one of my first trips this year was to visit our operations there.

In Mozambique, small-scale local farmers are responsible for about 90% of food production but many of these farmers have very little certainty about the price at which they can sell their crops. They often have to sell at distressed prices immediately after harvest and without any certainty of income, their ability to reinvest in their business is very limited. They badly need a solution to the volatility of food prices.

In order to address this problem, banks support an agricultural cooperative called Ikuru.

The banks provide a loan so that Ikuru can guarantee the price for crops from local farmers before they harvest.

This price guarantee gives farmers enough financial security to reinvest in more seeds, more fertiliser and to continue farming all year round.

Supporting Ikuru helps create a stable supply of food at stable prices for the people of Mozambique.

At the same time it allows us to grow our business there in a responsible way.

Here in the UK, over a third of farmers want to invest in renewable energy in order to reduce their energy costs and to generate income by selling electricity back to the grid.

We recently created a £100m fund to encourage them to make that investment. We're now working with the National Farmers Union and others to consider loan applications.

This helps to reduce carbon emissions so it's good for the environment, it contributes to the UK's long term energy security, it helps farmers reduce their costs and secure an additional income, and it also makes commercial sense for us.

This is a perfect example of how good environmental practice can make good business sense as well.

My third example concerns a series of lending clinics that we run around the UK, helping businesses to apply for the funding they need to invest and grow.

This is one small part of reinvigorating the UK economy.

The clinics provide an opportunity to meet business angels who can provide capital. They also help people to build a business case, to think about how they could use a loan. To think about how they will manage repayments.

Gavin Smith, for example, runs a small greetings card business with turnover of about £700,000. He wanted to expand but was uncertain how to do so, in particular how to build a credible business plan.

He heard about the clinics on the radio and came along for some advice.

It turned out to be good for him and good for us. He now has a business plan. We have a new customer.

Those three examples focus on commercial lending - investment banks also create shared value: One of our utility clients in the US, was an early investor in alternative energy. Today they are one of the largest developers of wind-farms in the world.

They were only able to make this investment by using commodity derivatives to protect their profits against swings in future energy prices over a 10-year period.

Think also about how an oil producing country like Mexico manages volatile oil prices.

In recent years oil prices have risen to $145 a barrel, they then fell to $40 a barrel - today they're at about $90 a barrel.

Helping Mexico to lock in the oil price before it fell, enabled them to preserve their credit rating, preserve their budget, and preserve their education programme.

These stories illustrate all three things that being a good citizen entails for me: It's about treating customers and clients with integrity, it's about helping them to create jobs and economic growth, and it's about making a contribution to the communities we serve.

I've used these examples from banking because this is the world that I know best. But I can assure you, other businesses are thinking in a similar vein.

I recently sat on a panel discussing food sustainability in Africa with Paul Polman, the chief executive of Unilever. This is what he has to say:

"We have ambitious plans to grow our company, creating jobs and income for all whose livelihoods are linked to our success.

"But growth at any cost is not viable. We have to develop new ways of doing business which will increase the social benefits from our activities."

Indra Nooyi of PepsiCo, who was with Paul and I on the panel - she calls her approach "Performance with Purpose" where purpose is woven into every activity in the company.

This has led PepsiCo to revise their product range, prioritise saving water and energy, and place a special emphasis on treating employees well and creating employment opportunities.

In 1970 Milton Friedman - who happens to be one of my favourite economists - wrote an influential article saying that the only social purpose of business is to increase its profits.

He dismissed well-intentioned philanthropy as "hypocritical window dressing".

I disagree with him on this.

The ideas I've talked about this evening are commercial ideas that address a social need. In other words -business leaders are asking themselves - given what we do, what we're good at, and where we operate, what are the issues where we can add the greatest value to both society and our company?

There's increasing momentum behind them and ongoing debate taking place in boardrooms and at conferences around the world.

Consensus is growing that businesses must increase profits in a way that creates sustainable shareholder value, not just short-term gain.

And for me, the best way to create sustainable shareholder value is to focus on the interests of the customers, clients and the communities that we serve.

I can tell you honestly that this is not always easy or straightforward.

The challenge for all businesses lies in balancing our obligations to all their stakeholders and there are often some difficult trade-offs.

I can't talk for every business but let me give you some examples of the sort of dilemmas that banks face.

One of our clients is a haulage firm who has banked with us for about 40 years. Last year they lost one of their major customers and their turnover plummeted.

They reduced their fleet size, the number of employees, and number of depots but they were still unable to meet their lending agreements.

We extended overdraft facilities of almost half a million pounds and we introduced turnaround professionals to work with them in order to cut costs, implement efficiencies and find new clients Ultimately market conditions deteriorated and the strategy failed.

We took a risk to support a client with whom we'd worked for 40 years. As a result we lost £750,000.

There's also the challenge of lending to new businesses. In the first six months of this year, banks supported the start up of 265,000 new businesses in the UK.

Think about that number - 265,000 businesses starting in the UK this year because of a loan from a bank.

Of course lending is what we're here for. But think about this: 50% of start ups close within three years so the risks in this business are considerable.

Balancing our responsibility to both customers and shareholders can be challenging, and remember those shareholders include pension funds - pension funds that help millions of people around the world save for their retirement.

I have also spent some time thinking about what it means to be a good citizen when part of the business is local - so the community is tangible - and when part of it is global - so the community is harder to define.

Of course it's easier to determine responsibilities on a local basis and there's often political pressure to do just that - politicians, after all, represent local constituencies.

But being a better citizen might mean weighing our obligations to a global community as well as to one that's local.

As chief executive of a bank with international operations I think of our community as all those we impact - not just those locations where we live and work.

I've talked this evening about three things that can help to restore trust:

Building a better understanding of how businesses and banks work together to generate economic growth; accepting responsibility for what has gone wrong; and using the lessons learned to become better citizens.

Restoring trust is especially important now because this is the moment. This is the moment when banks, businesses and governments absolutely must work together to move the onus from the public to the private sector, to create jobs and economic growth.

For banks and businesses to play their full role they must restore trust. That is why I care so much about citizenship.

Last week the Confederation of British Industry published a report that painted a vision for "the UK's army of mid-sized businesses" - a vision of innovation, growth and international trade. With the right encouragement, the right skills and with access to capital for long-term growth, they believe this sector can generate £50bn over the next 10 years.

These businesses account for two-thirds of new jobs. These businesses account for 60% of private sector employment. They hold the key to kick starting economic recovery.

We have a strong and imaginative business community here in the UK. We should all commit to supporting them with confidence.

As the leader of a bank, with 150,000 colleagues - a bank that has been headquartered here in the UK for 320 years - I am ready to commit, we are ready to commit.

I know many of you will listen to what I've said and question how much things have actually changed in the last three years.

There has been substantial change but I'm also the first to admit that we don't have all the answers.

I believe over time we will judge the success of businesses, including banks, on the basis of broader measures and values.

I hope this occasion generates further debate about how we can engage meaningfully with the customers, clients and communities that we serve.

To the question "can banks be good citizens?" the answer must be "yes". But I'm mindful of what was said to me three years ago: "Bob, think about the fact that no-one will believe you."

We're in the early stages of working to restore trust.

I'd like to be able to say we're achieving that, but I know that for you, seeing is believing.

You may not be able to see what's different today, but over time I very much hope you will see that and more.

Thank you very much.

Richard Tudway (Letters, 10th October 2008) is correct in linking the current financial crisis to failures in corporate governance. And weak oversight by boards is certainly part of it. Against this background, the secretary-general of the Organisation for Economic Co-operation and Development, Angel Gurría, recently launched a global drive to improve corporate governance.

The initiative will build on the OECD principles of corporate governance and also engage international organisations, business associations and other key stakeholders. The task is to address immediate reactions to present malpractices and to establish a longer-term road map for effective implementation and monitoring.

The OECD will make a statement on its findings and recommendations about the corporate governance lessons from the financial crisis following the next meeting of the OECD steering group on corporate governance, on November 19-20.

Through this effort, the OECD will play an important role in fostering a sound business culture and rebuilding confidence discredited by bad corporate governance practices in individual companies.

Marcello Bianchi,
Chairman, OECD Steering Group on Corporate Governance

Lightning Source UK Ltd.
Milton Keynes UK
UKOW07f0306230615

253960UK00002B/17/P

9 780993 135606